Contents

HOW TO USE THIS COURSE

Breakthrough Business German is the ideal course for business people who have little or no previous knowledge of German. Here are some of its main features:

- The key recordings have been made on location in German companies. The starting point for each unit is conversations and interviews with German people employed in a range of jobs.
- The language and the situations are, therefore, authentic – you are taken from boardrooms to the factory floor, from commercial exhibitions to banks financing small businesses.
- Business people have lives outside their jobs, and care is taken to provide training in the language which will help you to survive in hotels, restaurants and on the streets of German-speaking countries as well as in companies.
- The main emphasis throughout is on listening, speaking and reading – the skills you will find most useful in contacts with the German business world.
- Before producing the course, we talked to hundreds of people about *how* they learn languages. The result is that great care has been taken with the *Breakthrough Business* series to ensure that you get enough opportunities to practise the language. We have included in each unit a variety of activities that get you involved in using the German that has been introduced to you in the authentic dialogues.
- This is not a grammar course. You first understand and then you use the language; only then are the main grammar features introduced to provide some cement and to explain how the language works.
- Included in each unit is up-to-date information to ensure you are familiar with key features of the German business scene.

General hints

- Have confidence in us. Real language is complex and there are certain things in each unit which are not explained in detail and which you may find difficult to understand, particularly on the first hearing. We will build up your knowledge slowly, emphasizing only what you really need to remember at each stage and making a distinction between language you need to use and language where you only need to understand the gist.
- Try to practise regularly, but in short periods. 20–30 minutes a day is usually better than 3–4 hours once a week.
- To develop your speaking skills, do say the words and phrases out loud. This articulation of the language is important in building up a degree of confidence and fluency.
- If you don't understand something, don't panic. Leave it for a while. Learning a language is a bit like doing a jigsaw puzzle; it all eventually falls into place.
- Don't be afraid to write in the book and add your own notes.
- Go back over the units you have already studied. You'll often surprise yourself at how much you understand and it helps remind you of the vocabulary.
- If you are not attending language classes, try to pair up with someone else and learn with them.
- If this is the first time you have used a recording to help you learn a language, practise using the pause and repeat-play controls on your cassette or CD player.
- Learning German may take more time than you thought. Just be patient and, above all, don't get angry with yourself.

How the course is organized and how to make the most of each unit

There are twelve units, each one focusing on a particular aspect of business German. Each unit is divided up in the same way. In the first section, you get a number of authentic recordings with transcripts of what is said, together with notes and vocabulary. Each recording is followed by three or four exercises, some practising comprehension, some practising speaking. When the new location recordings have been introduced, explained and practised, all the main words and phrases are brought together in a list called *Key words and phrases*. Then come short sections which focus on grammar, reading, background information and some final 'open-ended' speaking practice.

The book contains step-by-step instructions for working through the course: when to use the book or recording on its own, when to use them together. As the course progresses you may well evolve your own pattern of study and that's fine. As a starting point, here's how we suggest you approach each unit.

Dialogues

First, listen to each of the key dialogues without stopping the recording, just to get a feel for the task ahead. Then go over the dialogue bit by bit in conjunction with the explanatory notes and vocabulary. You should get into the habit of playing the recordings repeatedly to give yourself time to think, listen to sentences a couple of times and repeat them after the speaker. When you feel confident you have at least understood what the dialogue is about and you have become familiar with the most important phrases, move on and do the associated exercises.

Practise what you have learned

These exercises have been carefully chosen to practise key vocabulary and structures. During the course you will come across many different types of exercises. Our presenter, Wolf, will guide you through what to do and there are clear instructions in the book.

Key words and phrases

By the time you get to this section you should be reasonably familiar with most of the words and phrases listed. Use the list to test yourself, covering up and checking what you know, first the English and then the German column. This should ensure that you can remember the most important items.

Read and understand and *Did you know?*

In these sections you will be able to read the kind of written material – signs, faxes, publicity brochures, etc. – that you are likely to come across in Germany and you are given some up-to-date information on the organization of business and commerce.

Your turn to speak

This final activity is open-ended. It is an opportunity for you to adapt the language of the unit to your own particular circumstances, so there are normally no 'correct' answers. When you've had a go at this guided speaking activity, you will hear a model version on the recording. This will show you what somebody else said and give you a few extra ideas.

Answers

The answers to all the exercises (except where the answers are given on the recording) can be found at the end of each unit.

Grammar summary

This is included at the back of the book as a reference tool.

Vocabulary

At the back of the book is a German–English and English–German vocabulary. This does not replace a dictionary, of course, but you should be able to use it as an alphabetical reference for most of the words you need.

Hints on pronunciation and spelling

On the whole German words are pronounced as they are written. You need to beware of one or two letters: **v** is pronounced like an **f** and **w** like a **v**. So the word for 'father' is **Vater**, spoken like *fater*, and the word for 'wolf' is **Wolf**, but pronounced *volf*. The combination **ch** is sometimes pronounced rather like **sh** and sometimes like a throaty **k**, depending on the vowels preceding it. Rather than learning theoretical rules, just listen carefully to the recording and imitate the German speakers. If you do this, you should soon pick up German pronunciation. Sometimes in spoken German a final **e** is 'swallowed' by the speaker. This is shown by an **e** in brackets, e.g. **ich geb(e)**.

German uses basically the same letters as English, though note that *all* nouns are written with a capital letter. The letter **ß** is like a double **s** and it is found in the middle and at the end of words. The vowels **a, o** and **u** can sometimes be found with two dots over them: **ä, ö, ü** (called umlauts). They have the effect of changing the sound of the word from **a, o, u** to **ae, oe**, or **ue**, and they also affect the meaning, so keep an eye on umlauts.

All of us involved in producing *Breakthrough Business German* hope you will enjoy the course and find it useful.

Viel Spaß!

Symbols and abbreviations

For cassettes
If your cassette recorder has a counter, set it to zero at the start of each unit and then note the number in the headphone symbol at the start of each dialogue. This will help you to find the right place on the tape when you want to wind back.

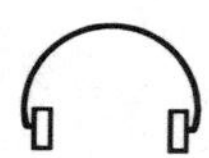

For CD players
Your player will locate each unit as a track number. Note the number from your display in the headphone symbol at the start of each dialogue. This will help you find the right place on your disc when you want to repeat play.

➧ This indicates the most important words and phrases.

m.	masculine	sing.	singular
f.	feminine	pl.	plural
n.	neuter	lit.	literally

1 TALKING ABOUT YOURSELF

You will learn

- to introduce yourself
- to say where you come from
- to say where you work and what you do
- to answer questions about the purpose of your visit
- to say the time of day
- to say 'yes' or 'no' politely

and you will be given some information on Germany, Austria and Switzerland.

Study guide

To help you keep a check on your progress, mark off the various tasks as you complete them.

- **Dialogue 1 + Practise what you have learned**
- **Dialogue 2 + Practise what you have learned**
- **Dialogue 3 + Practise what you have learned**
- **Dialogue 4 + Practise what you have learned**
- Make sure you know the **Key words and phrases**
- Study the **Grammar** section
- Do the exercises in **Read and understand**
- Read **Did you know?**
- **Your turn to speak**

Before you start, do make sure you've read the introduction, which explains the format of the course and how to make the most of it.

Dialogues

1 *Conversation in a hotel lobby*

Tom Miller Guten Abend.
Kurt Richter Guten Tag.
Tom Miller Ist der Sitz hier noch frei?
Kurt Richter Bitte sehr.
Tom Miller Mein Name ist Tom Miller.
Kurt Richter Angenehm. Mein Name ist Kurt Richter. Sie sind aber nicht von hier?
Tom Miller Nein, ich komme aus USA, aus Boston.
Kurt Richter Und was machen Sie hier in Bochum?
Tom Miller Ich bin Vizepräsident von Bancosoft.
Kurt Richter Ah. Bei der Bank.
Tom Miller Nein, das ist ein Softwarehaus. Wir verkaufen Computerprogramme.
Kurt Richter Ich arbeite auch bei der Bank. Bei der Westfalenbank. Hier ist meine Karte.
Tom Miller Oh, das ist interessant. Ich geb(e) Ihnen gerne auch meine Karte.
Kurt Richter Danke schön.

das Gespräch conversation, talk
die Hotelhalle hotel lobby

Guten Abend Good evening. **Guten Tag** literally means 'Good day', but is used for either 'Good morning' or 'Good afternoon' or even 'Good evening'. **Guten Morgen** (Good morning) is used until mid-morning; **Guten Abend** (Good evening) from about 6 o'clock to bedtime; **Gute Nacht** (Good night) is only used before you go to bed or when you leave someone late at night.

Ist der Sitz hier noch frei? Is the seat here still free?

Bitte sehr You will come across **bitte** quite a lot. Basically it means 'please' but here it is used idiomatically to mean 'Please sit down'. **Sehr** usually means 'very'.

Mein Name ist Tom Miller My name is Tom Miller. The easiest way of giving your name. When you address people formally, you use the polite form of address – **Herr** for 'Mr', **Frau** for 'Mrs' or 'Ms' and **Fräulein** for 'Miss' – and drop the first name. In a formal situation it would be more usual to say simply **Mein Name ist Miller**.

Angenehm How do you do (lit. pleasant). This is very formal.

Sie sind aber nicht von hier? You are not from here, are you? The intonation turns this statement into a question. The two businessmen use the formal **Sie** (see grammar, p. 17).

Nein, ich komme aus USA, aus Boston No, I'm from the USA, from Boston. (He should have said **aus den USA**.)

Und was machen Sie in Bochum? And what are you doing in Bochum? **Machen** means both 'to make' and 'to do'.

Ich bin Vizepräsident von Bancosoft I am vice-president of Bancosoft

Bei der Bank At the bank

Nein, das ist ein Softwarehaus No, it's a software company

Wir verkaufen Computerprogramme We sell computer programs

Ich arbeite auch bei der Bank I also work at a bank

Das ist interessant (That's) interesting

Ich geb(e) Ihnen gerne auch meine Karte Let me give you my card too (lit. I give to you gladly also my card).

Danke schön Thank you (very much). There is no difference between **danke** and **danke schön**. People usually respond with **bitte** or **bitte sehr,** for which there is no exact English equivalent. The nearest is 'It's OK' or 'It's a pleasure'.

Practise what you have learned

This part of the unit is designed to help you cope with the language you have met in the dialogues, in particular with the key phrases and structures. You will need both the recording and the book to do the exercises. Read the instructions in the book carefully before doing the exercises or listening to the recording again.

1 Complete these sentences. (Answers on p. 24.)

(a) **Ich komme aus Boston. Mein Name ist** ____________

(b) **Ich komme aus Bochum. Mein Name ist** ____________

2 Can you match the two halves of the sentences? The beginnings are in the left-hand column and the endings are on the right. (Answers on p. 24.)

(a) **Ich arbeite ...**
(b) **Ich bin ...**
(c) **Ich gebe ...**
(d) **Ich komme ...**
(e) **Sie sind ...**
(f) **Wir verkaufen ...**

(i) **... aus den USA.**
(ii) **... Vizepräsident bei Bancosoft.**
(iii) **... auch bei der Bank.**
(iv) **... Computerprogramme.**
(v) **... Ihnen gern auch meine Karte.**
(vi) **... aber nicht von hier.**

3 Now for the first speaking activity. Check the introduction on p. 5 before you start. Switch on the recording and follow the instructions given by Wolf. Use the prompts to answer the questions aloud during the pause. When you have given your answer, you will hear the correct version.

4 We have recorded several business people greeting each other. What time of day is it? Listen to one couple at a time and mark the correct box in the grid below. You can always go back and repeat play if you haven't understood. (Answers on p. 24.)

	morning	daytime	evening	night
(a) 1st couple				
(b) 2nd couple				
(c) 3rd couple				
(d) 4th couple				

Dialogues

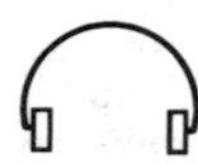

2 *Waiting in the airport lounge*

Kurt Richter Guten Tag, fliegen Sie auch nach London?
Ann Stuart Ja, ich flieg(e) auch nach London.
Kurt Richter Wohnen Sie in London?
Ann Stuart Nein, ich flieg(e) von London weiter nach Glasgow.
Kurt Richter Sind Sie das erste Mal in Deutschland?
Ann Stuart Nein, ich fahre regelmäßig jedes Jahr nach Deutschland seit vier Jahren.
Kurt Richter Mein Name ist Kurt Richter. Ich arbeite bei der Dortmunder Kronen-Brauerei.
Ann Stuart Und mein Name ist Stuart, ich bin beschäftigt als Verkaufsleiterin für Textilien.

➧ **die Flughafenhalle** airport lounge

Fliegen Sie auch nach London? Are you also going to London?

➧ **Ja, ich flieg(e) auch nach London** is an informal and yet polite reply. **Ja** on its own would have been impolite.

➧ **Wohnen Sie in London?** Do you live in London? The most common way of forming a question is to say the equivalent of 'Live you in London?'

➧ **Nein, ich flieg(e) von London weiter nach Glasgow.** No, I'll fly on from London to Glasgow. **Weiter** (further) indicates the continuation of something, e.g. **weiter machen** means 'to carry on doing something'.

Sind Sie das erste Mal in Deutschland? Is this your first visit to Germany?

➧ **Nein, ich fahre regelmäßig jedes Jahr nach Deutschland seit vier Jahren** No, I've been to Germany regularly every year during the past four years.

Dortmunder Kronen-Brauerei Kronen Brewery in Dortmund, one of Germany's leading brewers of light beers.

➧ **Ich bin beschäftigt als Verkaufsleiterin für Textilien** I work as a sales manageress in the textile industry. **Ich bin beschäftigt als** is an alternative for **ich arbeite als** (I work as) or simply **ich bin** (I am).

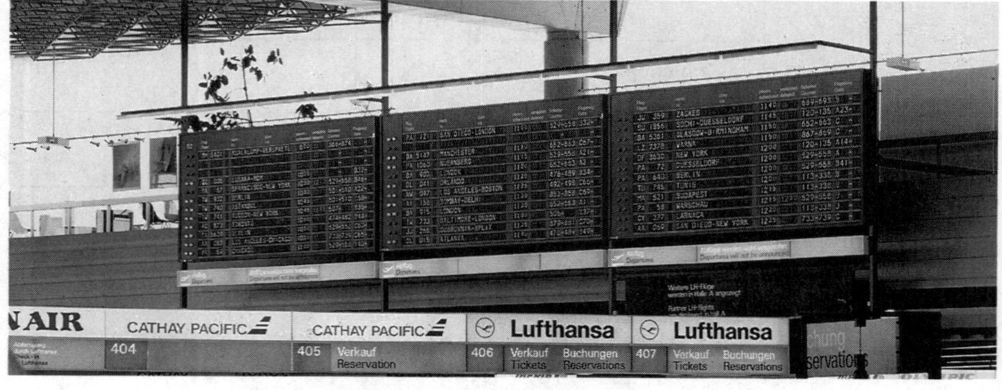

Practise what you have learned

5 Answer these questions in the spaces provided, then compare your answers with the ones given on the recording. Listen to these two examples on the recording before you start.

Example 1: **Fliegen Sie nach London?**
Ja, ich fliege nach London.

Example 2: **Fliegen Sie nach Berlin?**
Nein, ich fliege nicht nach Berlin.

(a) **Fliegen Sie weiter nach Glasgow? Ja,** ____________________

(b) **Kommen Sie aus den USA? Nein,** ____________________

(c) **Fahren Sie nach London? Ja,** ____________________

(d) **Arbeiten Sie in Boston? Nein,** ____________________

(e) **Sind Sie bei der Bank beschäftigt? Ja,** ____________________

(f) **Verkaufen Sie Computerprogramme? Ja,** ____________________

(g) **Wohnen Sie in Bochum? Nein,** ____________________

6 In each of the following sentences the last few words are missing. Try to match the beginnings on the left with the endings on the right. (Answers on p. 24.)

(a) **Fliegen Sie auch...?**
(b) **Sind Sie das erste Mal...?**
(c) **Wohnen Sie...?**
(d) **Ich arbeite...**
(e) **Ich bin beschäftigt als Verkaufsleiterin...**
(f) **Fahren Sie regelmäßig...?**

(i) **... in Bochum**
(ii) **... in Deutschland**
(iii) **... nach Deutschland**
(iv) **... bei der Kronen-Brauerei**
(v) **... nach London**
(vi) **... für Textilien**

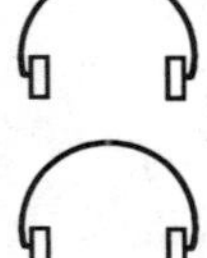

7 We are going to do the dialogue again. This time you act the role of Mrs Stuart. Follow the prompts.

8 Listen to this conversation between Frau Baum and Herr Koch in an airport lounge. Put a cross in the appropriate box next to the sentences below, depending on whether you think they are true (**richtig**) or false (**falsch**). (Answers on p. 24.)

	richtig	**falsch**
(a) Herr Koch is flying to London.		
(b) Frau Baum is heading for München (Munich).		
(c) Frau Baum works in München (Munich).		
(d) She works at a bank.		
(e) Herr Koch works in a brewery.		

Dialogues

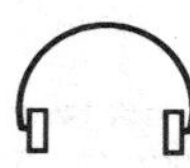

3 *In the departure lounge*

Jürgen Krause	Guten Morgen.
Peter Hock	Guten Morgen. Fliegen Sie auch nach Gatwick?
Jürgen Krause	Ja, ich fliege nach Gatwick, aber ich muß dann weiter nach Edinburgh. Ich hab(e) in Dundee zu tun – ich besuche dort Kunden. Ich bin Verkaufsleiter. Übrigens, meine Name ist Jürgen Krause.
Peter Hock	Freut mich, mein Name ist Peter Hock. Ich bin Vertriebsleiter für Chemieprodukte. Waren Sie schon mal in Schottland?
Jürgen Krause	Nein, das ist mein erster Besuch, aber ich bin schon oft in England gewesen. Kennen Sie das Ruhrgebiet?
Peter Hock	Ja, ein bißchen. Ich kenne Essen und ich kenne Bochum.
Jürgen Krause	Oh, dann kennen Sie meine Heimatstadt. Ich komme aus Bochum.
Peter Hock	Das ist interessant. Andere Regionen in Deutschland kenne ich leider nicht.

übrigens by the way
das Chemieprodukt chemical product
die Heimatstadt home town
die Region region
leider unfortunately

Aber ich muß dann weiter nach Edinburgh But I have to go on to Edinburgh. **Ich muß** means 'I must' or 'I have to'. Here the verb **fahren** (to travel) or **fliegen** (to fly) is left out because it is obvious what Herr Krause means.

Ich hab(e) **in Dundee zu tun** I have business to attend to in Dundee. The literal meaning of **tun** is 'to do'.

Ich besuche dort Kunden I'm going to visit clients/customers there

Freut mich is short for **es freut mich**, lit. 'it pleases me'. It's less formal than **angenehm**.

Waren Sie schon mal in Schottland? Have you been to Scotland before? (lit. Were you already in Scotland?). **Mal** is a common filler word often left untranslated.

Nein, dies ist mein erster Besuch No, this is my first visit

Aber ich bin schon oft in England gewesen But I have often been to England

Kennen Sie das Ruhrgebiet? Do you know the Ruhr area? The **Ruhrgebiet** is an industrial area named after the Ruhr river, which flows into the Rhine.

Ja, ein bißchen Yes, a little (bit). Useful in a lot of situations, e.g.: **Sprechen Sie Deutsch?** (Do you speak German?) **Ja, ein bißchen.** (Yes, a little (bit)).

Ich kenne Essen und ich kenne Bochum I know Essen and I know Bochum

Oh, dann kennen Sie meine Heimatstadt Oh, then you know my home town

Andere Regionen in Deutschland kenne ich leider nicht Unfortunately, I don't know any other regions in Germany

Practise what you have learned

9 Study the example and then complete the following sentences. Read them out loud. (Answers on p. 24.)

Ja, ________________ nach Gatwick. (I fly)
Ja, ich fliege nach Gatwick.

(a) ________________ **weiter nach Edinburgh fliegen.** (I must)

(b) ________________ **in Dundee zu tun.** (I have)

(c) ________________ **dort Kunden.** (I visit)

(d) ________________ **Verkaufsleiter.** (I am)

(e) ________________ **Essen und Bochum.** (I know)

10 Can you remember what Herr Krause and Herr Hock said about themselves? Play dialogue 3 again and fill in the blanks. (Answers on p. 24.)

Herr Krause:

(a) **Ich bin** ________________

(b) **Ich besuche** ________________ **in Dundee.**

(c) **Das ist mein erster** ________________ **(in Schottland).**

(d) **Dann kennen Sie meine** ________________

Herr Hock:

(e) **Ich bin** ________________ **für Chemieprodukte.**

(f) **Ich kenne** ________________ **und** ________________

(g) **Andere** ________________ **kenne ich leider nicht.**

11 In this speaking activity you are going to play the part of Peter Hock. He is talking about his job and what he is doing in Scotland.

Dialogues

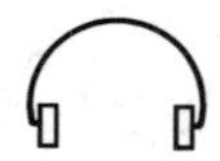

4 *At the hotel reception*

Receptionist Guten Tag. Kann ich Ihnen helfen?
Guest Guten Tag, ich möchte zu Frau Zimmermann. Können Sie mir ihre Zimmernummer sagen?
Receptionist Moment. Ich schau(e) mal nach ... Frau Zimmermann, ja, wohnt Zimmer 814.
Guest In welchem Stock?
Receptionist Das ist der achte Stock, und dann gehen Sie zur siebten Tür auf der rechten Seite. Sie benutzen am besten den Aufzug.
Guest Okay. Achter Stock. Zimmernummer 807?
Receptionist 814.
Guest Gut, vielen Dank.
Receptionist Bitte sehr.

die Zimmernummer room number
der Stock level/floor
die Tür door
der Aufzug lift/elevator

Kann ich Ihnen helfen? Can I help you?, the receptionist asks the guest (**der Gast**) at the hotel reception (**die Hotelrezeption, der Empfang**). This is a very common way of offering help or information (**die Information**) in almost any situation.

Ich möchte zu Frau Zimmermann I would like to see Frau Zimmermann (i.e. go and see her in her room). **Ich möchte gern** 'I would like to' is a very important phrase.

Können Sie mir die Zimmernummer sagen? Can you tell me her room number? Germans tend not to use **bitte** (please) quite as much as English speakers when making a request or asking for help.

Moment is short for **Einen Moment, bitte** 'Just a moment, please'.

Ich schau(e) mal nach (colloquial) I'll just check

Wohnt Zimmer 814 is short for **Sie wohnt in Zimmer 814**. Lit. 'She is living in room 814'.

In welchem Stock? On which floor?

Das ist der achte Stock That's (on) the eighth floor

Und dann gehen Sie zur siebten Tür auf der rechten Seite And then you go to the seventh door on your right. **Auf der rechten Seite** is 'on your right'; **auf der linken Seite** is 'on your left'; **rechts** means 'right' or 'on the right', and **links** 'left' or 'on the left'.

Sie benutzen am besten den Aufzug You are best to use the lift/elevator

Gut, vielen Dank OK, thanks. **Gut** (usually 'good') is used here to accept the receptionist's suggestion to use the lift/elevator and also to bring the conversation to an end.

Vielen Dank Many thanks. A common alternative to **danke** or **danke schön**.

Practise what you have learned

12 Play the dialogue again and fill in the missing words in the sentences below. Don't worry if you have to play it through a few times. (Answers on p. 24.)

(a) **Ich möchte gern zu** ______________________

(b) **Können Sie mir** ______________________ **sagen?**

(c) **Ich schau(e)** ______________________

(d) **Das ist der** ____________ **Stock.**

(e) **Dann gehen Sie zur** ____________ **Tür auf der** ____________ **Seite.**

(f) **Sie benutzen** ______________________ **den Aufzug.**

13 Complete these sentences by filling in the verb. Look back at the dialogue if you need help. (Answers on p. 24.)

(a) ____________ **ich Ihnen helfen?**

(b) **Ich** ____________ **zu Frau Zimmermann.**

(c) ____________ **Sie mir ihre Zimmernummer sagen?**

(d) **Ich** ____________ **mal nach.**

(e) **Frau Zimmermann** ____________ **im achten Stock.**

(f) **Sie** ____________ **am besten den Aufzug.**

14 Your turn to speak. This time you are a guest at the hotel reception. Use the prompts on the recording.

15 Listen to the directions and then put a cross in the box next to the statements below that are exactly *the same* as they were on the recording. (Answers on p. 24.)

(a) **Ich kann Ihnen helfen.** ☐

(b) **Frau Zimmermann ist nicht im Hotel.** ☐

(c) **Sie hat die Zimmernummer 814.** ☐

(d) **Sie fliegen mit dem Aufzug.** ☐

(e) **Das ist der achte Stock.** ☐

(f) **Es ist die siebte Tür auf der linken Seite.** ☐

Key words and phrases

Here are the most important words and phrases which you have met in this unit. You should make sure that you know them as they will keep cropping up. Practise reading them aloud.

Guten Morgen	Good morning
Guten Tag	Good morning / Good day / Good afternoon / Hello
Guten Abend	Good evening
Gute Nacht	Good night
Herr	Mr
Frau	Mrs/Ms
Fräulein	Miss
Mein Name ist ...	My name is ...
Ich komme aus ...	I come / I'm from ...
Ich fliege nach ...	I fly / I'm flying to ...
Ich fahre nach ...	I go / I'm going to ...
Ich arbeite / bin (beschäftigt) bei ...	I'm working / employed / work at ...
Ich muß ...	I must ...
Ich möchte gern ...	I would like to ...
machen	to make/do
tun	to do
Ich besuche dort Kunden	I'm going to visit / I'm visiting customers/clients there
Ich besuche Kunden in Dundee	I'm going to visit / I'm visiting customers/clients in Dundee
Hier ist meine Karte	Here is my card
Ich gebe Ihnen meine Karte	Let me / I'll give you my card
Waren Sie schon mal ...?	Have you ever been ...?
Kann ich Ihnen helfen?	Can I help you?
Können Sie mir sagen ...?	Can you tell me ...?
Das ist interessant	(That's) Interesting
Das ist mein erster Besuch	That's my first visit
Das ist der achte Stock	That's on the eighth floor
auf der rechten / linken Seite	on the right/left (hand side)
rechts / links	right/left
Freut mich / Angenehm	How do you do? / It's a pleasure / I'm pleased to meet you
Verkaufsleiter(in) für Textilien	sales manager(ess) for textiles
Vertriebsleiter(in) für Chemieprodukte	sales manager(ess) for chemical products
bitte (sehr)	please / you're welcome
danke (schön) / vielen Dank	thank you (very much) / many thanks
ein bißchen	a little (bit)
jedes Jahr	every year

Grammar

The word grammar can strike terror into many hearts, but it is not the aim of this course to go into great detail about grammar points. The grammar section in each unit will present the basics and show how the language works so that you have firm ground to build on. The grammar summary at the end of the book provides further information in the form of a table and gives definitions of the basic grammar terms (see pp. 223-225).

The verb sein *(to be)*

In Unit 1 you came across several forms of this important verb. Here are all the present tense forms. As in English, it is irregular.

ich bin	I am	**wir sind**	we are
du bist	you are	**ihr seid**	you (pl.) are
er/sie/es ist	he/she/it is	**sie sind**	they are
		Sie sind	you are (polite, sing./pl.)

The polite form of **Sie sind** 'you are' is used for one person or for several people. **Sie** is written with a capital letter when it means 'you'.

In German there are three ways of saying 'you are':

du bist	to a friend or child
ihr seid	to more than one friend or child
Sie sind	to one or more adults you don't know well

You will also have realized from the above that there are several meanings of the word **sie**. Without a capital it can mean 'she' (**sie ist Verkaufsleiterin**) or 'they' (**sie besuchen Berlin**). With a capital it means 'you' (**Was machen Sie?**).

The most important forms for you to learn at this stage are: **ich bin**, **er/sie/es ist**, **sie sind**, and the polite forms **Sie sind** or, in a question, **Sind Sie ...?**

Regular verbs

Here are some of the regular verbs we came across in the dialogues. Most of these form the present tense according to the same pattern: the infinitive ending **-en** is replaced by the appropriate endings (underlined below).

besuchen to visit

ich besuche	I visit	**wir besuchen**	we visit
du besuchst	you visit	**ihr besucht**	you (pl.) visit
er/sie/es besucht	he/she/it visits	**sie besuchen**	they visit
		Sie besuchen	you visit (polite, sing. or pl.)

machen	to make/do
wohnen	to live
verkaufen	to sell
arbeiten	to work
sagen	to say/tell
benutzen	to use/utilize

More on jobs

Most job designations in German end in **-er**. For job designations for women you simply add **-in**, as shown in the table below.

Job designation (male)	Job designation (female)	Translation
der Lehrer	**die Lehrerin**	teacher
der Verkäufer	**die Verkäuferin**	sales assistant
der Sachbearbeiter	**die Sachbearbeiterin**	clerk
der Abteilungsleiter	**die Abteilungsleiterin**	head of department
der Exportleiter	**die Exportleiterin**	export manager
der Geschäftsführer	**die Geschäftsführerin**	(general) manager
der Sekretär	**die Sekretärin**	secretary
der Assistent	**die Assistentin**	assistant
der Chef	**die Chefin**	boss
der Direktor	**die Direktorin**	director/executive manager
der Präsident	**die Präsidentin**	president
der Kunde	**die Kundin**	client/customer

Although this is the general pattern, there are some exceptions. For example, a male employee is **ein Angestellter** but a female employee is **eine Angestellte**. However, when the definite article is used, the forms are identical: **der Angestellte** und **die Angestellte**.

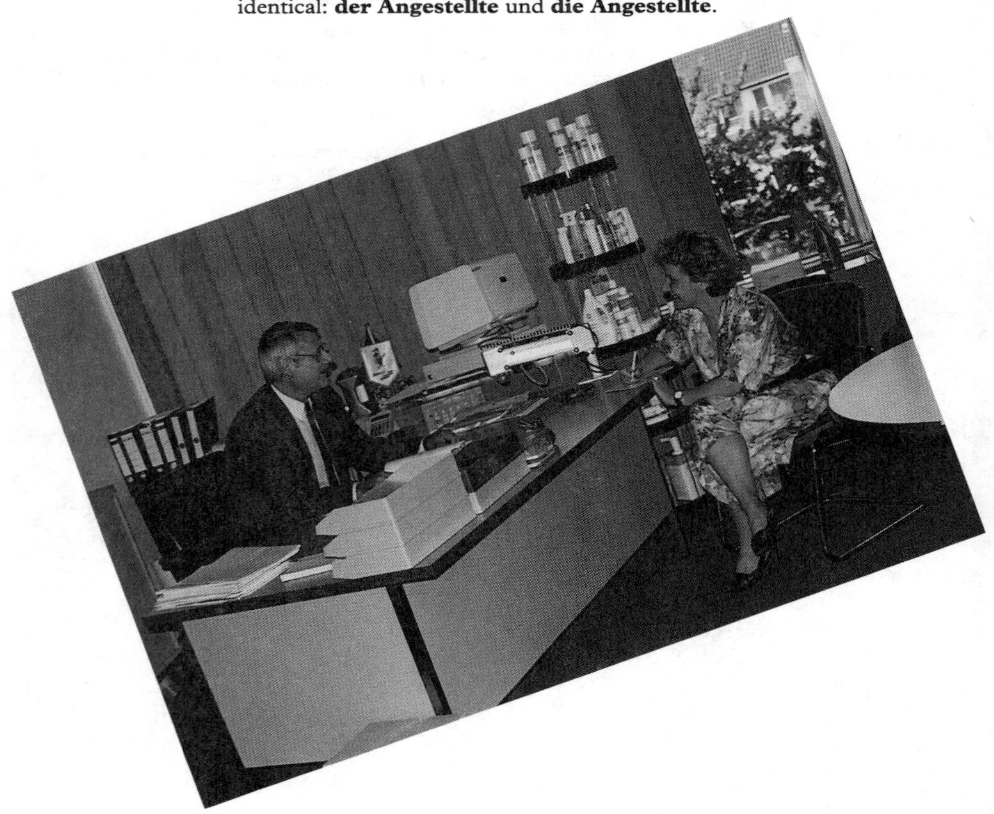

Read and understand

16 Here are four business cards. Study them carefully and then complete the box below. (Answers on p. 24.)

GASOLIN®

Hans-Hermann Brunholt
Exportleiter
GASOLIN GmbH • Lübeck • Büro Bochum

Am Hain 2
Postfach 10 08 11
D-4630 Bochum 1

Telefon 02 34 / 31 26 86
Telex 26 549 gasol d

H & W SPRACHENDIENST GMBH
KORNELIA BUSCHEY
GESCHÄFTSFÜHRERIN

BÜRO
HARDENSTEINER WEG 3C
5810 WITTEN 3
TEL. 0 23 02 - 7 56 67

PRIVAT
BONIFATIUSSTRASSE 9
4630 BOCHUM 7
TEL. 02 34 - 28 53 49

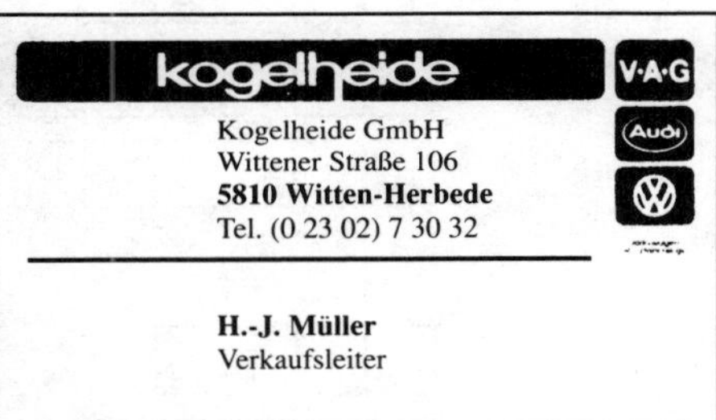
kogelheide
V·A·G
Audi

Kogelheide GmbH
Wittener Straße 106
5810 Witten-Herbede
Tel. (0 23 02) 7 30 32

H.-J. Müller
Verkaufsleiter

NORBERT J. BÖHM
Direktor des Bankhauses
Trinkaus & Burkhardt

4000 Düsseldorf 1 • Königsallee 21/23 • Telefon (02 11) 9 10 22 07

	Job designation	*Place of work*
Herr Müller		
Herr Böhm		
Frau Buschey		
Herr Brunholt		

17

Try to fill in this word puzzle. You'll find all the words you need jumbled up in the box below. The keyword is the name of a country. (Answers on p. 24.)

(a) **Ist dieser ... noch frei?**

(b) **Das ist mein erster ...**

(c) **Frau Zimmermann wohnt im ... Stock.**

(d) **Ich bin schon ... in England gewesen.**

(e) **Hier ist meine ...**

(f) **Ich muß dann ... nach Edinburgh.**

(g) **Andere Regionen kenne ich ... nicht.**

(h) **Herr Miller kommt aus den ...**

(i) **Herr Richter arbeitet bei der ...**

(j) **Ich fahre ... Jahr nach Deutschland.**

Keyword:

(a)	(b)	(c)	(d)	(e)	(f)	(g)	(h)	(i)	(j)

jedes **weiter** **leider** **Karte** **USA** **achten** **Sitz** **oft** **Bank** **Besuch**

Did you know?

Germany: a brief survey

The Federal Republic of Germany is made up of 16 **Länder** (states): the original ten **Länder** in the West, Berlin, and the five newly created **Länder** in what was the German Democratic Republic. With a population of close to 80 million it is one of the most densely populated countries in the world.

Germany derives its national income from farming and forestry, from building and manufacturing, and above all from services. Most sectors in the manufacturing industry are highly mechanized or automated and on the whole are very efficient. It is true to say, however, that not all plants in the former GDR are up to western standards. Although the manufacturing sector has witnessed persistent growth in absolute terms ever since 1945, its share in employment and its contribution to the gross national product has decreased. This is due to the decline of traditional industries such as coal, steel and shipbuilding, but also to the increasing speed of automation. The service sector, on the other hand, has expanded rapidly and now provides employment for nearly 50 per cent of the working population.

Germany relies heavily on foreign trade because of its geographical position in the centre of Europe and its lack of raw materials. The member states of the European Community take up the lion's share of German exports – mainly finished products from the car-manufacturing, chemical, engineering, electrical and electronics, optical and also agricultural sectors. Germany imports a similar range of products, in addition to the fuel and raw materials it requires. The supplying countries are almost the same as the countries that buy German goods.

Trade with the countries of the former Eastern bloc accounts for a fair share of the combined German foreign trade volume. The percentage figure for the trade with third-world countries is almost negligible, as is the case in other industrialized countries. In the past there has usually been a considerable surplus in the balance of visible trade, while at the same time the balance of invisible trade (services, financial transactions, insurance, tourism) has been in deficit. On the whole, however, the current account has been favourable.

Austria

Austria is a federal state comprising eight **Länder** plus the federal state of Vienna, which also is the capital. The landscape is characterized by the mountainous regions in the West and the gently sloping forest regions in the East, through which the river Danube winds its way to the Hungarian plains. With a population of about 7.6 million, it derives its income mainly from industrial production and the service industries, which are dominated by the tourist trade. Germany, its northern neighbour, is by far the most important trade partner and accounts for about a third of Austrian trade. Although Austria is not a member of the European Community (entry is under consideration), more than half its trade is with members of the EC, whereas EFTA countries account for less than 15 per cent of its trade. Usually the adverse balance of visible trade is offset by a huge surplus on invisible trade, the bulk of which is earned in the tourist sector.

Switzerland

Unlike its neighbours in the North and East, Switzerland has enjoyed centuries of political stability and national integrity – despite the fact that it is a confederation of 22 cantons which are not united by a common heritage, language or religion. The landscape is dominated by mountainous regions in the West (Jura), the Alps in the South and East and the plateau area in North and Central Switzerland. It is partly because of the natural borders created by the landscape that its 6.5 million inhabitants have no common language. German is spoken in the more densely populated and more heavily industrialized regions in the North and East, French in the South West and Italian in the alpine regions in the South. Its economic structure is similar to that of Austria. Manufacturing and the service industries each contribute between 40 and 45 per cent to the gross national product, with the share of manufacturing gradually declining. At roughly 65 per cent the EC-countries' share in Swiss foreign trade is quite considerable. The tourist trade is the most important industry in the services sector.

Your turn to speak

In this section the exercises are open-ended, so you can adapt them to cover your own situation – there is no right or wrong. However, we will give you some guidelines or phrases you should try to use. On the recording there will always be a model version, spoken by Paul and Maria, of what you could have said. But these are just suggestions. Your version might be quite different. A few useful phrases are given at the start of each exercise. Read the instructions carefully. When you have said your version aloud, return to the recording and listen to a model version.

18

You have just been asked to introduce yourself. Say the time of day, who you are, where you live, who you work for and in what capacity. Here are some phrases you might wish to use:

guten Morgen/Tag
Mein Name ist ...
Ich komme/bin aus ...
Ich arbeite bei ... / Ich bin beschäftigt bei ...

19 You come to a company for the first time and introduce yourself to the receptionist or to the person you have come to see. Say the time of day, who you are, where you work and in what capacity. Hand over your card. You might wish to use the phrases given in the last exercise. Here are a few extra ones:

Ich besuche Kunden ...
Hier ist meine Karte
Ich gebe Ihnen meine Karte

Don't forget to listen to the model version on the recording once you have had a go.

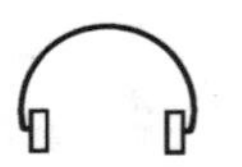

20 You have just made the acquaintance of someone in the hotel bar. This person has just introduced himself. Start by saying how pleased you are to make the acquaintance, introduce yourself and ask whether the guest knows your country or whether this is his first visit. Say your version out loud, then listen to the version given on the recording. Here are some useful phrases:

Angenehm
Freut mich
Kennen Sie ...?
Ist dies Ihr erster Besuch ...?

Answers

Practise what you have learned

Exercise **1** (a) Tom Miller (b) Kurt Richter

Exercise **2** (a) iii (b) ii (c) v (d) i (e) vi (f) iv

Exercise **4** (a) daytime (b) evening (c) morning (d) night

Exercise **6** (a) v (b) ii (c) i (d) iv (e) vi (f) iii

Exercise **8** *richtig:* (b), (c), (e); *falsch:* (a), (d)

Exercise **9** (a) Ich muß... (b) Ich habe... (c) Ich besuche... (d) Ich bin... (e) Ich kenne...

Exercise **10** (a) Verkaufsleiter (b) Kunden (c) Besuch (d) Heimatstadt (e) Vertriebsleiter (f) Essen; Bochum (g) Regionen

Exercise **12** (a) Frau Zimmermann (b) ihre Zimmernummer (c) mal nach (d) achte (e) siebten; rechten (f) am besten

Exercise **13** (a) Kann (b) möchte (c) Können (d) schau(e) (e) wohnt (f) benutzen

Exercise **15** You should have put a cross next to (a), (c) and (e).

Read and understand

Exercise **16** Müller: Verkaufsleiter/Witten-Herbede; Böhm: Direktor/Düsseldorf; Buschey: Geschäftsführerin/Witten; Brunholt: Exportleiter/Bochum

Exercise **17** (a) **S**itz (b) Besuch (c) ac**h**ten (d) **o**ft (e) Kar**t**e (f) wei**t**er (g) **l**eider (h) US**A** (i) Ba**n**k (j) je**d**es. Keyword: Schottland.

2

ASKING FOR AND UNDERSTANDING DIRECTIONS

You will learn

- to say where you are from
- to state the purpose of your visit
- to ask for and understand directions
- to ask for information to be repeated
- to use the cardinal and ordinal numbers from 1 to 20

and you will be given information on the transport services in Germany.

Study guide

Dialogue 1 + Practise what you have learned
Dialogue 2 + Practise what you have learned
Dialogue 3 + Practise what you have learned
Dialogue 4 + Practise what you have learned
Numbers
Make sure you know the **Key words and phrases**
Study the **Grammar** section
Do the exercise in **Read and understand**
Read **Did you know?**
Do the exercise in **Your turn to speak**

Dialogues

1 *An American businessman arrives at the company reception*

Mr Wilson	Guten Morgen.
Receptionist	Guten Morgen
Mr Wilson	Mein Name ist Wilson. Ich komme von der United Savings Bank in Dallas, Texas, und würde gern Herrn Falk sprechen.
Receptionist	Ja, würden Sie dann bitte den Aufzug benutzen. Und zwar fahren Sie da in die zweite Etage und gehen dann links den Korridor entlang. Es ist dann die sechste Tür. Und dort ist das Vorzimmer von Herrn Falk, wo Sie sich dann bitte melden.
Mr Wilson	Aha, also jetzt mit dem Aufzug und dann in die dritte Etage ...?
Receptionist	Nein, in die zweite.
Mr Wilson	In die zweite Etage, und wie war ...?
Receptionist	Sie müssen sich dann links halten.
Mr Wilson	Links ...?
Receptionist	Links den Korridor entlang ...
Mr Wilson	... und den Korridor ...
Receptionist	... und dann die sechste Tür.
Mr Wilson	Ja, das werd(e) ich finden. Vielen Dank.
Receptionist	Bitte sehr.

der Geschäftsmann businessman
➧ **die Etage** floor/level
➧ **das Vorzimmer** secretary's office/anteroom

➧ **Ich würde gern Herrn Falk sprechen** I would like to speak to Herr Falk. **Ich möchte gern Herrn Falk sprechen** would be a common alternative, though it is not as polite.

➧ **Würden Sie dann bitte den Aufzug benutzen** Would you then please use the lift

➧ **Und zwar fahren Sie da in die zweite Etage** And you then go up to the second floor. **Zwar** is a filler word, meaning 'then'. **Da** is also used as a filler word; in this context it means 'with the lift'.

➧ **und gehen dann links den Korridor entlang** and then go left along the corridor. When you hear **entlang**, you know you are being told to go down or along somewhere, e.g. **die Straße entlang** (down/along the street).

Es ist dann die sechste Tür Lit. 'It's then the sixth door'

➧ **und dort ist das Vorzimmer von Herrn Falk** and there's Mr Falk's anteroom. In a business context it means 'That's where you'll find Mr Falk's secretary'.

➧ **wo Sie sich dann bitte melden** where you will then please report. **Sich melden** is a useful verb in this context: **Melden Sie sich bitte im Vorzimmer von Herrn Falk** 'Please report to Mr Falk's secretary'; or **Bitte melden Sie sich bei der Rezeption** 'Please report to reception'.

und dann in die dritte Etage and then (I go) to the third floor

und wie war ...? and how was ...? or: and what was ...? An open question asking for all the information to be repeated.

➧ **Sie müssen sich dann links halten** And then you must keep to the left. 'Keep to the right' is **sich rechts halten**.

➧ **Ja, das werd(e) ich finden** Yes, I'll find that

Practise what you have learned

1 Complete the sentences below using the information given in the dialogue. If you don't remember, listen to the recording again. (Answers on p. 42.)

(a) **Mr Wilson kommt von** ____________________

(b) **Er würde gern** ____________________ **sprechen.**

(c) **Herr Wilson muß** ____________________ **benutzen.**

(d) **Er geht** ____________________ **entlang.**

(e) **Das Vorzimmer von Herrn Falk ist** ____________________

2 The sentences below are all jumbled up. See if you can sort them out. (Answers on p. 42.)

(a) **ist Name Wilson mein**
(b) **sprechen gern würde ich Herrn Falk**
(c) **den Aufzug bitte würden Sie benutzen**
(d) **fahren und zwar in die zweite Etage Sie**
(e) **den Korridor Sie dann links entlang gehen**
(f) **ist von Herrn Falk das Vorzimmer dort**
(g) **ich das finden ja, werde**

3 Choose the correct verb to describe what people do or want to do. (Answers on p. 42.)

(a) **Ich gehe / fliege / komme aus Dallas, Texas.**
(b) **Kann ich bitte Herrn Falk sprechen / melden / sagen.**
(c) **Sie gehen / halten / fahren also mit dem Aufzug.**
(d) **In der dritten Etage müssen Sie sich links melden / gehen / halten.**
(e) **Dort hat / ist / kann dann das Vorzimmer.**

4 Try to find out where you have to go. Use the prompts on the recording so that you can take the role of Mr Wilson.

5 Listen to this conversation between Frau Birgel and a company receptionist. Put a cross next to the statements which are different from the correct version on the recording. (Answers on p. 42.)

(a) **Guten Tag. Kann ich Ihnen sagen?** ☐

(b) **Ich möchte gern Frau Beyer sprechen.** ☐

(c) **Das Zimmer von Frau Beyer ist im dritten Stock.** ☐

(d) **Sie gehen dann links den Korridor entlang.** ☐

(e) **Die Zimmernummer ist 606.** ☐

Dialogues

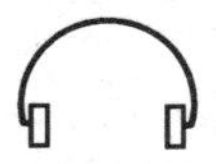

2 *At reception*

Receptionist Guten Tag. Kann ich Ihnen helfen?
Frau Thier Guten Tag. Mein Name ist Thier. Ich habe einen Termin bei Frau Steinbacher.
Receptionist Ja, Frau Steinbacher erwartet Sie im Konferenzraum. Dafür gehen Sie den Gang geradeaus und dann rechts, die dritte Tür links.
Frau Thier Den Gang geradeaus und dann links.
Receptionist Nein, dann rechts, und der Konferenzraum ist die dritte Tür links.
Frau Thier Ich gehe also den Gang rechts und dann die wievielte Tür?
Receptionist Die dritte Tür links.
Frau Thier Okay. Danke schön.
Receptionist Bitte sehr.

der Termin date/appointment
der Konferenzraum conference room
jemanden erwarten to expect someone

Ich habe einen Termin bei ... I have an appointment with ...

Frau Steinbacher erwartet Sie im Konferenzraum Frau Steinbacher is expecting you in the conference room

Dafür gehen Sie den Gang geradeaus In order to get there you walk straight along this corridor. **Dafür** is a colloquial way of saying 'in order to get there'; **Gang** is a synonym of **Korridor**; and **geradeaus** means 'straight ahead'.

die dritte Tür links the third door on the left

Ich gehe also den Gang rechts? So I take the corridor on the right? **Gehen** is 'to go' on foot.

Und dann die wievielte Tür? And then, which door? **Wieviel** normally means 'how much', but it can also be used as an adjective, as here.

Okay is fairly common, especially among younger people.

Practise what you have learned

6 Can you remember what was said in the dialogue? Answer the questions on the recording in German, using the prompts. Say your answers aloud and listen to the correct answers given after each pause.

7 Choose a word from the box below to complete these sentences (you won't need all the words). (Answers on p. 42.)

(a) **Ich habe einen ______________ bei Frau Steinbacher.**

(b) **Frau Steinbacher ist im ______________**

(c) **Dafür gehen Sie den ______________ geradeaus.**

(d) **Es ist dann die dritte ______________ links.**

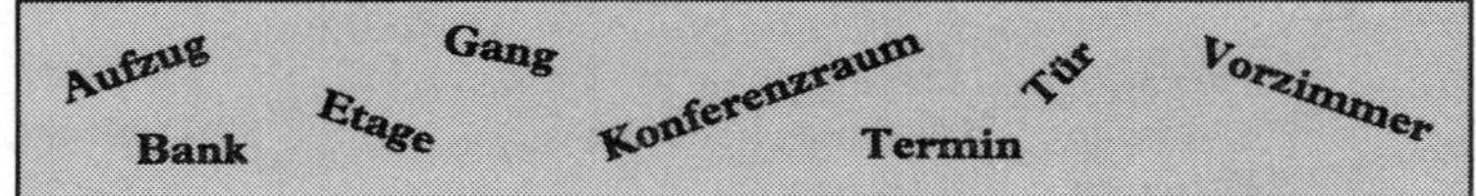

Aufzug
Gang
Konferenzraum
Tür
Vorzimmer
Bank
Etage
Termin

8 Try to be polite! Circle the most polite version. (Answers on p. 42.)

(a) (i) **Ich möchte gern Frau Steinbacher sprechen.**
(ii) **Ich werde Frau Steinbacher sprechen.**
(iii) **Ich muß Frau Steinbacher sprechen.**

(b) (i) **Würden Sie bitte den Aufzug benutzen.**
(ii) **Benutzen Sie den Aufzug.**
(iii) **Können Sie den Aufzug benutzen?**

(c) (i) **Melden Sie sich dann im Vorzimmer.**
(ii) **Melden Sie sich dann bitte im Vorzimmer.**
(iii) **Sie müssen sich dort zum Vorzimmer melden.**

(d) (i) **Ist dieser Sitz noch frei? Ja.**
(ii) **Ist dieser Sitz noch frei? Ja, bitte sehr.**
(iii) **Ist dieser Sitz noch frei? Ja, doch.**

9 Take the role of Frau Münzer in this dialogue with the company receptionist. The phrases you will need are printed below, but they are listed in the wrong order. You can check you've got them in the right order as you listen to the recording.

Wie komme ich da am besten hin?
Dritte Etage, und dann rechts und die wievielte Tür?
Also, die fünfte Tür links. Zimmernummer 312.
Guten Tag. Mein Name ist Münzer. Ich habe einen Termin mit Herrn Rauch.

Dialogues

3 *Asking the way to the town hall*

Visitor Entschuldigen Sie, können Sie mir sagen, wie ich zum Rathaus komme?

Passer-by Mhm, ja, da gehen Sie am besten hier die Straße entlang, dort hinten an dem Blumenladen vorbei und dann kommen Sie auf einen großen Platz ...

Visitor ... also immer geradeaus, ja?

Passer-by Ja, immer, immer geradeaus, an diesem Blumenladen vorbei, auf einen großen Platz. An diesem Platz gehen Sie rechts und dann etwas weiter linker Hand ist das Postamt und gegenüber, auf der rechten Seite dann, da ist das Rathaus.

Visitor Also immer geradeaus und dann rechts, auf der linken Seite das Postamt und rechts ist das Rathaus.

Passer-by Genau. Genau so.

Visitor Gut, danke schön.

Passer-by Bitt(e) schön.

Visitor Wiederseh(e)n.

- **das Postamt** post office
- **gegenüber** opposite

- **Entschuldigen Sie bitte** Excuse me please. It also means 'I'm sorry'.
- **Können Sie mir sagen ...?** Can you tell me ...?
- **... wie ich zum Rathaus komme?** ... how I get to the town hall? 'How do I get to the hotel?' would be **Wie komme ich zum Hotel?**

Da gehen Sie am besten ... Then the best is to go/walk ...

- **hier die Straße entlang** (here) along this road
- **dort hinten** over there (lit. there behind)

an dem/diesem Blumenladen vorbei past the/this flower shop. Both **Laden** and **Geschäft** mean 'shop', e.g. **Bäckerladen/-geschäft** (baker's shop), **Metzgerladen/-geschäft** (butcher's shop), **Gemüseladen/-geschäft** (greengrocer's shop), **Schreibwarenladen/-geschäft** (stationer's shop). The combination **an ... vorbei** gives the sense of going past something, e.g. **am Hotel vorbei** means 'past the hotel'.

- **und dann kommen Sie ...** and then you get to ... **Kommen** means 'to come', but it is also used to translate 'to get to' in this context.
- **auf einen großen Platz** to a big square. **Auf** usually means 'on'.
- **Also immer geradeaus, ja?** Here **also** is a filler meaning 'so'. **Also** does not mean the same as the English *also* or *too*. **Immer** literally means 'always'. **Geradeaus** means 'straight ahead' or 'keep straight on'.

An diesem Platz gehen Sie rechts At this square you turn right

und dann etwas weiter and then a bit further along

linker Hand is an alternative for **links** or **auf der linken Seite**, all of which mean 'on your left'. The same patterns can be used for **auf der rechten Seite** 'on your right'.

Genau. Genau so That's correct. Quite correct

- **Wiederseh(e)n** is short for **Auf Wiederseh(e)n**, meaning 'Goodbye'

Practise what you have learned

10 Here are the translations of some phrases from the dialogue. Translate them back into German, using the text of the dialogue if you need help. Read your answers aloud and then check them against the recording.

(a) Can you tell me how I get to the town hall?

____

(b) Go along this street here.

____

(c) And then you come to a big square.

____

(d) At that square you go right.

____

(e) And on the right is the town hall.

____

11 Complete the following sentences by translating the English phrases given in round brackets. Look back at dialogue 3 if you can't remember these phrases in German. (Answers on p. 42.)

(a) **Sie gehen am besten hier** ________________ (along the road)

(b) **Sie kommen dort hinten an** ____________ (the flower shop) **vorbei.**

(c) **Sie kommen dann auf** ____________________ (a big square)

(d) **Sie finden etwas weiter linker Hand** __________ (the post office)

(e) **Sie gehen dann rechts. Und da ist** ____________ (the town hall)

12 Can you explain these traffic signs? Your sentence should follow this pattern: **Sie müssen (nach) ... fahren** or **Sie müssen (nach) ... und dann ... fahren.** The correct answers are given on the recording.

(a) (b) (c) (d) (e) (f)

13 Listen to the recording and indicate whether the statements below are **richtig** (true) or **falsch** (false). (Answers on p. 42.)

	richtig	falsch
(a) **Sie gehen am besten am Blumenladen entlang.**		
(b) **An dem großen Platz müssen Sie links gehen.**		
(c) **Am Postamt gehen Sie also rechts.**		
(d) **Die Brauerei ist dann rechter Hand.**		
(e) **Der Blumenladen ist dann etwas weiter rechts.**		

Dialogues

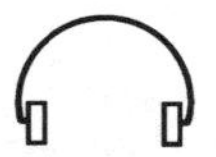

4 *Getting to the station*

Visitor Entschuldigen Sie, können Sie mir vielleicht sagen, wie ich von hier zum Bahnhof komme?

Passer-by Ja, Sie gehen jetzt hier über den Rathausplatz, kommen dann auf die Bahnhofstraße. Das ist eine Fußgängerzone. Die gehen Sie etwa 500 Meter rechts runter. Auf der linken Seite finden Sie dann den Berliner Platz. Über den gehen Sie, und kommen dann an der Hauptpost vorbei und laufen dann direkt auf den Wittener Hauptbahnhof zu.

Visitor Also von hier über den Marktplatz, dann rechts in die Bahnhofstraße und nach 500 Metern über den Berliner Platz zur Hauptpost, und dann komme ich zum Bahnhof.

Passer-by Ganz genau.

Visitor Ja, vielen Dank.

Passer-by Bitte schön.

die Bahnhofstraße Station Road
über across/over
der Rathausplatz Town Hall Square
der Berliner Platz Berlin Square
die Fußgängerzone pedestrian precinct/area
die Hauptpost main post office

vielleicht perhaps. Here it expresses politeness rather than uncertainty.

von hier zum Bahnhof from here to the station. The opposite of **von hier** is **von dort** (from there). **Bahnhof** usually refers to the railway station. The bus or coach station would be **der Busbahnhof** or **der Omnibusbahnhof**.

kommen dann auf then (you'll) get to

Die gehen Sie etwa 500 Meter rechts runter You'll then walk down this road on your right for about 500 metres (i.e. **die Bahnhofstraße,** which is part of a pedestrian precinct).

Auf der linken Seite finden Sie ... On the left (side) you'll find ...

Über den gehen Sie You walk across that (lit. Over that walk you)

und laufen dann direkt auf den Wittener Hauptbahnhof zu and then you walk straight ahead to Witten main station. **Laufen** literally means 'to run' but it is often used colloquially for **gehen**.

Also von hier über den Marktplatz From here across the market square. **Rathausplatz** and **Marktplatz** are being used interchangeably here. As in previous dialogues, the verb is omitted in this summing up of information.

Practise what you have learned

14 Here is a list of landmarks. Put a cross next to those that were *not* mentioned in the dialogue. (Answers on p. 42.)

(a) **Bäckerladen**	☐	(f) **Fußgängerzone**	☐
(b) **Bank**	☐	(g) **Hauptbahnhof**	☐
(c) **Berliner Platz**	☐	(h) **Hauptpost**	☐
(d) **Blumenladen**	☐	(i) **Marktplatz**	☐
(e) **Denkmal**	☐	(j) **Rathausplatz**	☐

15 Can you remember? Complete the sentences below, choosing the appropriate phrase from the jumbled list (you won't need all of them). (Answers on p. 42.)

(a) **Können Sie mir sagen, wie ich von hier ________________ komme?**

(b) **Sie gehen jetzt hier ________________**

(c) **Dann kommen Sie ________________**

(d) **________________ finden Sie dann den Berliner Platz.**

(e) **Dann kommen Sie ________________ vorbei.**

(f) **Sie laufen direkt ________________ zu.**

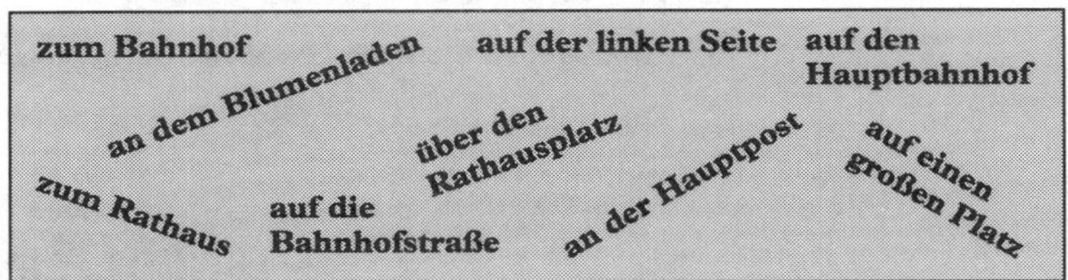

zum Bahnhof
an dem Blumenladen
auf der linken Seite
auf den Hauptbahnhof
über den Rathausplatz
auf einen großen Platz
zum Rathaus
auf die Bahnhofstraße
an der Hauptpost

Continued on next page.

16 How do you get to the station? Answer these questions with **ja** (yes) or **nein** (no). (Answers on p. 42.)

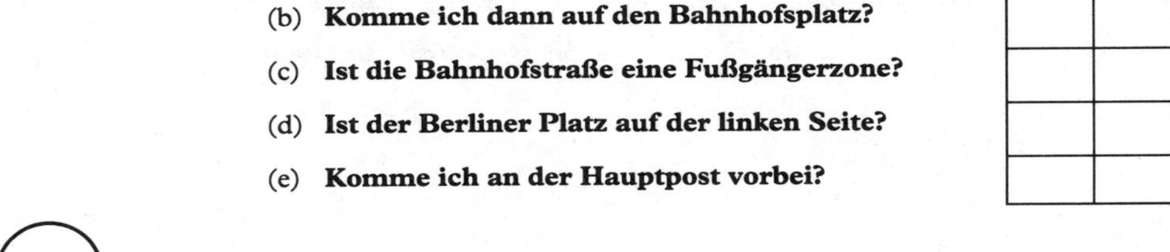

(a) **Muß ich jetzt hier über den Rathausplatz gehen?**

(b) **Komme ich dann auf den Bahnhofsplatz?**

(c) **Ist die Bahnhofstraße eine Fußgängerzone?**

(d) **Ist der Berliner Platz auf der linken Seite?**

(e) **Komme ich an der Hauptpost vorbei?**

	ja	nein
(a)		
(b)		
(c)		
(d)		
(e)		

17 Your turn to speak. Can you explain the way? With the help of the prompts, answer the questions on the recording.

18 Listen to this explanation of how to get to the main post office. Mark the statements that are *different* from the ones you hear. (Answers on p. 42.)

(a) **Wie komme ich am besten zum Bahnhof?**

(b) **Sie gehen also hier die Straße entlang.**

(c) **Dann kommen Sie zu einem Hauptpostamt.**

(d) **Ich fahre also diese Straße entlang.**

(e) **Dann gehen Sie noch 200 Meter geradeaus.**

(f) **Da ist dann das Hauptpostamt.**

Numbers

On the recording you will hear how to pronounce the numbers given in this table. Read them aloud once or twice.

Cardinal numbers			*Ordinal numbers*		
0	**null**	nil/zero			
1	**eins**	one	1.	**erster**	first
2	**zwei**	two	2.	**zweiter**	second
3	**drei**	three	3.	**dritter**	third
4	**vier**	four	4.	**vierter**	fourth
5	**fünf**	five	5.	**fünfter**	fifth
6	**sechs**	six	6.	**sechster**	sixth
7	**sieben**	seven	7.	**siebter**	seventh
8	**acht**	eight	8.	**achter**	eighth
9	**neun**	nine	9.	**neunter**	ninth
10	**zehn**	ten	10.	**zehnter**	tenth
11	**elf**	eleven	11.	**elfter**	eleventh
12	**zwölf**	twelve	12.	**zwölfter**	twelfth
13	**dreizehn**	thirteen	13.	**dreizehnter**	thirteenth
14	**vierzehn**	fourteen	14.	**vierzehnter**	fourteenth
15	**fünfzehn**	fifteen	15.	**fünfzehnter**	fifteenth
16	**sechzehn**	sixteen	16.	**sechzehnter**	sixteenth
17	**siebzehn**	seventeen	17.	**siebzehnter**	seventeenth
18	**achtzehn**	eighteen	18.	**achtzehnter**	eighteenth
19	**neunzehn**	nineteen	19.	**neunzehnter**	nineteenth
20	**zwanzig**	twenty	20.	**zwanzigster**	twentieth

19

Listen to the recording where you will hear announcers informing passengers about delays. Fill in the spaces below, using words rather than digits. You may need to know the following words: **der Flug** 'flight'; **der Zug** 'train'; **die Minute** 'minute'; **die Verspätung** 'delay'.
(Answers on p. 42.)

(a) **Der Zug aus Essen hat** ______________ **Minuten Verspätung.**

(b) **Der Zug aus Witten hat** ______________ **Minuten Verspätung.**

(c) **Der Zug aus Berlin hat** ______________ **Minuten Verspätung.**

(d) **Der Flug aus London hat** ______________ **Minuten Verspätung.**

(e) **Der Flug aus Paris hat** ______________ **Minuten Verspätung.**

20

On the recording you will hear the results of the first division of the German soccer league. Listen to the radio newsreader and fill in the results for these matches.

(a) **Karlsruher SC – SV Werder Bremen**	:
(b) **SG Wattenscheid 09 – Fortuna Düsseldorf**	:
(c) **FC Bayern München – Hertha BSC Berlin**	:
(d) **Bayer 04 Leverkusen – Hamburger SV**	:

Continued on next page.

(e) **FC St. Pauli – 1. FC Köln**

(f) **VfB Stuttgart – Borussia Mönchengladbach**

(g) **1. FC Nürnberg – Borussia Dortmund**

(h) **Bayer 05 Uerdingen – Eintracht Frankfurt**

(i) **1. FC Kaiserslautern – VfL Bochum**

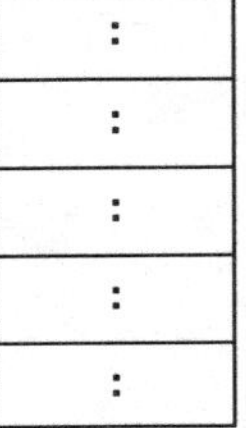

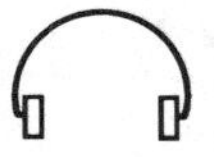

21

You are phoning your German business friend during your business trip to Germany. Your friend is abroad on holiday and wants to know about the weekend football results of his favourite teams. Tell him how München, Köln, Bochum, Dortmund and Düsseldorf played. Start by saying: **Die Ergebnisse sind ...** (the results are ...). When you have given your version out loud, listen to the radio newsreader again for the correct version.

22

Your friend would also like to know the positions of the teams in the league table. Listen to the recording so that you know how to start, then complete the report using the information in the league table below.

1. Kaiserslaut.	31	17	10	4	**62:39**	+23	**44:18**
2. B.München	31	17	8	6	**69:36**	+33	**42:20**
3. Wer.Bremen	31	12	14	5	**41:25**	+16	**38:24**
4. Hamburg.SV	31	15	7	9	**53:34**	+19	**37:25**
5. 1. FC Köln	31	13	10	8	**46:30**	+16	**36:26**
6. Etr.Frankfurt	31	13	9	9	**55:38**	+17	**35:27**
7. VfB Stuttgart	31	12	10	9	**49:39**	+10	**34:28**
8. Leverkusen	31	10	13	8	**43:40**	+ 3	**33:29**
9. F.Düsseldorf	31	11	10	10	**36:41**	- 5	**32:30**
10. Wattenscheid	31	8	14	9	**39:48**	- 9	**30:32**
11. Karlsruhe	31	8	13	10	**42:47**	- 5	**29:33**
12. M'gladbach	31	6	17	8	**42:51**	- 9	**29:33**
13. B.Dortmund	31	7	14	10	**38:54**	-16	**28:34**
14. VfL Bochum	31	8	10	13	**45:47**	- 2	**26:36**
15. FC St. Pauli	31	6	14	11	**30:42**	-12	**26:36**
16. FC Nürnberg	31	8	9	14	**35:51**	-16	**25:37**
17. B.Uerdingen	31	5	12	14	**31:49**	-18	**22:40**
18. Hertha Berlin	31	2	8	21	**32:77**	-45	**12:50**

23

Listen to the recording. Four people are dialling telephone numbers. Which of the two numbers given for each person are they dialling? Mark the correct ones. (Answers on p. 42.)

(a)	(b)	(c)	(d)
25681	31692	42427	57649
32681	55693	22437	47849

Key words and phrases

Ich würde gern ...	I would like ...
Würden Sie bitte ...	Would you please ...
Können Sie mir sagen ...	Can/Could you tell me ...
Entschuldigen Sie (bitte)	Excuse me (please) / I'm sorry
der Aufzug	lift/elevator
der Korridor / der Gang	corridor
die Tür	door
das Vorzimmer	anteroom / secretary's office
das Rathaus	town hall
der Bahnhof	station
der Hauptbahnhof	main/central station
das Postamt / die Post	post office
das Hauptpostamt / die Hauptpost	main post office
der Platz	square
der Marktplatz	market square
die Fußgängerzone	pedestrian precinct
der Laden / das Geschäft	shop/store
sich melden	to report
finden	to find
kommen zu	to get to
sich links / rechts halten	to keep to the left/right
benutzen	to use
in die zweite Etage fahren	to go up to the second floor
dort ist	there you'll find
einen Termin haben	to have an appointment
jemanden erwarten	to expect someone
vielleicht	perhaps/maybe
am besten	(the) best
etwas weiter	a (little) bit further along
hier	here
von hier	from here
dort	there
dort hinten	over there / in the distance
entlang	along
geradeaus	straight ahead
an ... vorbei	past
gegenüber	opposite
Wo?	Where?
Wie?	How?
Wieviel?	How much? / How many?
Wievielte ...?	Which ...?
auf Wiederseh(e)n	goodbye

Grammar

The verb haben *(to have)*

Haben and **sein** (to be) are two of the most important verbs in German. Both are irregular, but not difficult to remember. Pay special attention to the **ich, er/sie/es** and **sie** (plural) forms, as well as the polite **Sie** form. These are the ones which you will probably need most. Here are all the forms of **haben** in the present tense.

ich habe	I have	**wir haben**	we have
du hast	you have	**ihr habt**	you (pl.) have
er/sie/es hat	he/she/it has	**sie haben**	they have
		Sie haben	you have (polite, sing./pl.)

24 Fill in the right forms of **haben**. (Answers on p. 42.)

(a) **Ich ____________ einen Termin.**

(b) **Sie ____________ in Dundee zu tun.** (**sie** = 'she')

(c) **Ja, wir ____________ zehn Minuten Verspätung.**

(d) **Sie ____________ Kunden in Schottland.** (**Sie** = 'you')

(e) **Bochum ____________ ein Hauptpostamt.**

Irregular verbs

Most German verbs are regular, as we have seen in Unit 1. The endings are added to the stem, i.e. the infinitive ending **-en** is replaced by the appropriate endings (see Unit 1). There are some exceptions to this rule. Here are some examples. Make sure you remember these forms.

heißen to be called	**melden** to report	**fahren** to travel
ich heiße	**ich melde**	**ich fahre**
du heißt	**du meldest**	**du fährst**
er/sie/es heißt	**er/sie/es meldet**	**er/sie/es fährt**
wir heißen	**wir melden**	**wir fahren**
ihr heißt	**ihr meldet**	**ihr fahrt**
sie heißen	**sie melden**	**sie fahren**
Sie heißen	**Sie melden**	**Sie fahren**

25 Fill in the correct verb forms. (Answers on p. 42.)

(a) **Ich ____________ den Aufzug.** (benutzen)

(b) **Und zwar ____________ Sie mit dem Fahrstuhl in die dritte Etage.** (fahren)

(c) **Wir ____________ uns im Vorzimmer.** (melden)

(d) **Ihr ____________ links den Korridor entlang.** (gehen)

(e) **Du ____________ an dem Blumenladen dort hinten vorbei.** (kommen)

(f) **Ich ____________ als Verkaufsleiterin.** (arbeiten)

(g) **Sie ____________ Kunden in Essen.** (besuchen) (**sie** = 'she')

(h) **Dann ____________ Sie direkt auf den Bahnhof zu.** (gehen)

Read and understand

Have a good look at this key to the Bochum town plan. You will notice that a lot of words are similar to the English equivalents.

i	**Information**
	Polizei (police)
	Krankenhaus (hospital)
	Post (post office)
	Telefonzelle (public phone)
	Hotel
TAXI	**Dauerstandplatz** (overnight taxi rank)
	Straßenbahn (tram)
	U-Stadtbahn (underground/subway)
	Bus
U	**U-Bahn-Haltestelle** (underground/subway station)
S	**S-Bahn-Haltestelle** (suburban railway stop)
P	**Parkplatz** (car park)
P	**Parkhaus** (multi-storey car park)
P	**Tiefgarage** (underground car park)
	Vorgeschriebene Fahrtrichtung (compulsory direction)
	Einbahnstraße (one-way street)
	Fußgängerzone (pedestrian precinct)

When you are sure you have understood all the symbols, have a look at the map on the next page showing the centre of Bochum.

Here's a list of words and abbreviations used in the map:

ZOB (Zentraler Omnibusbahnhof)	central bus station
DB (Deutsche Bundesbahn)	German federal railways
Hbf (Hauptbahnhof)	main/central station
...pl. (... platz)	... square
... str. (... straße)	... street
... sch. (... schule)	... school
Kfm. Sch. (Kaufmännische Schule)	commercial school
Ev. K. (evangelische Kirche)	Protestant church
IHK (Industrie- und Handelskammer)	Chamber of Industry and Commerce
Verkehrsverein	tourist information

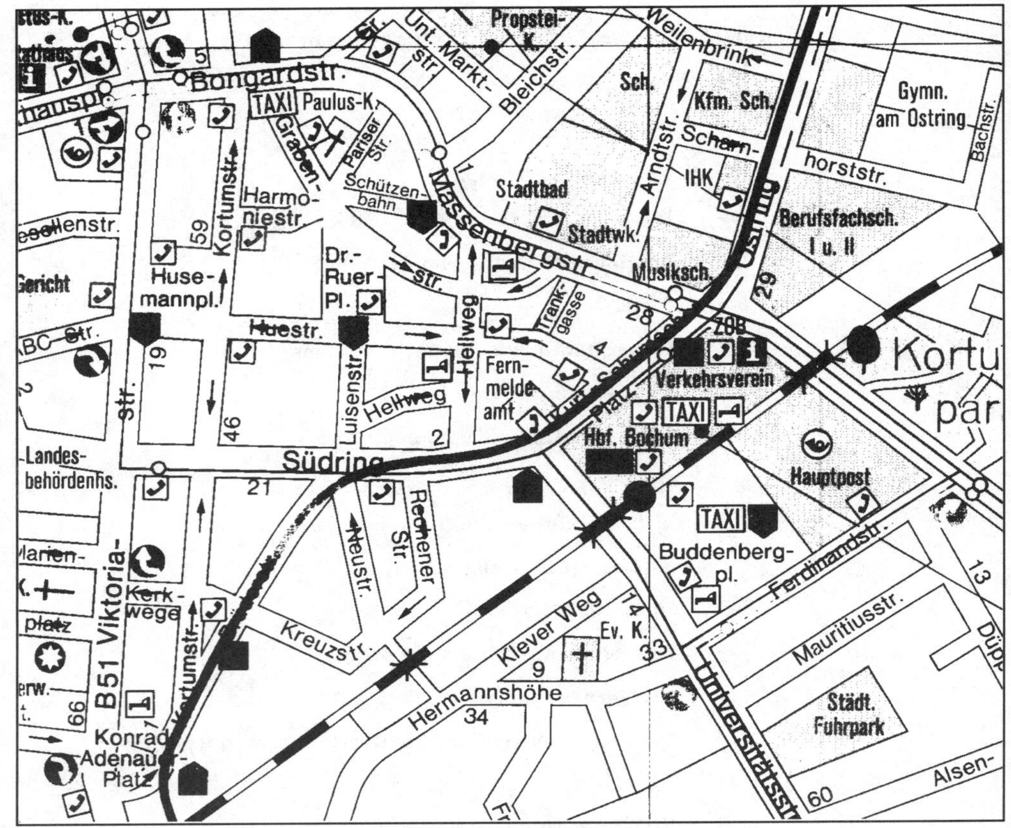

26 Try to find Bochum **Hauptbahnhof**. Which facilities (**Einrichtungen**) can you find at or next to the central station? Mark off the items on this list.

(a) **Blumenladen**
(b) **Hotel**
(c) **Industrie- und Handelskammer**
(d) **Krankenhaus**
(e) **Marktplatz**
(f) **Parkplatz**
(g) **Polizei**
(h) **Postamt**
(i) **S-Bahn-Haltestelle**
(j) **Taxi**
(k) **Telefonzelle**
(l) **U-Bahn-Haltestelle**
(m) **Verkehrsverein**
(n) **Zentraler Omnibusbahnhof**

Did you know?

Transport services in Germany

As in most other industrial countries, the railways' share in both passenger and freight handling has declined in the past 40 years in line with the extension and improvement of the road network. Timetable changes, hourly links between big industrial centres and higher speeds have halted, and in some areas reversed, the decline in the number of passengers on long-distance routes. The development of local and regional integrated transport systems has also helped to slow down the decline. It is the freight services of the **Bundesbahn** that have been hardest hit. They are criticized for being inflexible, too slow and too expensive. Attempts are being made to improve the overall performance of the rail system.

The massive extension of the road system, especially the construction of a very dense motorway network (more than 10,500 km (c. 6,560 miles) of motorways and 35,000 km (c. 21,875 miles) of federal trunk roads are now open), has attracted a lot of business away from the rail network. Fast and reliable door-to-door links have made it possible for businesses to reduce warehousing facilities, especially as most towns in Germany can be reached by road within eight to ten hours. The network is particularly dense in the Rhine/Ruhr agglomeration and in the Berlin, Hamburg, Hannover, Frankfurt, Stuttgart and München conurbations.

Navigable rivers such as the Rhine and its tributaries (Neckar, Main, Mosel, Ruhr), the Weser, the Elbe and the Oder, together with a comprehensive canal system which is still being enlarged to give access to the Danube and which provides valuable east–west links in an inland waterway system in which rivers flow from south to north, form a welcome backbone for low-cost transportation of bulk freight. Inland waterway transport is a major competitor for rail transport. The inland waterway network allows direct access to all major German, Dutch and Belgian seaports and inland to the Swiss, Czechoslovak and French import and export trade. Duisburg is possibly the busiest river port in Europe, if not the world.

The air transport network is well established with more than fifteen international airports. Frankfurt is the busiest of them and handles about 25 million passengers per year, which is about 40 per cent of the total. It also has the necessary facilities to handle the bulk of German air freight. The national airline and a number of independent carriers offer regular and efficient services to all the world's trade and tourist centres.

Since reunification in 1990, a massive investment programme has begun in order to adapt the German communications network to changing patterns of demand, to modernize transport facilities in eastern Germany and to re-establish the east–west communication lines which were destroyed or dismantled as a result of the Second World War.

Communications in Austria and Switzerland

The pattern of communications in landlocked Austria and Switzerland is largely dependent on their geographical features and the fact that the communications networks in both countries, which are not members of the EC, are used for the transit of goods and passengers between Germany and Italy. The road and rail networks in both countries are highly developed. The geographical problems have largely been overcome by complex systems of tunnels, which make fast road and rail transport possible irrespective of the weather. Electrification and the construction of motorways (most of these for north–south routes) have also helped to speed up the flow of traffic.

Your turn to speak

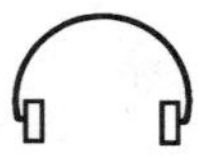

28 As in Unit 1 there are several possibilities and no single 'correct' answer. In order to do the exercises in this section you will have to refer to the map on p. 40.

(a) You are approached by a young man who does not know his way around Bochum. Give him directions from Kurt-Schumacher-Platz to the main post office. Before you start, revise the phrases in dialogues 3 and 4.

(b) Explain the shortest route from Bochum main station to Husemannplatz.

(c) Explain how you can get from Bochum main station to the local Chamber of Industry and Commerce.

Answers

Practise what you have learned

Exercise **1**	(a) der United Savings Bank (b) Herrn Falk (c) den Aufzug (d) den Korridor (e) die sechste Tür
Exercise **2**	(a) Mein Name ist Wilson (b) Ich würde gern Herrn Falk sprechen (c) Würden Sie bitte den Aufzug benutzen (d) Und zwar fahren Sie in die zweite Etage (e) Dann gehen Sie den Korridor links entlang (f) Dort ist das Vorzimmer von Herrn Falk (g) Ja, das werde ich finden
Exercise **3**	(a) komme (b) sprechen (c) fahren (d) halten (e) ist
Exercise **5**	You should have put a cross next to (a), (c) and (d).
Exercise **7**	(a) Termin (b) Konferenzraum (c) Gang (d) Tür
Exercise **8**	(a) i (b) i (c) ii (d) ii
Exercise **11**	(a) die Straße entlang (b) dem Blumenladen (c) einen großen Platz (d) das Postamt (e) das Rathaus
Exercise **13**	*falsch:* (a), (c), (e); *richtig:* (b), (d)
Exercise **14**	You should have put a cross next to (a), (b), (d) and (e).
Exercise **15**	(a) zum Bahnhof (b) über den Rathausplatz (c) auf die Bahnhofstraße (d) auf der linken Seite (e) an der Hauptpost (f) auf den Hauptbahnhof
Exercise **16**	(a) ja (b) nein (c) ja (d) ja (e) ja
Exercise **18**	You should have put a cross next to (a), (c), (d) and (e)

Numbers

Exercise **19**	(a) acht (b) fünf (c) zwölf (d) fünfzehn (e) zwanzig
Exercise **20**	(a) 1:1 (b) 2:0 (c) 7:3 (d) 2:2 (e) 2:0 (f) 1:1 (g) 1:1 (h) 2:3 (i) 4:1
Exercise **23**	(a) 25681 (b) 55693 (c) 22437 (d) 47849

Grammar

Exercise **24**	(a) habe (b) hat (c) haben (d) haben (e) hat
Exercise **25**	(a) benutze (b) fahren (c) melden (d) geht (e) kommst (f) arbeite (g) besucht (h) gehen

Read and understand

Exercise **26**	(b), (h), (i), (j), (k), (l), (m), (n)

3

TALKING ABOUT YOURSELF AND OTHERS

You will learn

- to make conversation at the company reception
- to understand and follow complex instructions
- to respond to offers of hospitality
- to talk about visits to German-speaking countries
- to enquire about exchanging money
- to understand and use job titles.

and you will be given information on how to address people.

Study guide

- **Dialogue 1 + Practise what you have learned**
- **Dialogue 2 + Practise what you have learned**
- **Dialogue 3 + Practise what you have learned**
- **Dialogue 4 + Practise what you have learned**
- Make sure you know the **Key words and phrases**
- Study the **Grammar** section
- Do the exercise in **Read and understand**
- Read **Did you know?**
- Do the exercises in **Your turn to speak**

Dialogues

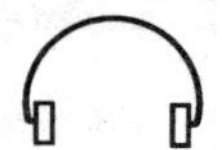

1 *Keeping an appointment*

Receptionist Guten Morgen, was kann ich für Sie tun?
Mr Masters Ich bin Herr Masters von der Firma Homecraft Ltd aus Wolverhampton. Ich habe für heute morgen, zehn Uhr, einen Termin mit Frau Köpl. Kann ich sie vielleicht sprechen?
Receptionist Ich ruf(e) mal eben an. Einen Moment, bitte.
Mr Masters Ja, danke.
Receptionist Wagelaar, Rezeption, guten Morgen. Hier ist ein Herr Masters von der Firma Homecraft aus Wolverhampton. Er hat für zehn Uhr einen Termin mit Frau Köpl. Geht das klar? ... Ja, gut. Ich schick(e) ihn rauf. Danke schön. Wiederhör(e)n. ... Frau Köpl erwartet Sie. Wenn Sie mit dem Aufzug in die vierte Etage fahren, dann links den Korridor entlang und die dritte Tür rechts.
Mr Masters Also mit dem Aufzug in die vierte Etage, dann links den Korridor entlang and vierte Tür rechts.
Receptionist Nein, die dritte Tür rechts.
Mr Masters Ach ja, die dritte Tür. Gut. Vielen Dank.
Receptionist Nichts zu danken. Wiedersehen.
Mr Masters Auf Wiedersehen.

der Moment moment

von der Firma Homecraft Ltd aus Wolverhampton from Homecraft Ltd of Wolverhampton. The preposition **aus** here indicates that the company is based in Wolverhampton. **Ich komme aus Köln** (I come from Cologne) indicates that you either live there or were born there, whereas **Ich komme von Köln** usually means that you have just come from there.

Ich habe für heute morgen einen Termin mit Frau Köpl I have an appointment with Frau Köpl this morning. **Für heute morgen** means 'for this morning'; **für heute nachmittag** 'for this afternoon'; **für heute abend** 'for tonight'.

➧ **Kann ich sie vielleicht sprechen?** Could I perhaps see her, please? (lit. Can I her perhaps speak). Note that **sie** is not written with a capital because it refers to Frau Köpl – it's not the polite form for 'you'.

➧ **Ich ruf(e) mal eben an** I'll just give her a ring

Wagelaar, Rezeption. Guten Morgen It is customary in German-speaking countries to mention one's name and department or section when making or answering a phone call.

Hier ist ein Herr Masters There is a Mr Masters here

für zehn Uhr for ten o'clock

➧ **Geht das klar?** Is that OK? A colloquial phrase to obtain a confirmation of something.

Ja, gut Yes, fine. Alternatively: **Ja, prima**.

Ich schick(e) ihn rauf I'll send him up (colloquial). Note the use of the present tense.

Wiederhör(e)n is only used at the end of a phone call. It is short for **Auf Wiederhören!** 'Till I hear you again'.

Frau Köpl erwartet Sie Frau Köpl is expecting you. There is no equivalent in German to the English continuous progressive form (is ...-ing).

Wenn Sie mit dem Aufzug ... fahren ... An invitation or suggestion to use the lift.

Ach ja Yes, of course

➧ **Nichts zu danken** Don't mention it (lit. Nothing to thank). Alternatively: **Gern geschehen** 'It's a pleasure'.

Practise what you have learned

1 Complete these sentences. Put the missing words into the boxes. The letters in the tinted boxes make up one of the words you have already filled in. (Answers on p. 60.)

(a) **Ich habe für ...**

... einen Termin mit Frau Köpl.

(b) **Kann ich sie vielleicht ...**

(c) **Frau Köpl ... Sie.**

(d) **Geht das ... ?**

(e) **... Sie mit dem Aufzug in die vierte Etage.**

(f) **Dann gehen Sie den Korridor ...**

(g) **Das ist die dritte Tür ...**

(h) **... zu danken.**

Keyword:

(a) (b) (c) (d) (e) (f) (g) (h)

2 How good are you at remembering the numbers? (Answers on p. 60.)

(a) **Der Termin mit Frau Köpl ist für __________ Uhr.**

(b) **Herr Masters muß mit dem Aufzug in die __________ Etage fahren.**

(c) **Es ist die __________ Tür rechts.**

(d) **Frau Zimmermann wohnt im __________ Stock.**

3 Your turn to speak. Can you make the correct responses? Take the role of Mr Masters and use the prompts for your part of the dialogue.

4 Listen to the conversation between Frau Braun and the receptionist and then decide whether the statements made below are **richtig** (true) or **falsch** (false). (Answers on p. 60.) You will hear the following new words: **Zu wem?** 'To whom?'; **bei uns** 'in our company'; **sondern** 'but'; **im Export** 'in the export department'; **Ach so** 'Oh, I get it'; **sich hinsetzen** 'to sit down'.

	richtig	falsch
(a) **Frau Braun wohnt bei der Firma Baumann.**		
(b) **Frau Braun hat einen Termin für elf Uhr.**		
(c) **Einen Herrn Baumann haben wir nicht bei uns.**		
(d) **Herr Baum ist als Vertriebsleiter beschäftigt.**		
(e) **Herr Baum hat Besuch.**		
(f) **Herr Baum kommt in fünfzehn Minuten.**		
(g) **Frau Baum kann sich hier nicht hinsetzen.**		

Dialogues

2 *Mr Carter is met at reception*

Mr Carter Guten Morgen.
Receptionist Guten Morgen.
Mr Carter Mein Name ist Carter, und ich komme von der United Investments Inc. in Boston und wollte gerne Herrn Körner sprechen.
Receptionist Ja, einen kleinen Moment, bitte. Ich ruf(e) nur kurz durch. ... Ja, hier ist Martina. Hallo Brigitte. Herr Carter ist hier und wollte gern Herrn Körner sprechen. Kannst du ihn kurz abholen? ... Ja, ich geb(e) ihm Bescheid. Bis gleich. Tschüß. ... Herr Carter, könnten Sie noch einen kleinen Moment Platz nehmen?
Mr Carter Selbstverständlich.
Receptionist Sie werden gleich abgeholt von Fräulein Halsband, der Sekretärin.
Mr Carter Danke schön.
Receptionist Bitte.

Secretary Guten Morgen, sind Sie Herr Carter?
Mr Carter Ja, guten Morgen.
Secretary Mein Name ist Halsband. Ich bin die Sekretärin von Herrn Körner.
Mr Carter Wie war der Name noch einmal?
Secretary Halsband.
Mr Carter Guten Morgen, Fräulein Halsband.
Secretary Guten Morgen. Kommen Sie dann bitte mit.
Mr Carter Gerne.
Secretary Wie war die Reise?

und wollte gerne Herrn Körner sprechen and was wanting to speak to Herr Körner. Note that **wollte** is often used to express the idea of 'would like to'.

➧ **Ich ruf(e) nur kurz durch** I'll give him a quick ring (lit. I call only shortly through) – i.e. to let him know he has a visitor. **Rufen** means 'to call'.

Ja, hier ist Martina Hello, this is Martina. **Ja** usually means 'yes', but here it is simply a casual way of answering the phone.

➧ **Kannst du ihn kurz abholen?** Lit. 'Can you him quickly fetch? **Kurz** is unnecessary and makes this phrase colloquial. Such phrases are common: **Ich gehe kurz (mal) einkaufen** (I'm just going shopping, but I won't be long) or: **Ich gehe kurz (mal) in die Stadt** (I'm just going into town).

➧ **Ich geb(e) ihm Bescheid** I'll tell him / let him know. You often hear **Ich sag(e) ihm Bescheid** (I'll let him know / tell him).

➧ **Bis gleich** Lit. 'Until immediately'. This is a very common phrase meaning 'See you later'.

Tschüß Bye. Cheerio. This is informal but very common, and is often used instead of **Auf Wiedersehen** and **Auf Wiederhören**, particularly by younger people.

Könnten Sie noch einen kleinen Moment Platz nehmen? Would you take a seat for a moment? A very polite invitation to sit down (**Platz nehmen**) and wait.

Selbstverständlich is a conventional response meaning 'Yes, of course'. It would be quite appropriate to say: **Ja, danke** or **Ja, vielen Dank** or **Ja natürlich, danke**.

➧ **Sie werden gleich abgeholt von Fräulein Halsband** Fräulein Halsband will be here in a minute to take you up (lit. you will immediately be collected by Fräulein Halsband). The literal meaning of **gleich** is 'immediately', but it is usually understood as 'soon'; **abholen** is 'to fetch/collect someone'.

Sind Sie Herr Carter? Are you Mr Carter?

Ich bin die Sekretärin von Herrn Körner I'm Herr Körner's secretary

➧ **Wie war der Name noch einmal?** What was your name again?

➧ **Kommen Sie dann bitte mit** Come with me then, please / Would you please come with me

➧ **Wie war die Reise?** How was the journey?

Practise what you have learned

5

Match the English and German sentences. (Answers on p. 60.)

(a) Come with me then, please.
(b) I was wanting to speak to Herr Körner.
(c) Can you quickly come and collect him?
(d) Fräulein Halsband will be here in a minute to take you up.
(e) I'll give him a quick ring.
(f) Could you wait a moment please?
(g) What was the name again?

(i) **Ich wollte gerne Herrn Körner sprechen.**
(ii) **Ich rufe nur kurz durch.**
(iii) **Kannst du ihn kurz abholen?**
(iv) **Könnten Sie noch einen Augenblick warten?**
(v) **Sie werden gleich von Fräulein Halsband abgeholt.**
(vi) **Wie war der Name noch einmal?**
(vii) **Kommen Sie dann bitte mit.**

6

What is your reaction to these requests and comments? See if you can match them up. (Answers on p. 60.)

(a) **Was kann ich für Sie tun?**
(b) **Können Sie bitte einen Moment Platz nehmen?**
(c) **Sie werden gleich abgeholt.**
(d) **Sind Sie Herr Carter?**
(e) **Kommen Sie dann bitte mit.**

(i) **Danke schön.**
(ii) **Ja, gerne.**
(iii) **Ja, ich bin Herr Carter.**
(iv) **Ja, selbstverständlich.**
(v) **Ich wollte gern Herrn Körner sprechen.**

7

Your turn to speak. Take the role of a visitor to a German company. Use the prompts to help you give the correct answers.

8

Listen to the conversation at the reception between Herr Bertram and the receptionist. Then decide who said the following sentences and put a cross in the appropriate box. (Answers on p. 60.) **Einen Augenblick bitte** means 'just a moment please' and **der Fahrstuhl** is another word for 'lift/elevator'.

	Herr Bertram	*Receptionist*
(a) **Zu wem möchten Sie bitte?**		
(b) **Herr Willms ist nicht in seinem Zimmer.**		
(c) **Wo ist Herr Willms denn?**		
(d) **Das kann ich Ihnen auch nicht sagen.**		
(e) **Ist die Sekretärin von Herrn Willms vielleicht da?**		
(f) **Nein, das Zimmer kenne ich nicht.**		
(g) **Sie fahren also mit dem Fahrstuhl in den vierten Stock.**		
(h) **Vielen Dank. Auf Wiedersehen.**		

Dialogues

3 *Arriving at the office*

Secretary Guten Tag.
Herr Grimshaw Guten Tag, mein Name ist Donald Grimshaw von der General Oxygen Company Ltd. Ich habe um zehn Uhr einen Termin mit Herrn Schönfeld.
Secretary Oh ja, ich weiß. Sie sind aber pünktlich! Es tut mir leid, der Herr Schönfeld ist leider gerade in einer Besprechung. Möchten Sie einen Moment warten?
Herr Grimshaw Ja, bitte.
Secretary Darf ich Sie bitten, Platz zu nehmen?
Herr Grimshaw Ja, gern.
Secretary Möchten Sie Ihren Mantel ablegen?
Herr Grimshaw Ja, bitte.
Secretary So, kann ich Ihnen eine Tasse Kaffee anbieten?
Herr Grimshaw Oh ja, bitte.
Secretary Nehmen Sie Milch und Zucker?
Herr Grimshaw Nein danke. Ich trinke ihn schwarz.
Secretary Bitte sehr ... Ist das Ihr erster Besuch in Deutschland?
Herr Grimshaw Nein, ich bin des öfteren in Deutschland.
Secretary Waren Sie denn auch schon mal in Witten?
Herr Grimshaw Nein, ich bin heute zum ersten Mal bei Ihnen hier.
Secretary Und wie gefällt es Ihnen?
Herr Grimshaw Ich muß sagen, sehr gut.
Secretary Das ist schön. Oh, ich sehe, da kommt der Herr Schönfeld gerade. Kleinen Moment bitte, ich sage ihm gleich Bescheid.
Herr Grimshaw Ja, vielen Dank.

eine Tasse Kaffee cup of coffee
die Milch milk
der Zucker sugar

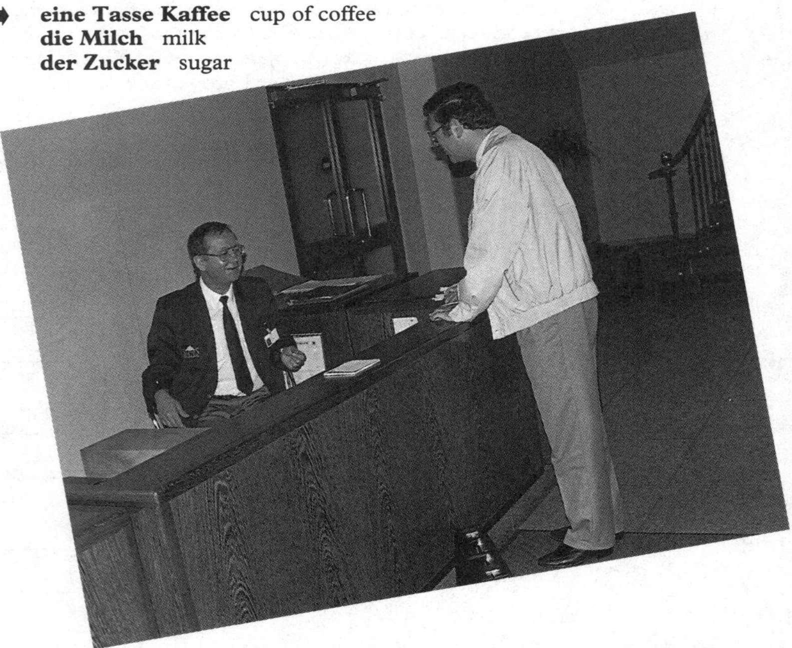

Oh ja, ich weiß Yes, of course. I know. **Ich weiß** is a present tense form of the irregular verb **wissen** (to know).

Sie sind aber pünktlich You *are* punctual. **Aber** usually means 'but' – it is used idiomatically here.

der Herr Schönfeld is a somewhat colloquial expression. The article (**der**) is not normally used with names.

ist gerade in einer Besprechung is in a meeting right now. **Eine Besprechung** refers to a meeting that may be called at short notice and as a rule is fairly informal. **Eine Sitzung** is a meeting with a fixed agenda to which participants have been invited in writing.

Möchten Sie einen Moment warten? Would you like to wait a moment? As in English, although this looks like a question, it is actually a request.

Darf ich Sie bitten, Platz zu nehmen? Lit. May I you ask a seat to take?

Möchten Sie Ihren Mantel ablegen? Won't you take off your coat?

Kann ich Ihnen eine Tasse Kaffee anbieten? May I offer you a cup of coffee? or **Möchten Sie eine Tasse Kaffee?** 'Would you like a cup of coffee?'. **Anbieten** means 'to offer'; **eine Tasse Kaffee**, 'a cup of coffee'.

Nehmen Sie Milch und Zucker? Do you take milk and sugar?

Ich trinke ihn schwarz I drink it black

Bitte sehr is an idiomatic phrase meaning 'Here you are'. It's what you say when you offer someone something. The expected reply would be **danke sehr / danke schön** or simply **danke**.

Ihr erster Besuch your first visit. The verb 'to visit' is **besuchen** (see p. 17); and the German for 'visitor' is **der Besucher**.

Ich bin des öfteren in Deutschland I come fairly often to Germany. **Öfter** (often) is better and simpler than **des öfteren**.

Waren Sie denn auch schon mal in Witten? Have you ever been to Witten before? Witten is a town south-east of Bochum.

Und wie gefällt es Ihnen? And how do you like it? (lit. And how pleases it to you?) One possible answer, **Es gefällt mir** 'I like it' (lit. It pleases to me), is a key construction for expressing likes/dislikes.

Ich muß sagen (Yes,) I must say

Das ist schön That is good. **Schön** is used in many different contexts. It can also mean 'nice/pretty'.

Da kommt der Herr Schönfeld gerade Herr Schönfeld is just coming. **Gerade** means 'just'.

Ich sage ihm gleich Bescheid I'll tell him at once (that you're here)

Now turn over for the exercises based on dialogue 3.

Practise what you have learned

9 Can you match the German and English versions of these polite questions? (Answers on p. 60.)

(a) **Kann ich Ihnen helfen?**
(b) **Darf ich Sie bitten, Platz zu nehmen?**
(c) **Möchten Sie Ihren Mantel ablegen?**
(d) **Darf ich Ihnen eine Tasse Kaffee anbieten?**
(e) **Nehmen Sie Milch und Zucker?**
(f) **Sind Sie zum ersten Mal in Deutschland?**
(g) **Kennen Sie Witten schon?**

(i) May I ask you to take a seat?
(ii) Do you take milk and sugar?
(iii) May I help you?
(iv) Do you already know Witten?
(v) May I offer you a cup of coffee?
(vi) Is this your first time in Germany?
(vii) Would you like to take your coat off?

10 Match the questions on the left with the answers on the right. Read your answers aloud, then listen to the recording to see if you got them in the correct order.

(a) **Um wieviel Uhr ist der Termin mit Herrn Schönfeld?**
(b) **Wo ist Herr Schönfeld gerade?**
(c) **Trinkt Herr Grimshaw den Kaffee schwarz?**
(d) **Ist er öfter in Deutschland?**
(e) **Kennt er Witten schon?**
(f) **Wie gefällt es ihm?**

(i) **Ja, Herr Grimshaw trinkt den Kaffee schwarz.**
(ii) **Es gefällt ihm sehr gut.**
(iii) **Der Termin mit Herrn Schönfeld ist um zehn Uhr.**
(iv) **Nein, er kennt Witten nicht.**
(v) **Herr Schönfeld ist gerade in einer Besprechung.**
(vi) **Ja, Herr Grimshaw ist des öfteren in Deutschland.**

11 Your turn to speak. Take the role of the visitor, Peter Hock, using the prompts for your part of the conversation.

12 Listen to the conversation between Herr Schumann, a secretary, and Frau Reich, who works as a representative. Put a cross next to the sentences below that Herr Schumann has actually said. (Answers on p. 60.)

(a)	**Guten Morgen, Frau Langer.**	
(b)	**Sie sind aber pünktlich heute.**	
(c)	**Die Reise war sehr angenehm.**	
(d)	**Ich will Ihnen jetzt den Mantel abnehmen.**	
(e)	**Sie möchten jetzt sicher etwas zu trinken?**	
(f)	**Kann ich bitte eine Tasse Kaffee haben?**	
(g)	**Frau Langer hat gerade eine Besprechung.**	
(h)	**Sie kommt in etwa zwanzig Minuten.**	

Dialogues

4 *Trying to change money at the hotel reception*

Receptionist Guten Morgen, kann ich Ihnen helfen?
Guest Ja gerne. Ich möchte gern einige Pfund eintauschen. Kann ich das bei Ihnen hier machen?
Receptionist Das tut mir leid, das ist hier leider nicht möglich.
Guest Das ist schade. Wo kann ich das denn tun? Können Sie mir vielleicht sagen, wo eine Bank in der Nähe ist?
Receptionist Ja, wir haben gleich hier in der Nähe verschiedene Banken, z.B. die Sparkasse ...
Guest Mhm ...
Receptionist ... oder die Westfalenbank ...
Guest Ah ja.
Receptionist ... und weiter, ein Stückchen weiter noch die Dresdner Bank und die Deutsche Bank.
Guest Mhm. Können Sie irgendeine der Banken empfehlen?
Receptionist Von der Nähe her können Sie am ehesten die Westfalenbank erreichen, sie öffnet auch schon um halb neun.
Guest Halb neun. Ach ja, da muß ich noch (ei)ne halbe Stunde warten. Hm, das ist ärgerlich, Mist.
Receptionist Das ist aber die erste.

der Geldtausch exchange of money **ärgerlich** annoying

Ich möchte gern einige Pfund eintauschen I would like to change a few pounds. **Einige** can mean either 'a few' or 'some'.

Kann ich das ... hier machen? Can I do that here?

Das tut mir leid I'm sorry (often shortened to **Tut mir leid**)

Das ist hier leider nicht möglich That is unfortunately not possible here. **Leider** means 'unfortunately', **möglich** 'possible'.

Das ist schade That's a pity. A useful and common phrase to express regret.

Wo kann ich das denn tun? Where can I do that then?

Können Sie mir vielleicht sagen, wo eine Bank in der Nähe ist? Could you perhaps tell me where there is a bank close by? **In der Nähe** means 'close by / nearby / in the neighbourhood' or even 'not far off'. The expression is often used as a preposition, e.g. **in der Nähe der Bank**, 'near the bank'.

gleich hier just outside (lit. immediately here)

verschiedene Banken several/various banks

Sparkasse savings bank. German savings banks are usually in public ownership and controlled by the municipal authorities. **Sparen** means 'to save'.

Westfalenbank is a private bank named after the region in which it is based, i.e. **Westfalen** (Westphalia), which is part of the federal state of Northrhine Westphalia.

Deutsche Bank and **Dresdner Bank** are two of the big three private banks in Germany, the third being **Commerzbank**.

und weiter, ein Stückchen weiter and further, a little bit further on

Turn over for the rest of the notes and the exercises for this dialogue.

Können Sie irgendeine der Banken empfehlen? Can you recommend any of the banks? **Irgendein** is usually translated by *some* or *any*; **empfehlen** is 'to recommend'.

Von der Nähe her as far as proximity is concerned

können Sie am ehesten die Westfalenbank erreichen the Westfalenbank is the one you'll get to most quickly. **Erreichen** is 'to get to / reach', and **am ehesten** is 'most quickly/ easily'.

Sie öffnet auch schon um halb neun It opens also at half past eight already. For more on times see p. 111-112.

Da muß ich noch (ei)ne halbe Stunde warten So I (still) have to wait half an hour

Das ist ärgerlich That is (very) annoying.

Mist Damn it

Das ist aber die erste But it's the first (to open)

COMMERZBANK

Practise what you have learned

13 Circle the correct answer. In some cases there is more than one possibility. (Answers on p. 60.)

(a) **Was möchte der Gast gern eintauschen?**

(i) **einige Dollar** (ii) **einige Pfund** (iii) **einige D-mark**

(b) **Kann er bei der Rezeption Geld eintauschen?**

(i) **ja** (ii) **ja, nur Dollar** (iii) **nein**

(c) **Wo kann er Geld eintauschen?**

(i) **bei der Sparkasse** (ii) **am Hauptbahnhof** (iii) **bei der Bank**

(d) **Welche Banken kennt die Frau an der Hotelrezeption?**

(i) **Westfalenbank** (ii) **Berliner Bank** (iii) **Commerzbank**

(iv) **Deutsche Bank** (v) **Dresdner Bank** (vi) **Sparkasse**

(e) **Welche Bank öffnet um halb neun?**

(i) **Deutsche Bank** (ii) **Kundenkreditbank** (iii) **Westfalenbank**

14 Jumbled up in the box below are all the missing words from these sentences. The English equivalent is given in round brackets to help you fill in the correct word. (Answers on p. 60.)

(a) **Ich möchte gern __________ Pfund eintauschen.** (some)

(b) **Kann ich das bei Ihnen __________ machen.** (here)

(c) **Das ist hier __________ nicht möglich.** (unfortunately)

(d) **Können Sie mir __________ sagen, wo ich eine Bank finde.** (perhaps)

(e) **Wir haben __________ hier verschiedene Banken.** (right)

(f) **Ein Stückchen __________ ist die Dresdner Bank.** (further along)

(g) **Die Westfalenbank können Sie __________ erreichen.** (the easiest)

(h) **Sie öffnet __________ um halb neun.** (already)

am ehesten **hier** **schon** **gleich** **weiter** **einige** **leider** **vielleicht**

15 In this speaking exercise, you take the role of the guest. Use the prompts for your parts of the dialogue.

16 Listen to the statements on the recording and compare them with the sentences printed below. Indicate in the boxes whether the ones below are **richtig** (true) or **falsch** (false). (Answers on p. 60.)

	richtig	falsch
(a) **Der Gast möchte am Postamt Geld eintauschen.**		
(b) **Das ist bei der Hotelrezeption leider nicht möglich.**		
(c) **Die Frau an der Rezeption sagt, in der Nähe sind vielleicht Banken und Sparkassen.**		
(d) **Die Deutsche Bank und die Commerzbank sind am ehesten zu erreichen.**		
(e) **Die Banken und Sparkassen öffnen um neun Uhr, nur die Westfalenbank öffnet schon um halb neun.**		

Key words and phrases

Was kann ich für Sie tun?	What can I do for you?
Kann ich sie vielleicht sprechen?	Could I perhaps talk to her?
Möchten Sie einen Moment warten?	Would you please wait a moment?
Könnten Sie Platz nehmen?	Would you take a seat?
Darf ich Sie bitten ...?	Would you please ...? / May I ask you to ...?
Möchten Sie den Mantel ablegen?	Would you like to take off your coat?
Kann ich Ihnen eine Tasse Kaffee anbieten?	May I offer you a cup of coffee?
Nehmen Sie Milch und Zucker?	Do you take milk and sugar?
Wie gefällt es Ihnen?	How do you like it?
Kannst du ihn abholen?	Can you meet/fetch him? / Can you pick him up?
Geht das klar?	Is that OK?
Wie war der Name noch einmal?	What was the name again?
Wie war die Reise?	How was the journey?
Kommen Sie bitte mit	Come with me please
Sie werden abgeholt	Someone will come to fetch you
Ja, gut / ja, prima	Yes, (that's) fine
Gern geschehen / Nichts zu danken	It's a pleasure / You're welcome / Don't mention it
Bis gleich	See you later
Auf Wiederhören	Goodbye (on phone)
Da kommt er gerade	He's just coming
Ich rufe mal eben an	I'll just give (him/her) a quick ring
Ich sage ihm gleich Bescheid	I'll tell him at once
Ich gebe ihm Bescheid	I'll let him know
Ich muß eine halbe Stunde warten	I have to wait half an hour
Ich möchte einige Pfund eintauschen	I would like to change a few pounds
in einer Besprechung sein	to be in a meeting
ich weiß	I know / I'm aware of that
Es tut mir (sehr) leid	I'm (very) sorry
Das ist leider nicht möglich	Unfortunately, that's not possible
Das ist schade	That's a pity
Das ist ärgerlich	That's annoying
in der Nähe	nearby / near here / close by
um halb neun	at half past eight
um zehn Uhr	at ten o'clock
pünktlich	punctual

Grammar

German nouns

Nouns are easy to identify in German as they are always written with a capital initial letter, e.g. **der Markt** (the market).

Gender There are three categories of nouns, called genders: masculine, feminine and neuter. You can tell the gender of a noun by the article, i.e. the word for either 'the' or 'a(n)': **der /ein** (masculine), **die/eine** (feminine), **das/ein** (neuter). Sometimes the gender is obvious, e.g. **der Vater** (the father) is masculine and **die Mutter** (the mother) is feminine. But in many instances the gender seems quite arbitrary. You are strongly advised to learn the gender together with the noun and, in order to help you, the genders are always indicated when new vocabulary is introduced. (In the vocabulary list at the back of the book the genders are shown as *m.* for masculine, *f.* for feminine and *n.* for neuter.)

In compounds, i.e. nouns composed of two or more separate nouns, the gender is always that of the last one: **das Postamt, der Besuchstermin, der Geldtausch, die Hotelrezeption**.

Case Unfortunately, knowing the gender of a noun, whether it is masculine, feminine or neuter, is not the end of the problem. There is also the concept of 'case': this is a grammatical term which basically explains the function of a particular word in a sentence. So you need to know two things: what gender a noun is and what its function is within the sentence. (If you are already confused or you don't like grammar, move on to the next section. Just remember that you will come across some slightly different ways of saying 'the' and 'a' as the course progresses. If you are interested and want to be correct, read on.)

There are three cases you need to know about at the moment: the nominative, the accusative and the dative. The **nominative** is used when the noun is the subject of a phrase. The **accusative** is used when it is the direct object of the phrase. The **dative** is used to express the idea of 'to the' (e.g. 'to the gentleman' is **dem Mann**) and also in conjunction with many prepositions (words like **zu** (to), **mit** (with), **von** (from)). Here are some examples which show the function of each noun.

Die Sekretärin	**gibt**	**dem Gast**	**eine Tasse Kaffee.**
The secretary	gives	(to) the guest	a cup of coffee.
↑		↑	↑
subject (nominative)		*indirect object (dative)*	*direct object (accusative)*

Die Sekretärin	**bringt**	**den Gast**	**zu dem Konferenzzimmer.**
The secretary	brings	the guest	to the conference room.
↑		↑	↑
subject (nominative)		*direct object (accusative)*	*preposition with dative*

In dictionaries and in this course a noun itself is always introduced as though it were in the nominative, e.g. **der Markt** *m.* 'the market', **die Reise** *f.* 'the journey', **das Büro** *n.* 'the office'.

The combination of gender and case is shown in table form below and in the grammar summary (see p.224). If this seems very complicated, *don't worry.* Just be aware that you may find different words for 'the' and 'a' as the course progresses.

	masculine	*feminine*	*neuter*
nominative	**der/ein Markt**	**die/eine Reise**	**das/ein Büro**
accusative	**den/einen Markt**	**die/eine Reise**	**das/ein Büro**
dative	**dem/einem Markt**	**der/einer Reise**	**dem/einem Büro**

Here are two exercises to help you see how this works in practice.

17

Choose the correct words for 'the'. The gender is given in brackets after the noun to help you, and you can always look back to the dialogues if you are not sure about the case. (Answers on p. 60.)

(a) **Würden Sie bitte ________ Aufzug** (m.) **benutzen.**

(b) **Er fährt mit ________ Fahrstuhl** (m.).

(c) **Jetzt gehen Sie ________ Korridor** (m.) **entlang.**

(d) **Ich kenne ________ Zimmernummer** (f.).

(e) **Leider kann er ________ Reise** (f.) **nicht machen.**

(f) **Linker Hand finden Sie ________ Rathaus** (n.).

(g) **Auf ________ linken Seite** (f.) **ist ________ Postamt** (n.).

18

Now choose the correct word for 'a'. (Answers on p. 60.)

(a) **Ich habe ________ Termin** (m.) **mit Frau Köpl.**

(b) **Warten Sie bitte ________ kleinen Moment** (m.).

(c) **Wir haben ________ Konferenzraum** (m.) **in der dritten Etage.**

(d) **Er ist leider gerade in ________ Besprechung** (f.).

(e) **Möchten Sie ________ Tasse** (f.) **Kaffee?**

(f) **Wo ist hier ________ Bank** (f.) **in der Nähe?**

(g) **Kennen Sie ________ Computerprogramm** (n.) **für Banken?**

(h) **Herr Richter hat ________ Büro** (n.) **mit ________ Vorzimmer** (n.).

(i) **Bancosoft ist ________ Softwarehaus** (n.).

Read and understand

Der Stellenmarkt Die Stellenangebote

The job market Vacancies

Have a look at these job descriptions taken from the vacancies pages of a German newspaper. The 'job market' is **der Stellenmarkt** and 'vacancies' are **die Stellenangebote**. All these descriptions relate to management and clerical jobs, or to jobs involving buying (**Kaufen**) and selling (**Verkaufen**). Many of them are easily recognizable because they are taken from the English; some may be familiar from earlier units. The job descriptions which end in **-kaufmann** refer to administrative functions with a specialization, e.g. a **Speditionskaufmann** is a 'qualified clerk in the haulage industry'; an **Exportkaufmann** is a 'qualified clerk in the export trade'.

19 Classify the job descriptions and list them under these three headings:

(a) Senior management jobs
(b) Jobs involving administrative or clerical work
(c) Jobs involving buying or selling

Diplom-Volkswirt
Günther Sussieck
Steuerberater
Diplom-Ökonom
FRITZ FUHR
Vereidigter Buchprüfer
Steuerberater
Diplom-Kaufmann
Jochen Meyer
Steuerberater
Rolf Dettmann
Rechtsanwalt

Did you know?

Saying hello and goodbye

Business visitors are likely to use the greetings which you have already come across in the first three units: **Guten Morgen, Guten Tag**, etc. On an informal level people often drop the **Gute(n)**, saying **Morgen, Tag, N'Abend, Nacht**. Colleagues may say **Hallo** when they arrive and **Tschüß** (bye) or **Tschau** when they leave. In southern Germany and Austria a lot of people say **Grüß Gott**, literally 'greet (you) God'. In business contexts these colloquial forms are also used, although on the whole **Auf Wiedersehen** (goodbye) and **Auf Wiederhören** (at the end of a telephone conversation) are preferred. At lunchtime people in companies often greet each other by saying **Mahlzeit** , literally 'mealtime'. In Austria good friends often greet each other with **Servus**; and in Switzerland you may hear the Swiss-German (**Schwyzerdütsch** or **Schweizerdeutsch**) variant **Gruezi** (**Grüß Sie/Euch/Dich**).

Germans usually shake hands when they greet someone and when they depart. It is customary to greet women first – even if there are men of senior rank in the group.

Frau and *Fräulein*

For official purposes the distinction between **Frau** and **Fräulein** is no longer made. **Frau** is now used for both married and unmarried women; there is no equivalent to the English 'Ms'. Some people though still use **Fräulein** for young, unmarried women, and it is used in certain service sectors, e.g. to attract the attention of a waitress.

Titles

If someone has a title, especially an academic one, it is common to use it together with the person's surname, e.g. **Frau Doktor Zimmermann** or **Herr Professor Richter**. However, doctors of medicine are usually addressed as **Frau/Herr Doktor**. At formal meetings, participants address the chair by saying **Herr Vorsitzender** or **Herr Präsident**, without mentioning the name of the person concerned. Other titles such as **Diplom-Betriebswirt** (qualified business administrator), **Diplom-Volkswirt** (qualified economist) or **Diplom-Kaufmann** (graduate in commerce) are as a rule only printed on cards or used on name tags and door labels.

First name or surname?

In the business world it is still fairly common among people in management positions to address each other by their surnames and also to use **Sie**, the polite form of address. This is particularly true for business contacts outside one's own company, and it would be expected from foreigners. If someone asks you to address them by their first name and use **du** instead of **Sie**, this usually implies a fair degree of familiarity. However, people who work together or who belong to some kind of group (e.g. members of a sports club, students) call each other **du** straight away. To be on the safe side, stick to **Sie** + surname unless you are asked to use **du**.

Your turn to speak

Now it's your turn to speak again. As in the previous units these exercises are open-ended. Use the phrases and structures from the dialogues, as well as those listed below, to help you work out what you want to say. Then say your version aloud before you listen to the model versions on the recording.

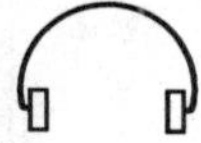

20 You are visiting business friends in a German-speaking country. Introduce yourself to the person you've come to see. State your name and the company you're working for. Say what your position is.

Mein Name ist ...
Ich bin bei ... beschäftigt
Ich bin Vertriebsleiter/Exportleiter, etc.
Ich bin Geschäftsführer bei der Firma ...

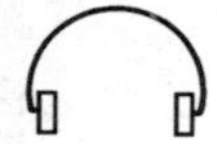

21 You are at a business meeting. Introduce your colleague who is responsible for marketing.

Und dies ist Herr/Frau/Fräulein ...
Herr/Frau/Fräulein ... arbeitet in der ...abteilung unserer Firma
Herr/Frau/Fräulein ... ist in der ...abteilung (unserer Firma) beschäftigt
Herr/Frau/Fräulein ... ist Leiter(in) der ...abteilung (in) unserer Firma

Answers

Practise what you have learned

Exercise 1	(a) heute morgen (b) sprechen (c) erwartet (d) klar (e) Fahren (f) entlang (g) rechts (h) Nichts Keyword: erwartet
Exercise 2	(a) zehn (b) vierte (c) dritte (d) achten
Exercise 4	*richtig:* (b), (c), (e); *falsch:* (a), (d), (f), (g)
Exercise 5	(a) vii (b) i (c) iii (d) v (e) ii (f) iv (g) vi
Exercise 6	(a) v (b) iv (c) i (d) iii (e) ii
Exercise 8	*Receptionist:* (a), (b), (d), (g); *Herr Bertram:* (c), (e), (f), (h)
Exercise 9	(a) iii (b) i (c) vii (d) v (e) ii (f) vi (g) iv
Exercise 12	You should have put a cross next to (b), (e) and (g).
Exercise 13	(a) ii (b) iii (c) i, iii (d) i, iv, v, vi (e) iii
Exercise 14	(a) einige (b) hier (c) leider (d) vielleicht (e) gleich (f) weiter (g) am ehesten (h) schon
Exercise 16	*richtig:* (b), (e); *falsch:* (a), (c), (d)

Grammar

Exercise 17	(a) den (b) dem (c) den (d) die (e) die (f) das (g) der, das
Exercise 18	(a) einen (b) einen (c) einen (d) einer (e) eine (f) eine (g) ein (h) ein, einem (i) ein

Read and understand

Exercise 19	(a) Abteilungsleiter/in, Einkaufsleiter, Exportleiter, Fertigungsleiter, Geschäftsführer, Leiter(in) der Finanzen, Leiter(in) Marketing, Personalleiter/Personalleiterin, Technischer Leiter (b) Assistentin, Buchhalter, Bürogehilfin, Bürokauffrau, Bürokaufmann, Europasekretärin, Fremdsprachenkorrespondent, Industriekaufmann, Marketing-Assistentin, Sachbearbeiter, Sekretärin, Speditionskaufmann (c) Außendienst-Mitarbeiter, Einkäufer (Rohstoffe), Handelsvertreter, Kunden-Betreuerin, Verkaufsberater, Verkaufssachbearbeiter(in), Verkaufs-Ingenieur/in Vertriebsingenieur

4 AT THE HOTEL

You will learn

- to enquire about a room in a hotel
- to check in and register at a hotel
- to ask to be shown a room
- to enquire about hotel facilities for business people
- to use numbers from 20 to 100

and you will be given information on where to stay in Germany, Switzerland and Austria.

Study guide

- **Dialogue 1 + Practise what you have learned**
- **Dialogue 2 + Practise what you have learned**
- **Dialogue 3 + Practise what you have learned**
- **Dialogue 4 + Practise what you have learned**
- Make sure you know the **Key words and phrases**
- Study the **Grammar** section
- Do the exercises in **Read and understand**
- Read **Did you know?**
- Do the exercises in **Your turn to speak**

Dialogues

1 *Checking in at a hotel*

Herr Müller	Guten Tag.
Receptionist	Guten Tag. Bitte schön?
Herr Müller	Ich habe ein Zimmer vorbestellt.
Receptionist	Auf welchen Namen, bitte?
Herr Müller	Das ist Müller, von der Firma Steinbrink.
Receptionist	Ja, ich schau(e) mal nach ... Das war ein Einzelzimmer?
Herr Müller	Ja.
Receptionist	Für eine Nacht?
Herr Müller	Ja, richtig.
Receptionist	Wenn Sie dann bitte das Formular ausfüllen würden.
Herr Müller	Ja, selbstverständlich.
Receptionist	Ja, und dann brauchte ich hier unten noch eine Unterschrift bitte.
Herr Müller	Ah ja ... So, bittschön.
Receptionist	Danke sehr. Das ist dann die Nummer vierzehn. Die ist im ersten Stock.
Herr Müller	Ja, ist das ein ruhiges Zimmer?
Receptionist	Das Zimmer ist ruhig. Ja, das geht also zum Park raus. Und wenn Sie in den ersten Stock wollen, der Aufzug ist direkt hinter Ihnen.
Herr Müller	Jawohl. Ganz schönen Dank dann.

- **das Einzelzimmer** single room **die Nummer** number
- **ruhig** quiet

Bitte schön? Yes, please? Short way of asking what a customer wants.

- **Ich habe ein Zimmer vorbestellt** I have booked a room. **Vorbestellen** means 'to book/ reserve'.
- **Auf welchen Namen, bitte?** In which name, please? **Welche/welcher/welches** mean 'which', e.g. **Welche Tür?** (Which door?); **Welches Hotel?** (Which hotel?). The endings change like those of adjectives used with the indefinite article (see p. 225).

Das war ... That was ... **War** is a form of the verb **sein** (to be) in the past tense.

- **Für eine Nacht?** For one night?
- **richtig** in this context means 'That's right/correct'
- **das Formular ausfüllen** to fill in/out the form
- **Dann brauchte ich noch eine Unterschrift** Then I still need a signature. The verb **brauchen** means 'to need/require'.
- **Hier unten** Here, at the bottom (lit. down here)

So, bittschön is a contracted form of **So, bitte schön**, 'Well, here you are'. Intonation is used to distinguish between its two possible meanings: 'What can I do for you?' and 'Here you are'.

Das geht also zum Park raus It faces onto the park side (lit. It goes therefore towards the park out). **Rausgehen** is short for **herausgehen**. Note that in German verbs with a prefix such as **hinaus-**, **heraus-**, **zu-**, **an-**, **ein-** usually split up like this, with the prefix at the end of the sentence, e.g. **ich fülle aus**, from **ausfüllen**.

- **Wenn Sie ... wollen** If you'd like / you want. Forms such as **ich möchte, wir möchten** also express intention but are more polite. Remember the question in the first dialogue: **Was möchten Sie?** 'What would you like?'
- **direkt hinter** directly behind

jawohl was originally a very emphatic way of saying 'yes', now it is a regional alternative of **ja**.

Ganz schönen Dank dann is a very emphatic form of saying 'thank you'. **Schön,** meaning 'nice/beautiful' is not normally used in connection with **Dank**.

Practise what you have learned

1 Decide whether these statements are **richtig** (true) or **falsch** (false). Put a cross in the appropriate box. (Answers on p. 80.)

	richtig	falsch
(a) **Das Zimmer ist nicht vorbestellt.**		
(b) **Herr Müller arbeitet bei der Firma Steinbrink.**		
(c) **Herr Müller möchte ein Doppelzimmer haben.**		
(d) **Das Zimmer ist für drei Nächte vorbestellt.**		
(e) **Er muß ein Formular ausfüllen.**		
(f) **Der Aufzug ist direkt hinter Herrn Müller.**		

2 Complete these sentences by filling in the correct form of the verb given in round brackets. (Answers on p. 80.)

(a) **Was ______________ Sie bitte?** (mögen)

(b) **Ich ______________ ein Zimmer vorbestellt.** (haben)

(c) **Der Name ______________ Müller.** (sein)

(d) **Ich ______________ mal nach.** (schauen)

(e) **______________ Sie bitte das Formular ausfüllen?** (können)

(f) **Der Aufzug ______________ direkt hinter Ihnen.** (sein)

3 Can you remember what was said in the dialogue? Check that you know the answers to the following questions, then turn on the recording and have a go at answering them aloud.

(a) What did Herr Müller say he had done about the room?
(b) What kind of room had he booked?
(c) For how long did Herr Müller want to stay?
(d) What does the receptionist ask Herr Müller to do to register?
(e) Can you remember the room number?
(f) Can you remember whether it was a quiet room?

Continued on next page.

4 Listen to the conversation between a hotel receptionist and a guest. Then decide which of the statements below is correct and circle the correct answers. (Answers on p. 80.) But first study the new vocabulary.

Zimmer frei haben to have vacancies
die Dusche shower
WC toilet
für 128 Mark for 128 marks
des Haupthaus main building
der Anbau annex
allerdings however
die Toilette toilet
der Flur corridor
ansonsten otherwise
gleich in the same way

eingerichtet furnished
lieber rather/preferably
einmal just/once
natürlich of course / obviously
das Telefon telephone
das Fernsehen television set
die Minibar mini-bar
der Fernseher televison set
prima excellent/fine/splendid
der Schlüssel key

(a) **Im Hotel sind** (i) **Einzelzimmer frei.**
(ii) **Einzel- oder Doppelzimmer frei.**
(iii) **Doppelzimmer frei.**

(b) **Das Zimmer im Haupthaus hat** (i) **Dusche und WC.**
(ii) **einen Park.**
(iii) **eine Dusche auf dem Flur.**

(c) **Die Zimmer im Anbau sind** (i) **im achten Stock.**
(ii) **ruhig.**
(iii) **gleich eingerichtet.**

(d) **Die Zimmer im Anbau sind** (i) **gut eingerichtet.**
(ii) **ohne Dusche und Toilette.**
(iii) **ohne Fahrstuhl.**

(e) **Der Gast muß** (i) **sich eintragen.**
(ii) **sich anmelden.**
(iii) **sich hinsetzen.**

(f) **Das Zimmer 82 ist im** (i) **elften Stock.**
(ii) **achten Stock.**
(iii) **ersten Stock.**

WOHNEN IN ÜBER 100 VARIATIONEN

WINGST
im Land Hadeln (75 km nordwestlich von Hamburg) Niedersachsen
Waldschlößchen Dobrock

Dialogues

2 *Filling in a registration form*

Receptionist Wenn Sie dann bitte mal das Anmeldeformular ausfüllen würden?
Guest Ja. Können Sie mir vielleicht helfen? Ich kann nicht gut Deutsch.
Receptionist Ja, selbstverständlich. Hier wird der Nachname eingetragen.
Guest Der Name.
Receptionist Ja. Dann kommt hier der Vorname hin.
Guest Ja.
Receptionist Tragen Sie hier Ihren Beruf ein.
Guest Der Beruf.
Receptionist Ja. Und hier die vollständige Adresse. Das fängt an mit der Stadt ...
Guest Die Stadt.
Receptionist ... und der Postleitzahl.
Guest Postleitzahl.
Receptionist Ja. Und dann die Straße.
Guest Die Straße.
Receptionist Und die Straßennummer.
Guest Und die Nummer, mhm.
Receptionist Und hier kommt die Nationalität hin.
Guest Ja.
Receptionist Und dann tragen Sie hier unten das Geburtsdatum ein ...
Guest Das Geburtsdatum.
Receptionist ... und ob Sie mit oder ohne Ehefrau anreisen.
Guest Ohne Ehefrau.
Receptionist Dann hätte ich gerne noch hier unten eine Unterschrift.
Guest Und die Unterschrift.
Receptionist Danke sehr.

das Anmeldeformular registration form
der Beruf job/profession
die Postleitzahl postal code (zip code)
die Nationalität nationality
das Geburtsdatum date of birth

Können Sie mir vielleicht helfen? Lit. 'Can you me perhaps help?' – a very polite request.

Ich kann nicht gut Deutsch means 'My German isn't very good'. The opposite would be **Ich kann gut Deutsch** (I'm able to speak and understand German well). **Können** here means 'to be able to'.

Hier wird der Nachname eingetragen Here the surname is entered. **Eintragen** is 'to enter (on a form)'.

Dann kommt hier der Vorname hin The first name is entered here (lit. Then comes here the first name)

die vollständige Adresse full/complete address

Das fängt an mit der Stadt You begin with the town (lit. It starts with the town). **Anfangen** means 'to begin/start'.

die Straßennummer (lit. street number) is sometimes used instead of **Hausnummer** (house number).

mit oder ohne Ehefrau with or without wife. **Ohne** means 'without'. 'Husband' is **Ehemann**.

Dann hätte ich gerne noch ... Lit. 'Then would I still like ...' A useful phrase when you want to ask for things one after the other. **Ich hätte gern** is 'I would like to have'.

Now turn over for the exercises based on dialogue 2.

Practise what you have learned

5 Can you remember what the guest was told to enter on the form? Keeping to the same order as the dialogue, complete these sentences. Choose from the nouns in the box below (you won't need all of them). (Answers on p. 80.)

(a) **Hier wird der ______________ eingetragen.**

(b) **Dann kommt hier der ______________ hin.**

(c) **Tragen Sie hier Ihren ______________ ein.**

(d) **Die vollständige Adresse fängt an mit der ______________**

und der ______________

(e) **Und dann kommt die ______________ und die Hausnummer.**

(f) **Tragen Sie hier unten das ______________ ein.**

(g) **Dann hätte ich gerne noch hier unten eine ______________**

die Stadt
das Geburtsdatum
die Nationalität
die Nummer
der Beruf
der Nachname
der Vorname
die Postleitzahl
die Straße
die Unterschrift

6 Use the personal details in the box below to complete this form. **Der Wohnort** is 'place of residence' and **der Geburtsort** is 'place of birth'. (Answers on p. 80.)

(a) **Vorname**	(b) **Nachname** ....
(c) **Straße**	(d) **Hausnummer** ....
(e) **Postleitzahl**	(f) **Wohnort** ....
(g) **Geburtsdatum**	(h) **Geburtsort** ....
(i) **Nationalität**	(j) **Beruf** ....
(k) **beschäftigt bei**	

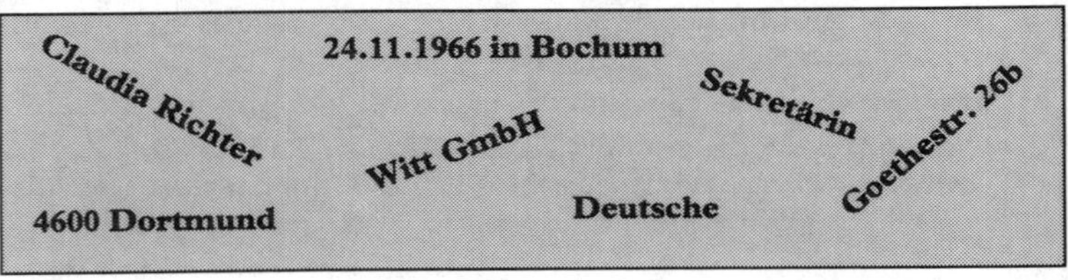

Claudia Richter
24.11.1966 in Bochum
Sekretärin
Witt GmbH
Goethestr. 26b
4600 Dortmund
Deutsche

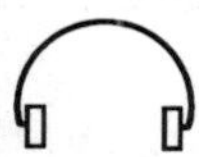

7 In this dialogue the receptionist is helping you fill in a registration form. Give her the necessary information in German.

Parkhotel Witten Fremdenverzeichnis	Zimmer-Nr. Pers.-Zahl	Ankunft Abreise	Voraussichtliche Aufenthaltsdauer
Name Nom	Vorname Christianname / Prénom		Beruf / Titel Profession
Wohnort Residence / Domicile ( ) Leitzahl	Straße Nr. No. Street / No. Rue		Nationalität Nationality / Nationalité
Geburtsdatum Date of birth Date de naissance	mit / ohne Ehefrau with / without Mrs avec / sans Mme.	Vorname Christian-name Prénom	mit Kindern (Zahl) with children (number) avec enfants (nombre)
Bemerkungen			

8 Listen to this conversation between a bank clerk and a customer who wishes to apply for a personal loan. Then fill in the missing information below. (Answers on p. 80.)

New vocabulary
das Antragsformular application form
der Familienname family name / surname
verdienen to earn
ungefähr approximately
brutto gross
monatlich per month
Bescheid bekommen to be informed (i.e. to receive information about a decision)

(a) **Die Kundin bei der Bank heißt:**

Familienname: ____________________ **Vorname:** ________________

(b) **Die Kundin wohnt:**

Straße und Hausnummer: ____________________________________

Wohnort mit Postleitzahl: ____________________________________

(c) **Der 2.6.1960 ist das** ________________ **der Kundin und Essen**

ist der ____________________________

(d) **Die Kundin ist bei der** ________________**beschäftigt.**

(e) **Sie verdient ungefähr DM 4300 brutto** ________________________

Dialogues

3 *The receptionist shows the guest her room*

Receptionist So, dann zeige ich Ihnen jetzt mal das Zimmer. Es ist das Zimmer 31. Wir sind hier im dritten Stock.
Guest Gut, ja.
Receptionist Und wenn Sie dann bitte mal eintreten möchten.
Guest Ja, danke schön.
Receptionist So, dann ist das hier vorne das Badezimmer.
Guest Ja.
Receptionist Mit Badewanne hier.
Guest Oh, das sieht ja prima aus. Gut.
Receptionist Und hier vorne ... sind dann ... ist dann das Schlafzimmer.
Guest Ja, das sieht ja nett aus.
Receptionist So, dann haben wir noch die Minibar. Die ist hier unten im Schrank.
Guest Ja.
Receptionist Und den Fernseher. Der wird also ganz normal bedient.
Guest Gut, alles klar, prima.
Receptionist Ja, dann verabschiede ich mich.
Guest Ja, tschüß.
Receptionist Angenehmen Aufenthalt.
Guest Danke schön.
Receptionist Wiederseh(e)n.

das Badezimmer bathroom
die Badewanne bath/bathtub
das Schlafzimmer bedroom
alles klar all right (lit. everything clear)
sich verabschieden to say goodbye

Dann zeige ich Ihnen jetzt mal das Zimmer Well, I'll show you your room now (lit. Then show I you now the room). Note the use of the present tense, even though **jetzt** (now) indicates that the action is about to begin. **Zeigen** is 'to show'.

Wenn Sie dann bitte mal hier eintreten möchten If you would then please be so kind as to come in here. A very polite, almost stilted, invitation to enter (**eintreten**) the room. **Mal** and **hier** are filler words here.

hier vorne is a colloquialism meaning 'right here'.

Das sieht ja prima aus That looks really good

Das sieht ja nett aus That does look nice

hier unten im Schrank here at the bottom of the cupboard.

Der wird ganz normal bedient It is operated quite normally (like any other). **Bedienen** is 'to operate/handle'.

Angenehmen Aufenthalt is short for **Ich wünsche Ihnen einen angenehmen Aufenthalt** 'I wish you a pleasant stay'. **Wünschen** means 'to wish'; **angenehm** is 'pleasant'; and **der Aufenthalt** 'stay'.

Practise what you have learned

9 Circle the correct ending for each sentence. (Answers on p. 80.)

(a) **Das Badezimmer ist**
- (i) **hier unten.**
- (ii) **hier vorne.**
- (iii) **hier oben.**

(b) **Das Badezimmer hat**
- (i) **eine Rezeption.**
- (ii) **eine Minibar.**
- (iii) **eine Badewanne.**

(c) **Die Minibar ist**
- (i) **im dritten Stock.**
- (ii) **unten im Schrank.**
- (iii) **bei der Rezeption.**

(d) **Ich wünsche Ihnen**
- (i) **eine angenehme Reise.**
- (ii) **einen angenehmen Aufenthalt.**
- (iii) **einen angenehmen Flug.**

10 Can you remember details of the room? Answer the questions in German in complete sentences, using the English prompts.

11 Listen to this dialogue and then complete the sentences below, matching each sentence with one of the phrases on the right. (Answers on p. 80.) You do not need to learn all the new vocabulary, but it will help you get the gist of the dialogue.

New vocabulary
die Garderobe coat stand
das Bad bath(room)
das Handtuch towel
genug enough/sufficient
aufschreiben to write down
die Abreise departure
das Fernsehgerät television set
das Programm programme
empfangen to receive
die Fernbedienung remote control
ab wann from when on
frühstücken to have breakfast
zwischen between

(a) **Die Garderobe und der Schrank sind gleich ...**
(b) **Das Bad mit Dusche und WC ist ...**
(c) **Die Minibar ist hier unten ...**
(d) **... hier können Sie alle Programme empfangen.**
(e) **Die Rezeption erreichen Sie ... neun.**
(f) **Sie können ... frühstücken.**

(i) **Mit dem Fernsehgerät ...**
(ii) **... mit der Nummer ...**
(iii) **... im Schreibtisch.**
(iv) **... auf der anderen Seite.**
(v) **... hinter der Tür.**
(vi) **... zwischen 6.30 und 10 Uhr.**

Dialogues

4 *Using the hotel's business facilities*

Herr Müller	Guten Tag.
Receptionist	Guten Tag, Herr Müller.
Herr Müller	Darf ich bitte Ihr Faxgerät benutzen?
Receptionist	Ja, selbstverständlich.
Herr Müller	Und dann muß ich ein paar Photokopien machen.
Receptionist	Das können Sie auch bei uns.
Herr Müller	Das ist nett. Können Sie mir bitte für morgen eine Sekretärin und eine Dolmetscherin bestellen?
Receptionist	Ja, aber da muß ich mich dann erst erkundigen, wieviel das kostet. Und für welche Sprache brauchen Sie die Dolmetscherin?
Herr Müller	Für Spanisch bitte.
Receptionist	Spanisch. Da muß ich dann auch erst nachfragen, wieviel ... eh, ob wir also spanischsprechende Dolmetscher hier in Witten haben. Das kann ich Ihnen dann aber heute abend sagen.
Herr Müller	Gut, das ist nett. Dann komme ich heute abend vorbei.
Receptionist	Machen Sie das, Herr Müller.
Herr Müller	Wiedersehen.
Receptionist	Ja, Wiederschau(e)n.

➧ **die Dienstleistung** service/facility
➧ **die Photokopie** photocopy
der Dolmetscher/ die Dolmetscherin interpreter
die Sprache language
Spanisch Spanish (language)
spanischsprechend Spanish-speaking
➧ **nachfragen** to enquire / ask again
ob whether/if

➧ **Darf ich bitte Ihr Faxgerät benutzen?** May I please use your fax machine? **Darf ich bitte ...?** (May I ...?) is a very common phrase to ask permission to do something. If you are not sure whether they have a fax machine, you would say **Haben Sie vielleicht ein Faxgerät?**

➧ **ein paar** some/a few

Das ist nett That is very kind (lit. That's nice). A common form of saying 'Thank you'.

für morgen for tomorrow. Note the following difference in capitalization and meaning: **morgen** means 'tomorrow' and **der Morgen** (as in **Guten Morgen**) means 'the morning'.

Können Sie bitte ... bestellen? Could you please arrange for ... to be available? The commonest meaning of **bestellen** is 'to order', especially goods or a meal in a restaurant; it is also commonly used for 'to book', e.g. a table in a restaurant or theatre tickets.

➧ **Da muß ich mich dann erst erkundigen** In that case I'll have to make some enquiries first (lit. There must I myself then first inform). Note that the verb **sich erkundigen** (to inform oneself/enquire) is reflexive in German (see grammar, p. 129).

wieviel das kostet how much that costs

Das kann ich Ihnen dann aber heute abend sagen I'll let you know tonight (lit. That can I you then but tonight tell). **Heute abend** means 'this evening' or 'tonight'; you can easily form similar compounds in German (see p. 111).

Dann komme ich heute abend vorbei Then I'll come by this evening. **Vorbeikommen** is 'to go/walk past' or 'to see someone'. Verbs with separable prefixes are explained in Unit 5.

Machen Sie das Do that. A common phrase to signal agreement to a proposal.

Wiederschau(e)n Bye. An alternative to **Wiedersehen**.

Practise what you have learned

12 Can you remember the services Herr Müller requires? Complete these sentences. (Answers on p. 80.)

(a) **Herr Müller sagt: 'Darf ich bitte Ihr ________________ benutzen?'**

(b) **Er muß dann auch ein paar ________________ machen.**

(c) **Der Empfang soll für morgen eine ________________ und eine ________________ bestellen.**

(d) **Für welche ________________ brauchen Sie die Dolmetscherin?**

(e) **Der Empfang muß nachfragen, ob es in Witten ________________ Dolmetscher gibt.**

(f) **Das kann die Frau am Empfang ________________ sagen.**

13 Form questions that would give you the following answers. Write your version down first, then listen to the recording for the correct question.

(a) ________________

Ja, wir haben noch Zimmer frei.

(b) ________________

Nein, ein Einzelzimmer haben wir leider nicht mehr.

(c) ________________

Das Zimmer kostet DM 98,– mit Frühstück.

(d) ________________

Ja, das ist ein ruhiges Zimmer.

(e) ________________

Nein, das Zimmer hat leider keine Minibar.

(f) ________________

Ja, unser Faxgerät können Sie gern benutzen.

(g) ________________

Sie können zwischen 6.30 Uhr und 10 Uhr frühstücken.

(h) ________________

Nein, bei uns können Sie leider kein Geld eintauschen.

14 Frau Richter is in a small hotel in Witten and requires some help. Take the role of Frau Richter and use the prompts for your part of the dialogue.

15 Listen to the statements on the recording and compare them with the sentences below. Put a cross next to the ones which are *different* from the ones you hear. (Answers on p. 80.)

(a) **Darf ich bitte Ihr Kopiergerät benutzen?** ☐

(b) **Dann muß ich noch eine paar Photokopien machen.** ☐

(c) **Können Sie für morgen früh eine Assistentin bestellen?** ☐

(d) **Für morgen brauche ich auch noch einen Dolmetscher.** ☐

(e) **Ich brauche den Dolmetscher für Französisch.** ☐

Key words and phrases

Was möchten Sie?	What would you like?
Ich möchte/hätte gern ...	I would like ...
Haben Sie noch Zimmer frei?	Do you have any vacancies?
Ich habe ein Zimmer vorbestellt	I booked a room in advance
Auf welchen Namen, bitte?	In which name, please? / What was the name, please?
Ein Einzel- oder Doppelzimmer?	A single or a double room?
mit Dusche und WC	with shower and toilet
für eine Nacht	for one night
Haben die Zimmer Fernsehen und Telefon?	Do the rooms have television and telephone?
Ist das ein ruhiges Zimmer?	Is it a quiet room?
ein Zimmer für ... Mark	a room for ... marks
das Formular ausfüllen	to fill in the form
Wenn Sie wollen ...?	If you like ...?
die Unterschrift	signature
Können Sie mir vielleicht helfen?	Could you perhaps help me?
Angenehmen Aufenthalt	Enjoy your stay / Have a pleasant stay
Ich kann nicht gut Deutsch	I don't speak German very well / My German isn't very good
Der Aufzug ist dort hinten	The lift is over there
Für welche Sprache?	For which language?
Das ist nett	That's very kind
Ich muß mich erst erkundigen	I'll have to make some enquiries first
bei der Abreise	when you leave
alles klar	alright / everything OK
richtig	(that's) correct
Bitte schön?	Yes, please?
das Anmeldeformular	registration/application form
der Nachname / Familienname	surname / family name
der Vorname	first name
die Adresse	address
der Wohnort	place of residence
die Stadt	town/city
die Hausnummer	house number
die Postleitzahl	post code / zip code
das Geburtsdatum	date of birth
der Geburtsort	place of birth
die Ehefrau / der Ehemann	wife/husband
der Beruf	job/occupation/profession
die Dienstleistung	service/facility
das Faxgerät	fax machine
das Photokopiergerät	photocopier
Photokopien machen	to make photocopies
anrufen / telefonieren	to ring/phone/call
bezahlen	to pay
aufschreiben	to write down
bestellen	to order
nachfragen	to ask (again)
zeigen	to show/demonstrate
eintreten	to enter / come in
hier unten / hier vorn(e)	down here / right here
direkt hinter	directly behind
ein paar	a few
heute morgen	this morning
heute mittag	this lunchtime
heute nachmittag	this afternoon
heute abend	tonight / this evening

Grammar

Prepositions

Prepositions are useful words such as 'in', 'at', 'on', 'to', 'with'. In this course you have already met quite a few German prepositions, e.g.:

mit with	**von** from
für for	**zu** to
auf on	**bei** at, near
in in	

However, there is a snag. After prepositions the words for 'the' or 'a' often change. So, you get **der Mann** but **mit d<u>em</u>/ein<u>em</u> Mann**; **die Firma** but **von d<u>er</u>/ein<u>er</u> Firma** (see the explanation about gender and case on p. 55).

After some of the most common prepositions, you find the dative case, e.g. **mit d<u>em</u> Direktor** (with the Director), **aus d<u>em</u> Haus** (out of the house); **von ein<u>er</u> Frau** (from/of a woman); **zu d<u>em</u> Zimmer** (to the room).

After a few prepositions you find the accusative case (remember it's only with masculine – **der** – nouns that there is a problem): e.g. **durch d<u>en</u> Park** (through the park); **ohne ein<u>en</u> Kaffee** (without a coffee); **für d<u>en</u> Direktor** (for the Director).

To confuse the situation even more, some prepositions such as **an, hinter, vor, unter, auf** and **in** can be followed by either the accusative or dative case. For example:

Ich gehe in die Bank (accusative) but **Ich arbeite in einer Bank** (dative). Where there is motion (I go to the bank) the accusative follows; where you are simply in the bank and staying there (I work in a bank), the preposition is followed by the dative.

Some of the very common prepositions merge with the article as shown:

an	+	**dem**	=	**am**	**an**	+	**das**	=	**ans**
in	+	**dem**	=	**im**	**in**	+	**das**	=	**ins**
von	+	**dem**	=	**vom**	**bei**	+	**dem**	=	**beim**
zu	+	**dem**	=	**zum**	**zu**	+	**der**	=	**zur**

This rather confusing grammar point is raised so that you don't think there are lots of typing errors or that you have misheard something. At this stage it is enough to be aware of the problem so that you can understand what you read or hear. Gradually you'll get a feel for using the correct version and if you are really interested you can check in a grammar book or the grammar summary on p. 225.

The negative

There are two ways of expressing the negative in German. You have already come across the word **nicht** (not) in earlier units. In simple sentences it follows straight after the verb:

Sind Sie Herr Richter? – Nein, ich bin <u>nicht</u> Herr Richter.
Are you Herr Richter? – No, I'm not Herr Richter.

Wohnen Sie hier? – Nein, ich wohne <u>nicht</u> hier.
Do you live here? – No, I don't live here.

You will sometimes find **nicht** in a different position – not after the verb, but at the end of the sentence or somewhere in the middle.

Ich kenne die Adresse nicht. I don't know the address.

Ich fahre heute morgen nicht nach Bochum. I'm not going to Bochum this morning.

If the negation refers to a noun, then you use the word **kein** (no), which has the same gender and case endings as **ein** (a).

Hat das Zimmer eine Dusche? – Nein, das Zimmer hat <u>keine</u> Dusche.
Does the room have a shower? – No, the room has no shower / does not have a shower.

Haben Sie einen Termin mit Frau Köpl? – Nein, ich habe <u>keinen</u> Termin mit Frau Köpl.
Do you have an appointment with Frau Köpl? – No, I have no appointment with Frau Köpl / don't have an appointment with Frau Köpl.

For 'not a' use a form of **kein** and *not* **nicht ein**:

Ich habe keinen Kunden in Deutschland.
I have no / do not have a customer in Germany.

16

Fill in the prepositions given in round brackets and put the article in the correct case. You may have to merge the preposition and the article. Go back and look at the grammar section in Unit 3 and study the forms of the article before attempting this exercise. (Answers on p. 80.) You may find the grammar summary (p. 224) useful too.

Example **Ich komme** _______ (die) **Firma Steinbrink.** (von)
Ich komme von der Firma Steinbrink.

(a) **Der Gast möchte ein Zimmer** _______ (das) **Haupthaus.** (in)

(b) **Die Dusche und Toilette sind** _______ (der) **Flur.** (auf)

(c) **Das Zimmer ist** _______ (der) **achten Stock.** (in)

(d) **Das Zimmer ist** _______ (der) **Namen Müller vorbestellt.** (auf)

(e) **Das ruhige Zimmer geht** _______ (der) **Park hinaus.** (zu)

(f) **Die Adresse fängt** _______ (die) **Stadt an.** (mit)

(g) **Am besten gehen Sie** _______ (der) **Blumenladen vorbei.** (an)

(h) **Dann kommen Sie** _______ (der) **Marktplatz.** (auf)

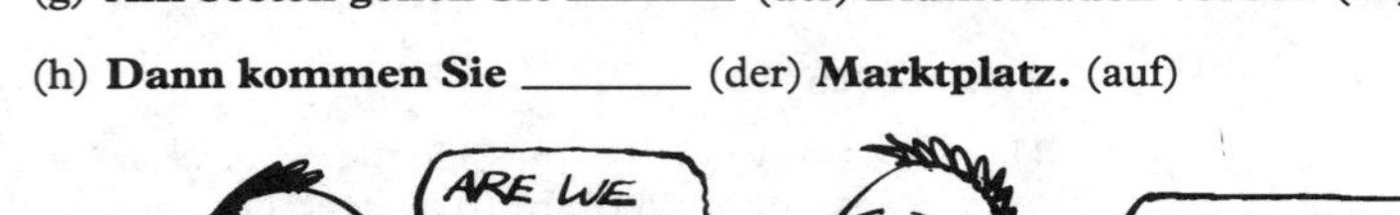

17

Complete the answers to these questions, using either **nicht** or **kein** as appropriate. (Answers on p. 80.)

(a) **Haben Sie vorbestellt? – Nein, ich habe ______________ vorbestellt.**

(b) **Hat das Zimmer ein Telefon? – Nein, das Zimmer hat ______________**

(c) **Kennen Sie Frau Müller? – Nein, ich kenne ______________**

(d) **Fliegen Sie nach Berlin? – Nein, ich fliege ______________**

(e) **Gehen Sie zum Postamt? – Nein, ich gehe ______________**

(f) **Nehmen Sie Milch** (f.) **zum Kaffee? – Nein, ich nehme ______________**

(g) **Wohnen Sie in Bochum? – Nein, ich wohne ______________**

(h) **Öffnet die Bank um acht Uhr? – Nein, die Bank öffnet ______________**

Numbers

In Unit 2 we looked at numbers up to 20. In this unit we will work upwards from 20. Listen to the numbers on the recording and then read them out loud.

Cardinal numbers			*Ordinal numbers*		
20	**zwanzig**	twenty	20.	**zwanzigster**	twentieth
21	**einundzwanzig**	twenty-one	21.	**einundzwanzigster**	twenty-first
22	**zweiundzwanzig**	twenty-two	22.	**zweiundzwanzigster**	twenty-second
23	**dreiundzwanzig**	twenty-three	23.	**dreiundzwanzigster**	twenty-third
	etc.			*etc.*	
34	**vierunddreißig**	thirty-four	30.	**dreißigster**	thirtieth
45	**fünfundvierzig**	forty-five	40.	**vierzigster**	fortieth
56	**sechsundfünfzig**	fifty-six	50.	**fünfzigster**	fiftieth
67	**siebenundsechzig**	sixty-seven	60.	**sechzigster**	sixtieth
78	**achtundsiebzig**	seventy-eight	70.	**siebzigster**	seventieth
89	**neunundachtzig**	eighty-nine	80.	**achtzigster**	eightieth
90	**neunzig**	ninety	90.	**neunzigster**	ninetieth
100	**(ein)hundert**	one hundred	100.	**(ein)hundertster**	(one) hundredth

18

Write out the numbers in the following sentences in full and read the sentences aloud. (Answers on p. 80.)

(a) **Der Gast wohnt in Zimmer Nummer 43.** ______________

(b) **Der Konferenzraum hat die Nummer 68.** ______________

(c) **Das Einzelzimmer mit Dusche kostet 75 Mark.** ______________

(d) **Nach etwa 100 Metern kommen Sie auf den Marktplatz.** ______________

(e) **Die Dolmetscherin kostet 95 Mark.** ______________

Read and understand

19 Study this extract from the brochure of Parkhotel in Witten and read the statements that follow. Are they **richtig** (true) or **falsch** (false)? Mark the appropriate boxes. (Answers on p. 80.)

Die Zimmer haben Bad, Dusche, WC, Radio, Telefon, Minibar und Fernseher.
Es gibt auch Konferenzräume für 10 bis 60 Personen.

Preise pro Tag einschließlich Frühstücksbuffet

Einzelzimmer	135, - DM
Doppelzimmer	176, - DM
Kinder bis 10 Jahre	frei

Telefoneinheit 0,60 DM

	Vollpension	Halbpension
für Erwachsene	38, - DM	19, - DM
für Kinder bis 10 Jahre	18, - DM	9, - DM

Wir wünschen Ihnen einen angenehmen Aufenthalt

New vocabulary

das Radio radio
der Preis price
bis (up) to
pro Tag daily/per day
einschließlich inclusive
das Frühstücksbuffet breakfast buffet
das Kind child
die Telefoneinheit telephone unit
die Vollpension full board
die Halbpension half board

	richtig	falsch
(a) **Die Zimmer haben Dusche, WC und Fernseher.**		
(b) **Das Hotel hat keine Konferenzräume.**		
(c) **Das Einzelzimmer kostet 135, - DM.**		
(d) **Die Telefoneinheit kostet 0,70 DM.**		
(e) **In den Zimmern ist keine Minibar.**		
(f) **Das Hotel wünscht einen angenehmen Aufenthalt.**		

20 Here is a list of the types and facilities of some hotels in Bochum. Study the list, the abbreviations and the pictograms and then answer the questions. (Answers on p. 80.)

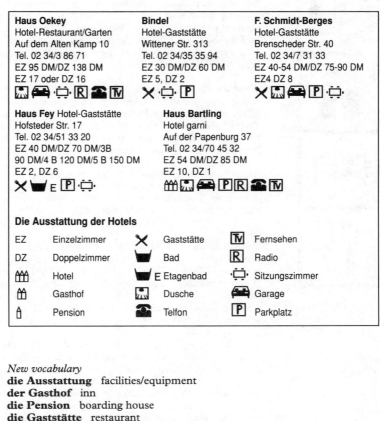

Haus Oekey
Hotel-Restaurant/Garten
Auf dem Alten Kamp 10
Tel. 02 34/3 86 71
EZ 95 DM/DZ 138 DM
EZ 17 oder DZ 16

Bindel
Hotel-Gaststätte
Wittener Str. 313
Tel. 02 34/35 35 94
EZ 30 DM/DZ 60 DM
EZ 5, DZ 2

F. Schmidt-Berges
Hotel-Gaststätte
Brenscheder Str. 40
Tel. 02 34/7 31 33
EZ 40-54 DM/DZ 75-90 DM
EZ4 DZ 8

Haus Fey Hotel-Gaststätte
Hofsteder Str. 17
Tel. 02 34/51 33 20
EZ 40 DM/DZ 70 DM/3B
90 DM/4 B 120 DM/5 B 150 DM
EZ 2, DZ 6

Haus Bartling
Hotel garni
Auf der Papenburg 37
Tel. 02 34/70 45 32
EZ 54 DM/DZ 85 DM
EZ 10, DZ 1

Die Ausstattung der Hotels

EZ	Einzelzimmer	Gaststätte	Fernsehen
DZ	Doppelzimmer	Bad	Radio
	Hotel	E Etagenbad	Sitzungszimmer
	Gasthof	Dusche	Garage
	Pension	Telfon	Parkplatz

New vocabulary
die Ausstattung facilities/equipment
der Gasthof inn
die Pension boarding house
die Gaststätte restaurant
das Etagenbad bathroom for each floor
das Sitzungszimmer conference room
die Garage garage

(a) **Welche Ausstattung hat das Hotel Haus Fey?**

____

(b) **Was kosten die Einzel- und Doppelzimmer im Hotel Bindel?**

Einzelzimmer______________ **Doppelzimmer** ______________

(c) **Haben die Zimmer im Haus Oekey Telefon und Fernseher?** ________

(d) **Welche Zimmer hat das Haus Bartling und was kosten sie?**

____

(e) **Was ist die Telefonnummer vom Hotel Schmidt-Berges?**

____

____

Did you know?

Accommodation in Germany

Big hotels of a high standard can be found everywhere in Germany, Austria, Switzerland and, increasingly, in the former GDR. Apart from the obvious locations near airports, stations or in big commercial centres, there is an amazing number of such high quality hotels in more remote rural and scenically attractive areas. They often cater for conferences and seminars and are usually run as family businesses. As such they are often part of a voluntary chain which allows them to maintain their identity and at the same time enjoy the benefits of the joint marketing efforts of such an association.

The bulk of the hotel establishments are small family businesses which you can find everywhere in Germany. They are usually well equipped, very efficiently managed and offer a reasonably priced personalized service. Recently big hotel chains have begun to capture the lower end of the business by offering a standardized range of basic facilities at comparatively low rates in newly built hotels.

Small family hotels frequently incorporate a restaurant. These **Gasthöfe** (inns) provide good average hotel standards and moderately priced meals. It is in these **Gasthöfe** that you are likely to find regional specialities. The names of such inns – which frequently include the words **Haus** (house) or **Hof** (courtyard) – often reflect their regional character.

Boarding houses (**Pensionen**) tend to be in tourist resorts. The rooms are not always equipped with showers or toilets, but most will have a television room or a lounge. They are usually a very cheap form of accommodation. While preferring to cater for visitors who stay for longer than a couple of days, they will also readily take in overnight guests, especially in the off-season. They can usually be relied upon to provide an evening meal (not always cooked). A lot of them are licensed to sell drinks.

Occasionally people offer private accommodation (**Gästezimmer**, 'guest rooms'); vacancies are advertised by a notice in the windows or in the front garden saying **Zimmer frei** or simply **Gästezimmer**.

Hotel information is available in various forms. The annual hotel-guides are generally reliable although the ratings are sometimes a matter of taste. Most towns of a reasonable size will have a **Verkehrsverein** or **Verkehrsbüro** (tourist information office) which is open during normal office hours. At most international airports and at big railway stations there is a counter with the sign **Zimmernachweis** (accommodation register). And information is usually given free of charge.

Except in the off-season, advance booking is advisable. This is especially true for the big towns – all the available hotels for miles around may be fully booked because of trade fairs held regularly in cities such as Hamburg, Hannover, Düsseldorf, Köln, Frankfurt, Stuttgart, München and Berlin.

Your turn to speak

As in the previous units, these exercises are open-ended.

21

You have to provide information about yourself for an insurance proposal form. State your full name and address, your date and place of birth, where you work and what you do. Here are some useful phrases:

Mein Name/Vorname/Nachname ist ...
Meine Adresse ist ...
Mein Geburtsdatum/Geburtsort ist ...
Ich bin bei ... beschäftigt
Ich arbeite bei ...
Ich bin ... von Beruf / Von Beruf bin ich ...

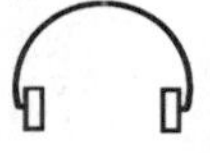

22

Provide the same information about your husband or wife or about a friend (**der Freund / die Freundin**). Here again are some useful phrases:

Mein Mann / Meine Frau ist ...
Mein Freund / Meine Freundin ist ...

Die Adresse		
Das Geburtsdatum	**meines Mannes/Freundes**	**ist ...**
Der Geburtsort	**meiner Frau/Freundin**	
Der Beruf		

Mein Mann / Meine Frau arbeitet bei ...
Mein Freund / Meine Freundin arbeitet bei ...

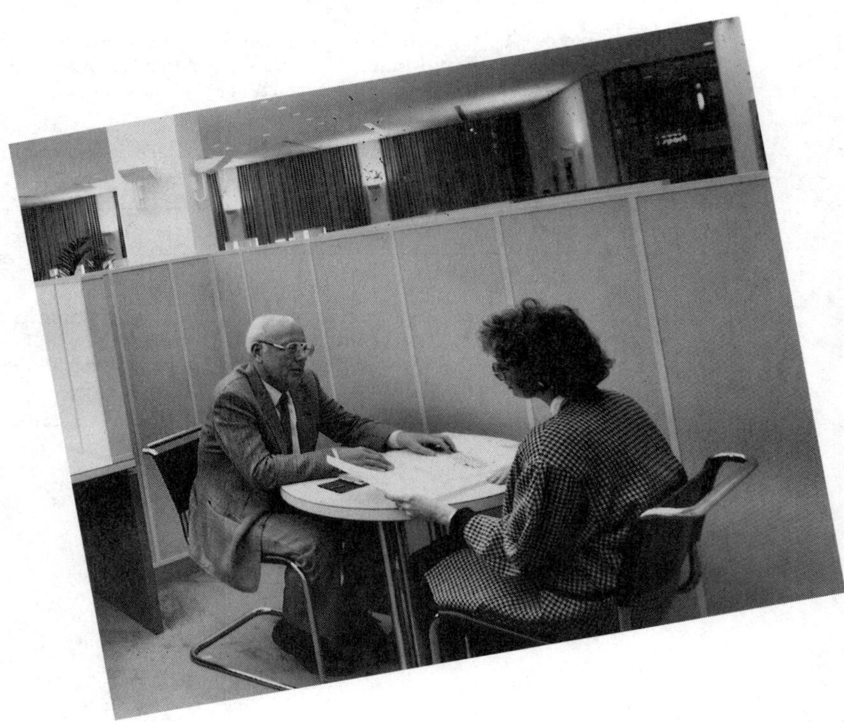

Answers

Practise what you have learned

Exercise 1	*richtig:* (b), (e), (f); *falsch:* (a), (c), (d)
Exercise 2	(a) möchten (b) habe (c) ist (d) schau(e) (e) können (f) ist
Exercise 4	(a) ii (b) i (c) iii (d) ii (e) i (f) ii
Exercise 5	(a) Nachname (b) Vorname (c) Beruf (d) Stadt, Postleitzahl (e) Straße (f) Geburtsdatum (g) Unterschrift
Exercise 6	(a) Claudia (b) Richter (c) Goethestr. (d) 26b (e) 4600 (f) Dortmund (g) 24.11.1966 (h) Bochum (i) Deutsche (j) Sekretärin (k) Witt GmbH
Exercise 8	(a) Brandt, Heike (b) Wasserstr. 42, 463 Bochum (c) Geburtsdatum, Geburtsort (d) Opel AG (e) monatlich
Exercise 9	(a) ii (b) iii (c) ii (d) ii
Exercise 11	(a) v (b) iv (c) iii (d) i (e) ii (f) vi
Exercise 12	(a) Faxgerät (b) Photokopien (c) Sekretärin, Dolmetscherin (d) Sprache (e) spanischsprechende (f) heute abend
Exercise 15	You should have put a cross next to (a), (c) and (e).

Grammar

Exercise 16	(a) im (b) auf dem (c) im (d) auf den (e) zum (f) mit der (g) am (i) auf den
Exercise 17	(a) nicht (b) kein Telefon (c) Frau Müller nicht/keine Frau Müller (d) nicht nach Berlin (e) nicht zum Postamt (f) keine Milch zum Kaffee (g) nicht in Bochum (h) nicht um acht Uhr
Exercise 18	(a) dreiundvierzig (b) achtundsechzig (c) fünfundsiebzig (d) (ein)hundert (e) fünfundneunzig

Read and understand

Exercise 19	*richtig:* (a), (c), (f); *falsch:* (b), (d), (e)
Exercise 20	(a) Gaststätte, Etagenbad, Parkplatz, Sitzungszimmer (b) Einzelzimmer 30 DM, Doppelzimmer 60 DM (c) ja (d) Einzelzimmer 54 DM, Doppelzimmer 85 DM (e) 02 34/7 31 33

5 AT THE BANK AND IN A RESTAURANT

You will learn

- to change money at a bank
- to use your credit card to obtain cash at the bank
- to order and pay for drinks and a meal
- to ask simple questions

and you will be given some information on food and drink in Germany.

Study guide

Dialogue 1 + Practise what you have learned
Dialogue 2 + Practise what you have learned
Dialogue 3 + Practise what you have learned
Dialogue 4 + Practise what you have learned
Make sure you know the **Key words and phrases**
Study the **Grammar** section
Do the exercises in **Read and understand**
Read **Did you know?**
Do the exercises in **Your turn to speak**

Dialogues

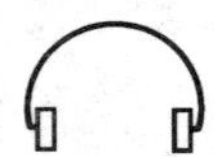

1 *Changing currency at a bank*

Cashier Guten Morgen. Was kann ich für Sie tun?
Customer Guten Morgen. Bin ich bei Ihnen richtig, am Sortenschalter?
Cashier Ja.
Customer Ich habe 500 Dollar, die ich gerne in D-Mark wechseln möchte.
Cashier Mhm, kein Problem. Der Kurs heute ist 1,655 für einen Dollar.
Customer Mhm.
Cashier Wie darf ich Ihnen das Geld auszahlen?
Customer Wie Sie möchten.
Cashier Spielt keine Rolle. So, der Computer hat einen Betrag errechnet von DM 827,50. Ich darf's Ihnen hinzählen: ein-, zwei-, drei-, vier-, fünfhundert, 550, 600, 650, 700, 750, 800, 820 und 7,50 DM – 5, 6, 7, 10, 20, 30, 40, 50. Bitte schön.
Customer Besten Dank. Bekomme ich noch einen Beleg von Ihnen?
Cashier Ja, der Computer druckt ihn gerade aus.
Customer Danke schön.
Cashier Bitte schön. Hier ist Ihr Beleg.
Customer Vielen Dank.
Cashier Bitte sehr.
Customer Auf Wiederschau(e)n.
Cashier Wiederschau(e)n.

➧ **der Devisenschalter / der Sortenschalter** foreign exchange counter
der Computer computer
der Kassierer cashier

Bin ich bei Ihnen richtig? Am I in the right place? (lit. Am I with you right?)

die ich gerne wechseln möchte which I'd like to change. **Wechseln** is 'to change'.

➧ **Kein Problem** is short for **Das ist kein Problem** 'That's no problem'.

➧ **Der Kurs heute ist ...** The (exchange) rate today is ... **Der Kurs** is short for **der Wechselkurs** or **der Devisenkurs** 'the exchange rate'. **Kurs** is also used for the price of stocks and shares.

1,655. Note how this is said: **eins Komma sechs fünf fünf.** Please note that, instead of the digital point, a digital comma is used in German. In figures over 1000 you will sometimes see a full point or space used to separate the thousands, e.g. 10.240 or 170 800.

➧ **Wie darf ich ...?** How may I ...? A very polite form of request, similar to **Darf ich Platz nehmen?** 'May I sit down?'.

➧ **Geld auszahlen** to pay out money. **Zahlen** means 'to pay'.

➧ **Spielt keine Rolle** Any way you like (lit. plays no role). Short for **Das spielt keine Rolle** 'It doesn't matter'.

hat einen Betrag errechnet von DM 827,50 has calculated an amount of ...

Ich darf's Ihnen hinzählen Lit. 'I may it you down count'. Again a very polite phrase to introduce the transaction of counting. Note the difference between **zahlen** (to pay) and **zählen** (to count). **Darf's** is short for **darf es**.

Bekomme ich noch einen Beleg von Ihnen? Do I also get a receipt? (lit. Get I also a receipt from you?). **Der Beleg** is 'the receipt'. It would have been much politer to say **Könn(t)en Sie mir bitte noch den Beleg geben?**

Der Computer druckt ihn gerade aus The computer is just printing it. **Gerade** (just) indicates that an action is just taking place. **Drucken** is 'to print'; **ausdrucken** 'to print out'.

Practise what you have learned

1 Look back at the dialogue and find out whether these statements are **richtig** (true) or **falsch** (false). Mark the appropriate box. (Answers on p. 98.)

		richtig	falsch
(a)	**Die Bank hat keinen Sortenschalter.**		
(b)	**Der Kunde möchte englische Pfund eintauschen.**		
(c)	**Der Kurs heute ist DM 1,655 für einen Dollar.**		
(d)	**Der Kassierer hat den Betrag errechnet.**		
(e)	**Der Kassierer zahlt DM 827,50 an den Kunden aus.**		
(f)	**Der Kunde möchte keinen Beleg.**		
(g)	**Der Computer druckt den Beleg gerade aus.**		

2 Complete the sentences on the left using the phrases on the right. (Answers on p. 98.)

(a) **Ja, Sie sind hier richtig ...**
(b) **Ich möchte gern 500 Dollar ... wechseln.**
(c) **... ist 1,655 für einen Dollar.**
(d) **Wie darf ich Ihnen ... auszahlen?**
(e) **Der Computer hat ... von DM 827,50 errechnet.**
(f) **Ja, Sie bekommen noch ... von mir.**
(g) **... druckt ihn gerade aus..**

(i) **einen Beleg**
(ii) **einen Betrag**
(iii) **der Computer**
(iv) **in D-Mark**
(v) **das Geld**
(vi) **der Kurs**
(vii) **am Sortenschalter**

3 Below you will find some invoice amounts written in figures. Say them out loud and listen to the recording for the correct version.

(a) DM 46,50 (b) DM 21,70 (c) DM 525,— (d) DM 15,19
(e) DM 153,72 (f) DM 75,95 (g) DM 184,15 (h) DM 290,—

4 In this dialogue you play the role of a client in a bank who wants to change some money. Follow the prompts. You may need to know that **umrechnen** means 'to convert' and **die Umrechnungstabelle** is 'the conversion table'.

5 Listen to the recording where people are counting out money. Try to work out what the final amounts are and write them down in figures. (Answers on p. 98.)

(a) DM ____________ (b) DM ____________ (c) DM ____________

Dialogues

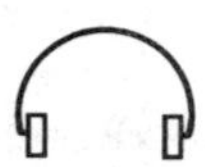

2 *Getting cash with a credit card*

Cashier Guten Morgen. Kann ich etwas für Sie tun?

Customer Guten Morgen. Ich denke schon. Ich habe eine Kreditkarte von der Amexco und möchte gerne 2000 Mark abheben. Ist das möglich?

Cashier Das ist möglich. Welche Kreditkarte haben Sie? Die normale oder die Goldkarte?

Customer Ich habe(e) die Goldkarte.

Cashier Ja, dann kann ich Ihnen 2000 Mark auszahlen, ich muß nur vorher bei der American Express in Frankfurt anrufen. Und das kostet Sie zehn Mark Gebühren. Aber sonst kann ich Ihnen das Geld dann sofort geben.

Customer Das ist in Ordnung. Bitte rufen Sie dort an. Und – eh – ich werde solange warten.

Cashier Ja, kleinen Moment bitte. ... So, es ist alles in Ordnung. Die 2000 Mark kann ich Ihnen auszahlen. Soll ich die zehn Mark einbehalten oder wollen Sie mir die zehn Mark extra geben?

Customer Nein, nein, behalten Sie die ruhig ein.

Cashier Gut. Dann darf ich Ihnen das Geld auszahlen. Möchten Sie (e)s in Hundertern?

Customer Geben Sie mir bitte einen Tausender, einen Fünfhunderter und den Rest in Hundertern, bitte.

Cashier Ja, eintausend, fünfhundert, sechs, sieben, acht, neun, fünfzig, siebzig, neunzig, eintausendneunhundertundneunzig Mark. Bitte schön.

Customer Danke schön. Auf Wiederschau(e)n.

- **das Bargeld** cash
- **abheben** to withdraw
- **sofort** at once / immediately
- **der Rest** remainder/rest

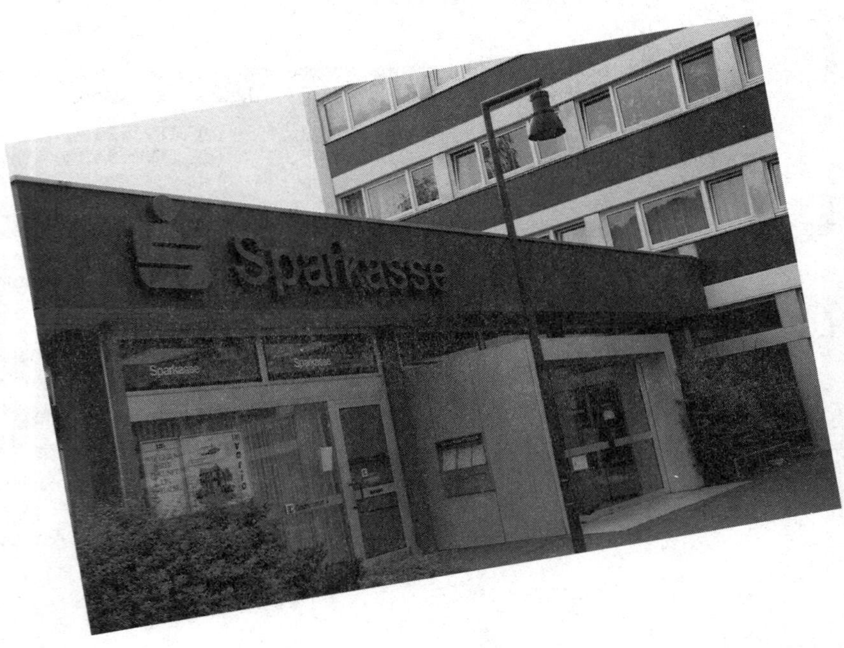

Ich denke schon Yes, I think you can (lit. I think already)

Welche Kreditkarte haben Sie? – Die normale oder die Goldkarte? Which credit card do you have? – The ordinary one or the gold card?

Dann kann ich Ihnen 2000 Mark auszahlen Then I can give you 2000 marks (lit. Then can I you 2000 marks pay out). **Geld auszahlen** is 'to pay out money'.

Ich muß nur vorher ... in Frankfurt anrufen The only thing is I have to ring ... in Frankfurt first (lit. I must only before ... in Frankfurt ring)

Das kostet Sie zehn Mark Gebühren Lit. 'That costs you ten marks charges'. **Das kostet mich ...** means 'that costs me ...'. **Die Gebühr** is 'the charge'.

aber sonst but apart from that (lit. but otherwise). This phrase is used frequently to begin a statement.

Das ist in Ordnung That is OK

Bitte rufen Sie dort an Please ring them up (lit. Please ring there). Although he uses the word **bitte,** this is still an instruction.

solange here: until you have finished. In other contexts the word **solange** means 'as long as'.

Ich werde warten I'll wait

Soll ich die zehn Mark einbehalten? Shall I keep the ten marks? **Einbehalten** means 'to take off from the amount to be paid out'. **Soll** is a form of **sollen**, 'shall', which, like English *shall*, is used together with another verb.

Wollen Sie mir die zehn Mark extra geben? Do you want to give me the ten marks separately.

Behalten Sie die ruhig ein means 'You might as well take off the ten Marks'. **Ruhig** normally means 'quiet', but it is often used as an expression of approval, as here.

Dann darf ich Ihnen das Geld auszahlen Then may I count out the money to you. Again, this polite phrase expresses the intention to do something rather than a request for permission.

Möchten Sie (e)s in Hundertern? Would you like it in 100s (i.e. 100 mark notes)? Similarly: **in Fünfzigern** (in 50s), **in Zwanzigern** (in 20s), **in Zehnern** (in 10s), etc.

Now turn over for the exercises based on dialogue 2.

Practise what you have learned

6 Which of these statements is correct? Circle the appropriate answer. (Answers on p. 98.)

(a) **Der Kunde hat eine Kreditkarte von** (i) **Amexco.**
(ii) **Diner's Club.**
(iii) **Access.**

(b) **Er möchte** (i) **200 Mark abheben.**
(ii) **2000 Mark abheben.**
(iii) **2200 Mark abheben.**

(c) **Der Kassierer ruft bei der American Express** (i) **in Hamburg an.**
(ii) **in Frankfurt an.**
(iii) **in Stuttgart an.**

(d) (i) **Der Beleg kostet 10 Mark.**
(ii) **Das Formular kostet 10 Mark.**
(iii) **Die Gebühr kostet 10 Mark.**

(e) **Der Kassierer** (i) **behält das Geld ein.**
(ii) **hebt das Geld ab.**
(iii) **tauscht das Geld um.**

(f) **Der Kunde möchte** (i) **vier Fünfhunderter.**
(ii) **zwei Tausender.**
(iii) **einen Tausender, einen Fünfhunderter und den Rest in Hundertern.**

7

Choose the appropriate words from the box to complete these sentences – you won't need all of them. (Answers on p. 98.)

(a) **Der Kunde möchte gern 2000 Mark** ______________

(b) **Er hat die Goldkarte und nicht die** ______________ **Kredikarte.**

(c) **Der Kassierer muß nur** ______________ **in Frankfurt anrufen.**

(d) **Dann kann er das Geld** ______________

(e) **Der Kunde muß 10 Mark** ______________ **bezahlen.**

(f) **Der Kassierer soll die Gebühren** ______________

(g) **Der Kassierer soll das Geld nicht in** ______________ **auszahlen.**

abheben **auszahlen** **geben** **Geld** **Gebühren** **normale** **einbehalten** **vorher** **extra** **anrufen** **Hundertern** **sofort**

8

Your turn to speak. Repeat some of the statements made by the client (**der Kunde**) and the cashier (**der Kassierer**). Use the prompts.

9

Listen to this dialogue at the bank counter and then fill in the blanks in the sentences with the appropriate words from the box below – you won't need all of them. (Answers on p. 98.) But first study the new vocabulary.

New vocabulary

die Schweiz Switzerland
schweizer Swiss
der Franken franc
umtauschen to exchange
auskommen to manage
reichen to be sufficient
mitnehmen to take (with you)
auf jeden Fall in any case
ausrechnen to work out

(a) **Ich muß morgen in die** ______________ **fahren.**

(b) **Ich brauche noch ein paar schweizer** ______________

(c) **Mit** ______________ **schweizer Franken komme ich aus.**

(d) **Ich kann aber für morgen noch etwas** ______________

(e) **Ich muß ja morgen schon** ______________

bestellen **besuchen** **Franken** **Schweiz** **Türkei** **fahren** **dreitausend** **fliegen** **Gulden** **zweitausend**

Dialogues

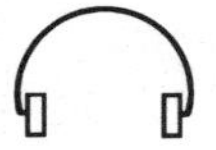

3 *Ordering drinks*

Waitress Guten Tag.
Customer Guten Tag.
Waitress Möchten Sie schon (et)was zu trinken bestellen?
Customer Ja, das wäre nett. Wollen wir mal eben gucken.
Waitress Ja.
Customer So, das wären, glaub(e) ich, drei Alt.
Waitress Drei Alt, ja.
Customer Vier Pils.
Waitress Nehmen Sie Pils oder Pils leicht?
Customer Pils.
Waitress Pils, ist recht.
Customer Und drei kleine Pils.
Waitress Ja, drei kleine Pils.
Customer Zweimal Mineralwasser.
Waitress Apollinaris, nicht?
Customer Ja, ist in Ordnung. Und zwei Cola bitte.
Waitress Und zwei Cola. Vielen Dank.
Customer Und könnten Sie uns dann vielleicht die Karte bringen?
Waitress Das bring(e) ich.
Customer Danke schön.
Waitress Bitte schön.
Customer Danke.

Andreas Pils
3 Cola 9,–
2 Pils 7,20
2 Alt 3,60
1 Wasser 2,30
22,10
nach bester Tradition

die Bedienung waitress/waiter
leicht light
das Mineralwasser mineral water

Möchten Sie schon (et)was zu trinken bestellen? Would you like to order something to drink already? **Etwas zu trinken** means 'something to drink'.

Das wäre nett That would be nice (i.e. 'Yes, please')

Wollen wir mal eben gucken Let's just see quickly. **Wollen wir ...** means 'Let's (do something)', e.g. **Wollen wir nach Frankfurt fahren?** 'Let's go to Frankfurt?'.

Das wären ... That would be ...

glaub(e) ich I think (lit. believe I). **Glauben** means 'to believe/think'.

Alt is short for **das Altbier**, which is similar to British ale and, like most German beers, usually served chilled. It is commonly found in the Rhine and Ruhr regions.

Pils is a popular beer similar in taste and brewing method to the Czechoslovak Pilsener (hence the name).

Nehmen Sie ...? Would you like ...? (lit. Take you ...?). The verb **nehmen** is commonly used to get over the idea of choosing or selecting.

Pils, ist recht All right, Pils (i.e. a confirmation of the order)

drei kleine Pils three small Pils. In Germany beer is served in different-sized glasses: 0.2 litre (**klein**), 1/3 litre, 1/2 litre or a full litre glass.

Apollinaris is a brand of mineral water

Und könnten Sie uns dann vielleicht die Karte bringen? And could you then perhaps bring us the menu? **Die Karte** is the short form for **die Speisekarte**, 'the menu'.

Das bring(e) ich I'll do that. To be grammatically correct, the reference to the previous sentence should be 'die'.

Practise what you have learned

10 See if you can remember how these sentences ended. Listen to the recording again if you need help. (Answers on p. 98.)

(a) **Möchten Sie schon etwas zu trinken** ______________

(b) **Wollen wir mal eben** ______________

(c) **So, das wären,** ______________ **, drei Alt.**

(d) ______________ **Pils oder Pils leicht?**

(e) **Und könnten Sie uns vielleicht** ______________ **bringen?**

11 Complete the following sentences with the appropriate phrases from the list below. (Answers on p. 98.)

(a) ______________ **bitte zwei Cola haben?**

(b) ______________ **gern etwas zu trinken bestellen.**

(c) ______________ **vielleicht noch ein Zimmer frei?**

(d) ______________ **Ihnen eine Tasse Kaffee anbieten?**

(e) ______________ **mir bitte ein Pils bringen?**

(f) ______________ **Pils oder Pils leicht?**

Wir möchten **Haben Sie** **Können Sie** **Darf ich** **Nehmen Sie** **Kann ich**

12 Your turn to speak. How do you order drinks? Use the prompts to help you phrase your order correctly. The word for 'drink' is **das Getränk** (pl. **die Getränke**).

13 Listen to this conversation in a restaurant between a customer and a waiter. Then decide whether the statements made below are **richtig** (true) or **falsch** (false). (Answers on p. 98.) But first study the new vocabulary.

New vocabulary

gewählt chosen
das Schnitzel pork chop
der Salatteller mixed salad
der Schinken ham
das Ei egg
der Hawaii Toast toast topped with cheese, ham and pineapple
Pommes frites (pl.) chips/French fries
die Bratkartoffeln (pl.) fried/sauté potatoes

	richtig	falsch
(a) **Das sind zwei Schnitzel.**		
(b) **Dann dreimal den Salatteller.**		
(c) **Mit Schinken, aber kein Ei.**		
(d) **Und einmal bitte Hawaii Toast.**		
(e) **Und zwei Hamburger bitte.**		
(f) **Mit Pommes frites.**		

Dialogues

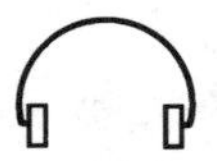

4 *Paying for the meal*

Customer Fräulein?
Waitress Ja?
Customer Ich möchte gern zahlen.
Waitress Ja, ich komm(e) sofort
Customer Ja, danke.
Waitress Zahlen Sie zusammen?
Customer Ja.
Waitress Das waren drei Jägerschnitzel.
Customer Richtig.
Waitress Und drei große Salatteller.
Customer Genau.
Waitress Ein Hawaii Toast. ...
Customer Dann haben wir's alles.
Waitress Geschmeckt hat's Ihnen auch?
Customer Das war sehr lecker. Herzlichen Dank.
Waitress Schön.
Customer Das hat gut geschmeckt.
Waitress Schönen Dank ... So, das sind dann 303 Mark* genau.
Customer Gut, machen Sie 310 draus.
Waitress Danke schön.
Customer Bitte sehr.
Waitress Hat es Ihnen gefallen bei uns?
Customer Doch, das war sehr schön. Ich glaub(e), da kommen wir noch mal wieder.
Waitress Sehr nett. Vielen Dank.

*The final bill seems rather high because the waitress did not go through all the food and drink they had ordered.

das Jägerschnitzel pork chop with mushroom sauce
wiederkommen to come again
noch (ein)mal once again

Fräulein? Lit. 'Miss'. This is the common way to attract the waitress' attention. A waiter would be called **Herr Ober** or simply **Ober**.

Ich möchte gern zahlen I would like to pay. This is the usual way to ask for the bill/check.

Ich komm(e) sofort Lit. 'I come at once', meaning 'I'll be with you in a minute'. **Sofort** can mean 'at once' or 'in a minute/second'.

Zahlen Sie zusammen? Lit. 'Pay you together', i.e. 'Are you paying for everything together?'.

Das waren ... You had ... Lit. 'That were ...' . **Waren** is a past tense form of the verb **sein**.

Dann haben wir's alles Then we've got everything (lit. Then have we it everything). **Wir's** is short for **wir es**.

Geschmeckt hat's Ihnen auch? You enjoyed your meal then? **Geschmeckt** is a form of **schmecken** 'to be good / to taste good'. A more neutral question is: **Hat es Ihnen geschmeckt?** Once again, the word **es** has merged with the preceding word.

Das war sehr lecker That was very nice. **Lecker** (tasty) is only used for food and drink.

Herzlichen Dank Thank you very much indeed (lit. Hearty thanks). This is much more emphatic than **vielen Dank**, which you have already met.

Das hat geschmeckt is another way of saying **Das war sehr lecker** or **Das hat lecker geschmeckt**.

Das sind dann 303 Mark genau That's exactly 303 marks then. The verb is in the plural because the speaker is talking about more than one mark.

Machen Sie 310 draus Call it 310 (lit. Make you 310 of that). **Draus** is short for **daraus** (of/from that). In Germany the service charge is usually included in the price, but rounding up a restaurant bill is nevertheless very common.

Hat es Ihnen gefallen bei uns? Did you like it here? In this context **bei uns** means 'at our restaurant', but it can also mean 'at our house'.

doch is a very strong affirmative here, meaning 'yes, of course'.

Sehr nett That's very kind (lit. very nice). Short for **Das ist sehr nett von Ihnen**, 'That's very kind of you (to say so)'.

Practise what you have learned

14 Who said what? Mark the appropriate boxes for the phrases used by the waitress and the customer. (Answers on p. 98.)

	waitress	*customer*
(a) **Ich möchte gern zahlen.**		
(b) **Das hat gut geschmeckt.**		
(c) **Ja, ich komme sofort.**		
(d) **Zahlen Sie zusammen?**		
(e) **Dann haben wir's alles.**		
(f) **Sehr nett. Vielen Dank.**		
(g) **Doch, das war sehr schön.**		
(h) **Und drei große Salatteller.**		

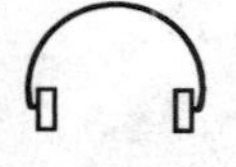

15 Your turn to speak. Answer the questions on the recording using sentences from the dialogue. You will be prompted in English, as usual.

16 Listen to the short dialogue on the recording and then match together the questions and answers below. (Answers on p. 98.)

(a) **Was möchte der Gast haben?**
(b) **Wie lange soll der Gast warten?**
(c) **Was hatte der Gast zu trinken?**
(d) **Wieviel muß der Gast zahlen?**
(e) **Was soll die Bedienung wechseln?**

(i) **zwei Altbier und eine Tasse Kaffee**
(ii) **21 Mark**
(iii) **hundert Mark**
(iv) **die Rechnung**
(v) **zwei Minuten**

Key words and phrases

Das ist kein Problem	That's no problem
Das spielt keine Rolle	That/it doesn't matter
Wie darf ich ...?	How may I ...?
Ich muß anrufen	I have to / must phone/call
Das kostet ... Mark	That costs ... marks
Der Kurs ist ...	The (exchange) rate is ...
Dollar/Pfund in D-Mark wechseln	to change dollars/pounds into deutschmarks
Geld auszahlen	to pay out money
Geld abheben	to withdraw money
der Schalter	counter
der Devisenschalter / der Sortenschalter	foreign exchange counter
der Beleg	receipt/voucher
das Bargeld	cash
die Kreditkarte	credit card
die Gebühr	charge
der Rest	rest/remainder
in Hundertern	in 100-mark notes
in Zehnern	in 10-mark notes
aber sonst	but apart from that
etwas zu trinken	something to drink
etwas zu essen	something to eat
Nehmen Sie ...?	Do you take ...? / Would you like ...?
Könnten Sie uns die Karte bringen?	Could you bring us the menu, please?
Haben Sie gewählt?	Have you made your choice?
Ich möchte gern zahlen	I would like to pay
Zahlen Sie zusammen?	Are you paying everything together?
Das sind dann ... Mark genau	That's exactly ... marks then
Machen Sie ... Mark draus	Call it ... marks
Hat es Ihnen geschmeckt?	Was it nice? / Did you like the food?
Das war lecker	That was nice / That tasted very nice
Hat es Ihnen gefallen?	Did you like it?
Herzlichen Dank	Thank you very much indeed
die Bedienung	waitress/waiter/service
die Rechnung	bill/check/invoice
das Getränk	drink
glauben	to think/believe

Grammar

Irregular verbs

In Units 1 and 2 we studied the forms of some verbs in the present tense. Here are the present tense forms of some irregular verbs. The verbs where the *stem* itself changes are known as strong verbs (see grammar summary, p.223).

nehmen to take	**laufen** to run	**geben** to give
ich nehme	**ich laufe**	**ich gebe**
du nimmst	**du läufst**	**du gibst**
er/sie/es nimmt	**er/sie/es läuft**	**er/sie/es gibt**
wir nehmen	**wir laufen**	**wir geben**
ihr nehmt	**ihr lauft**	**ihr gebt**
sie nehmen	**sie laufen**	**sie geben**
Sie nehmen	**Sie laufen**	**Sie geben**

Note that most of the problems are in the **du** or the **er/sie/es** forms. As you go through the course you will come across other irregular verbs, but they are usually easy to recognize.

Verbs with separable prefixes

Many German verbs are made up of a prefix and a full verb. For example, **eintreten** (to enter) is made up of the prefix **ein** (into) and the main verb **treten** (lit. to tread) or **ankommen** (to arrive), which is made up of the prefix **an** (to) and **kommen** (to come). To form the present and past tenses the two parts are separated: **ich trete ein** (I enter), **du trittst ein** (you enter), **wir kommen an** (we arrive), etc. In a sentence the prefix **ein** usually moves to the end. Have a look at these examples:

Ich <u>trete</u> in das Zimmer <u>ein</u>. I enter the room. (**eintreten** 'to enter')

Er <u>kommt</u> am Bahnhof in Bochum <u>an</u>.
He arrives at the station in Bochum. (**ankommen** 'to arrive')

Ich <u>rufe</u> um sieben Uhr <u>an</u>.
I'll phone/call at seven o'clock. (**anrufen** 'to phone/call')

There are a lot of these verbs. Very often the prefix is like a preposition, e.g. **<u>aus</u>zahlen** (to pay out), **<u>aus</u>rechnen** (to work out), **<u>durch</u>fahren** (to go/drive through), etc. Just remember to separate such verbs and to place the prefix at the end of the sentence.

Questions

Questions can be formed in a number of ways. Very often words such as **Was?** (What?), **Wo?** (Where?) or **Wie?** (How?) are used to obtain specific information:

Wo ist das Hotel? Where is the hotel?
Was kostet das Bier? What does the beer cost?
Wie komme ich zum Bahnhof?* How do I get to the station?

*The verb in German usually comes in second place.

Welcher/welche/welches (which) is a useful word for asking questions. You might also need **wieviel(e)** (How many?). The endings change a bit but you needn't worry about that at the moment. Here are some examples:

Welches Zimmer haben Sie? Which room do you have?
Wieviele Etagen hat das Hotel? How many floors does the hotel have?

Another way is simply to use the equivalent of the English construction 'Have you ...?', etc.

Haben Sie ein gutes Zimmer? Have you / Do you have a good room?

Kennen Sie den Weg zum Bahnhof?
Do you know the way to the station?

Gehen Sie jetzt zum Hotel? Are you going to the hotel now?

Fliegen Sie nach Stuttgart? Are you flying to Stuttgart?

17

Translate these questions into English.

(a) **Wo ist das Postamt?**

____

(b) **Was/Wieviel kostet das Zimmer?**

____

(c) **Wie funktioniert der Fernseher?**

____

(d) **Wo finde ich den Konferenzraum?**

____

(e) **Was trinkt sie?**

____

(f) **Wie ist das Zimmer im sechsten Stock?**

____

(g) **Wieviele Pils bestellt sie?**

____

(h) **Welche Nummer hat das Zimmer?**

____

(i) **Wieviele Dollar tauscht der Kunde?**

____

(j) **In welchem Stock ist der Konferenzraum?**

____

Read and understand

18 Study this menu and find out what there is to eat. Some of the dishes have been mentioned before. Other words that you may not know are listed below.

New vocabulary

geöffnet open/opening hours
der Dienstag Tuesday
der Samstag Saturday
Sonntags on Sundays
Montags on Mondays
der Ruhetag closing/rest day
die Hühnersuppe chicken soup
die Zwiebelsuppe onion soup
das Würstchen sausage
der Kartoffelsalat potato salad
der Brathering grilled herring
das Rührei scrambled egg
heiß hot
die Fleischwurst pork sausage
der Schinkenteller plate of boiled and smoked ham
die Soße sauce
die Ananas pineapple
der Käse cheese
das Zigeunerschnitzel pork chop with peppers and tomatoes
alle all
inklusive (**inkl.**) inclusive
die Mehrwertsteuer (**Mwst.**) value added tax (VAT)
die Bedienung service (charge)

SEIT 1729
DORTMUNDER KRONEN
Alte Braukunst – junge Marken

GEÖFFNET
Dienstag – Samstag von 16.00 – 1.00 Uhr
Sonntags von 11.00 – 1.00 Uhr
Montags – Ruhetag

Speisekarte

Hühnersuppe	3,80 DM
Zwiebelsuppe	3,80 DM
Würstchen mit Kartoffelsalat	4,80 DM
Bratheringe mit Bratkartoffel	7,30 DM
Rührei mit Bratkartoffel	7,20 DM
Heiße Fleischwurst mit Kartoffelsalat	7,20 DM
Schinkenteller mit Ei	7,20 DM
Spaghetti mit Soße Bolognese	6,60 DM
Schinkentoast mit Ananas und Käse	5,20 DM
Zigeunerschnitzel mit Pommes	10,80 DM
Jägerschnitzel mit Pommes	11,80 DM

Alle Preise inkl. Mwst. und Bedienung

Now give one-word answers to these questions. (Answers on p. 98.)

(a) **Wieviele Suppen gibt es auf der Speisekarte?** __________

(b) **Was kostet das Rührei mit Bratkartoffeln?** __________

(c) **Gibt es Kartoffelsalat zum Zigeunerschnitzel?** __________

(d) **Gibt es auf der Speisekarte einen Salatteller?** __________

(e) **Was kostet der Schinkenteller mit Ei?** __________

(f) **Was gibt es zum Schinkentoast zu essen?** __________

(g) **Sind die Preise mit Mehrwertsteuer und Bedienung?** __________

19 And here is a list of drinks that you can buy in the same **Gaststätte**. Have a good look at the new vocabulary and then complete the sentences below. (Answers on p. 98.)

New vocabulary

die Getränkekarte list of beverages
das Malz malt beer
der Korn corn schnapps
der Jägermeister brand of herb-based schnapps
der Wacholder juniper schnapps
alkoholfrei non-alcoholic / alcohol free
der Apfelsaft apple juice
der Orangensaft orange juice
der Traubensaft grape juice
Kaffee Hag brand of decaffeinated coffee
die Schokolade chocolate
schwarzer Tee black tea
der Kräutertee herb tea
das Kännchen pot (of coffee/tea)

SEIT 1729

DORTMUNDER KRONEN

Alte Braukunst – junge Marken

GETRÄNKEKARTE

Pils	0,2 l	1,30 DM
Alt	0,2 l	1,30 DM
Malz	0,2 l	1,30 DM
Korn 2 cl		1,30 DM
Jägermeister		1,60 DM
Wacholder		1,50 DM

ALKOHOLFREI

Cola	0,2 l	1,50 DM
Fanta	0,2 l	1,50 DM
Mineralwasser		1,50 DM
Apfelsaft		2,— DM
Orangensaft		2,20 DM
Traubensaft		2,20 DM

HEISSE GETRÄNKE

Tasse Kaffee	1,50 DM
Tasse Kaffee Hag	1,50 DM
Tasse Schokolade	1,50 DM
Glas schwarzen Tee	1,50 DM
Glas Kräutertee	1,50 DM
Kännchen Kaffee	3,— DM

Alle Preise inkl. Mwst. und Bedienung

(a) **Auf der Karte gibt es sechs alkoholfreie ...** ☐☐☐☐☐☐■☐

(b) **Sie können auch ein ... Kräutertee trinken.** ☐☐■☐

(c) **Für ... und ... müssen Sie 2,20 bezahlen.**
☐☐☐☐☐☐☐☐☐■☐ / ☐☐☐☐☐☐☐☐☐■☐

(d) **Ein Glas Fanta ... 1,50 DM.** ☐☐☐☐■☐

(e) **Alle ... sind inklusive Mehrwertsteuer und Bedienung.**
☐☐☐☐☐■

The letters in the tinted boxes will give you the name of a popular drink.

What is it? ____________________

Did you know?

Food and drink

Snacks

The range of snacks at street stalls and kiosks, snack-bars and in fast-food restaurants in Germany has grown over the years, but the more traditional fare includes a variety of rolls (**das Brötchen**), filled with slices of sausage, ham, cheese or fish, plus hot dogs with bread (**Würstchen mit Brot**), fried sausages (**Bratwurst**), fried chicken (**Brathähnchen**) and chips / French fries (**Pommes frites**). In addition to the American-style fast-food chains there are now also a fair number of Italian, Greek, Yugoslav and occasionally even Turkish snack-bars where national specialities can be bought. Kiosks and stalls in the street are called **Würstchenbude** or **Schnellimbiß**, and a snack-bar is an **Imbißstube**.

Main meals

In Germany the main meal of the day is lunch, served around one o'clock. If possible, the Germans stick to their hot **Mittagessen** even at work (many firms provide canteens), otherwise they will have a hot meal in the evening. The evening meal (**Abendessen** or **Abendbrot**) is around seven p.m. and usually consists of slices of cold meat, sausage or cheese on bread. The tradition of coffee and cake – **Kaffee und Kuchen** – is gradually dying out, partly as a result of changes in leisure activities. On family occasions and for other special events, however, there will be quite a spread of all sorts of home-baked cakes and biscuits.

The tradition of **Bratwurst, Sauerkraut, Kartoffeln** and **Bier** – often associated with the German way of life – is still very much alive in some tourist centres (Pfalz, München), where they are part of the regional specialities, and in quite a few restaurants at the lower end of the market. The regional and local specialities are too numerous to be mentioned here. The best thing is to try them out – just ask for **Spezialitäten**.

Drinks

Beer and coffee are still the most popular drinks in Germany. At business meetings it is fairly common to offer coffee and sometimes tea. At more important meetings a selection of cold drinks may be available. With the exception of beer, alcoholic drinks are not normally served, not even in staff restaurants unless there is a formal function.

In some regions of Germany wine is the preferred drink. The best-known wines are **Rheinwein** (wines from the Rhine area, called **Hock** in Britain) and **Moselwein** (wines from the Moselle). Both can be rather sweet, although owing to changes in taste there are now also lighter, drier and fruitier varieties. Other well-known German wines are grown on the banks of the rivers **Nahe, Saar** and **Ruwer** (all tributaries to the Rhine). It is also well worth trying wines from other wine-growing areas: **Frankenwein** (from the area south-east of Frankfurt), or the **Württemberger** (the area north of Stuttgart), **Badische** (area along the western slopes of the Black Forest), **Pfälzer** and **Rheinhessen Weine** (area south-west of Frankfurt, on the left bank of the Rhine). Most of the German wines are white. Some very good wines are also produced in Austria and Switzerland.

Your turn to speak

20 You are visiting business friends in a German-speaking country. At lunchtime you invite them to a small and informal restaurant near the firm's premises for a snack and drinks. Order different drinks for the people in your party – there are five of you in all. Use the list of drinks on p. 96. You may find these phrases helpful:

Ich möchte zuerst die Getränke bestellen
Das sind also ...
Können Sie uns dann auch noch die Karte bringen, bitte?

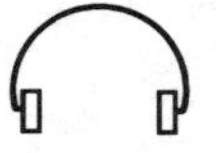

21 And now order the food for the people in your party, and say that you would like the food quickly. Use the menu on p. 95. Here are a few useful phrases:

Und jetzt möchte ich schnell etwas zu essen bestellen
Wir hätten gern einmal/zweimal/dreimal ...
Und dann noch ...

Answers

Practise what you have learned

Exercise 1	*richtig:* (c), (e), (g); *falsch:* (a), (b), (d), (f)
Exercise 2	(a) vii (b) iv (c) vi (d) v (e) ii (f) i (g) iii
Exercise 5	(a) DM 575,— (b) DM 44,22 (c) DM 18,03
Exercise 6	(a) i (b) ii (c) ii (d) iii (e) i (f) iii
Exercise 7	(a) abheben (b) normale (c) vorher (d) auszahlen (e) Gebühren (f) einbehalten (g) Hundertern
Exercise 9	(a) Schweiz (b) Franken (c) zweitausend (d) bestellen (e) fahren
Exercise 10	(a) bestellen (b) gucken (c) glaube ich (d) Nehmen Sie (e) die Karte
Exercise 11	(a) Kann ich (b) Wir möchten (c) Haben Sie (d) Darf ich (e) Können Sie (f) Nehmen Sie
Exercise 13	*richtig:* (b), (d); *falsch:* (a), (c), (e), (f)
Exercise 14	*waitress:* (c), (d), (f), (h); *customer:* (a), (b), (e), (g)
Exercise 16	(a) iv (b) v (c) i (d) ii (e) iii

Grammar

Exercise 17	(a) Where is the office? (b) How much does the room cost? (c) How does the TV work? (d) Where do I find the conference room? (e) What is she drinking? (f) What is the room on the sixth floor like? (g) How many Pils does she order? (h) Which number is the room? (i) How many dollars does the client change? (j) On which floor is the conference room?

Read and understand

Exercise 18	(a) zwei (b) 7,20 DM (c) nein (d) nein (e) 7,20 DM (f) Ananas und Käse (g) ja
Exercise 19	(a) Getränke (b) Glas (c) Orangensaft/Traubensaft (d) kostet (e) Preise; the drink is *Kaffee.*

6 UNDERSTANDING DATES AND TIMES

You will learn

- to plan a business trip
- to enquire about the times of departure and arrival
- to book a trip in a travel agency
- to discuss and arrange appointments and meetings

and you will be given information about national holidays, opening hours and working patterns in the German-speaking countries.

Study guide

Dialogue 1 + Practise what you have learned
Dialogue 2 + Practise what you have learned
Dialogue 3 + Practise what you have learned
Dialogue 4 + Practise what you have learned
Make sure you know the **Key words and phrases**
Study the **Grammar** section
Do the exercises in **Read and understand**
Read **Did you know?**
Do the exercises in **Your turn to speak**

Dialogues

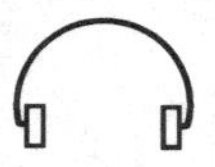

1 *Getting travel information by phone*

Clerk Reiseauskunft der Deutschen Bundesbahn Bochum. Ludwig, guten Morgen.

Herr Berger Schönen guten Morgen, Herr Ludwig. Berger, hier. Ich hätte gerne eine Zugauskunft. Ich müßte morgen nach Braunschweig fahren, und zwar morgens früh.

Clerk Kleinen Moment, bitte ... Es gibt eine Verbindung durchgehend von Bochum um 7.25 ... mit dem D-Zug in Richtung Warschau. Der Zug wäre um 10.55 in Braunschweig und fährt in Bochum ab Gleis 5.

Herr Berger 10.55 an Braunschweig. Ja gut.

Clerk 10.55 in Braunschweig.

Herr Berger Das ist prima. Und für die Rückfahrt, haben Sie da am späten Nachmittag eine Verbindung?

Clerk Am späten Nachmittag von Braunschweig?

Herr Berger Von Braunschweig, ja.

Clerk Es gibt die Möglichkeit, von Braunschweig um 18.44 durchgehend nach Bochum zu fahren.

Herr Berger Das hört sich gut an – 18.44.

Clerk 18.44 ab Braunschweig mit einer Ankunftszeit in Bochum 22.19 Uhr.

Herr Berger Und in Bochum um 22.19 Uhr. Okay. Eh ... was kostet die Fahrt?

Clerk Der Preis für die Hin- und Rückfahrt beträgt 124 D-Mark.

Herr Berger 124 D-Mark. Danke. Auf Wiederhör(e)n.

- **die Zugauskunft** train information
  und zwar that is
- **die Verbindung** connection
- **durchgehend** through
- **die Fahrt** trip/journey/travel

Reiseauskunft der Deutschen Bundesbahn German Federal Railways travel information. **Die Auskunft** means 'information' and **die Reiseauskunft** is 'travel information'. It is common practice in Germany to state your name and, where appropriate, the name of your company when you answer the phone.

Schönen guten Morgen, ... Berger hier. A more emphatic way of saying 'good morning'. The enquirer mentions his name – a common form of politeness, even in this context.

Ich hätte gern ... I would like ... A very polite request, also useful in a shop or restaurant. **Ich hätte** comes from the verb **haben** (to have).

Ich müßte ... fahren is a tentative way of saying **ich muß fahren**, 'I must travel'.

morgens früh early in the morning. **Früh** means 'early'.

D-Zug – a fast train for which a supplement has to be paid. This type of train is being replaced by the new **InterRegio** trains. **Der Zug** means 'train'.

in Richtung in the direction of, i.e. 'bound for'

Der Zug wäre ... The train would be ...

und fährt in Bochum ab Gleis 5 and leaves (in) Bochum from platform 5. **Abfahren** is 'to depart'/leave.

am späten Nachmittag late in the afternoon. Similarly, **am späten Morgen** (late in the morning), etc. To express the idea of early in the afternoon, use **früh**, e.g. **am frühen Nachmittag**.

Haben Sie da ...? Do you have ...? **Da** is a filler here.

Es gibt die Möglichkeit ... There is the possibility ... A very common phrase if you wish to offer an alternative. In the sentence that follows the verb is used in the infinitive, as in English, but in German you add **zu**: **nach Bochum zu fahren** (to go to Bochum). **Es gibt**, 'there is/are' is a very useful phrase.

Das hört sich gut an That sounds good. **Anhören**, meaning 'to listen (to)', is used idiomatically here.

mit einer Ankunftszeit Lit. 'with an arrival time' (timetable jargon)

der Preis für die Hin- und Rückfahrt beträgt ... the price for the journey there and back amounts to ... **Die Hinfahrt** is 'the journey there', **die Rückfahrt** 'the journey back. **Beträgt** is a present tense form of **betragen**, 'to come/amount to'.

Now turn over for the exercises based on dialogue 1.

Practise what you have learned

1 Complete these sentences using the words from the box below.
(Answers on p. 118.)

(a) __________ **der Deutschen Bundesbahn. Guten Morgen.**

(b) **Ich hätte gern eine** __________

(c) **Es gibt eine** __________ **durchgehend von Bochum um 7.25.**

(d) **Und für die** __________ **, haben Sie da am späten** __________ **eine Verbindung?**

(e) **Es gibt die** __________ **, um 18.44 von Braunschweig nach Bochum zu fahren.**

(f) **Mit einer** __________ **in Bochum 22.19.**

(g) **Der** __________ **für die Hin- und Rückfahrt beträgt 124 D-Mark.**

Ankunftszeit **Reiseauskunft** **Preis** **Möglichkeit** **Rückfahrt** **Verbindung** **Nachmittag** **Zugauskunft**

2 Fill in the correct form of the the verb in round brackets.
(Answers on p. 118.)

(a) __________ **ich bitte eine Zugauskunft haben?** (können)

(b) **Ich** __________ **morgen nach Berlin fahren.** (wollen)

(c) **Um 7.25** __________ **es eine durchgehende Verbindung.** (geben)

(d) **Der Zug** __________ **von Gleis 5** __________ (abfahren)

(e) __________ **Sie auch am späten Nachmittag eine Verbindung?** (haben)

(f) **Wieviel** __________ **die Hin- und Rückfahrt nach Braunschweig?** (kosten)

(g) **Der Preis für die Hin- und Rückfahrt nach Braunschweig** __________ **124 D-Mark.** (betragen)

3 Take the role of the traveller and, following the prompts, ask about trains from Frankfurt to Bonn.

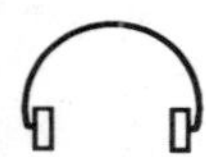

4 Listen to the recording and decide which of the statements below were made by the railway clerk and which by the enquirer. Put a cross in the appropriate boxes. (Answers on p. 118.) But first study the new vocabulary. Don't worry, you are not expected to learn all these words. Just use them to get the gist of the dialogue.

New vocabulary

die Zuginformation train information
möglichst if possible
der Tag day
(**Ab**) **Wann?** When?
der Donnerstag Thursday
vormittags in the morning
umsteigen to change
der Bahnsteig platform
wechseln to change
insgesamt altogether
die Person person
allein alone
der Zuschlag surcharge / extra charge / supplement

		enquirer	*clerk*
(a)	**Ich hätte gern eine Zuginformation von Witten nach Frankfurt.**		
(b)	**Wann möchten Sie denn gerne bitte fahren?**		
(c)	**Morgen, also Donnerstag.**		
(d)	**Dann fahren Sie ab Witten 8.13.**		
(e)	**In Hagen ist die Ankunft 8.26.**		
(f)	**Muß ich in Hagen umsteigen?**		
(g)	**Die Ankunft in Frankfurt ist 11.23.**		
(h)	**Und wieviel kostet das insgesamt?**		
(i)	**Inklusive InterCity-Zuschlag kostet das 135 Mark.**		

Dialogues

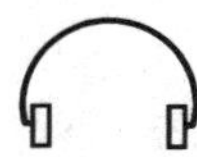

2 *Making a booking in a travel agency*

Customer Guten Tag.
Travel Agent Guten Tag.
Customer Ich möchte gerne eine Zugverbindung von Bochum nach Brüssel haben und dort in Brüssel zwei Tage Aufenthalt machen.
Travel Agent Ja.
Customer Können Sie da was für mich zusammenstellen, bitte?
Travel Agent Aber gerne. Sie können ab Bochum mit dem Zug fahren um 9.19, steigen in Köln um, 10.42 ist die Ankunft.
Customer Ja.
Travel Agent 11.15 geht's weiter. Brüssel-Midi erreichen Sie dann um 14.07. Der Preis für den Erwachsenen beträgt 84 Mark.
Customer Schön. Und Aufenthalt in Brüssel ..., können Sie da ein Hotel für mich buchen?
Travel Agent Ja. Da hätten wir das Hotel Delta anzubieten. Eine Nacht inklusiv Frühstück kostet 89 Mark pro Person.
Customer Gut. Das hört sich gut an. Können Sie da bitte die Buchung für mich vornehmen?
Travel Agent Ja, gerne.
Customer Eine Frage noch. Kann ich per Kreditkarte bezahlen?
Travel Agent Die Hotelübernachtung können Sie selbstverständlich mit der Kreditkarte bezahlen. Die Bundesbahn ist da leider noch nicht angeschlossen. Das müßte ich bitte bar kassieren.

die Buchung booking/reservation
das Reisebüro travel agency
➧ **die Zugverbindung** (train) connection
zusammenstellen to put together
➧ **der/die Erwachsene** adult/grown-up
➧ **buchen** to book
➧ **pro Person** per person
➧ **die Hotelübernachtung** hotel accommodation / overnight stay in a hotel
angeschlossen linked

➧ **Aufenthalt machen** to stay (lit. to make a stay)

Können Sie da (et)was für mich zusammenstellen? Can you put something together for me?

➧ **Da hätten wir ... anzubieten** There we could offer ... **Wir hätten ... anzubieten** is also used in restaurants or shops to draw attention to what is available.

➧ **eine Buchung vornehmen** to make a booking. A slightly more formal alternative to **buchen** 'to book'.

➧ **Eine Frage noch** is short for **Ich habe noch eine Frage**, 'I still have a question'.

per Kreditkarte bezahlen to pay by credit card

➧ **Das müßte ich bitte bar kassieren** I must ask you to pay cash for that, please. **Kassieren** means 'to take (your) money'; **bar** means 'cash'. Note also: **bar bezahlen** 'to pay cash'.

Practise what you have learned

5 Can you work out the sequence in which these sentences occurred in the dialogue? Put the correct letters next to the numbers. (Answers on p. 118.)

(a) **Ich möchte ... dort in Brüssel zwei Tage Aufenthalt machen.**
(b) **Das müßte ich bitte bar kassieren.**
(c) **Da hätten wir das Hotel Delta anzubieten.**
(d) **Die Hotelübernachtung können Sie ... mit der Kreditkarte bezahlen.**
(e) **Ich möchte gerne eine Zugverbindung von Bochum nach Brüssel haben.**
(f) **Kann ich per Kreditkarte bezahlen?**
(g) **Können Sie da was für mich zusammenstellen?**
(h) **Brüssel-Midi erreichen Sie dann um 14.07.**
(i) **Können Sie da bitte die Buchung für mich vornehmen?**
(j) **Der Preis für den Erwachsenen beträgt 84 Mark.**

1	
2	
3	
4	
5	
6	
7	
8	
9	
10	

6 Have a look at these statements and decide whether they are **richtig oder falsch** (true or false). (Answers on p. 118.)

(a) **Er möchte in Brüssel drei Tage Aufenthalt machen.**
(b) **Der Zug nach Brüssel fährt um 9.19 in Bochum ab.**
(c) **Sie müssen in Düsseldorf umsteigen.**
(d) **In Köln fahren Sie um 10.42 weiter.**
(e) **Die Fahrt kostet 84 Mark für den Erwachsenen.**
(f) **Der Preis für die Übernachtung im Hotel Delta beträgt 69 Mark pro Person.**
(g) **Sie können die Fahrkarte mit der Kreditkarte bezahlen.**

richtig	falsch

7 You are planning a business trip and so you need to get some information from the travel agent. The prompts on the recording will tell you which questions to ask.

8 Listen to a telephone conversation in which a secretary makes travel arrangements for her boss. Frau Schumann has left this memo for her boss. See if you can complete her notes. (Answers on p. 118.)

New vocabulary
die Flugnummer flight number
Hotel der Mittelklasse middle-range hotel
der Rückflug return flight
zur Auswahl haben to have to offer / have a choice of

BUCHUNG

(a) Flug von .... nach ....
(b) Einen .... Aufenthalt
(c) .... ab Dortmund
(c) Ankunft in Gatwick ....
(e) Flugnummer ....
(f) Hotel kostet ....

Dialogues

3 *Discussing this week's appointments*

Herr Thiel Frau Wagelaar, können wir mal die Termine besprechen, die wir diese Woche haben?

Frau Wagelaar Ja, Herr Thiel. Für Montag haben wir um 10.00 Uhr die Besprechung mit den Außendienstmitarbeitern.

Herr Thiel Ja.

Frau Wagelaar Um 12.00 den Besuch von Herrn Clarkson aus Kanada – wegen der Lizenz.

Herr Thiel Ja ... Wer holt Herrn Clarkson ab?

Frau Wagelaar Eh, das kann ich übernehmen, wenn Sie möchten.

Herr Thiel Gut. Ist Herr Clarkson pünktlich? Wissen Sie das, mit welcher Maschine er kommt?

Frau Wagelaar Gewöhnlich kommt die Maschine pünktlich an, denke ich.

Herr Thiel Gut.

Frau Wagelaar Am Dienstag haben wir dann um 8.00 Uhr die Abteilungsbesprechung.

Herr Thiel Ja.

Frau Wagelaar Und um 14.00 Uhr die Besprechung mit der Geschäftsführung wegen der Jahresplanung.

Herr Thiel Gut.

Frau Wagelaar Mittwoch wäre dann ...

Herr Thiel Eh, das lassen wir mal ...

➧ **der Termin** appointment
➧ **der Terminkalender** appointments/business diary
➧ **die Woche** week
➧ **der Außendienstmitarbeiter** field worker / travelling salesman
die Außendienstmitarbeiter (pl.) field staff/travellers
wegen because of
die Lizenz licence
Wer? Who?
➧ **gewöhnlich** usual(ly)
➧ **die Abteilungsbesprechung** departmental meeting
➧ **die Geschäftsführung** management (board)
die Jahresplanung planning for the year

für Montag haben wir um 10.00 Uhr ... on Monday we have at ten o'clock ... It's also very common to say **am Montag**. Note the expression for the time is **um 10 Uhr**.

die Besprechung mit den Außendienstmitarbeitern discussion with the field staff. **Mitarbeiter** (fellow worker) is a fairly new word in German and was originally meant to denote a degree of parity between management and labour. ➧ **Besprechen** is 'to discuss / talk over'.

Das kann ich übernehmen I can do that / take that on. Slightly more formal than **Das kann ich tun/machen**.

... mit welcher Maschine er kommt? ... with which plane he will arrive? **Die Maschine** normally means 'machine'; here it is short for **die Flugmaschine**.

Gewöhnlich kommt die Maschine pünktlich an Normally the plane arrives on time

denke ich is often used instead of **glaube ich** to mean 'I believe'. **Denken** means 'to think'.

Mittwoch wäre dann ... On Wednesday there will be ... **Wäre** is a form of **sein,** used here to refer to the future. A very useful phrase for talking about something arranged for the future is **Ist ... vorgesehen**. For example, **Am Dienstag ist die Besprechung vorgesehen,** 'The discussion is scheduled for Tuesday'. **Vorgesehen** is a form of **vorsehen,** to plan/schedule/envisage'.

Practise what you have learned

9 Cross out the days of the week which are not mentioned in the dialogue. (Answers on p. 118.)

Montag	Dienstag	Mittwoch	Donnerstag	Freitag	Samstag	Sonntag

10 Here are some sentences from the dialogue, but the words and phrases in each one are muddled up. Rearrange them so that they make sense. Listen to the dialogue again to check your answers. (The words in brackets are understood in the context of the dialogue.)

(a) **für Montag die Besprechung um 10.00 Uhr haben wir mit den Außendienstmitarbeitern**
(b) **wegen der Lizenz aus Kanada um 12.00 den Besuch von Herrn Clarkson (haben wir)**
(c) **an gewöhnlich pünktlich kommt die Maschine**
(d) **am Dienstag die Abteilungsbesprechung dann um 8.00 Uhr haben wir**
(e) **wegen der Jahresplanung mit der Geschäftsführung und um 14 Uhr (haben wir) die Besprechung**

11 Your turn to speak. Tell your colleague about your business appointments for the week, using the information provided below to form complete sentences. The verb part for each sentence is given in round brackets. The correct answers are given on the recording. **Die Messe** means 'trade fair/exhibition/show' and **das Mittagessen** is 'lunch / midday meal'.

(a) **Montag, 9.00 Uhr: Besprechung mit Frau Seiler** (habe ich)
(b) **Dienstag, 6.00 Uhr: Fahrt zur Hannover Messe** (ist ... vorgesehen)
(c) **Mittwoch, 14.00 Uhr: Sitzung der Abteilungsleiter** (ist)
(d) **Donnerstag, 10.00 Uhr: Besuch von Herrn Reuter von der Firma Stein** (ist ... vorgesehen)
(e) **Donnerstag, 13.00 Uhr: Mittagessen mit Herrn Richter im Parkhotel** (ist)
(f) **Freitag, 11.00 Uhr: Besprechung in der Abteilung** (habe ich)

12 Listen to the dialogue on the recording, then decide whether the statements below are **richtig oder falsch** (true or false). (Answers on p. 118.) But first study the new vocabulary to help you get the gist of the conversation.

New vocabulary
notiert noted down
der Gesprächspartner opposite number / contact
korrekt that's right/correct
der Feiertag public holiday
der Auszubildende trainee/ apprentice
die Abteilung department
der Vertreter representative

	richtig	falsch
(a) **Fräulein Disselkamp und Herr Seiler besprechen die Termine für diese Woche.**		
(b) **Fräulein Disselkamp hat noch nichts notiert.**		
(c) **Dienstag ist ein Termin mit der Firma Sauer in Frankfurt.**		
(d) **Der Gesprächspartner ist Frau Brehmer.**		
(e) **Mittwoch um 10 Uhr ist das Gespräch mit den Auszubildenden der Abteilung.**		
(f) **Um 12.00 Uhr kommt dann noch ein Vertreter der Firma Bauer ins Haus.**		
(g) **Donnerstag ist der 1. Mai. Das ist ein Feiertag.**		

Dialogues

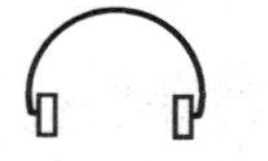

4 *Arranging a date for the next meeting*

Herr Seiler Ich glaube, wir müssen die Sitzung schließen, die Zeit läuft uns davon. Wie sieht es mit einem neuen Termin in vierzehn Tagen aus? Gleicher Tag, gleiche Uhrzeit. Würde das gehen, Herr Theile?

Herr Theile Nein, bei mir würde das nicht gehen. Ich habe einen auswärtigen Termin.

Herr Seiler Mhm. Herr Thiel?

Herr Thiel Ich stehe da zur Verfügung.

Herr Seiler Fräulein Tonscheidt?

Frl. Tonscheidt Ich hab(e) den Besuch eines Kunden hier im Hause.

Herr Seiler Wie sieht denn die nächste Woche dann aus?

Frl. Tonscheidt Das ist Buß- und Bettag.

Herr Seiler Ach so – geht nicht. Und die folgende Woche? Nee, da hab(e) ich ja selber einen Termin. Wie sieht es dann in der ersten Dezemberwoche aus?

Herr Theile Das geht bei mir in Ordnung.

Frl. Tonscheidt Bei mir würd's auch passen.

Herr Thiel Das geht bei mir auch in Ordnung.

Herr Seiler Prima, schön. Also, treffen wir uns dann.

die Uhrzeit time
auswärtig external/outside
zur Verfügung stehen to be available
sich treffen to meet

Wir müssen die Sitzung schließen We must close the meeting

Die Zeit läuft uns davon Time is running out (lit. The time runs us away)

Wie sieht es mit einem neuen Termin in vierzehn Tagen aus? How about a new date in a fortnight? **Wie sieht es aus mit ...?** is a very common phrase to express the English *How about ...?* **Aussehen** is 'to look like', and **in vierzehn Tagen** means 'in a fortnight'.

Gleicher Tag, gleiche Uhrzeit On the same day, at the same time. Similarly: **gleicher Ort, gleiche Zeit** 'at the same place, at the same time'.

Würde das gehen? Lit. 'Would that go?', i.e. 'Would that be possible?' A less formal alternative is **Geht das?**

ein auswärtiger Termin an appointment outside the company

die nächste Woche and **die folgende Woche** both mean 'next week'.

Buß- und Bettag Day of Penitence and Prayer. A public holiday in mid-Novenber.

da habe ich ja selber einen Termin Then I myself have a meeting. **Selber** usually stands together with words such as **ich, du, er** and so on and means 'I myself', 'you yourself', 'he himself'.

die erste Dezemberwoche the first week in December. In the business world people tend to refer to weeks by numbering them and saying, for example, **in der zehnten (Kalender-) Woche,** 'in the tenth calendar week'.

Das geht bei mir in Ordnung That's OK with me. This is a long way of saying **Ja, das geht**.

Bei mir würd's auch passen Lit. 'With me would it also suit. **Würd's** is short for **würde es**. **Passen** means 'to suit' or 'to be suitable'. A more straightforward alternative is **Es paßt mir**.

Also, treffen wir uns dann Well then, let's meet then. This is similar to the constructions used when giving directions, e.g. **Gehen Sie geradeaus** or **Bringen Sie mir ein Bier** or **Fahren Sie mit dem Aufzug**.

Practise what you have learned

13 Can you work out which of these sentences did *not* appear in this dialogue? Put a cross in the appropriate boxes. (Answers on p. 118.)

(a) **Wir wollen die Besprechung schließen.**
(b) **Wie sieht es mit einem neuen Termin in vierzehn Tagen aus?**
(c) **Gleicher Tag, gleiche Uhrzeit.**
(d) **Ich habe einen Termin bei der Firma Witt.**
(e) **Ich stehe da zur Verfügung.**
(f) **Ich besuche einen Kunden hier im Hause.**
(g) **Wie sieht es dann in der zweiten Aprilwoche aus?**
(h) **Das geht bei mir in Ordnung.**
(i) **Bei mir geht es auch nicht.**

14 Complete the sentences on the left by matching them with the appropriate words and phrases from the list on the right. (Answers on p. 118.)

(a)	**Wie sieht es mit einem neuen Termin ... aus?**	(i)	**in Ordnung**
(b)	**Gleicher Tag, gleiche ...?**	(ii)	**hier im Hause**
(c)	**Ich habe ... Termin**	(iii)	**in vierzehn Tagen**
(d)	**Ich habe den Besuch eines Kunden ...**	(iv)	**einen Termin**
(e)	**Wie sieht denn ... dann aus?**	(v)	**einen auswärtigen**
(f)	**Da habe ich ja selber ...**	(vi)	**Uhrzeit**
(g)	**Das geht bei mir ...**	(vii)	**die nächste Woche**

15 On the recording you will be asked if various meetings are convenient for you. Say your answers aloud after the prompts. If you find it helpful to write your answers down, use the pause control to give yourself more time.

16 Two secretaries arrange for their bosses to meet. Study the new vocabulary and then listen to the dialogue. Circle the correct answers to the questions below. (Answers on p. 118.)

New vocabulary
im Auftrage on behalf of
ausgemacht fixed/arranged
holen to fetch/get
der Terminplan appointments diary
eingetragen entered/filled in
gerade just now
bestätigen to confirm

(a) Who is Doerthe's boss?
(i) **Herr Thiel** (ii) **Herr Weiß** (iii) **Herr Seiler**

(b) What had Herr Thiel and Herr Weiß arranged?
(i) **eine Besprechung** (ii) **ein Gespräch** (iii) **einen Termin**

(c) What is the date of the appointment?
(i) **8. Juni** (ii) **28. Juni** (iii) **28. Juli**

(d) Had Martin made a note of the appointment in his diary?
(i) **no** (ii) **not sure** (iii) **yes**

(e) What did Doerthe want to do?
(i) **change the date** (ii) **confirm the appointment**
(iii) **cancel the appointment**

(f) What will Martin do?
(i) **tell Herr Weiß** (ii) **write to Herr Weiß** (iii) **ring Herr Thiel**

Key words and phrases

Ich müßte von ... nach ... fahren	I would like to travel from ... to ...
Wann möchten Sie fahren?	When would you like to travel?
Der Zug fährt ab Gleis ...	The train leaves from platform ...
Sie müssen in ... umsteigen	You must change trains at ...
Sie erreichen ... um ... Uhr	You'll get to ... at ... o'clock
Der Zug fährt ... ab Bochum	The train leaves Bochum at ...
Der Zug fährt durch **Das ist eine durchgehende Verbindung**	It's a through train
Das hört sich gut an	That sounds good
Wenn das geht	If that's possible
Es gibt die Möglichkeit	There is the possibility ...
die Reiseauskunft	travel information
die Zugauskunft / die Zuginformation	train information
die Ankunft / die Ankunftzeit	arrival / time of arrival
die Abfahrt / die Abfahrtzeit	departure / time of departure
die Fahrt	trip/journey/travel
die Hinfahrt	journey there / outward journey
die Rückfahrt	journey back / return journey
die Hin- und Rückfahrt	return journey / journey there and back
der Zug	train
der Zuschlag	supplement/surcharge
Wir hätten ... anzubieten	We could offer you ...
Wie teuer wäre das?	How much would that be?
der Preis für einen Erwachsenen	price for an adult
in Höhe von	amounting to
pro Person	per person
pro Nacht	a/per night
bar kassieren	to ask someone to pay cash
bar bezahlen	to pay cash
per Kreditkarte bezahlen	to pay by credit card
eine Buchung vornehmen	to make a booking/reservation
buchen	to book/reserve
zur Auswahl haben	to have to offer / have to choose from
die Hotelübernachtung	overnight accommodation in a hotel
der Aufenthalt	stay
der Terminkalender / der Terminplan	appointments diary/schedule
der auswärtige Termin	appointment outside the company
einen Termin besprechen	to discuss a date
einen Termin ausmachen	to fix a date
einen Termin bestätigen	to confirm a date
Wie sieht es aus mit ...?	How about ...?
vorgesehen	planned/scheduled/fixed
Das kann ich übernehmen	I can do that / see to that
Die Zeit läuft uns davon	Time is running out
eine Sitzung schließen	to close a meeting
die Abteilungsbesprechung	departmental meeting
der Vertreter	representative
der Außendienstmitarbeiter	field worker
die Geschäftsführung	management
im Auftrage	on behalf of / for
Eine Frage noch	I still have a question
Würde das gehen?	Would that be possible?
Das geht nicht	That's not possible
Es paßt mir	It suits me / It is suitable
betragen	to be / amount to
die Uhrzeit	time

Grammar

Times, days and months

Here is a summary of useful words and phrases relating to times and dates. Try to learn as much of this essential vocabulary as you can, and practise by reading the words and phrases aloud.

der Tag	day	**tags(über)**	during the day
der Morgen	morning	**morgens**	in the morning
der Vormittag	morning	**vormittags**	in the morning
der Mittag	midday/lunchtime	**mittags**	at midday/lunchtime
der Nachmittag	afternoon	**nachmittags**	in the afternoon
der Abend	evening	**abends**	in the evening
die Nacht	night	**nachts**	at night

am frühen/späten Morgen **früh/spät am Morgen**	early/late in the morning
am frühen/späten Vormittag **früh/spät am Vormittag**	early/late in the morning
am frühen/späten Nachmittag **früh/spät am Nachmittag**	early/late in the afternoon
am frühen/späten Abend **früh/spät am Abend**	early/late in the evening

gestern	yesterday	**morgen**	tomorrow
heute	today	**übermorgen**	the day after tomorrow

gestern **heute**	**morgen**	yesterday this	morning
gestern **heute** **morgen**	**vormittag**	yesterday this tomorrow	morning
gestern **heute** **morgen**	**mittag**	yesterday this tomorrow	lunchtime
gestern **heute** **morgen**	**nachmittag**	yesterday this tomorrow	afternoon
gestern **heute** **morgen**	**abend**	yesterday this tomorrow	evening
gestern **heute** **morgen**	**nacht**	yesterday night tonight tomorrow night	

der Tag	day	**die Woche**	week
der Monat	month	**das Jahr**	year
das Vierteljahr	quarter (of the year)	**das Halbjahr**	half (of the year)

Die Uhr (the clock)

die Sekunde second **die Minute** minute **die Stunde** hour

Es ist zwei Uhr. It's two o'clock.

Es ist fünf (Minuten) nach zwei. It's five (minutes) past two.

Es ist zehn (Minuten) nach zwei. It's ten (minutes) past two.

Es ist viertel nach zwei. It's a quarter past two.

Es ist zwanzig (Minuten) nach zwei. It's twenty (minutes) past two.

Es ist fünf (Minuten) vor halb drei. It's twenty-five (minutes) past two.

Es ist halb drei. It's half past two.

Es ist fünf (Minuten) nach halb drei. It's twenty-five (minutes) to three.

Es ist zwanzig (Minuten) vor drei. It's twenty (minutes) to three.

Es ist viertel vor drei. It's a quarter to three.

Es ist zehn (Minuten) vor drei. It's ten (minutes) to three.

Es ist fünf (Minuten) vor drei. It's five (minutes) to three.

Die Jahreszeiten (seasons)

der Frühling / das Frühjahr	spring/lent	**der Sommer**	summer
der Herbst	autumn/fall	**der Winter**	winter

Die Wochentage (days of the week)

Montag	Monday	**montags**	on Mondays
Dienstag	Tuesday	**dienstags**	on Tuesdays
Mittwoch	Wednesday	**mittwochs**	on Wednesdays
Donnerstag	Thursday	**donnerstags**	on Thursdays
Freitag	Friday	**freitags**	on Fridays
Samstag/Sonnabend	Saturday	**samstags/sonnabends**	on Saturdays
Sonntag	Sunday	**sonntags**	on Sundays

Die Monate (months of the year)

Januar	January	**Juli**	July
Februar	February	**August**	August
März	March	**September**	September
April	April	**Oktober**	October
Mai	May	**November**	November
Juni	June	**Dezember**	December

The days of the week and the months of the year all have the article **der** (the), which means that they are *masculine*.

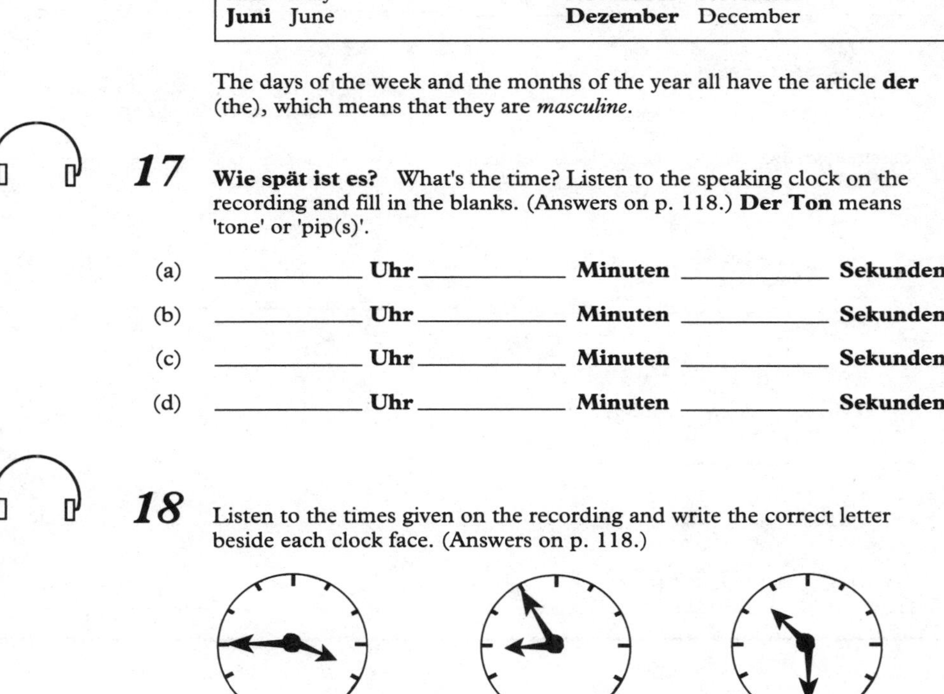

17 **Wie spät ist es?** What's the time? Listen to the speaking clock on the recording and fill in the blanks. (Answers on p. 118.) **Der Ton** means 'tone' or 'pip(s)'.

(a) ____________ **Uhr** ____________ **Minuten** ____________ **Sekunden**

(b) ____________ **Uhr** ____________ **Minuten** ____________ **Sekunden**

(c) ____________ **Uhr** ____________ **Minuten** ____________ **Sekunden**

(d) ____________ **Uhr** ____________ **Minuten** ____________ **Sekunden**

18 Listen to the times given on the recording and write the correct letter beside each clock face. (Answers on p. 118.)

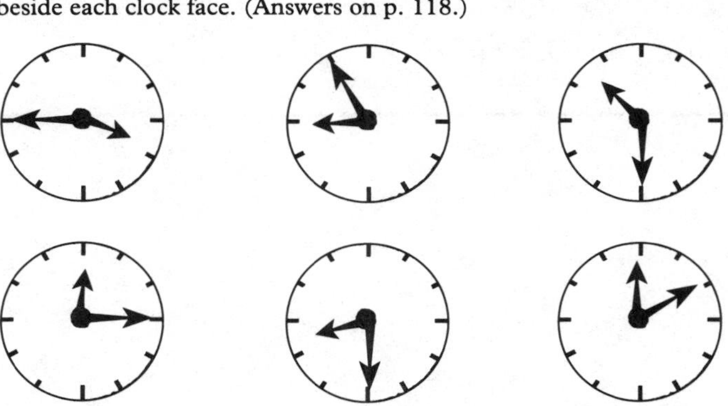

Read and understand

19 Here is an extract from Herr Seiler's appointments diary. See how much of it you can understand before you look at the new vocabulary.

New vocabulary

Wochennotizen notes for the week
die Sitzplatzreservierung seat reservation
der Nichtraucher non-smoker
die Theaterkarte theatre ticket
der Geburtstag birthday
absagen to cancel
telefonieren to phone
Industrie- und Handelskammer chamber of industry and commerce
der Devisenhandel foreign exchange dealing
ganztägig all day / the whole day
der Empfang reception
die Besichtigung guided tour / visit
die Hauptversammlung (annual) general meeting

April 18. Woche 118-124

Wochennotizen
Flüge für München buchen!
Sitzplatzreservierung Nichtraucher
Termin für Montag absagen
Eisen & Stahl, Düsseldorf
Theaterkarten für Samstag bestellen

27 Montag
10⁰⁰ Vorstandssitzung
15⁰⁰ IHK, Industrie- und Handelskammer, Bochum

28 Dienstag
8¹⁵ mit Hr. Jäger telefonieren
17⁰⁰ Deutsche Bank, Köln
- Herr Grafenhain

29 Mittwoch
12⁰⁰ Mittagessen mit Hr. Jung (Devisenhandel)
Geburtstag Hr. Schiffkowski
Empfang

SA 5.02 SU 19.38
MA 2.42 MU 13.59

April/Mai

Donnerstag 30
ganztägig in München
15⁰⁰ Besichtigung Löwenbräu
W / Hauptversammlung

Maifeiertag Freitag 1

● Samstag 2

Sonntag 3

20

Here is an extract from a timetable of the **Deutsche Bundesbahn** together with the key. Have a good look at the key first and then study the timetable. **Täglich** means 'daily' and **außer** 'except'. Put a circle round the correct answers. (Answers p. 118.)

Zeichenerklärung (Key)

ICE	***InterCity Express***
EC	***EuroCity***
IC	***InterCity***
IR	***InterRegio***
D	***Schnellzug*** (express train)
E	***Eilzug*** (fast train)
①	Montag
②	Dienstag
③	Mittwoch
④	Donnerstag
⑤	Freitag
⑥	Samstag (Sonnabend)
⑦	Sonntag
Ⓢ	Ⓢ-Bahn
	Kurswagen (through coach)
	Schlafwagen (sleeper)
✕	Zugrestaurant (restaurant)
🍷	Speisen u. Getränke im Zug erhältlich bzw. bei der DR "Büfettwagen" (buffet trolley)
[U]	Umsteigen (change trains)
⚒	an Werktagen (workdays)
†	an Sonntagen und allgemeinen Feiertagen (Sundays and Bank Holidays)

Essen

	km 382 →			Hamburg Hbf		
	km 382 →				Hmb-Altona	
	ab	Zug		an	an	Bemerkungen
Ⓖ	**0.40**	***D***	1931	**5.04**	**5.24**	[45]
Ⓗ	**4.28**	Ⓢ		**8.06**	**8.19**	[45] [U] Dortm ***IC***✕
Ⓘ	**5.21**	***E***	3201	**9.06**	**9.19**	[45] [72] [U] Dortm ***IC*** ✕
Ⓙ	**5.28**	Ⓢ		**9.06**	**9.19**	[45] [U] Dortm ***IC***✕
	6.59	***IC***	608		**10.19**	✕ [45] [U] Dortm ✕
	7.06	***IC***	533	**9.56**		✕
Ⓕ	**7.59**	***IC***	635	**11.06**	**11.19**	✕ [45]
	8.59	***IC***	833	**12.06**	**12.19**	✕ [45]
	9.27	***D***	1035	**13.26**		✕ [45]
	9.59	***IC***	639	**13.06**	**13.19**	✕ [45]
	10.59	***IC***	604	**14.06**	**14.19**	✕ [45] [U] Dortm ✕
	11.35	***IR***	2059	**15.06**	**15.19**	✕ [45] [U] Dortm ***IC***✕
Ⓕ	**11.59**	***IC***	506	**15.06**	**15.19**	✕ [45] [U] Dortm ✕
	12.59	***IC***	822	**16.06**	**16.19**	✕ [45]
	13.59	***IC***	524	**17.06**	**17.19**	✕ [45]
	14.59	***EC***	108	**18.06**	**18.19**	✕ [45] [U] Dortm ***IC***✕
	15.59	***IC***	620	**19.06**	**19.19**	✕ [45]
	16.59	***EC***	102	**20.06**	**20.19**	✕ [45] [U] Dortm ✕
Ⓓ	**17.25**	***IC***	612	**20.16**	**20.29**	✕ [45]
Ⓔ	**17.59**	***EC***	106	**21.06**	**21.19**	✕ [45] [U] Dortm ***IC***✕
	18.59	***EC***	28	**22.06**	**22.19**	✕ [45]
	19.59	***IC***	724	**23.06**	**23.19**	✕ [45]
Ⓚ	**20.25**	***IC***	714	**23.26**	**23.39**	✕ [45]
	20.59	***EC***	4	**0.06**	**0.19**	✕ [45] [U] Dortm ✕
	23.11	***D***	233	**2.58**		🍷

Ⓓ = ① bis ⑤, nicht 24. XII. bis 1. I., 17. bis 20. IV.
Ⓔ = täglich außer ⑥, nicht 24. bis 31. XII., 17. bis 19. IV.
Ⓕ = ① bis ⑥, nicht 25. XII. bis 1. I., 18. bis 20. IV.
Ⓖ = ① bis ⑥, auch 31. V., nicht 25., 26. XII., 1. I., 18. bis 20. IV.
Ⓗ = ⚒ außer ⑥, nicht 1. XI., 24., 31. XII.
Ⓘ = ⚒, nicht 1. XI., 25. XII. bis 1. I., 18. bis 20. IV.
Ⓙ = ⚒ außer ⑥, nicht 1. XI., 24. XII. bis 1. I., 18. bis 20. IV.
Ⓚ = ⑦, nicht 29. XII., 19. IV.
[45] = Zug hält auch in Hamburg-Harburg
[72] = Essen-Altenessen

(a) **Wann komme ich in Hamburg Hauptbahnhof an, wenn ich um 7.06 in Essen abfahre?**

(i) 10.00 (ii) 9.56 (iii) 10.07

(b) **Kann ich sonntags mit dem Zug um 7.59 nach Hamburg fahren?**

(i) **ja** (ii) **nein**

(c) **Fährt der Zug um 11.35 ab Essen täglich?**

(i) **ja** (ii) **nein**

(d) **Kann ich auch mit einem D-Zug nach Hamburg fahren?**

(i) **ja** (ii) **nein**

(e) **Wie oft fährt ein EuroCity-Zug nach Hamburg?**

(i) einmal (ii) dreimal (iii) fünfmal

(f) **Wo muß ich umsteigen, wenn ich um 5.28 von Essen nach Hamburg fahre?**

(i) **in Bochum** (ii) **in Bremen** (iii) **in Dortmund**.

Did you know?

National holidays

Compared with some other countries you may find that the number of national holidays (**Feiertage**) is fairly high in Germany. Here is a list of them. As some of the holidays move from year to year depending on the calendar, dates are only given for those holidays that do not change.

Neujahr New Year's Day (1 January)
Karfreitag Good Friday
Ostertag Easter Sunday
Ostermontag Easter Monday
Maifeiertag Labour Day (1 May)
Christi Himmelfahrt Ascension Day (Thursday c.40 days after Easter)
Pfingstsonntag und Pfingstmontag Whit Sunday and Whit Monday
Tag der Wiedervereinigung German Reunification Day (3 October)
Buß- und Bettag Day of Penitence and Prayer (Wednesday in the 3rd week of November)
1. und 2. Weihnachtstag Christmas Day and Boxing Day

Most of these holidays are also observed in Switzerland, although Easter and Whit Mondays are normal working days; and the Day of Penitence is kept on the third Sunday in September. In Austria, where there are many more religious holidays due to the fact the vast majority of Austrians are Roman Catholic, the following days are also kept: 15 August, **Mariä Himmelfahrt** (Ascension of Mary), 2 November, **Allerseelen** (All Souls), and 8 December, **Mariä Empfängnis** (Immaculate Conception). The Swiss national holiday is 1 August, and in Austria it is 26 October.

Opening hours

Shops

Shops usually open around 9 a.m. (baker, butcher, newsagent open even earlier) and shut at either 6 or 6.30 p.m. Some close for lunch, though not in town centres. On Saturdays shops are open in the morning only, except on the first Saturday of the month, when town-centre and large, out-of-town shops stay open until 4 p.m. (**Langer Samstag**). These same shops usually stay open longer on Thursday evenings. This is referred to as **der Dienstleistungsabend** (service evening). With minor local differences the same shop opening hours will be found in Switzerland and Austria.

Banks and offices

Most bank branches in Germany are open 9–4, Monday–Friday; some of them may stay open a little longer on Thursdays too. Some offices, especially local authority offices and often main post offices, open very early. But as opening hours vary considerably it is advisable to enquire first. Banking hours in Switzerland tend to be shorter, with the vast majority of banks closing at 3 p.m. In Austria, on the other hand, most banks stay open until 6 p.m., but there is usually a two hour break for lunch. This is also true for a lot of offices in Austria, whereas office hours in Switzerland are similar to those in Germany.

Working hours

Work starts at any time between 6 and 9 a.m. and finishes between 2 and 5.30 p.m., or even later in the retail trade. Office workers tend to have later starting and finishing hours than factory workers. Very often the former are on flexitime (**die Gleitzeit**). Shift-work systems (**die Wechselschicht**) usually operate 2 or 3 eight-hour shifts, with the first one starting at 6 a.m., the second at 2 p.m. and the third, where it exists, at 10 p.m. The same can be said of Switzerland and Austria. Office hours often depend on the duration of the lunchtime break.

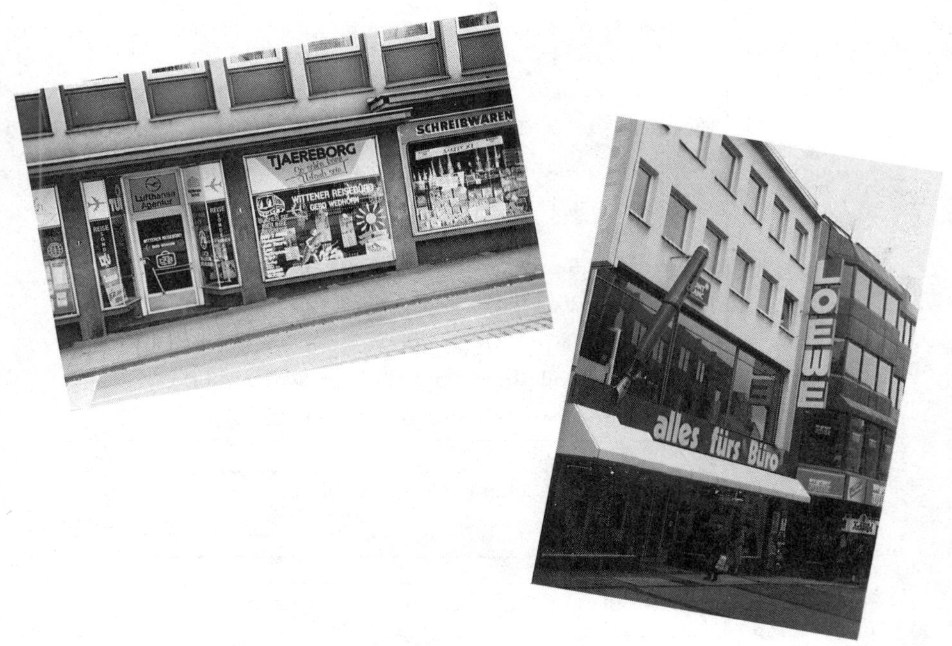

Your turn to speak

Now it's your turn to speak again. Have a go at these open-ended exercises and then listen to the recording to hear what you might have said.

21 You need some travel information for a business trip. Tell the travel agent when and where you want to go and ask about travel and accommodation possibilities. Here are some useful phrases:

Ich muß von ... nach ... fliegen/fahren
Können Sie mir vielleicht eine durchgehende Verbindung sagen
Ich hätte gern eine Reiseauskunft
Ich will ... Tage dort bleiben und brauche auch Informationen über Hotels

22 Over lunch you discuss your business appointments for next week with your business partner. Start by telling her/him that you already have some appointments next week. You may find these phrases helpful:

Am Montag um ... Uhr ist / muß ich / habe ich ...
Für Dienstag (um ... Uhr) ist ... vorgesehen/angesetzt
... habe ich einen auswärtigen Termin
... habe ich eine Besprechung mit ... von ...

Answers

Practise what you have learned

Exercise **1**	(a) Reiseauskunft (b) Zugauskunft (c) Verbindung (d) Rückfahrt, Nachmittag (e) Möglichkeit (f) Ankunftszeit (g) Preis
Exercise **2**	(a) Kann/Könnte (b) will (c) gibt (d) fährt ... ab (e) Haben (f) kostet (g) beträgt
Exercise **4**	*enquirer:* (a), (c), (f), (h); *clerk:* (b), (d), (e), (g), (i)
Exercise **5**	(a) 2 (b) 10 (c) 6 (d) 9 (e) 1 (f) 8 (g) 3 (h) 4 (i) 7 (j) 5
Exercise **6**	*richtig:* (b), (e); *falsch:* (a), (c), (d), (f), (g)
Exercise **8**	(a) Dortmund, London (b) Tag (c) 11.45 (d) 12.15 (e) VG 309 (f) 155 DM
Exercise **9**	Donnerstag, Freitag, Samstag, Sonntag
Exercise **12**	*richtig:* (a), (c), (g); *falsch:* (b), (d), (e), (f)
Exercise **13**	(a), (d), (f), (g), (i)
Exercise **14**	(a) iii (b) vi (c) v (d) ii (e) vii (f) iv (g) i
Exercise **16**	(a) i (b) iii (c) ii (d) iii (e) ii (f) i

Grammar

Exercise **17**	(a) 7, 25, 30 (b) 10, 45, 10 (c) 12, 31, 55 (d) 22, 2, 7
Exercise **18**	(a) 12.15 (b) 8.30 (c) 15.45 (d) 20.55 (e) 10.30 (f) 14.00

Read and understand

Exercise **20**	(a) ii (b) ii (c) i (d) i (e) iii (f) iii

7 ON THE TELEPHONE

You will learn

- to explain who you are and whom you want to talk to
- to ask someone to take a message
- to pass on and understand telephone numbers
- to find out when someone is free
- to arrange a date for a visit
- to use a public telephone

and you will be given information about the telephone system in Germany.

Study guide

Dialogue 1 + Practise what you have learned
Dialogue 2 + Practise what you have learned
Dialogue 3 + Practise what you have learned
Dialogue 4 + Practise what you have learned
Make sure you know the **Key words and phrases**
Study the **Grammar** section
Do the exercise in **Read and understand**
Read **Did you know?**
Do the exercises in **Your turn to speak**

Dialogues

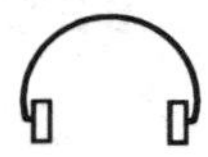

1 *Getting through to the switchboard*

Telephonist Wischmann & Co. KG. Guten Tag.
Frau Schwarz Schwarz, guten Morgen. Ich bin von der Firma Triebwasser GmbH in Kiel und möchte gerne Frau Körner von der Vertriebsabteilung sprechen. Geht das wohl?
Telephonist Einen kleinen Moment, Frau Schwarz, ich verbinde Sie.
Frau Schwarz Danke schön.
Telephonist Frau Schwarz? Es tut mir leid, die Frau Körner meldet sich nicht. Könnten Sie später noch einmal anrufen?
Frau Schwarz Ja natürlich. Ich probier's später nochmal. Danke schön. Wiederhör(e)n.
Telephonist Danke auch. Wiederhör(e)n.

die Vertriebsabteilung marketing/distribution department
später later

Wischmann & Co. KG The abbreviation **Co.** stands for **Compagnie** and means 'society' (**die Gesellschaft**). **KG** is short for **Kommanditgesellschaft** (limited partnership). This is a family group which has organized its business interests in a limited partnership.

Triebwasser GmbH The abbreviation **GmbH** is short for **Gesellschaft mit beschränkter Haftung** (private company with limited liability)

Geht das wohl? Is that possible perhaps? A very polite request. **Wohl** introduces an element of hesitation.

Ich verbinde Sie I'll put you through (lit. I connect you)

meldet sich nicht does not answer (the phone). **Sich melden** means 'to report'. A very useful telephone phrase.

Ich probier's später nochmal I'll try again later. In the phrase **probier's,** the final **e** of **probiere** and the initial **e** of **es** is 'swallowed' by the speaker. Such contractions are common in spoken German – see also dialogue 2. **Nochmal** is colloquial for **noch einmal; probieren** means 'to try'.

Telefonieren ohne Münzen

Telefonkarten erhalten Sie im Postamt

Practise what you have learned

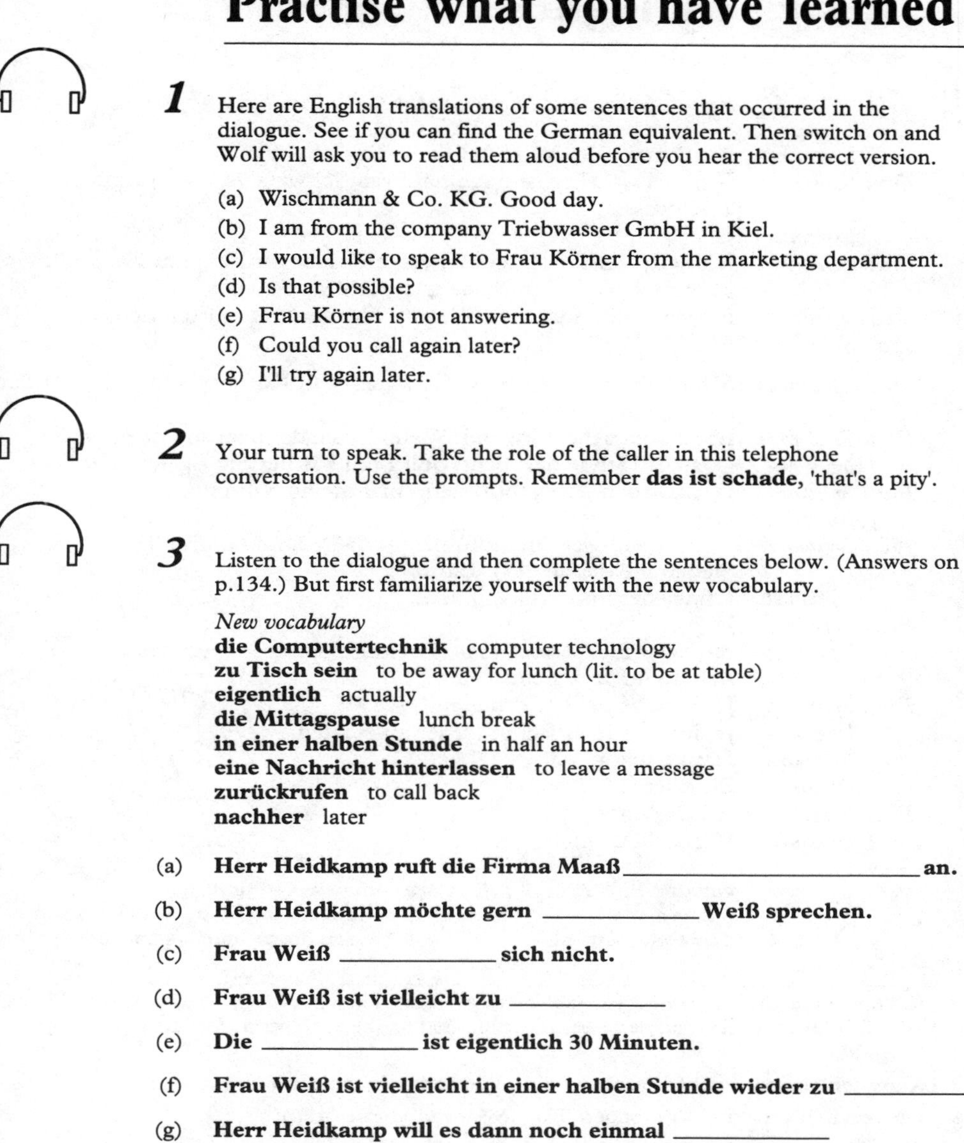

1 Here are English translations of some sentences that occurred in the dialogue. See if you can find the German equivalent. Then switch on and Wolf will ask you to read them aloud before you hear the correct version.

(a) Wischmann & Co. KG. Good day.
(b) I am from the company Triebwasser GmbH in Kiel.
(c) I would like to speak to Frau Körner from the marketing department.
(d) Is that possible?
(e) Frau Körner is not answering.
(f) Could you call again later?
(g) I'll try again later.

2 Your turn to speak. Take the role of the caller in this telephone conversation. Use the prompts. Remember **das ist schade**, 'that's a pity'.

3 Listen to the dialogue and then complete the sentences below. (Answers on p.134.) But first familiarize yourself with the new vocabulary.

New vocabulary
die Computertechnik computer technology
zu Tisch sein to be away for lunch (lit. to be at table)
eigentlich actually
die Mittagspause lunch break
in einer halben Stunde in half an hour
eine Nachricht hinterlassen to leave a message
zurückrufen to call back
nachher later

(a) **Herr Heidkamp ruft die Firma Maaß ____________ an.**

(b) **Herr Heidkamp möchte gern ____________ Weiß sprechen.**

(c) **Frau Weiß ____________ sich nicht.**

(d) **Frau Weiß ist vielleicht zu ____________**

(e) **Die ____________ ist eigentlich 30 Minuten.**

(f) **Frau Weiß ist vielleicht in einer halben Stunde wieder zu ____________**

(g) **Herr Heidkamp will es dann noch einmal ____________**

(h) **Herr Heidkamp kann auch eine Nachricht ____________**

Dialogues

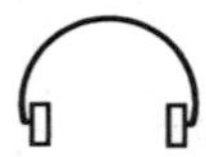

2 *Frau Schwarz gets through to the switchboard again*

Telephonist	Wischmann & Co. KG. Guten Tag.
Frau Schwarz	Guten Tag. Hier ist nochmal Frau Schwarz von der Firma Triebwasser.
Telephonist	Ja.
Frau Schwarz	Ich hatte vorhin schon mal vergeblich angerufen, um Frau Körner zu erreichen. Kann ich sie jetzt wohl sprechen?
Telephonist	Ich versuch's nochmal. Kleinen Moment bitte, Frau Schwarz.
Frau Schwarz	Mhm.
Telephonist	Mhm. Tut mir leid Frau Schwarz. Frau Körner meldet sich immer noch nicht.
Frau Schwarz	Es ist aber sehr dringend. Wann ist sie denn zu sprechen?
Telephonist	Das weiß ich leider nicht. Soll Frau Körner Sie zurückrufen?
Frau Schwarz	Ja, natürlich. Ich geb(e) dann mal meine Nummer an.
Telephonist	Das wäre nett.
Frau Schwarz	Das ist null vier einundfünfzig (0451). Dreiunddreißig (33). Siebenundvierzig (47). Eins (1).
Telephonist	Ich wiederhol(e) noch mal ...
Frau Schwarz	Ja.
Telephonist	Null vier fünf eins (0451). Dreiunddreißig siebenundvierzig eins (33 47 1).
Frau Schwarz	Ja. Und es ist sehr dringend!
Telephonist	Ja, ich werde es Frau Körner ausrichten.
Frau Schwarz	Danke schön.
Telephonist	Bitte sehr.
Frau Schwarz	Wiederhören.
Telephonist	Wiederhör(e)n.

vorhin earlier (on) / a short time ago
➧ **dringend** urgent
➧ **angeben** to give
➧ **wiederholen** to repeat / say again
➧ **ausrichten** to tell (someone) / pass on

➧ **Ich hatte vorhin schon mal vergeblich angerufen** I had already phoned (once) before in vain. **Ich hatte angerufen** describes an action that has been completed in the past. **Vergeblich** means 'in vain'.

➧ **Kann ich sie jetzt wohl sprechen?** Can I perhaps talk to her now?

➧ **Ich versuch's** I'll try. **Versuchen**, like **probieren**, means 'to try'.

Frau Körner meldet sich immer noch nicht Frau Körner is still not answering. **Immer noch nicht** is very emphatic and is commonly used when there is a repeated lack of success. Similarly: **Herr Braun ist immer noch nicht da** (Mr Brown still isn't there).

➧ **Wann ist sie denn zu sprechen?** Lit. 'When is she then to speak?' i.e., 'When will Frau Körner be available so that I can speak to her?' This impersonal phrase is commonly used as an alternative to the more direct and less polite **Wann kann ich bitte Frau Körner sprechen?**

➧ **Ich geb(e) dann mal meine Nummer an** I'll give you my number then. **Mal** makes this sentence very casual.

0451/33 47 1 Note the way the telephone number is given. The area code (**die Vorwahl (nummer)**) is often given in single-digit figures, whereas the subscriber's number (**die Rufnummer**) is normally given in double-digit figures. To avoid confusion between **zwei** and **drei**, which may sound similar on the phone, **zwei** is usually pronounced **zwo**. Similarly, **Juni** becomes **Juno**.

Practise what you have learned

4 Complete the sentences below. Choose the missing words from those in the box – you won't need all of them. (Answers on p. 134.)

(a) **Hier ist nochmal Frau Schwarz von der ____________ Triebwasser.**

(b) **Ich hatte vorhin schon einmal ____________ angerufen.**

(c) **Kann ich sie jetzt wohl ____________ ?**

(d) **Frau Körner ____________ sich immer noch nicht.**

(e) **Ich muß sie aber sehr ____________ sprechen.**

(f) **Ich weiß ____________ nicht, wann Frau Körner zu sprechen ist.**

(g) **Vielleicht kann Frau Körner ____________ , wenn sie im Büro ist?**

dringend **Firma** **leider** **meldet** **natürlich** **sprechen** **zurückrufen** **Durchwahl** **jetzt** **wiederholen** **vergeblich** **leid**

5 Here are some verb phrases that were used in the dialogue. Write down the full sentences in which they occurred. Then say them aloud and listen to the correct answers on the recording.

(a) **hatte ... angerufen**: ________________________

(b) **versuche es**: ________________________

(c) **meldet sich**: ________________________

(d) **ist ... zu sprechen**: ________________________

(e) **soll ... zurückrufen**: ________________________

(f) **gebe ... an**: ________________________

(g) **werde ... ausrichten**: ________________________

6 Your turn to speak. Here is a dialogue which is similar to the one you have just heard. Take the role of Frau Schwarz and use the prompts for your replies and requests. Try to respond straight away. You'll hear the answers on the recording.

7 Listen to Paul and Maria reading out some telephone numbers. Circle the numbers you hear. (Answers on p. 134.) **Die Durchwahl** means 'extension number'.

(a)	(i) 0211/35 53 35	(ii) 0221/53 35 53	(iii) 0211/53 35 53
(b)	(i) 400-2589	(ii) 700-2589	(iii) 700-2958
(c)	(i) 0611/96 43 57	(ii) 069/96 43 57	(iii) 069/43 57 96
(d)	(i) 040/24 42 1	(ii) 0401/24 48 42	(iii) 040/24 42 2498
(e)	(i) 020/17 17 71 4	(ii) 030/71 71 17 1	(iii) 030/17 71 71 4

Dialogues

3 *Making a call to the United States*

Visitor Entschuldigung. Ich müßte in die USA anrufen, nach Boston. Können Sie mir da helfen?
Passer-by Ja, natürlich doch. Lassen Sie uns direkt zur Telefonzelle gehen.
Visitor Ja.
Passer-by So. Hier oben steht die Telefonnummer für die USA. Das ist die null null eins (001).
Visitor Null null eins (001), ja.
Passer-by Jetzt nehmen Sie den Hörer. Hören Sie den Wählton?
Visitor Ich höre den Ton, ja.
Passer-by Jetzt werfen Sie das Geld ein. Sie können Ein-, Zwei- oder Fünfmarkstücke einwerfen.
Visitor So, das Geld habe ich eingeworfen.
Passer-by Jetzt wählen Sie die null null eins (001) für die USA. Die Nummer in Boston weiß ich leider nicht.
Visitor Ja, dann weiß ich Bescheid. Danke.
Passer-by Wiederseh(e)n.
Visitor Wiederseh(e)n.

- **der Hörer** receiver
- **hören** to hear / listen to
- **einwerfen** to insert
- **wählen** to dial

Entschuldigung Excuse me. This noun, which means 'apology' or 'excuse', is often used instead of **Entschuldigen Sie bitte** (Excuse me, please).

Ich müßte in die USA anrufen I must really make a phone call to the USA. He could just as well have said **Ich muß in die USA anrufen,** but this phrase sounds less urgent and does not convey the need for help.

Lassen Sie uns ... gehen Let's go ... The German sentence is much more formal than its English equivalent. **Geh(e)n wir** corresponds much more to the English translation of the original German phrase.

hier oben up here (lit. here up). Similarly: **hier unten** (down here), **da oben** (up there), **da unten** (down there).

steht die Telefonnummer there is the telephone number. **Stehen** means 'to stand' but forms of this verb are often used to mean 'there is/are' or 'there was/were'.

der Ton Lit. 'the sound'. Here it's an abbreviation of **der Wählton,** 'the dialling tone'.

Einmark-, Zweimark- oder Fünfmarkstück one-mark coin, two-mark or five-mark coin. The one-mark coin is often also referred to as **das Markstück.**

Das Geld habe ich eingeworfen The money, I have put in the slot. This unusual word order puts emphasis on **das Geld. Eingeworfen** is a form of **einwerfen** and means 'inserted'.

Dann weiß ich Bescheid Then I know (what to do). **Bescheid wissen** is a very common expression to convey the idea of having knowledge of something.

Practise what you have learned

8 Complete these sentences using words and phrases from the dialogue. (Answers on p. 134.)

(a) ______________, **ich müßte in die USA anrufen.**

(b) **Dann wollen wir direkt zur** ______________ **gehen.**

(c) **Hier oben steht die** ______________ **für die USA.**

(d) **Nehmen Sie bitte den** ______________

(e) **Wenn Sie den** __________ **hören, können Sie das Geld** __________

(f) **So, jetzt weiß ich** ______________

9 Now it's your turn to answer some questions on the phone. Answer politely, following the prompts.

10 Listen to a dialogue where Mr Humble, a British customer, is having difficulties with the language. Circle the correct ending for each statement. (Answers on p. 134.)
Die Englischkenntnisse means 'knowledge of English'; **(he)rausholen** is 'to get out / fetch from'; and **jemand** means 'someone'.

(a) **Herr Humble ist**
- (i) **von der Firma Bancosoft Ltd.**
- (ii) **von der Biggs Construction Ltd.**
- (iii) **von der Bovis Company Ltd.**

(b) **Er möchte**
- (i) **mit Herrn Klause telefonieren.**
- (ii) **Herrn Klause zurückrufen.**
- (iii) **Herrn Klause fragen.**

(c) **Herr Klause ist leider**
- (i) **in der Stadt.**
- (ii) **im Hotel.**
- (iii) **in einer Sitzung.**

(d) **Herr Humble kann**
- (i) **gut Deutsch.**
- (ii) **etwas Deutsch.**
- (iii) **kein Deutsch.**

(e) **Herr Humble möchte**
- (i) **seine Adresse hinterlassen.**
- (ii) **seine Durchwahl hinterlassen.**
- (iii) **seine Telefonnummer hinterlassen.**

Dialogues

4 *Using a cardphone*

Visitor Entschuldigen Sie, können Sie mir bitte das Kartentelefon erklären?
Passer-by Ja, ich will es versuchen. Haben Sie schon eine Karte gekauft?
Visitor Ja, hier.
Passer-by Ja, die nehmen Sie und stecken sie hier in den Schlitz. Sehen Sie?
Visitor Ja, und jetzt?
Passer-by Jetzt nehmen Sie den Hörer und Sie sehen, daß Sie für zwölf Mark telefonieren können.
Visitor Ah ja.
Passer-by Sie wählen also die Nummer ...? Wohin wollen Sie telefonieren?
Visitor Nach Großbritannien.
Passer-by Da schau(e)n Sie hier nach.
Visitor Null null vier vier (0044).
Passer-by Richtig. Nun wählen Sie Ihre Nummer und Sie können telefonieren.
Visitor Das ist schon alles?
Passer-by Nach dem Gespräch drücken Sie hier auf den grünen Knopf. Und dann kommt die Karte wieder.
Visitor Muß ich dann auflegen?
Passer-by Ja, Sie legen erst auf. Und dort ist Ihre Karte. Ganz einfach.
Visitor Vielen Dank.
Passer-by Bitte sehr.

das Kartentelefon cardphone
der Schlitz slot
alles all/everything
grün green
der Knopf button
drücken to press/push
das Gespräch conversation
auflegen to put down the receiver
einfach simple

Können Sie mir bitte ... erklären? Can you please explain to me ...? **Mir** is usually translated by 'to me'.

gekauft bought/purchased. This is a form of **kaufen** 'to buy/purchase'.

Karte refers to the plastic phonecard here.

Die nehmen Sie und stecken sie hier in den Schlitz You take it and put it here into the slot. **Die** here refers to **die Karte**. Note the difference between **S̲ie** meaning 'you' and **s̲ie** meaning 'it' (the card here).

telefonieren means the same as **anrufen**, 'to telephone'.

Wohin wollen Sie telefonieren? Lit. 'To where want you to ring?' **Wohin?** is a question word that refers to a place or geographical location.

Da schau(e)n Sie hier nach Look up here. **Nachschauen** means 'to have a look at'.

Das ist schon alles? That is all? **Schon** adds emphasis to the remark.

Und dann kommt die Karte wieder And then the card comes back. **Wiederkommen** is 'to come back'.

Ganz einfach Quite simple. **Ganz** used with adjectives means 'quite a lot' or 'very'.

Practise what you have learned

11 Can you remember what the people in the dialogue actually said? Circle the correct word or phrase. (Answers on p. 134.)

(a) **Können Sie mir bitte den Fernseher / das Kartentelefon / die Kreditkarte erklären?**

(b) **Haben Sie schon eine Karte gekauft / gewählt / bestellt?**

(c) **Jetzt nehmen / halten / geben Sie den Hörer.**

(d) **Sie sagen / wählen / versuchen also die Nummer.**

(e) **Nach der Besprechung / der Sitzung / dem Gespräch drücken Sie hier auf den grünen Knopf.**

(f) **Und dann kommt der Hörer / die Karte / das Telefon wieder.**

12 Your turn to speak. Listen to this text from a telephone answering machine (**der Anrufbeantworter**), then work out the message you would leave in response, saying who you are (**Mein Name ist ...**), giving your address (**Meine Anschrift ist ...**) and phone number (**Meine Rufnummer ist ...**) and asking to be called back (**Bitte rufen Sie zurück**). Study the new vocabulary first.

New vocabulary

der Anschluß (telephone) connection
unser our
gegenwärtig at present
das Büro ist nicht besetzt there is nobody at the office
jedoch however
nennen to state/mention
zunächst first
die Anschrift address

13 Study the new vocabulary before you listen to the conversation on the recording. Below is a translation of the conversation. Fill in the missing words in English. (Answers on p. 134.)

New vocabulary

die Maschinenfabrik engineering works
AG (die Aktiengesellschaft) plc (public limited company)
wohl likely/probably
den ganzen Tag all day (long)
dauern to last/take
die Pause break

Telephonist Bochum Engineering Works plc. Hallo.

Hicks Hallo. My name is Hicks from the Basic Company Ltd. May I ____(a)____ Frau Koch?

Telephonist Mm, I'm sorry. Frau Koch is ____(b)____ today. She will probably ... that will probably last the whole ____(c)____ .

Hicks Will there be a ____(d)____ ? Can Frau Koch call me back?

Telephonist Yes, the ... a break is planned from 12.30 to 2 o'clock.

Hicks And her extension number? Frau Koch's ____(e)____ ?

Telephonist The extension number is ... The ____(f)____ for Bochum is 0234 ... 315. And the extension number is 316.

Hicks OK. Thank you.

Telephonist ____(g)____

Key words and phrases

Ich bin von der Firma ...	I am from the ... company
Ich hatte vergeblich versucht ...	I had tried in vain ...
Ich hatte schon einmal angerufen	I had already phoned once before
Herr/Frau ... meldet sich nicht	Mr/Mrs ... is not answering (the phone) / There is no answer
Wann ist sie denn zu sprechen?	When can I speak to her then?
Kann ich sie jetzt wohl sprechen?	Can I perhaps speak to her now?
Ich probiere/versuche es später noch einmal	I'll try again later
Ich gebe meine Nummer an **Ich gebe Ihnen meine (Telefon-) Nummer**	I'll give you my (telephone) number
Geht das wohl?	Is/Will that be possible at all?
Ich verbinde Sie	I'll put you through
Das dauert den ganzen Tag	That takes / will take the whole day
eine Nachricht hinterlassen	to leave a message
Das habe ich notiert	I've made a note of that / noted that down
Ich richte es aus	I'll pass it on
Es ist sehr dringend	It's very urgent
Können Sie mir bitte erklären ...?	Can you please explain to me ...?
Wie war der Name bitte?	What's your name, please?
Können Sie Englisch?	Can you speak English?
Kann hier jemand ...?	Is there anyone here who can ...?
Dann weiß ich Bescheid	Then I know (what to do)
Das ist / Ist das schon alles?	Is that all?
die Englischkenntnisse (pl.)	knowledge of English
wiederholen	to repeat
anrufen/telefonieren	to call/ring/phone
zurückrufen	to call/ring back
die Nummer wählen	to dial the number
den Hörer (ab)nehmen	to pick up the receiver
auflegen	to put down the receiver
die Telefonzelle	telephone box/booth
der (Telefon)Anschluß	telephone connection
die Telefonnummer	telephone number
die Vorwahl(nummer)	area code
die Rufnummer	subscriber's number
die Durchwahl(nummer)	extension (number)
der Wählton	dialling tone
das Kartentelefon	cardphone
der Anrufbeantworter	telephone answering machine
Geld einwerfen	to insert a coin / coins
gekauft	bought/purchased
die Pause	break/interval
die Mittagspause	lunch break
einfach	simple/simply
gegenwärtig	at present
die Anschrift	address
nennen	to state/mention
hier oben	up here
das Markstück	one-mark coin
Entschuldigung	Excuse me, please

Grammar

Modal verbs

There are some common verbs which are usually found together with other verbs, e.g. **können** (can / to be able to), **müssen** (must / to have to), **wollen** (to want / intend to), **sollen** (shall / should / ought to), **dürfen** (may / to be allowed to). These are called modal verbs, and the table below shows their present tense endings.

	können to be able to	**müssen** to have to	**sollen** shall	**wollen** to want to	**dürfen** to be allowed to	**mögen/möchte** to like (to)
ich	**kann**	**muß**	**soll**	**will**	**darf**	**möchte**
du	**kannst**	**mußt**	**sollst**	**willst**	**darfst**	**möchtest**
er/sie/es	**kann**	**muß**	**soll**	**will**	**darf**	**möchte**
wir	**können**	**müssen**	**sollen**	**wollen**	**dürfen**	**möchten**
ihr	**könnt**	**müßt**	**sollt**	**wollt**	**dürft**	**möchtet**
sie	**können**	**müssen**	**sollen**	**wollen**	**dürfen**	**möchten**
Sie	**können**	**müssen**	**sollen**	**wollen**	**dürfen**	**möchten**

Note that after all the forms of these modals the second verb goes to the end of the sentence.

Ich möchte gern Herrn Richter sprechen.
I would like to speak to Herr Richter.

Er will mir etwas sagen.
He wants to tell me something.

14 Fill in the correct forms of the verbs in round brackets. (Answers on p. 134.)

(a) ________ **du eine Tasse Kaffee trinken?** (möchten)

(b) **In zehn Minuten** ________ **er gehen.** (dürfen)

(c) **Zuerst** ________ **Sie das Formular ausfüllen.** (müssen)

(d) **Die Sekretärin** ________ **den Besucher anmelden.** (sollen)

(e) **Wir** ________ **Ihnen das Zimmer leider nicht reservieren.** (können)

(f) **Der Chef** ________ **um 10.00 Uhr eine Besprechung machen.** (wollen)

Reflexive verbs

In English we have reflexive verbs such as *I wash myself, he kicks himself,* etc. In German you have the same reflexive verbs as in English plus a few more where the reflexive meaning is not so clear.

In some of the previous units we've come across reflexive verbs such as **sich freuen** (to be pleased), **sich erkundigen** (to obtain information), **sich melden** (to report), **sich rechts/links halten** (to keep to the left/right). The reflexive pronoun changes with the subject, so you get **ich wasche mich** (I'm washing myself) but **er wäscht sich** (he's washing himself). These reflexive pronouns are the same with all reflexive verbs. Here's one example: **sich melden** (to report).

ich melde mich	**wir melden uns**
du meldest dich	**ihr meldet euch**
er/sie/es meldet sich	**sie melden sich**
Sie melden sich	

15 Circle the correct pronoun. (Answers on p. 134.)

(a) **Morgen melden Sie sich / uns / mich um 8.30 Uhr.**

(b) **Wir treffen mich / uns / sich um 11.00 Uhr.**

(c) **Ich freue uns / euch / mich auf Ihren Besuch.**

(d) **Er erkundigt uns / euch / sich bei der Information.**

(e) **Halten Sie euch / sich / dich rechts.**

Read and understand

16 Here is a notice which you will find in public telephone boxes/booths and which tells you what you have to do to make a phone call. Study it carefully and do the exercise below. But first have a look at the new vocabulary.

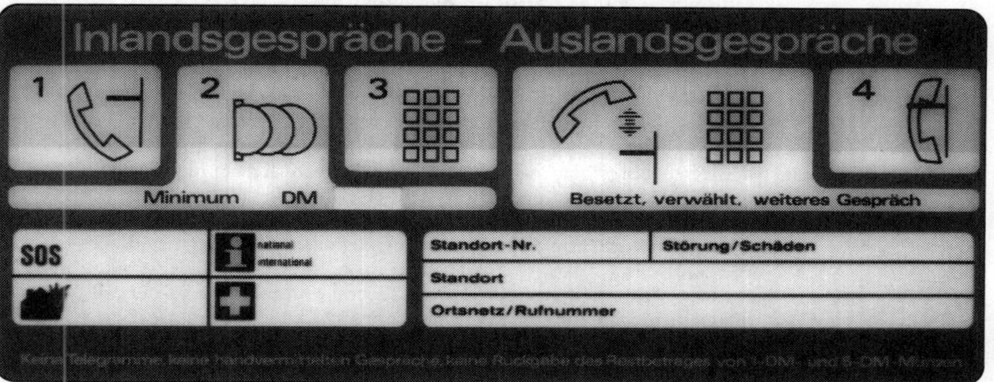

New vocabulary

das Inlandsgespräch domestic call
das Auslandsgespräch foreign call
besetzt engaged/busy
verwählt misdialled
weiteres Gespräch further call
die Standort-Nr. number of location
das Ortsnetz local network
die Störung fault
das Telegramm telegramme
handvermittelt operator-connected
die Rückgabe refund/return
der Restbetrag remainder
die Münze coin

Write down the words which are defined below. (Answers on p. 134.)

(a) You have to lift it to make a phone call. ____________________

(b) At least three have to be inserted into a public phone. ____________

(c) 1 DM and 5 DM coins which are not returned. ______________

(d) Types of calls that can be made from a public phone box/booth. ________

(e) It puts the phone out of order. ________________________

(f) Place where a public phone is situated. ___________________

(g) Call which requires the help of the operator. _______________

(h) Urgent message which cannot be sent from a public phone. __________

Did you know?

The telephone system

The postal and telecommunication services operate as three independent state-owned enterprises: **Postdienst** (postal services), **Postbank** (Post Office giro) and **Telekom** (telecommunications services).

The telephone network in western Germany is fully equipped for self-service trunk dialling; in eastern Germany it is being extended and modernized. Some of the area codes are easy to remember. Big cities such as Berlin, Frankfurt, Hamburg and München have three-digit area codes, compared with four digits for the other cities and market towns in more rural areas and five digits for the vast majority of towns and villages. In contrast, subscribers' numbers are six- to seven-digit in big towns and five-, four- and sometimes even three-digit elsewhere.

There is a good network of public phones. Like all postal buildings and installations and equipment the booths can easily be recognized because they are yellow. Most of them take coins of at least three denominations, starting with ten pfennigs. Charges depend on the length of the call, the distance and the time of day. There are reduced charges for calls made between 6 p.m. and 8 a.m. on workdays and generally on Saturdays, Sundays and public holidays.

Some important services and their numbers

die Telefonauskunft (telephone enquiries)	national	01188
	international	00118
das Fernamt (operator)	national	010
	international	0010
der Notruf/die Polizei (emergency call/police)		110
die Feuerwehr (fire and ambulance service)		112

Emergency calls are free of charge but if they are made from a public phone, coins must be inserted before the call can be made. The money is returned after the receiver has been replaced.

There are plenty of other 24-hour information services, including the time signal (**die Zeitansage**), information on television, cinema and theatre programmes, sports news, stock exchange news, weather forecast, road conditions, political news, etc. The numbers can be obtained from a telephone directory (**das Telefonbuch**).

The telephone services available in Austria and Switzerland are similar to those described above.

Benutzungs-hinweise

1. **Besetzt?**
   Nach kurzem Einhängen des Hörers
   - statt erneuter Wahl nur -Taste drücken
   oder
   - andere Rufnummer wählen.
2. **Verwählt?**
   Nach kurzem Einhängen des Hörers richtige Rufnummer wählen.

Instructions for use

1. **Line busy?**
   After briefly replacing the receiver
   - press button instead of re-dialling
   or
   - dial a different call number.
2. **Wrong number?**
   After briefly replacing the receiver dial the correct number.

Your turn to speak

17 You are phoning one of your customers. But there is nobody in the office and you are asked to leave a message on the telephone answering machine. Say who you are and the name of your firm. Give the name of the person you wanted to speak to and ask to be called back. Say that it's very urgent. Give your telephone number, including the area code and the extension. When you've had a go, listen to the model conversation on the recording. You may find the following phrases helpful:

Mein Name ist ... / Hier ist ... von der Firma ...
Ich muß dringend Herrn/Frau ... sprechen
Ich möchte gern Herrn/Frau ... sprechen
Es ist dringend
Bitte rufen Sie sofort zurück
Ich gebe Ihnen meine Telefonnummer
die Vorwahl, die Rufnummer, die Durchwahl

18 Here are four pictograms which tell you how to use a cardphone. Tell your friend in four or five sentences what you have to do. Use the **du** form. Here are some useful words and phrases:

den Hörer abnehmen
die Karte in den Schlitz stecken
die Nummer wählen
den Hörer auflegen
wiederkommen/zurückkommen

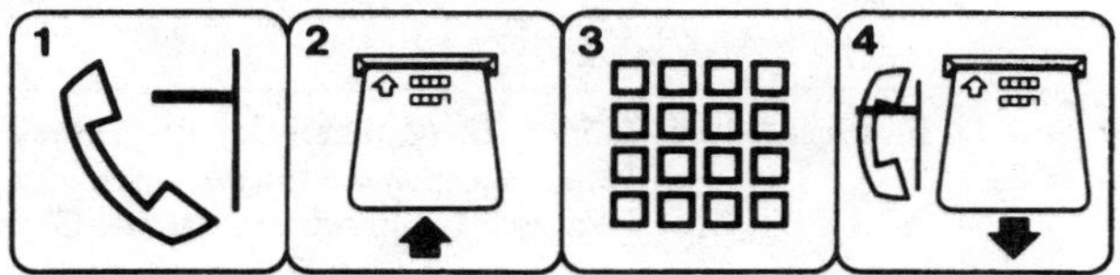

Answers

Practise what you have learned

Exercise **3** (a) Computertechnik GmbH (b) Frau (c) meldet (d) Tisch (e) Mittagspause (f) erreichen (g) probieren (h) hinterlassen

Exercise **4** (a) Firma (b) vergeblich (c) sprechen (d) meldet (e) dringend (f) leider (g) zurückrufen

Exercise **7** (a) iii (b) iii (c) ii (d) i and iii (e) iii

Exercise **8** (a) Entschuldigung (b) Telefonzelle (c) Telefonnummer (d) Hörer (e) Wählton, einwerfen (f) Bescheid

Exercise **10** (a) ii (b) i (c) iii (d) ii (e) iii

Exercise **11** (a) das Kartentelefon (b) gekauft (c) nehmen (d) wählen (e) dem Gespräch (f) die Karte

Exercise **13** (a) speak to (b) in a meeting (c) day (d) break (e) extension number (f) code (g) You're welcome

Grammar

Exercise **14** (a) möchtest (b) darf (c) müssen (d) soll (e) können (f) will

Exercise **15** (a) sich (b) uns (c) mich (d) sich (e) sich

Read and understand

Exercise **16** (a) Hörer (b) Münzen (c) Restbetrag (d) Inlandsgespräche und Auslandsgespräche (e) Störung (f) Standort (g) handvermitteltes Gespräch (h) Telegramm

8 WELCOMING A VISITOR

You will learn

- to introduce yourself to your business partner
- to state the purpose of your visit
- to talk about your journey and accommodation
- to accept hospitality
- to chair a meeting and introduce colleagues
- to understand about the functions of the various deapartments in a manufacturing company

and you will be given information about the business organization in German-speaking countries.

Study guide

- **Dialogue 1 + Practise what you have learned**
- **Dialogue 2 + Practise what you have learned**
- **Dialogue 3 + Practise what you have learned**
- **Dialogue 4 + Practise what you have learned**
- Make sure you know the **Key words and phrases**
- Study the **Grammar** section
- Do the exercise in **Read and understand**
- Read **Did you know?**
- Do the exercises in **Your turn to speak**

Dialogues

1 *Frau Köpl meets a visitor from America*

Frau Köpl Guten Morgen.
Mr Williams Guten Morgen. Mein Name ist Williams von der Firma Progress Inc. aus Chicago, Illinois.
Frau Köpl Ja, guten Morgen Herr Williams. Wir hatten heute einen Termin. Bitte kommen Sie doch rein.
Mr Williams Ja, herzlichen Dank.
Frau Köpl Bitte nehmen Sie Platz.
Mr Williams Ja, danke schön.
Frau Köpl Sie hatten ja sicher eine weite Reise?
Mr Williams Ja, das ist sicherlich richtig, ich bin ja gestern schon gestartet. Aber wir hatten einen fabelhaften Flug und keine Probleme.
Frau Köpl Wunderbar. Wo sind Sie hier untergebracht?
Mr Williams Ja, ich bin im Parkhotel. Das ist ein gutes Hotel, glaub(e) ich.
Frau Köpl Ja, das ist auch die beste Möglichkeit in Witten. Aus Ihrer Anmeldung konnte ich nicht ersehen, welche Funktion Sie in Ihrer Firma haben.
Mr Williams Ja, ich bin der Product Manager für Edelstahlarmaturen.
Frau Köpl Ah ja. Das klingt sehr interessant.

sicherlich certainly
fabelhaft splendid/excellent
wunderbar wonderful/splendid
beste best
die Anmeldung letter announcing the arrival
ersehen to see/gather
die Funktion function/position
die Edelstahlarmatur special steel fitting
klingen to sound

Wir hatten heute einen Termin We had an appointment today. **Hatten** is a past tense form of **haben** (to have).

Bitte kommen Sie doch rein Please do come in. A very common phrase. The adverb **doch** carries the same emphasis as the English *do*. **Rein** is a short form of **herein,** 'in(to the room)'.

Bitte nehmen Sie Platz Please, do have a seat. You could also say: **Nehmen Sie** (**doch**) **Platz bitte** or **Nehmen Sie** (**doch**) **bitte Platz**. The adverb **doch** makes this slightly more polite.

Sie hatten ja sicher eine weite Reise? You had certainly a long journey? **Reise** means 'journey' here but it may also refer to travel generally. **Ja,** like **doch** adds emphasis.

ich bin ... gestartet I set off. **Gestartet** is a form of **starten** 'to start/begin'.

Wo sind Sie hier untergebracht? Where are you staying here? **Untergebracht** is a form of **unterbringen** 'to house/accommodate'.

Aus Ihrer Anmeldung konnte ich nicht ersehen ... From your letter I could not make out ... (lit. from your announcement could I not see ...). **Anmeldung** here implies the notification of an impending visit.

Practise what you have learned

1 Can you work out what Mr Williams and Frau Köpl said? Complete these sentences. (Answers on p. 152.)

Frau Köpl:
(a) **Wir hatten heute** ____________________
(b) **Bitte** ____________________ **Platz.**
(c) **Sie hatten ja sicher** ____________________ **Reise.**
(d) **Wo sind Sie hier** __________ **?**
(e) **Das klingt** ____________________

Mr Williams:
(f) ____________________ **ist Williams.**
(g) **Das ist** __________ **richtig.**
(h) **Ich bin ja** ____________________ **gestartet.**
(i) **Wir hatten einen fabelhaften** ____________
(j) **Das ist ein** ____________________ **, glaube ich.**

2 Here are fragments of things that were said in the dialogue. Try and piece them together again so that they form meaningful sentences. Then listen to the dialogue again to check your answers.

(a) **einen hatten heute Termin wir**
(b) **bitte Sie doch kommen rein**
(c) **Reise eine hatten ja sicher Sie weite**
(d) **bin gestartet gestern schon ich ja**
(e) **aber einen fabelhaften Flug hatten keine Probleme und wir**
(f) **hier sind Sie untergebracht wo**
(g) **auch beste das die in ist Möglichkeit Witten**

3 In the short dialogue on the recording you are asked to take the role of Mr Johnson of Compusoft Inc. Use the prompts for your part.

4 Listen to the dialogue on the recording and then decide which of the statements below are correct.
(Answers on p. 152.)

(a) (i) **Herr Berns besucht Frau Braun.**
(ii) **Herr Braun besucht Herrn Berns.**
(iii) **Frau Berns besucht Herrn Braun.**

(b) **Frau Braun kennt Herrn Berns** (i) **schon etwas.**
(ii) **noch nicht.**
(iii) **sehr gut.**

(c) **Die Reise war** (i) **ganz gut.**
(ii) **ganz angenehm.**
(iii) **ganz dringend.**

(d) **Herr Berns ist** (i) **im Hotel Duisburger Hof untergebracht.**
(ii) **im Hotel Dortmunder Hof untergebracht.**
(iii) **im Hotel Bochumer Hof untergebracht.**

(e) (i) **Die Sekretärin bringt gleich einen Kaffee.**
(ii) **Die Bedienung bringt gleich einen Kaffee.**
(iii) **Die Assistentin bringt gleich einen Kaffee.**

(f) **Frau Braun möchte** (i) **neue Computerprogramme sehen.**
(ii) **neue Computerprogramme kaufen.**
(iii) **neue Computerprogramme zeigen.**

Dialogues

2 *Making the first business contact*

Frau Köpl Guten Morgen.
Mr Masters Guten Morgen, mein Name ist Masters von der Firma Homecraft Ltd. aus Wolverhampton. Ich bin hierher gekommen, um mit Ihnen über unsere Produkte zu sprechen.
Frau Köpl Mein Name ist Köpl. Herr Masters, wir stellen ja ähnliche Sachen her. Das war auch der Grund für die Terminvereinbarung. Bitte kommen Sie doch rein und nehmen Sie Platz.
Mr Masters Herzlichen Dank.
Frau Köpl Darf ich Ihnen etwas zu trinken anbieten?
Mr Masters Ja, gerne.
Frau Köpl Was hätten Sie denn gern?
Mr Masters Einen Kaffee, vielleicht?
Frau Köpl Gerne. Wie nehmen Sie ihn?
Mr Masters Mit Milch und Zucker, wenn es möglich ist, bitte.
Frau Köpl Ich bestelle. – Kann ich bitte zwei Kaffee haben: einen schwarz und einen mit Milch und Zucker. Danke. – Kaffee kommt sofort.
Mr Masters Danke schön.
Frau Köpl Können wir in der Zwischenzeit schon mit den geschäftlichen Dingen anfangen?
Mr Masters Ja, sicher doch.
Frau Köpl Gut, danke.

- ➧ **das Produkt** product/article
- ➧ **herstellen** to manufacture/produce/make
- ➧ **ähnlich** similar
- **die Sache** thing/object
- **länger** longer
- ➧ **in der Zwischenzeit** in the meantime
- ➧ **geschäftliche Dinge** business matters

ich bin hierher gekommen I've come here. **Gekommen** is a form of **kommen** 'to come'. As in many other languages, the perfect tense of some verbs is formed using the verb 'to be' rather than 'to have'. Hence **ich <u>bin</u> gekommen**. If you want to know more, see p. 199.

➧ **um mit Ihnen über unsere Produkte zu sprechen** in order to talk to you about our products. **Um ... zu** means 'in order to', so **um in die Stadt zu gehen** means 'in order to go into town', and **um den Direktor zu sehen** means 'in order to see the Director'.

Das war auch der Grund für die Terminvereinbarung That was also the reason for fixing this appointment.

➧ **Darf ich Ihnen etwas zu trinken anbieten?** May I offer you something to drink? You might answer **Ja gerne**, 'yes willingly' (as here), or **Ja, danke** (**Das ist sehr nett**). To refuse, you might say **Nein, danke**. (**Das ist wirklich sehr nett. Aber ich möchte nichts.**)

➧ **Wie nehmen Sie ihn?** How do you like it (your coffee)? Lit. 'How take you it?'

Ich bestelle I'm ordering, i.e. 'I'm going to order it straight away'.

➧ **Kann ich bitte zwei Kaffee haben?** Can I please have two coffees?

einen schwarz und einen mit Milch und Zucker one black and one with milk and sugar

Kaffee kommt sofort coffee comes immediately

Können wir ... schon ... anfangen? Can we already begin? The meaning is 'Is it alright if we now begin ...?'

Practise what you have learned

5 Which versions of the sentences below were used in the dialogue? Circle the appropriate words and phrases. (Answers on p. 152.)

(a) **Ich bin hierher gekommen/gegangen/gelaufen, um über unsere Dinge/Sachen/Produkte zu sprechen.**

(b) **Wir stellen ja gleiche/ähnliche/andere Sachen her.**

(c) **Darf ich Ihnen etwas zu trinken geben/holen/anbieten?**

(d) **Kann ich bitte zwei Kaffee haben/bestellen/buchen?**

(e) **Können wir schon ... mit den richtigen/geschäftlichen/dringenden Dingen anfangen?**

6 Choose the appropriate words from the box below to complete these polite sentences. (Answers on p. 152.)

(a) ______________ **kommen Sie doch rein.**

(b) ______________ **ich Ihnen etwas zu trinken anbieten?**

(c) **Was möchten Sie denn** ______________ **?**

(d) **Ich hätte gern eine Tasse Kaffee,** ______________

gern
bitte
wenn es möglich ist
darf

7 In this recorded dialogue you are asked to take the role of the visitor. Use the prompts for your responses. 'That's right' is **Das stimmt**.

8 Listen to Frau Köpl welcoming Mr Masters. Then look at the sentences and see if you can remember who said what. (Answers on p. 152.)

New vocabulary

das Zweigwerk branch plant
die Produktpalette product range
der Tee tea
etwas Kaltes something cold
vorläufig for the time being
Sie haben hierher gefunden? You found your way here?
zurück back

	Masters	*Köpl*
(a) **Ja, das ist mein Name.**		
(b) **Ich bin Verkaufsleiter des Zweigwerks in Wolverhampton.**		
(c) **... und wollte heute mit Ihnen sprechen über unsere Produktpalette.**		
(d) **Kommen Sie doch bitte rein und nehmen Sie Platz.**		
(e) **Kann ich Ihnen etwas zu trinken anbieten?**		
(f) **Ich glaube, ich trinke mal einen Kaffee, bitte.**		
(g) **Nehmen Sie mit Milch und Zucker?**		
(h) **Wie war die Reise?**		
(i) **Die Reise war sehr leicht.**		
(j) **Und wo sind Sie untergebracht?**		
(k) **Ich wohne im Parkhotel.**		

Dialogues

3 *Introducing various employees*

Frau Köpl Herr Masters, in unserem Hause sind für die verschiedenen Produktgruppen verschiedene Angestellte zuständig. Für den Bereich Sicherheitsarmaturen bin ich es selbst. Für den Bereich LPG und Edelstahl ist es Herr Karlow, für den Bereich Gasmischer und Analysatoren ist es unser Herr Waigl. Ich habe beide Herren gebeten, an unserem Gespräch heute teilzunehmen, und sie werden sich Ihnen jetzt selbst kurz vorstellen.

Mr Masters Ja, danke.

Herr Karlow Ja, guten Morgen, Herr Masters. Mein Name ist Karlow. Ich bin verantwortlich für die Produktlinie Edelstahlarmaturen und LPG-Produkte.

Mr Masters Mhm. Danke.

Herr Waigl Ja, Herr Masters. Mein Name ist Waigl, und ich bin im Hause Witt verantwortlich für den gesamten Apparatebau, d.h. Gasmischanlagen und Analysestationen.

Mr Masters Vielen Dank. Sie wissen sicherlich, mein Name ist Masters. Ich komme von der Firma Homecraft Ltd aus Wolverhampton und bin dort Verkaufsleiter für den ganzen Bereich von Armaturen.

Herr Karlow Ja, Frau Köpl hat uns vorinformiert.

Mr Masters Dann wissen Sie ja Bescheid.

- ➧ **die Produktgruppe** product group
- ➧ **zuständig** responsible/in charge
- ➧ **der Bereich** area/field/section
- **die Sicherheitsarmatur** safety valve
- **LPG** liquefied petroleum gas
- **der Edelstahl** special steel
- **der Gasmischer / die Gasmischanlage** gas mixing unit
- ➧ **das heißt (d.h.)** that is (i.e.)
- **der Analysator / die Analysestation** analyzer
- ➧ **teilnehmen** to take part
- ➧ **die Produktlinie** product line
- **die Armatur** instrument fixture

➧ **in unserem Hause** in our house. This is a very common phrase to refer to one's company.

➧ **bin ich es selbst** it is me who is responsible (lit. I am it myself). **Selbst** is used for emphasis here.

ist es unser Herr Waigl it is our Herr Waigl. This slightly patronizing expression is frequently used among business people when they talk of colleagues of slightly inferior rank.

➧ **Ich habe beide Herren gebeten, ...** I have asked both gentlemen ... **Gebeten** is a form of **bitten** 'to ask/request'.

➧ **Sie werden sich Ihnen jetzt selbst kurz vorstellen** They will now briefly introduce themselves to you (lit. They will themselves to you now themselves briefly introduce). Again **selbst** is used for emphasis and cannot be translated literally. **Sie werden sich vorstellen** is an example of the future tense, which we will look at in Unit 12.

➧ **Ich bin verantwortlich für ...** I'm responsible for / in charge of ...

für den gesamten Apparatebau for the whole field of instruments engineering. **Gesamt** means 'total/altogether'.

➧ **Sie wissen sicherlich ...** You will surely know ... Note that German uses the present tense here.

hat uns vorinformiert has informed us in advance. **Vorinformiert** is a form of **vorinformieren** 'to inform in advance'.

Practise what you have learned

9 Can you remember who was responsible for what? Fill in the missing names. (Answers on p. 152.)

(a) **Für den Bereich Sicherheitsarmaturen ist ______________ zuständig.**

(b) **______________ ist für den Bereich Edelstahl und LPG verantwortlich.**

(c) **Für den Bereich Gasmischer und Analysatoren ist ________ zuständig.**

(d) **___________ ist Verkaufsleiter für den ganzen Bereich von Armaturen.**

10 In each of the following sentences there is a word missing. The missing words are given in round brackets. All you have to do is put them in their correct position in the sentences. (Answers on p. 152.)

(a) **In Hause sind verschiedene Angestellte für verschiedene Produkte zuständig.** (unserem)
(b) **Ich habe Herren gebeten, an unserem Gespräch teilzunehmen.** (beide)
(c) **Sie stellen sich kurz selbst vor.** (Ihnen)
(d) **Name ist Waigl.** (mein)
(e) **Frau Köpl hat vorinformiert.** (uns)

11 Your turn to speak. You are head of the export department and it is up to you to introduce the members of the department to your visitor and ask him to introduce himself. The words and phrases you will need are given below, but you need to rearrange them. The first word(s) in each sentence is/are underlined. Say your solution aloud and compare it with the version on the recording.

Here are the names of a few European countries – you will need most of them for this exercise:

Belgien Belgium
Dänemark Denmark
Frankreich France
Großbritannien Great Britain
Holland Holland
Irland Ireland
Italien Italy
Luxemburg Luxembourg
Norwegen Norway
Österreich Austria
Portugal Portugal
Schweden Sweden
die Schweiz Switzerland
Spanien Spain

(a) **<u>So, Herr Parker,</u> zuerst vorstellen möchte ich Ihnen aus meiner Abteilung einige Mitarbeiter**
(b) **ist Frau Bäumler <u>Dies</u> für die Kunden <u>Sie ist</u> in Holland, Belgien, Luxemburg und Frankreich zuständig**
(c) **<u>Für Großbritannien und Irland</u> ist verantwortlich Herr Peters**
(d) **Herr Ostkamp <u>Und dies</u> ist in Spanien und Portugal arbeitet <u>Herr Ostkamp</u>**
(e) **ist Frau Bendick <u>Und</u> hier <u>Sie besucht</u> in der Schweiz, in Österreich und Italien Kunden**
(f) **jetzt bitte <u>Können Sie sich</u> selbst vorstellen, Herr Parker**

Continued on next page.

12 Now listen to the recording where four people introduce themselves. Find out who these people are and what they do, fill in their names in the sentences below. Some of the names occur more than once. (Answers on p. 152.)

New vocabulary
die Dame lady
begrüßen to welcome
vorschlagen to suggest/propose
die Pumpenproduktion production of pumps
der Versand dispatch (department)
bereits already
(**sich**) **kennenlernen** to get to know (each other)
telefonisch on the phone / by phone
den weiten Weg machen to travel so far
ins Gespräch gehen to start negotiations

Brandt	**Lehmann**	**Schneider**	**Stevens**

(a) **Herr ______________ freut sich, alle hier begrüßen zu dürfen.**

(b) **Frau ______________ ist verantwortlich für die Pumpenproduktion.**

(c) **Herr ______________ hat Herrn Stevens telefonisch kennengelernt.**

(d) **Herr ______________ möchte sich über Pumpen informieren.**

(e) **Frau ______________ ist Leiterin des Versands.**

(f) **Herr ______________ ist von der Firma Norton in Los Angeles.**

(g) **Herr ______________ schlägt vor, daß sie direkt ins Gespräch gehen.**

Dialogues

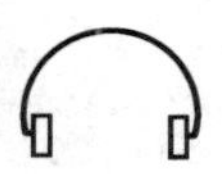

4 *Having a look round a company*

Herr Lehmann Ja, also hier unten befindet sich die Verwaltung. Auf der linken Seite ist beispielsweise die Buchhaltung, der Einkauf und ähnliche Abteilungen. Auf der rechten Seite befindet sich der Verkauf und die Werbeabteilung.

Mr Stevens Mit wieviel Personen?

Herr Lehmann In der Werbeabteilung sind wir drei und im Verkaufsinnendienst sind wir sieben.

Mr Stevens Ah ja.

Herr Lehmann Gut, dann gehen wir jetzt hier in die Arbeitsvorbereitung und von dort aus in den Betrieb. Ja, wir haben also zunächst einmal hier die mechanische Fertigung. Hier werden sämtliche Drehteile hergestellt.

Mr Stevens Wird das alles automatisch gemacht?

Herr Lehmann Die meisten Dinge werden von automatischen Maschinen hergestellt. Wir haben aber auch Einzelanfertigungen.

Mr Stevens Mhm.

Herr Lehmann Wir sind insgesamt 340 Mitarbeiter. Davon sind es 70 in der Verwaltung. Und der Rest sind Arbeitnehmer, die die Produkte fertigen.

Mr Stevens Und wie hoch ist der Jahresumsatz bei Ihnen?

Herr Lehmann Wir haben einen Gesamtumsatz von 58 Millionen D-Mark.

Mr Stevens Das ist interessant.

- ➧ **die Besichtigung** (guided) tour/visit
- ➧ **der Betrieb** premises/business unit/plant/factory
- ➧ **die Verwaltung** administration
- ➧ **der Verkauf** sales (office)
- **die Arbeitsvorbereitung** production scheduling
- **mechanisch** mechanical
- ➧ **die Fertigung** production/ manufacturing
- **die meisten** most of
- **davon** of these/which
- ➧ **der Gesamtumsatz** total turnover
- (**die**) **Million** million

➧ **Hier unten befindet sich ...** Down here there is ... **Sich befinden** (lit. to find itself) is a very useful alternative to **es gibt** (there is/are) when the meaning is 'is situated'. But people generally prefer the simpler form **Hier unten ist ...**

beispielsweise die Buchhaltung, der Einkauf und ähnliche Abteilungen for example, the book-keeping, the purchasing and similar departments

In der Werbeabteilung sind wir drei und im Verkaufsinnendienst sind wir sieben In the advertising department we are three and in the sales office we are seven. **Personen** (people) is understood.

Hier werden sämtliche Drehteile hergestellt All the lathe work is done here (lit. Here become all turned pieces manufactured). **Hergestellt** comes from **herstellen** 'to produce/ manufacture/make'.

Wird das alles automatisch gemacht? Is (lit. becomes) all that made automatically?

werden von automatischen Maschinen hergestellt are (lit. become) manufactured by automatic machines

wir haben auch Einzelanfertigungen Lit. 'We have also single-made units', i.e. 'We also manufacture single units / customized items'.

➧ **Wir sind insgesamt 340 Mitarbeiter** We are altogether 340 employees. **Mitarbeiter** literally means 'fellow worker' or 'co-worker'. It is used by management to refer to the workforce – with the implication of equality.

➧ **und der Rest sind Arbeitnehmer** Lit. 'and the remainder are employees'. The suggestion here is that the remainder are 'blue-collar workers'.

➧ **Und wie hoch ist der Jahresumsatz bei Ihnen?** And what's your annual turnover? (lit. And how high is the annual turnover with you?)

Now turn over for the exercises based on dialogue 4.

Practise what you have learned

13 Can you remember the facts and figures you heard in the dialogue? Match the questions on the left with the answers on the right. (Answers on p. 152.)

(a)	**Wieviele Mitarbeiter arbeiten in der Werbeabteilung?**	(i)	**7**
(b)	**Und wieviele sind im Verkaufsinnendienst?**	(ii)	**70**
(c)	**Wieviele Mitarbeiter sind in der Verwaltung?**	(iii)	**58 Millionen**
(d)	**Wieviele Mitarbeiter hat die Firma insgesamt?**	(iv)	**3**
(e)	**Wie hoch ist der Gesamtumsatz der Firma?**	(v)	**340**

14 Here is a list of departments. Mark those mentioned in the dialogue. (Answers on p. 152.)

(a) **Abteilung Arbeitsvorbereitung**
(b) **Buchhaltungsabteilung**
(c) **Einkaufsabteilung**
(d) **Exportabteilung**
(e) **Fertigungsabteilung**
(f) **Finanzabteilung**
(g) **Marketingabteilung**
(h) **Technische Abteilung**
(i) **Verkaufsabteilung**
(j) **Versandabteilung**
(k) **Vertriebsabteilung**
(l) **Werbeabteilung**

15 Your turn to speak. Take the role of the visitor. Use the prompts.

16 Listen to the dialogue and decide whether the statements below are **richtig oder falsch** (true or false). (Answers on p. 152.) The new vocabulary that you will need for the exercise is given here.

New vocabulary

allgemein general(ly)
die Produktion production/ manufacturing
als erstes first (of all)
anschließend and then / which is followed by
die Spinnerei spinning mill
die Weberei weaving mill
die Qualitätskontrolle quality control
beschäftigen to employ
viel(e) much/many
das ist (sehr) viel that's quite a lot
exportieren to export
die Ware(n) goods
eine ganze Reihe quite a few
das Land country
nicht nur ... sondern auch not only ... but also
Europa Europe
der Kontinent continent
das Zweigwerk branch plant / factory

		richtig	falsch
(a)	**Auf der einen Seite befindet sich die allgemeine Verwaltung mit der Werbeabteilung.**		
(b)	**Auf der anderen Seite ist die Buchhaltung mit der Versandabteilung.**		
(c)	**Erst kommt die Spinnerei, dann die Weberei.**		
(d)	**Danach kommen die Qualitätskontrolle und der Versand.**		
(e)	**In dem Betrieb arbeiten 480 Personen.**		
(f)	**Die Firma exportiert in eine ganze Reihe von Ländern.**		
(g)	**Die Firma exportiert nicht in andere Kontinente.**		
(h)	**Die Firma hat viele Zweigwerke.**		

Key words and phrases

Wir hatten heute einen Termin	We had an appointment today
Ich freue mich, Sie hier begrüßen zu dürfen	I am pleased to be able to welcome you here
Bitte kommen Sie doch rein	Please do come in
Bitte nehmen Sie (doch) Platz	Please (do) have a seat
Wie war die Reise?	How was the journey? / What was the journey like?
Wo sind Sie untergebracht?	Where are you staying?
Darf ich Ihnen etwas zu trinken anbieten?	May I offer you something to drink?
Was hätten Sie denn gern?	What would you like?
Wie nehmen Sie den Kaffee?	How do you like your coffee?
Mit Milch und Zucker?	With milk and sugar?
Wie hoch ist der Jahresumsatz bei Ihnen?	What's your annual turnover?
Das klingt/ist sehr interessant	That sounds/is very interesting
Das interessiert mich sehr	That interests me a lot
Darf ich vorschlagen ...?	May I suggest ...?
Ich möchte Ihnen (gern) ... zeigen	I would like to show you ...
Hier befindet sich ...	Here is ...
Ich bin damit einverstanden	I agree (to that)
an dem Gespräch teilnehmen	to take part in the discussion
sich (selbst) vorstellen	to introduce oneself
sich kennenlernen	to get to know one another
zuständig/verantwortlich sein für	to be responsible for / in charge of
über geschäftliche Dinge sprechen	to talk about / discuss business matters
in der Zwischenzeit	in the meantime / meanwhile
vorläufig	for the time being
sicherlich	certainly
beispielsweise	for example
das heißt (d.h.)	that means (i.e.)
allgemein	general(ly)
ähnlich	similar(ly)
weit	far/long
die Funktion	function
die Anmeldung	letter announcing the arrival
der Geschäftskontakt	business contact
die Terminvereinbarung	(fixing of an) appointment
zur Erläuterung	to explain / by way of explanation
die Vorstellung	introduction
der Bereich	area/field/section
in unserem Hause	in our company
der Mitarbeiter / der Arbeitnehmer	employee
der Gesamtumsatz	total turnover/sales
der Jahresumsatz	annual turnover/sales
das Werk	plant/factory
der Betrieb	business/enterprise/premises/plant/factory
das Zweigwerk / der Zweigbetrieb	branch plant/factory
die Produktion / die Fertigung	production/manufacturing
das Produkt	product/item
die Einzelanfertigung	single-unit production / customized manufacturing / single unit

die Produktpalette	(product) range
die Produktgruppe / die Produktlinie	line / product group
herstellen/fertigen	to make/produce/manufacture
exportieren	to export
die Abteilung	department
die Verwaltung	administration
die Buchhaltung	book-keeping (department)
der Einkauf / die Einkaufsabteilung	purchasing/buying (department)
der Verkauf / die Verkaufsabteilung	sales/selling (department)
der Versand / die Versandabteilung	dispatch (department)
die Werbeabteilung	advertising department
die Arbeitsvorbereitung	production scheduling
die Qualitätskontrolle	quality control

Grammar

Pronouns

Personal pronouns are used to replace nouns. They refer to people and things and have cases like proper nouns, as shown in the table in the grammar summary on p. 224.

Here are some examples to show you how personal pronouns are used.

Der Angestellte besucht den Kunden. The employee visits the client.
Er besucht ihn. He visits him.

Der Besucher gibt der Sekretärin die Karte.
The visitor gives (to) the secretary the card.
Er gibt sie ihr. He gives it to her.

17 Here are some phrases to make visitors feel welcome and to show hospitality. The pronouns are missing. Complete the sentences by choosing the correct pronoun from the box below. (Answers on p. 152.)

(a) **Kann ich ___________ etwas zu trinken anbieten?**

(b) **Es ist nett, Sie heute bei ___________ zu sehen.**

(c) **Wir möchten mit ___________ über unsere Produkte sprechen.**

(d) **Kommen ___________ doch bitte rein.**

(e) **Hier ist der Kaffee. Trinken Sie ________ mit Milch und Zucker?**

(f) **Ich freue mich, ___________ hier begrüßen zu dürfen.**

uns	**ihn**	**Sie**	**Ihnen**	**Sie**	**Ihnen**

Possessives

Although possessives are not as frequently used in German as in English, it is useful to be aware of the basic forms.

mein my
dein your
sein his
ihr her
sein its
unser our
euer your
ihr their
Ihr your (polite form)

The endings vary according to the gender (m./f./n.) and the number (sing./pl.). At this stage it is much too complicated to list all the forms here. Just be aware that there are different endings.

Here are some examples:

Mein Name ist Johnston. My name is Johnston.

Ich zeige Ihnen unsere Firma. I('ll) show you round our firm.

Ich will mit Ihnen über unsere Produkte sprechen.
I want to discuss our products with you.

Ich möchte mich über Ihre Produkte informieren.
I would like to inform myself about your products.

Read and understand

18 Here is an extract from a leaflet of the Aral AG in Bochum. Study it carefully, using the vocabulary list to help you get the gist, and then complete the sentences below. (Answers on p. 152.)

Aral Aktiengesellschaft: Ein Unternehmen mit Geschichte

Die Aral Aktiengesellschaft ist aus der Westdeutschen Benzol-Verkaufsvereinigung entstanden, die 1898 gegründet wurde. Aus der Mischung von **Ar**omaten (Benzole) und **Al**iphaten (Benzine) hat Aral seinen Namen bekommen und 1924 den ersten Superkraftstoff der Welt entwickelt. Mit neun Jahrzehnten Erfahrung ist Aral heute die führende Kraftstoffvertriebsgesellschaft. So kommt jeder vierte in der Bundesrepublik verkaufte Liter Benzin von Aral.

EINIGE ZAHLEN DER ARAL AKTIENGESELLSCHAFT

Absatz in Mio. t	**1989**	**1990**
Gesamtabsatz	10,11	10,46
davon Kraftstoffe	6,00	6,24
Dieselkraftstoffe	3,21	3,28
Gesamtumsatz in Mrd. DM		
Gesamtumsatz netto	11,58	12,45
Zahl der Mitarbeiter	918	879
Zahl der Tankstellen	2753	3040

New vocabulary

das Unternehmen enterprise/company
die Geschichte history/past
die Aktiengesellschaft (**AG**) public limited company (plc)
ist entstanden has emerged
westdeutsch West German
die Benzol-Verkaufsvereinigung benzene sales association
gegründet wurde was founded
der Superkraftstoff premium fuel
entwickeln to develop
das Jahrzehnt decade
die Erfahrung experience
führend leading
die Kraftstoffvertriebsgesellschaft fuel distributor
verkauft sold
der Liter litre
das Benzin petrol/gasoline
der Absatz sales
die Million (**Mio.**) million
der Kraftstoff fuel
der Dieselkraftstoff diesel fuel
die Milliarde (**Mrd.**) billion / thousand million
netto net
die Tankstelle petrol/gas station

(a) **Die Aral __________ ist aus der Westdeutschen Benzol-Verkaufsvereinigung entstanden.**

(b) **Sie hat 1924 den ersten __________ der Welt entwickelt.**

(c) **Mit neun __________ Erfahrung ist Aral heute die __________ Kraftstoffvertriebsgesellschaft.**

(d) **So kommt jeder vierte in der Bundesrepublik __________ Liter Benzin von Aral.**

(e) **1990 hat die Aral Aktiengesellschaft einen __________ von DM 12,453 Mrd. gehabt.**

Did you know?

Business enterprises are organized in much the same way in most of the industrialized countries. The internal organization depends very much on the size, the line of business, the number of staff, etc. The five main types of business organizations are explained here.

Die Einzelfirma (sole trader/proprietor)

This type of enterprise is very common for small businesses. The owner – an individual – is solely responsible for managing the business affairs, provides all the capital and is entitled to all the profits, but is also fully liable for the debts of this business. The enterprise is named after the owner and is easy to set up and close down.

Die offene Handelsgesellschaft / OHG (general partnership)

In this type of business, two or more owners provide the capital for the business. All the partners (**der Gesellschafter**) are personally involved in the management of the company, they are jointly and severally liable, and their liability is not limited. The company is registered with the local court. A balance sheet has to be prepared annually. The partners are legally entitled to a share in the profits, which amounts to at least 4 per cent of their capital contribution. The relationship between the partners is laid down in the articles of association, which have to be changed whenever a partner leaves the partnership. At least one of the names of the partners is used for the firm's name.

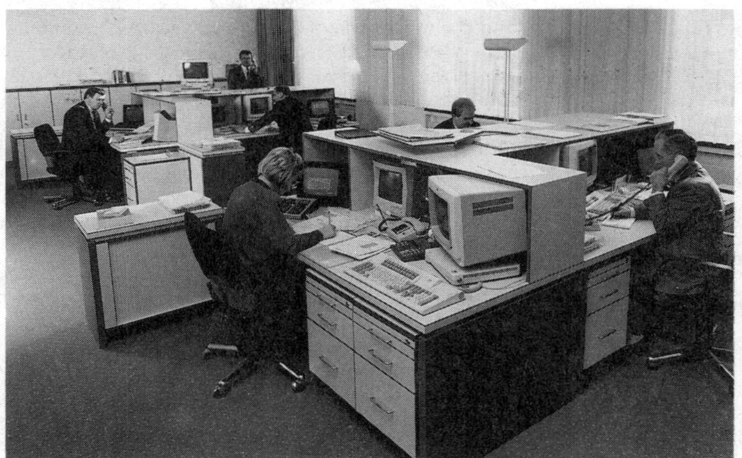

Die Kommanditgesellschaft / KG (limited partnership)

Here there are two kinds of partners, the general partner (**der Komplementär**) and the limited partner (**der Kommanditist**). The general partner is fully liable for all debts contracted on behalf of the business, whereas the liability of the limited partner is restricted to the amount of capital he or she has agreed to put into the business. In return the general partner is entitled to run the business. The limited partner has to be consulted about important business decisions. A balance sheet must be drawn up annually and the business must be registered with the local court. The relationship of the partners is laid down in the articles of association, which have to be changed whenever a partner leaves. The name of the general partner is part of the firm's name.

Die Gesellschaft mit beschränkter Haftung / GmbH (private limited company)

This type of company organization is most commonly used for small and medium-sized companies. The **GmbH** is a joint-stock company; it is a legal person, which means that it can sue and be sued. It may be founded by only one person and must have a minimum capital of 50,000 marks, with the minimum share being fixed at 500 marks. Each shareholder is liable only to the amount of capital subscribed. There are two organs in this private limited company: the general manager (**der Geschäftsführer**), who is responsible for the day-to-day business of the company, and the shareholders' meeting (**die Gesellschafterversammlung**), which must take place at least once a year and which appoints and supervises the management. It decides on the distribution of the profit. The company must be registered with the local court, where the annual report, the balance sheet and the profit and loss account must also be filed.

Die Aktiengesellschaft / AG (public limited company)

Most big German companies are organized in this form, although of the 2,300 public limited companies in Germany only about 500 are quoted on the stock exchange. The **AG** is a joint-stock company and a legal person. At least five people are required to form such a company. The minimum capital is 100,000 marks, divided into shares of at least 50 marks. There are three organs in this type of business enterprise: the shareholders' meeting (**die Aktionärsversammlung**), the supervisory board (**der Aufsichtsrat**) and the management (**der Vorstand**). The shareholders elect the supervisory board (although this right is restricted because of the legislation concerning employee participation – **die Mitbestimmung**); they decide on the distribution of the profit and the increase or decrease of the share capital; they discharge the executive and non-executive directors (**Vorstands- und Aufsichtsratsmitglieder**) and appoint the auditor (**der Rechnungsprüfer**). The **AG** must be registered with the local court, where the annual report, the balance sheet, the profit and loss account and the social report must be made available for public inspection.

There is one special form of company which has no equivalent in other countries: the **GmbH & Co. KG.** Here the private limited company, which has limited liability, acts as the general partner, who, by law, has unlimited liability in a limited partnership.

Most of these forms also exist in Switzerland, although the **GmbH** is not very common. Joint-stock companies are usually organized as **AG**s. The Swiss equivalent of the **OHG** is the **Kollektivgesellschaft**.

WITTENER REISEBÜRO

Your turn to speak

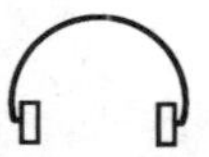

19 After the end of your business talks you offer to show your visitor round the premises of your company and you tell him/her about the different departments. Below are a few phrases you could use.

Wie versprochen zeige ich Ihnen jetzt ... (**wie versprochen** means 'as promised')
Hier links/rechts ist ...
... sehen Sie / befindet sich die ...abteilung
Hier unten / Da drüben ist ...
Und jetzt kommen wir zu/in ...
Auf der anderen Seite ...

20 Tell a business friend about the activities of your company and provide some important data about the turnover and the number of employees. Try to use a word that you haven't had before: **der Sitz**, 'headquarters'.

Unser Unternehmen hat seinen Sitz in ...
Wir haben noch Zweigwerke in ... / keine Zweigwerke
Wir produzieren ... / stellen ... her
Unser Jahresumsatz beträgt ...
Wir haben insgesamt ... Mitarbeiter
Davon arbeiten ... in der Verwaltung
... sind in der Produktion beschäftigt

Answers

Practise what you have learned

Exercise **1** (a) einen Termin (b) nehmen Sie (c) eine weite (d) untergebracht (e) sehr interessant (f) Mein Name (g) sicherlich (h) gestern schon (i) Flug (j) gutes Hotel

Exercise **4** (a) i (b) ii (c) ii (d) ii (e) i (f) i

Exercise **5** (a) gekommen, Produkte (b) ähnliche (c) anbieten (d) haben (e) geschäftlichen

Exercise **6** (a) bitte (b) darf (c) gern (d) wenn es möglich ist

Exercise **8** *Masters:* (b), (c), (f), (i), (k); *Köpl:* (a), (d), (e), (g), (h), (j)

Exercise **9** (a) Frau Köpl (b) Herr Karlow (c) Herr Waigl (d) Mr Masters

Exercise **10** (a) unserem Hause (b) beide Herren (c) sich Ihnen (d) Mein Name (e) hat uns vorinformiert

Exercise **12** (a) Lehmann (b) Schneider (c) Lehmann (d) Stevens (e) Brandt (f) Stevens (g) Lehmann

Exercise **13** (a) iv (b) i (c) ii (d) v (e) iii

Exercise **14** *Departments mentioned:* (a), (b), (c), (e), (i), (l)

Exercise **16** *richtig:* (c), (d), (f); *falsch:* (a), (b), (e), (g), (h)

Grammar

Exercise **17** (a) Ihnen (b) uns (c) Ihnen (d) Sie (e) ihn (f) Sie

Read and understand

Exercise **18** (a) Aktiengesellschaft (b) Superkraftstoff (c) Jahrzehnten, führende (d) verkaufte (e) Gesamtumsatz

9 SELLING YOUR PRODUCT

You will learn

- to make enquiries and arrange appointments over the phone
- to understand and record telephone messages
- to talk about products
- to discuss prices and terms
- to understand telex/fax messages

and you will be given some information about newspapers and periodicals in German-speaking countries.

Study guide

Dialogue 1 + Practise what you have learned
Dialogue 2 + Practise what you have learned
Dialogue 3 + Practise what you have learned
Dialogue 4 + Practise what you have learned
Make sure you know the **Key words and phrases**
Study the **Grammar** section
Do the exercises in **Read and understand**
Read **Did you know?**
Do the exercises in **Your turn to speak**

DER SPIEGEL

Die Presse

Unabhängige Tageszeitung für Österreich

Dialogues

1 *.Frau Axt calls a printer's to enquire about writing paper and business cards*

Frau Köpke Werbedruck GmbH, Köpke, guten Tag.
Frau Axt Firma Weiß, Regeltechnik, Axt, guten Tag.
Frau Köpke Guten Tag, Frau Axt.
Frau Axt Ich habe Ihre Anzeige in der Zeitung gelesen und möchte gerne Briefpapier in DIN A4, DIN A5 und Visitenkarten bei Ihnen bestellen.
Frau Köpke Ja. Die Preise richten sich nach Art und Umfang des Auftrags. Und ich schlage vor, daß wir Ihnen unseren Mitarbeiter, Herrn Krämer, vorbeischicken. Der kann dann alle Details mit Ihnen klären.
Frau Axt Ja, das halte ich für eine sehr gute Idee. Können wir direkt einen Termin vereinbaren?
Frau Köpke Ja natürlich. Montag vielleicht?
Frau Axt Moment, ich schau(e) mal im Kalender nach. Nein, Montag geht nicht. Wie wär's mit Dienstag um 12 Uhr?
Frau Köpke Gut. Dienstag 12 Uhr. Sagen Sie mir bitte Ihre Anschrift?
Frau Axt Ja. Das wäre die Markstraße 10, 4630 Bochum 1.
Frau Köpke Gut, Frau Axt. Ich hab's notiert. Herr Krämer wird Sie am Dienstag um 12 Uhr besuchen.
Frau Axt Ganz vielen Dank.
Frau Köpke Ich danke. Auf Wiederhören.
Frau Axt Wiederhör(e)n.

die Regeltechnik control engineering
➧ **die Anzeige** ad
➧ **die Zeitung** paper
das Briefpapier writing paper / (company) stationery
➧ **die Visitenkarte** business card
die Art type/kind
der Umfang volume/amount/size
➧ **der Auftrag** order
direkt immediately/straightaway
der Kalender diary/calendar

Werbedruck GmbH, the firm's name, is linked to the word **Druck**, 'print/printing'.

➧ **Ich habe Ihre Anzeige in der Zeitung gelesen** I (have) read your ad in the paper. **Gelesen** is the past participle of **lesen** 'to read'.

Briefpapier in DIN A4, DIN A5 stationery in A4, A5. These are standard European formats for writing paper. **DIN** stands for **Deutsche Industrienormen** (German industrial standards).

➧ **Die Preise richten sich nach ...** The prices depend on ... This phrase is common in a business context, although **nach** generally indicates a direction, e.g. **Ich fahre nach Bochum** (I go to Bochum).

Ich schlage vor, daß wir Ihnen unseren Mitarbeiter ... vorbeischicken Lit. 'I suggest that we you our employee ... past send', i.e. 'I suggest that our employee comes round to talk things over'. **Vorbeischicken** means 'to send round'.

➧ **Der kann dann alle Details mit Ihnen klären** He can then discuss all the details with you. **Das Detail** is still very much a foreign word in

German: it has preserved both the French pronunciation and also the plural ending **s. Klären** means 'to clarify/clear up'.

➧ **Ja, das halte ich für eine sehr gute Idee.** Yes, I think that's a very good idea. **Etwas halten für** means 'to consider sth. to be ... / to think sth. is ...

➧ **Können wir direkt einen Termin vereinbaren?** Can we immediately make an appointment? **Vereinbaren** means 'to arrange/agree'.

➧ **Montag geht nicht** Lit. 'Monday goes not', i.e. Monday is not possible. You'll often hear **Das geht nicht**, 'That's not possible / That's no good'.

➧ **Wie wär's mit ...?** How about ...? **Wie wäre es ...?** means 'How would it be ...?' **Wäre** indicates a tentative/polite suggestion, but you can also say **Wie ist es mit ...?**, as in dialogue 3.

Das wäre ... That would be ... A commonly used form of **sein** (to be) when addresses etc. are given.

➧ **Ich hab's notiert** I've noted that down. **Notieren** means 'to write down'; it does *not* have the wider meaning that the English equivalent has.

Herr Krämer wird Sie am Dienstag um 12 Uhr besuchen Herr Krämer will visit you on Tuesday at 12 noon. **Wird besuchen** is a form of the future tense which is explained in Unit 12 and in the grammar summary at the end of the book.

Practise what you have learned

1 Complete these sentences using the appropriate words from the box below – you won't need all of them. (Answers on p. 172.)

(a) **Frau Axt hat die ____________ in der ____________ gelesen.**

(b) **Sie möchte ____________ und ____________ bestellen.**

(c) **Frau Köpke schlägt vor, einen ____________ vorbeizuschicken.**

(d) **Frau Axt hält das für eine gute ____________**

(e) **Sie fragt, können wir direkt einen ____________ vereinbaren.**

(f) **Frau Köpke möchte noch die ____________ wissen.**

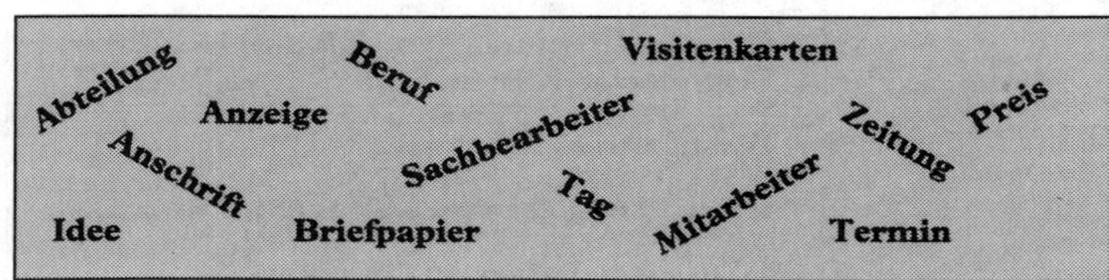

Abteilung
Beruf
Visitenkarten
Anzeige
Sachbearbeiter
Zeitung
Preis
Anschrift
Tag
Mitarbeiter
Idee
Briefpapier
Termin

Continued on next page.

2 Here are some sentences from the dialogue where the parts are all jumbled up. Put them in the right order to form complete sentences. Listen to the dialogue again to check your answers.

(a) **in der Zeitung gelesen habe Ihre Anzeige ich**
(b) **Briefpapier bei Ihnen ich gerne und möchte Visitenkarten bestellen in DIN A4, DIN A5**
(c) **des Auftrags richten sich nach die Preise Art und Umfang**
(d) **der dann klären mit Ihnen alle Details kann**
(e) **einen Termin wir direkt vereinbaren? können**
(f) **mir Ihre Anschrift sagen bitte Sie**

3 Your turn to speak. Take the role of Frau Bormann in this conversation and ask about the possibilities of buying office stationery for your company.

4 Listen to the recording and try to remember who said what. Indicate which of the sentences below were used by Herr Liedtke, from Handorf GmbH, and which by Frau Baumann, the prospective customer. (Answers on p. 172.) Don't worry, you are not expected to learn every word of the new vocabulary, just make sure you get the gist of the discussion.

New vocabulary
das Inserat ad
die IHK-Zeitschrift journal/periodical of the Chamber of Commerce
gesehen seen
das Verpackungsmaterial pack(ag)ing material
aller Art of all kinds
günstig favourable/low-priced/competitive
das Interesse interest
die Kartonage cartons/carton material(s)
das Packpapier wrapping paper
zuschicken to send
ausführlich exhaustive/full
der Prospekt leaflet/brochure
die Angelegenheit matter/problem/question
durchsprechen to discuss (in detail)

		Baumann	*Liedtke*
(a)	**Ich habe gerade Ihr Inserat in der IHK-Zeitschrift gesehen.**		
(b)	**Wir freuen uns über Ihr Interesse.**		
(c)	**Wir stellen also vor allem Kartonagen und Packpapier her.**		
(d)	**Ich schicke Ihnen gerne mal einen ausführlichen Prospekt zu.**		
(e)	**Ist es vielleicht möglich, daß Sie einen Ihrer Vertreter vorbeischicken?**		
(f)	**Wann paßt es Ihnen denn?**		
(g)	**Ich muß mal eben im Kalender nachschauen.**		
(h)	**Ja, das geht bei uns in Ordnung.**		
(i)	**Dann brauchen Sie noch unsere Adresse.**		

Dialogues

2 *Requesting a catalogue and price list*

Frau Schmidt	Schmidt Möbelfabrik GmbH & Co. KG. Guten Tag.
Frau Fischer	Bohlmann & Söhne. Fischer am Apparat. Guten Tag. Ich hab(e) Ihre Annonce gesehen in der Zeitung *Büro + Design* vom November. Und wir wollen ein neues Großraumbüro einrichten. Wäre es möglich, daß Sie uns einen Katalog mit Preisliste zusenden würden?
Frau Schmidt	Natürlich, selbstverständlich. Sind Sie interessiert an speziellen Büroeinrichtungen?
Frau Fischer	Ja, Schreibtische und Bürostühle dazu, natürlich auch Schreibmaschinentische.
Frau Schmidt	Ah ja, selbstverständlich. Dann schicke ich Ihnen unseren kompletten Katalog mit Preisliste.
Frau Fischer	Das wäre sehr nett. Wann kann ich damit rechnen?
Frau Schmidt	Ich denke, daß er morgen rausgehen kann. Wenn Sie mir noch bitte Ihre Anschrift angeben?
Frau Fischer	Ja, selbstverständlich. Das war Bohlmann & Söhne.
Frau Schmidt	Ja ...
Frau Fischer	Friedrichstraße 35.
Frau Schmidt	Friedrichstraße 35.
Frau Fischer	In 5000 Köln 21.
Frau Schmidt	5000 Köln 21. Sagen Sie mir Ihren Namen nochmal bitte?
Frau Fischer	Das war Fischer.
Frau Schmidt	Frau Fischer. Gut, Frau Fischer. Der Katalog geht morgen an Sie raus.
Frau Fischer	Ja, vielen Dank.
Frau Schmidt	Danke auch.
Frau Fischer	Wiederhör(e)n.
Frau Schmidt	Wiederhör(e)n.

die Möbelfabrik furniture factory
➧ **die Annonce** ad
das Großraumbüro open-plan office
einrichten to furnish
➧ **der Katalog** catalogue
➧ **die Preisliste** price list
➧ **zusenden/schicken** to send

speziell special
die Büroeinrichtung office furniture (and equipment)
der Bürostuhl office chair
der Schreibmaschinentisch typewriter desk
➧ **komplett** complete/full/comprehensive

Bohlmann & Söhne Bohlmann & sons. **Sohn** means 'son'.

➧ **Fischer am Apparat** Fischer speaking. A very common phrase used to identify an individual within a company.

Büro + Design (office + design) is the name of the publication.

Wäre es möglich, daß Sie ...? Lit. 'Would it be possible that you ...? This is the best possible way of saying 'Would it be possible for you to ...?

➧ **zusenden** to send. The prefix **zu** is occasionally omitted. People also often use the verb **schicken** (or **zuschicken**), which means the same, as in Frau Schmidt's reply: **Dann schicke ich Ihnen ...**

➧ **Wann kann ich damit rechnen?** Lit. 'When can I with it calculate?', i.e. 'When do you think it will reach me? / When can I expect to receive it?' **Damit** (with it), which includes the preposition **mit**, refers to the material mentioned in the previous sentence. The German phrase is **mit etwas rechnen**, 'to count on something / expect something'.

daß er morgen rausgehen kann that it will (lit. can) leave here tomorrow. She avoids making a binding commitment. The phrase would only be used in spoken German.

Now turn over for the exercises based on dialogue 2.

Practise what you have learned

5 Can you remember what Frau Schmidt and Frau Fischer said in the dialogue? Answer the following questions. (Answers on p. 172.)

(a) **Wo hat Frau Fischer die Annonce gesehen?**
Frau Fischer hat die Annonce ____________________ gesehen.

(b) **Was möchte die Firma Bohlmann & Söhne einrichten? Die Firma Bohlmann & Söhne möchte ____________________ einrichten.**

(c) **Was soll die Firma Schmidt Möbelfabrik zusenden? Die Firma Schmidt Möbelfabrik soll ____________________ zusenden.**

(d) **An was ist die Firma Bohlmann & Söhne interessiert? Die Firma Bohlmann ist an ____________________ interessiert.**

(e) **Was kann morgen rausgehen?**
Ein kompletter ____________________ kann morgen rausgehen.

(f) **Was soll Frau Fischer noch tun?**
Frau Fischer soll noch ____________________

6 Match the sentences on the left with the missing words on the right, and make sure you understand what the sentences mean. (Answers on p. 172.)

(a) **Gestern habe ich ... Annonce in der Zeitung gesehen.**
(b) **Ist es vielleicht möglich, daß Sie ... einen Katalog zusenden?**
(c) **Das beste ist, ich schicke ... den kompletten Katalog mit der Preisliste.**
(d) **Vielleicht können Sie ... noch ... Anschrift geben.**
(e) **Sagen Sie mir bitte noch einmal ... Namen.**
(f) **Der Katalog geht morgen an ... raus.**

(i) **Ihnen**
(ii) **Ihre**
(iii) **Ihren**
(iv) **mir**
(v) **Sie**
(vi) **uns**
(vii) **Ihre**

7 Take the role of Herr Wiehl in the dialogue on the recording and ask for a catalogue to be sent to you. Follow the prompts.

8 Listen to the dialogue on the recording and then match the questions on the left with the answers on the right. (Answers on p. 172.) But first study the new vocabulary.

New vocabulary
technisch technical
das Gerät device/machine
elektrisch electrical
das Informationsmaterial information material/literature
freundlich friendly/kind
das Angebot offer
schriftlich written
das Material material
weitere further

(a) **Wo hat Herr Aumann die Produkte gesehen?**
(b) **Was braucht Herr Aumann jetzt noch?**
(c) **Was will Frau Steiger Herrn Aumann zusenden?**
(d) **Welche Informationen braucht Herr Aumann noch?**
(e) **Für welche Maschinen braucht er die Informationen?**
(f) **Wen will Frau Steiger vorbeischicken?**
(g) **Was genügt Herrn Aumann zunächst?**

(i) **einen Außendienstmitarbeiter**
(ii) **einige technische Details**
(iii) **auf der Hannover Messe**
(iv) **einige Informationen**
(v) **einen Katalog**
(vi) **für die elektrischen Maschinen**
(vi) **das schriftliche Material**

Dialogues

3 *Arranging an appointment over the telephone*

Frau Schiffkowski Westfalenbank. Schiffkowski. Guten Tag.
Herr Riedl Guten Tag Frau Schiffkowski. Hier ist die Firma Auffermann, Riedl.
Frau Schiffkowski Guten Tag, Herr Riedl.
Herr Riedl Hhm. Ich wollte wegen eines Termins mich mit Ihnen abstimmen. Und zwar ist unsere neue Kollektion von Werbegeschenken fertig. Und ich wollte fragen, ob ich in der nächsten Woche bei Ihnen vorbeikommen kann?
Frau Schiffkowski Wann ist ... nächste Woche Montag? Wäre ... ach nee, da seh(e) ich g(e)rade, da sind die internen Sitzungen. Wie ist es mit Dienstag vormittag?
Herr Riedl Da bin ich leider verhindert.
Frau Schiffkowski Und nachmittags? Ach, da hat der Chef Kundenbesuch. Wie wär's denn mit Mittwoch um 14.00 Uhr?
Herr Riedl Das geht im Prinzip gut. Wenn's 'ne Stunde später wäre, wäre es noch besser.
Frau Schiffkowski Ja, okay. Dann nehmen wir Mittwoch 15.00 Uhr.
Herr Riedl Sehr schön.
Frau Schiffkowski Ich werd's ausrichten.
Herr Riedl Ja, vielen Dank, Frau Schiffkowski.
Frau Schiffkowski Danke. Wiederhör(e)n.
Herr Riedl Wiederschau(e)n.

- **die Kollektion** collection/range
- **das Werbegeschenk** (free) gift
- **fertig** ready/finished/completed
- **intern** internal/in-house
- **im Prinzip** in principle

Ich wollte wegen eines Termins mich mit Ihnen abstimmen Lit. 'I wanted because of an appointment myself with you to agree'. **Wollte** is the past tense of **wollen** (to want). This verb is often used to express an intention – 'I would like'. **Wegen eines Termins** means 'concerning a date / an appointment'. The word order of this sentence is quite unusual – just make sure you recognize **ein Termin** (an appointment) and **abstimmen** (to agree).

- **Ich wollte fragen, ob ...** is frequently used to introduce a question. The English equivalent is 'I wanted to ask whether ...'.

- **Da seh(e) ich g(e)rade ...** Oh, I just see ... This colloquial form is commonly used when something has escaped attention at first sight.

- **Wie ist es mit ...?** How about ...? Another colloquial way of making a suggestion.

Da bin ich leider verhindert Then unfortunately I am busy (lit. Then am I unfortunately prevented). In this context, **verhindert sein** means 'to be busy/engaged'.

Da hat der Chef Kundenbesuch Then the boss will be seeing visitors (lit. Then has the boss customer-visit). Note the difference in tense in German (present) and English (future). **Der Kundenbesuch** can mean 'the visit *of* a customer' or 'the visit *paid to* a customer'. **Kundenbesuch haben** means 'to have visitors' and **Kundenbesuch machen** means 'to go and visit/see customers'.

Wenn's 'ne Stunde später wäre, wär's noch besser If it were an hour later, it would be even better. The verb forms are complex but quite common, so these are useful phrases to learn. **Wenn's 'ne** is short for **wenn es eine**.

Dann nehmen wir ... Then let's take ... At the end of a discussion about possible dates you are more likely to hear **Dann sagen wir ...** (Then let's say/make it ...).

Now turn over for the exercises based on dialogue 3.

Practise what you have learned

9 Circle the correct answers to these questions. (Answers on p. 172.)

(a) **Wo arbeitet Frau Schiffkowski?** (i) **im Blumenladen**
(ii) **in der Werbeabteilung**
(iii) **in der Westfalenbank**

(b) **Was möchte Herr Riedl abstimmen?** (i) **einen Tag**
(ii) **einen Monat**
(iii) **einen Termin**

(c) **Was ist fertig?** (i) **die Kollektion von Werbegeschenken**
(ii) **die Liste mit den Werbegeschenken**
(iii) **der Katalog für die Werbegeschenke**

(d) **Wann will Herr Riedl vorbeikommen?** (i) **nächsten Montag**
(ii) **nächsten Monat**
(iii) **nächste Woche**

(e) **Was ist am Montag?** (i) **interne Sitzungen**
(ii) **die Sitzung mit den Mitarbeitern**
(iii) **die Sitzung mit den Kunden**

(f) **Warum geht Dienstag vormittag nicht?**
(i) **Herr Riedl ist beschäftigt.**
(ii) **Herr Riedl hat einen Termin vereinbart.**
(iii) **Herr Riedl ist verhindert.**

(g) **Und was macht der Chef am Dienstag nachmittag?**
(i) **Der Chef hat Kundenbesuch.**
(ii) **Der Chef besucht einen Kunden.**
(iii) **Der Chef ist beim Kundendienst.**

(h) **Welchen Termin vereinbaren Herr Riedl und Frau Schiffkowski?**
(i) **Mittwoch um 14.00 Uhr.**
(ii) **Dienstag um 15.00 Uhr.**
(iii) **Mittwoch um 15.00 Uhr.**

10 Complete the sentences below. (Answers on p. 172.)

(a) ____________________ **wegen eines Termins mich mit Ihnen** __________

(b) **Und** ______________________________ **, ob ich in der nächsten Woche bei Ihnen** _________________________________

(c) **Da** ____________________ **gerade, da sind die internen Sitzungen.**

(d) **Da** ____________________ **leider** ____________

(e) **Da** ______________________________ **Kundenbesuch.**

(f) **Wenn es eine Stunde später wäre,** ________________ **noch** __________

(g) **Dann** ___________________ **Mittwoch 15.00 Uhr.**

11 Your turn to speak. Take the role of an employee who wishes to arrange a meeting with a client. Use the prompts for your part of the dialogue.

12

Listen to two messages recorded on a telephone answering machine. Then put the words and phrases below in the correct order to make complete sentences. Read your answers aloud before you check them by listening to the messages again.

New vocabulary
zur Zeit at present
um Verständnis bitten to ask for (someone's) understanding
der Summton buzzing sound
sich interessieren für to be interested in
die Zusendung sending/forwarding
um Zusendung bitten to ask to send
ausführlich exhaustive/full/comprehensive

(a) **unser Anschluß nicht besetzt zur Zeit leider ist**
(b) **dafür um Verständnis bitten wir**
(c) **hinterlassen Sie können jedoch eine Nachricht**
(d) **bitte an Ihren Namen geben und Sie Ihre Telefonnummer**
(e) **wir gesehen in der Zeitung heute Ihr Inserat haben**
(f) **wir uns für Ihre Produkte interessieren**
(g) **eines ausführlichen Katalogs daher einer Preisliste und bitten wir um Zusendung**

Dialogues

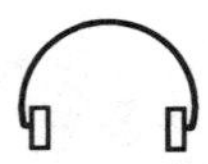

4 *Discussion at a trade fair*

Salesman Guten Tag, Sie interessieren sich für unsere Produkte?
Customer Ja. Ich sehe, daß Sie sich mit Gasarmaturen beschäftigen. Was kostet denn ein solches Gerät, bitte?
Salesman Der Listenpreis wird etwa 1800 Mark betragen.
Customer 1800 Mark. Ja, das klingt interessant. Geben Sie auch einen Wiederverkaufsrabatt?
Salesman Das hängt von der Verkaufsmenge ab.
Customer Aha. Ja, dann geb(e) ich Ihnen meine Karte und ich bitte Sie, mir ein detailliertes Angebot zu erstellen.
Salesman Das will ich gerne tun. Wann benötigen Sie dieses Angebot?
Customer Ja. Ich denke, in der nächsten Woche bin ich wieder im Haus. Wenn Sie es nächste Woche schaffen ...?
Salesman Das läßt sich einrichten.
Customer Ja, prima. Herzlichen Dank.
Salesman Auf Wiedersehen.
Customer Wiederschau(e)n.

die Messe trade fair / exhibition **solch** such

- **daß Sie sich mit Gasarmaturen beschäftigen** that you work/operate in the field of gas instruments
- **Der Listenpreis wird etwa 1800 Mark betragen** The list price will amount to about 1800 marks. The future tense **wird ... betragen** is unusual in German. It indicates that a final decision on the price has not yet been taken and/or is negotiable. **Der Listenpreis** means 'list price'.

Geben Sie auch einen Wiederverkaufsrabatt? Do you also give a trade discount? **Wiederverkaufsrabatt** really means 'resale discount'.

Dann geb(e) ich Ihnen ... Then I'll give you ... / Let me give you ...

- **Ich bitte Sie, mir ein detailliertes Angebot zu erstellen** Lit. 'I ask you (to) me a detailed offer to prepare'. This is a very important business phrase. **Detailliert** means 'detailed' and **das Angebot** is 'offer'.
- **Das hängt von der Verkaufsmenge ab** That depends on the quantity sold. **Die Menge** means 'quantity', so **die Verkaufsmenge** means 'quantity sold'. Similarly: **die Bestellmenge**, 'the quantity ordered'. **Abhängen von** is 'to depend on', e.g. **Es hängt vom Wetter ab** 'It depends on the weather'.
- **Das will ich gerne tun** It will be a pleasure for me to do that. A very polite phrase that is often used in such a formal situation.
- **in der nächsten Woche** next week. Note that the German phrase requires the preposition **in** and the appropriate endings.
- **bin ich wieder im Haus** Lit. 'am I again in the house'. German business people invariably use **im Haus(e)** for 'in their/my office' or 'in their/my company'.
- **Wenn Sie es nächste Woche schaffen?** If you manage (to get it done) next week? **Es schaffen** (to manage) is very common. Although the sentence is not complete, the meaning is clear.
- **Das läßt sich einrichten** That can be arranged/done. Another very common phrase.

Practise what you have learned

13 Can you remember what the two businessmen at the trade fair actually said? Circle the correct sentences. (Answers on p. 172.)

(a) (i) **Sie interessieren sich für unser Angebot?**
(ii) **Sie interessieren sich für unsere Produkte?**
(iii) **Sie interessieren sich für unsere Geräte?**

(b) (i) **Ich sehe, daß Sie Gasarmaturen herstellen.**
(ii) **Ich sehe, daß Sie Gasarmaturen verkaufen.**
(iii) **Ich sehe, daß Sie sich mit Gasarmaturen beschäftigen.**

(c) (i) **Was kostet denn ein solches Gerät?**
(ii) **Wie teuer ist denn ein solches Gerät?**
(iii) **Wieviel muß ich denn für ein solches Gerät bezahlen?**

(d) (i) **Der Messepreis wird etwa 1800 Mark betragen.**
(ii) **Der Katalogpreis wird etwa 1800 Mark betragen.**
(iii) **Der Listenpreis wird etwa 1800 Mark betragen.**

(e) (i) **Das hängt von der Verkaufsmenge ab.**
(ii) **Das hängt von der Qualität ab.**
(iii) **Das hängt vom Kunden ab.**

(f) (i) **Ich bitte Sie, mir ein ausführliches Angebot zu erstellen.**
(ii) **Ich bitte Sie, mir ein detailliertes Angebot zu erstellen.**
(iii) **Ich bitte Sie, mir ein genaues Angebot zu erstellen.**

14 Complete these sentences by filling in the correct form of the correct verb. Choose from the ones in the box below – you won't need all of them. (Answers on p. 172.)

(a) ___________ **Sie sich für unsere Produkte?**

(b) **Wir** ___________ **uns schon lange mit Gasarmaturen.**

(c) **Und wieviel soll solch ein Gerät** ___________ **?**

(d) **Der Listenpreis** ___________ **ungefähr 1800 Mark.**

(e) **Der Rabatt** ___________ **von der Verkaufsmenge** ___________

(f) **Bitte** ___________ **Sie mir ein detailliertes Angebot.**

(g) **Ich** ___________ **das Angebot in der nächsten Woche.**

(h) **Ja, in der nächsten Woche** ___________ **ich das.**

abhängen betragen einrichten interessieren benötigen erstellen geben kosten beschäftigen schaffen klingen

15 Your turn to speak. Take the role of a customer at the trade fair and enquire about the gas instrument displayed at the stand. Use the prompts. **Das Gasmischgerät** is a 'gas mixing device' and the word for 'especially' is **besonders**.

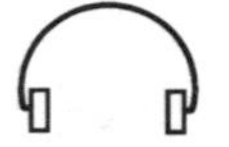

16

Listen to the recording and then do the exercise below. Decide whether the statements are **richtig oder falsch** (true or false). Study the new vocabulary first. (Answers on p. 172.)

New vocabulary

einen Moment Zeit haben to have a minute to spare
womit with what
neuest newest/latest
die Daten data
deswegen therefore/that's why
ideal ideal
besondere special/particular
der Messerabatt trade-fair discount
schlecht bad
liefern to supply/deliver
am Lager in stock
also therefore/thus
sich etwas überlegen to think something over

		richtig	falsch
(a)	**Der Kunde interessiert sich für Telefongeräte.**		
(b)	**Der Verkäufer gibt dem Kunden den neuesten Katalog.**		
(c)	**In der Preisliste sind alle technischen Daten.**		
(d)	**Das Büro ist viel zu groß.**		
(e)	**Es gibt einen Wiederverkaufsrabatt.**		
(f)	**Der Kunde muß in dieser Woche noch bestellen.**		
(g)	**Alle Geräte sind am Lager.**		
(h)	**Der Kunde braucht sich das nicht zu überlegen.**		

Key words and phrases

Ich habe in der Zeitung gelesen ...	I (have) read in the newspaper ...
Ich wollte fragen, ob ...	I wanted to ask whether ...
sich für etwas interessieren	to be interested in something
sich mit etwas beschäftigen	to work/operate in the field of
die Details klären	to discuss the details
um Zusendung bitten	to ask to be sent
Ich halte es für ...	I consider it to be ...
Das hängt von ... ab	That depends on ...
am Apparat	speaking
einen Termin vereinbaren	to make/arrange an appointment
Wie wäre/ist es mit ...?	How about ...?
Montag geht nicht	Monday is not possible
Da seh(e) ich gerade ...	Oh, I just see ... / I've just noticed ...
in der nächsten Woche	next week
Ich habe es notiert	I've noted that down
ein detailliertes Angebot erstellen	to make/prepare a detailed offer
Die Preise richten sich nach ...	The prices depend on ...
Der Listenpreis beträgt ...	The list price is/amounts to ...
Wann kann ich damit rechnen?	When can I count on receiving it (the material)?
es schaffen	(to be able) to manage it
wieder im Haus sein	to be in the office again
Das will ich gern tun	It will be a pleasure
Das läßt sich einrichten	That can be arranged/done
die Anzeige / die Annonce / das Inserat	ad
die Zeitung	newspaper
die Visitenkarte	business card
das Werbegeschenk	free gift (incentive)
das Gerät	device/machine/appliance
die Messe	trade fair / exhibition
der Auftrag	order
der Katalog	catalogue
der Prospekt	leaflet/brochure
die Preisliste	price list
der Listenpreis	list price
der Rabatt	discount
der Wiederverkaufsrabatt	trade discount
die Menge / die Verkaufsmenge	quantity / quantity sold
am Lager	in stock
liefern	to supply/deliver
(zu)senden / (zu)schicken	to send
komplett	complete/full/comprehensive
ausführlich	exhaustive/full/comprehensive
fertig	ready/finished/completed
günstig	favourable/low-priced/competitive
schriftlich	in writing
verhindert sein	to be busy/engaged
zur Zeit	at present

Grammar

Adjectives

Words such as **groß** (big), **klein** (small), **kurz** (short) and **lang** (long) are adjectives. They are used to describe things, people, express feelings etc. Therefore they are often used together with nouns or noun-like words. Here are some examples:

Die Fahrt ist lang. The journey is long.
Die Hotels sind gut. The hotels are good.
Die Bank ist offen. The bank is open.

If adjectives are used in front of nouns, they take endings such as **-e**, **-er**, **-es**, **-en** etc. These endings depend on the gender of the noun (i.e. whether the noun is masculine, feminine or neuter), the case (i.e. whether the noun is used in the nominative, the accusative or the dative) and finally also on whether the noun is used in the singular or the plural. For instance, you would say **die große Firma** or **eine kleine Bank**. Often the ending on the adjective is **-en**, e.g. **mit einem neuen Direktor** or **Ich habe den folgenden Brief** or **die besten Ideen** (pl.). At this stage just note that there are different endings. You should always be able to understand the meaning regardless of the ending. The rules are rather complicated but if you are interested, there's more detail in the grammar summary on p. 225.

Here is a list of some of the more useful adjectives which you have come across so far.

allgemein general
angenehm pleasant
ausführlich exhaustive
auswärtig external
bestimmt certain
detailliert detailed
deutsch German
direkt direct
dringend urgent
einfach simple
englisch English
falsch false
fertig ready
folgend following
französisch French
freundlich friendly
früh early
genau exact
gesamt total
gewöhnlich usual
groß big, large
günstig favourable
heiß hot
herzlich cordial
interessant interesting
intern internal
jede every
kalt cold
komplett complete
lang long
leicht light/easy
mittlere medium(-sized)
möglich possible
nett nice, kind
neu new
planmäßig scheduled
richtig right/correct
ruhig quiet
schlecht bad
schnell quick
schön nice
schriftlich written
sicher certain
spät late
speziell special
technisch technical
telefonisch by phone
verantwortlich responsible
verschieden several/different
zentral central

17

Find the adjectives in the sentences below and write them down in their basic form, i.e. without the ending. (Answers on p. 172.)

Example: **Das ist eine lange Fahrt.** lang

(a) **Dann schicke ich Ihnen unseren neuen Mitarbeiter vorbei.** ________
(b) **Das halte ich für eine sehr gute Idee.** ________
(c) **Mich interessiert ein detailliertes Angebot.** ________
(d) **Die günstigen Preise werden Sie interessieren.** ________
(e) **Kennen Sie schon unseren ausführlichen Prospekt?** ________
(f) **Wir benutzen nur festes Verpackungsmaterial.** ________
(g) **Wenn es sich um eine große Menge handelt, kann ich Ihnen auch einen Rabatt geben.** ________
(h) **Das telefonische Angebot interessiert uns sehr.** ________

Read and understand

18 Here is an offer written to a customer. Read the text and study the new vocabulary carefully, then complete the second letter with the correct phrases from the box. (Answers on p. 172.)

New vocabulary

Sehr geehrte Damen und Herren Dear Sir or Madam
beigefügt enclosed
gültig valid/current
die Rabattstaffel schedule of discounts
bisher hitherto/up to now
zukünftig in future
der Sicherungsautomat automatic flashback arrestor
stückzahlbezogen quantity-related
der Sonderpreis special price
netto net
vorgenannt above-mentioned
gelten to be valid
die Abnahme purchase
die Sendung consignment
ab Werk ex factory/plant/works
weiterhin furthermore
die Zusammenarbeit co-operation
verbleiben to remain
mit freundlichem Gruß yours faithfully/sincerely
die Anlage enclosure

WITT-GASETECHNIK GmbH & Co KG
SICHERHEITSARMATUREN UND APPARATEBAU
Postfach 2550
D 5810 Witten
Salinger Feld 4–8
☎ 02302/8901–0
Telex: 8229017 witt d
Telefax: 02302/89013

Sehr geehrte Damen und Herren,

beigefügt finden Sie unsere gültige Preisliste mit Rabattstaffel.

Wie bisher räumen wir Ihnen auch zukünftig auf den WITT-Sicherungsautomaten RF 53 N einen stückzahlbezogenen Sonderpreis ein:

ab	10 - 19 Stück = 21,90	netto/Stück
	20 - 49 Stück = 20,60	netto/Stück
	ab 50 Stück = 20,—	netto/Stück

Die vorgenannten Preise gelten ab heute, verstehen sich für Abnahmen in einer Sendung, ab Werk.

Wir freuen uns auf weiterhin gute Zusammenarbeit und verbleiben

mit freundlichem Gruß
W I T T - Gasetechnik
GmbH & Co. KG

____(a)____ Damen und Herren,

vielen Dank für Ihre ____(b)____ vom 21.3.1992. In der ____(c)____ finden Sie unseren Katalog und die gültige ____(d)____. Für unsere Geräte können wir Ihnen einen stückzahlbezogenen ____(e)____ anbieten.

Über Ihren ____(f)____ würden wir uns freuen.

Mit ____(g)____ Gruß,

Anfrage · Auftrag · freundlichem · Sehr geehrte · Sonderpreis · Anlage · Preisliste

19 Here is a fax to a customer. Read the text and study the new vocabulary. In the exercise below there's one word missing in each sentence. See if you can fill them in. (Answers on p. 172.)

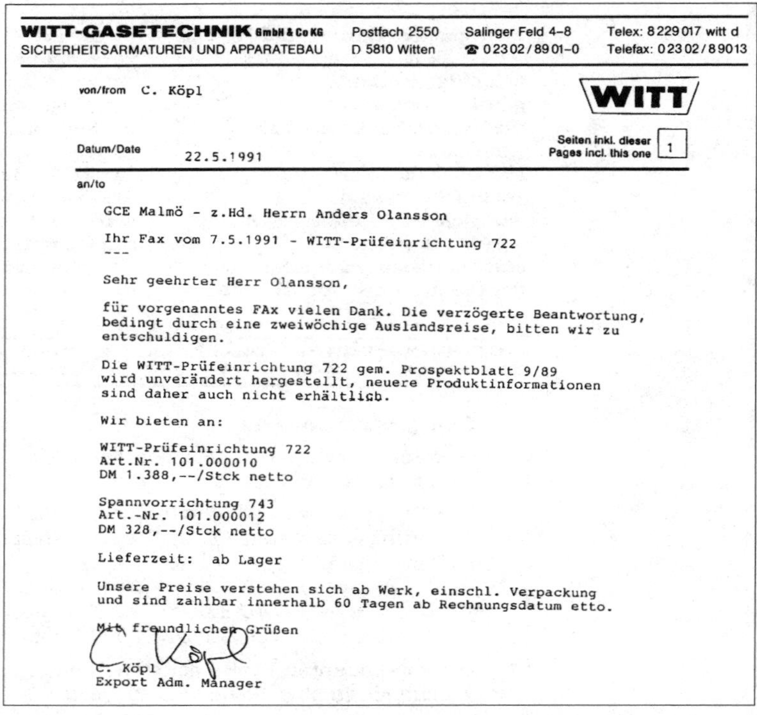

WITT-GASETECHNIK GmbH & Co KG
SICHERHEITSARMATUREN UND APPARATEBAU
Postfach 2550
D 5810 Witten
Salinger Feld 4–8
☎ 02302/8901–0
Telex: 8229017 witt d
Telefax: 02302/89013

von/from C. Köpl

WITT

Datum/Date 22.5.1991

Seiten inkl. dieser / Pages incl. this one: 1

an/to

GCE Malmö - z.Hd. Herrn Anders Olansson

Ihr Fax vom 7.5.1991 - WITT-Prüfeinrichtung 722

Sehr geehrter Herr Olansson,

für vorgenanntes FAx vielen Dank. Die verzögerte Beantwortung, bedingt durch eine zweiwöchige Auslandsreise, bitten wir zu entschuldigen.

Die WITT-Prüfeinrichtung 722 gem. Prospektblatt 9/89 wird unverändert hergestellt, neuere Produktinformationen sind daher auch nicht erhältlich.

Wir bieten an:

WITT-Prüfeinrichtung 722
Art.Nr. 101.000010
DM 1.388,--/Stck netto

Spannvorrichtung 743
Art.-Nr. 101.000012
DM 328,--/Stck netto

Lieferzeit: ab Lager

Unsere Preise verstehen sich ab Werk, einschl. Verpackung und sind zahlbar innerhalb 60 Tagen ab Rechnungsdatum etto.

Mit freundlichen Grüßen

C. Köpl
Export Adm. Manager

New vocabulary

das Fax fax
die Prüfeinrichtung testing device
verzögert delayed
die Beantwortung reply
bedingt durch caused by/due to
zweiwöchig of two weeks
die Auslandsreise trip abroad
(sich) entschuldigen to apologize
gem. = gemäß according to
das Prospektblatt leaflet/flyer
unverändert unchanged
die Produktinformation product information
daher therefore
erhältlich available
ab Lager ex warehouse
sich verstehen to be
einschl. = einschließlich inclusive
die Verpackung packing
zahlbar payable
das Rechnungsdatum date of invoice

(a) **Für was dankt Frau Köpl? Für das** ____________

(b) **Was bittet Frau Köpl zu entschuldigen? Die verzögerte** ____________

(c) **Warum ist die Beantwortung verzögert?**
Wegen einer zweiwöchigen ____________

(d) **Was ist nicht erhältlich? Neuere** ____________

(e) **Was ist die Lieferzeit? Ab** ____________

(f) **Wann muß man die Rechnung bezahlen? Innerhalb 60** ____________

Did you know?

Newspapers and business magazines

There is a wide choice of large, quality daily papers, such as the **Frankfurter Allgemeine Zeitung, Frankfurter Rundschau, Stuttgarter Zeitung, Süddeutsche Zeitung** and **Die Welt**. Circulation figures for these range from 250,000 to 450,000. In addition there is a large number of slightly smaller-format dailies with a considerable regional circulation (between 250,000 and 750,000). These include the **Augsburger Allgemeine, B.Z.** (Berlin), **Hamburger Morgenpost, Hannoversche Allgemeine Zeitung, Kölner Stadtanzeiger, Neue Osnabrücker Zeitung, Nürnberger Nachrichten, Rheinische Post** (Düsseldorf), **Westdeutsche Allgemeine Zeitung** (Essen). There are also the truly local papers, with a circulation ranging from 50,000 to 250,000.

WESTDEUTSCHE
ALLGEMEINE

The only truly national popular daily paper is **Die Bildzeitung**, which has a circulation of around 4.5 million and is interested above all in stories that appeal to a mass readership.

The vast majority of German papers call themselves free and independent. But usually the discerning reader can detect some form of political leaning to one of the big parties and/or to more liberal or conservative ways of thinking.

Advertising is a major source of income for all of these papers, and they also provide a means to distribute advertising leaflets. Most of the daily papers have a lot of additional advertising sections on Fridays or Saturdays. The **Frankfurter Allgemeine Zeitung**, for example, occasionally has 100 pages or more of job adverts in one weekend issue. Colour supplements offer additional advertising space, mainly for product advertising. Most dailies also distribute free brochures with the week's radio and television programmes.

All the dailies rely heavily on subscriptions. Deliveries are made through local networks (papers arrive by 7 o'clock in urban areas) or by post.

There are only a few evening papers in Germany now. The two worth mentioning are **Abendzeitung-8-Uhr-Blatt** and **Hamburger Abendblatt**, which are published in Munich and Hamburg respectively.

Süddeutsche Zeitung
MÜNCHNER NEUESTE NACHRICHTEN AUS POLITIK, KULTUR, WIRTSCHAFT UND SPORT

Handelsblatt
WIRTSCHAFTS- UND FINANZZEITUNG

Most of the quality papers carry a very comprehensive business section, with well-informed reports on business affairs, business sectors, companies and products, stock and commodity markets. The one specialized business paper, **Das Handelsblatt**, with a circulation of close to 150,000 is published five times a week and is the official stock-exchange gazette.

Only two of the papers with a nationwide circulation publish a Sunday paper: **Bild am Sonntag** and **Welt am Sonntag**, with a circulation of 2.6 million and 450,000 respectively. In addition there is **Sonntag aktuell**, published in Stuttgart, with a circulation of almost one million. Sports and leisure are the outstanding features in all three of them. There is a small number of fairly intellectual weeklies such as **Die Zeit** (575,000 copies), **Rheinischer Merkur** (125,000 copies) and **Bayernkurier** (168,000 copies), and there are weekly radio and TV magazines.

The 'freebies' distributed at weekly intervals often have a very local bias and are distributed to all the households in their area. Private individuals can place small ads for only a fraction of the price charged by commercial papers. They are also much used for advertising by local businesses.

Apart from this immense field of daily and weekly papers there is a wide range of monthly, sometimes very expensively produced, magazines and journals specializing in politics, business and finance, cars, general interest, leisure, fashion, home, sports, etc. All of them provide ample possibilities for advertising on a national scale; circulation ranges from 150,000 to more than 3.5 million.

Neue Zürcher Zeitung

The most widely read Austrian papers are the **Kurier** and **Neue Kronenzeitung**, both published in Vienna, with a circulation of 440,000 and 1,070,000 respectively. Some of the papers in Austria are more closely affiliated to one of the two big political parties. Of the Swiss German-language newspapers, **Neue Zürcher Zeitung** is probably the most influential nationally and internationally. Other important papers are **Berner Zeitung** and **Der Bund**, both published in Bern, and **Basler Zeitung**, all of which have a circulation of about 120,000.

In the context of press and advertising, it is worth mentioning the advent of new privately and commercially operated television programmes and local radio stations, which has contributed to an enormous increase of advertising in these media.

Your turn to speak

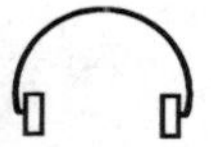

20 You are phoning one of your suppliers and the person you normally deal with is not in the office. Tell the secretary who you are and the company you work for. Ask her to get your regular contact to send you a new catalogue and price list. Explain that you are particularly interested in a certain product and would like to have all the technical data. End on a polite note of thanks. These phrases may be useful:

Mein Name ist ... von der Firma ...
Ich bin ... von der Firma ...
Kann ich vielleicht eine Nachricht hinterlassen?
Kann Herr/Frau ... mir bitte/vielleicht ... zusenden/schicken?
Ich brauche auch noch alle technischen Daten von ...

21 You receive a telephone call from a business customer who is interested in your products. Tell him that you are pleased he is interested in your products and that you will send information material. Explain that it is possible to grant a trade discount, but that depends on the size of the order. Finish by asking your customer whether he has any further questions and for the address of his company.

Ich freue mich, daß Sie sich für unsere ... /Produkte interessieren
Gern schicke ich Ihnen ... zu
Ich schicke/sende Ihnen gern unsere(n) ... (zu)
Ein Wiederverkaufsrabatt ist möglich
Das hängt vom Umfang des Auftrags ab / Das hängt davon ab, wie groß der Auftrag ist
Haben Sie noch weitere Fragen?

Answers

Practise what you have learned

Exercise **1** (a) Anzeige, Zeitung (b) Briefpapier, Visitenkarten (c) Mitarbeiter (d) Idee (e) Termin (f) Anschrift

Exercise **4** *Baumann:* (a), (e), (g), (i); *Liedtke:* (b), (c), (d), (f), (h)

Exercise **5** (a) in der Zeitung *Büro + Design* (b) ein neues Großraumbüro (c) einen Katalog mit Preisliste (d) an Schreibtischen, Bürostühlen und Schreibmaschinentischen (e) der komplette Katalog mit Preisliste (f) die Anschrift angeben

Exercise **6** (a) ii (b) vi (c) i (d) iv, vii (e) iii (f) v

Exercise **8** (a) iii (b) iv (c) v (d) ii (e) vi (f) i (g) vii

Exercise **9** (a) iii (b) iii (c) i (d) iii (e) i (f) iii (g) i (h) iii

Exercise **10** (a) ich wollte, abstimmen (b) ich wollte fragen, vorbeikommen kann (c) sehe ich (d) bin ich, verhindert (e) hat der Chef (f) wäre es, besser (g) nehmen wir

Exercise **13** (a) ii (b) iii (c) i (d) iii (e) i (f) ii

Exercise **14** (a) interessieren (b) beschäftigen (c) kosten (d) beträgt (e) hängt ab (f) erstellen (g) benötige (h) schaffe

Exercise **16** *richtig:* (b), (f), (g); *falsch:* (a), (c), (d), (e), (h)

Grammar

Exercise **17** (a) neu (b) gut (c) detailliert (d) günstig (e) ausführlich (f) fest (g) groß (h) telefonisch

Read and understand

Exercise **18** (a) Sehr geehrte (b) Anfrage (c) Anlage (d) Preisliste (e) Sonderpreis (f) Auftag (g) freundlichem

Exercise **19** (a) Fax (b) Beantwortung (c) Auslandsreise (d) Produktinformation(en) (e) Lager (f) Tagen (ab Rechnungsdatum)

10 GETTING WHAT YOU WANT

You will learn

- to ask for a quotation and negotiate terms
- to obtain information about discounts and after-sales service
- to discuss delivery periods
- to understand product information

and you will be given information about the Chambers of Industry and Commerce in Germany.

Study guide

Dialogue 1 + Practise what you have learned
Dialogue 2 + Practise what you have learned
Dialogue 3 + Practise what you have learned
Make sure you know the **Key words and phrases**
Study the **Grammar** section
Do the exercise in **Read and understand**
Read **Did you know?**
Do the exercises in **Your turn to speak**

Dialogues

1 *Negotiating prices and terms*

Herr Karloff Ja, Herr Waigl. Technisch ist mir jetzt alles klar mit Ihrem Gasmischer BM 2. Aber wie ist denn jetzt bitte der Preis?

Herr Waigl Der Bruttopreis beträgt 1600 D-Mark pro Stück bei Einzellieferung.

Herr Karloff Ist die Mehrwertsteuer im Preis enthalten?

Herr Waigl Nein, die müssen Sie bitte addieren.

Herr Karloff Okay. Wann können Sie liefern?

Herr Waigl Wir können innerhalb von drei Wochen liefern.

Herr Karloff Oh, das ist mir doch etwas lang. Besteht die Möglichkeit, es abzukürzen?

Herr Waigl Das Äußerste, was ich anbieten kann, wären 14 Tage.

Herr Karloff 14 Tage. Gut. Liefern Sie frei Haus oder ... ab Werk?

Herr Waigl Wir liefern generell ab Werk.

Herr Karloff Ah ja. Wieviel Skonto räumen Sie ein, bitte?

Herr Waigl Bei einer Zahlungsweise 10 Tage 2%, sonst 30 Tage netto.

Herr Karloff In Ordnung. Ich werde das prüfen und ich gebe Ihnen in einer Woche Bescheid.

- ➧ **der Bruttopreis** gross price
- ➧ **pro Stück** per unit/piece
- ➧ **die Einzellieferung** supply of single units
- ➧ **innerhalb von** within
- **etwas** here: somewhat
- ➧ **abkürzen** to shorten / cut short
- **das Äußerste** the utmost/best
- **generell** general(ly)

Technisch ist mir jetzt alles klar Lit. 'Technical(ly) is to me now everything clear', i.e. 'Technically I have now understood everything'.

Aber wie ist denn jetzt der Preis? But what about the price now?

Besteht die Möglichkeit ...? Lit. 'Exists the possibility ...?', i.e. 'Would it be possible ...?'

➧ **Ist die Mehrwertsteuer im Preis enthalten?** Is the value added tax included in the price?

Nein, die müssen Sie bitte addieren Lit. 'No, it must you please add'. An unusual but very businesslike phrase. Most Germans would say **Nein, die kommt noch hinzu** (No, it comes in addition).

wären 14 Tage would be a fortnight. **Wäre** (a form of **sein**) indicates a vague possibility. **14 Tage** is a common alternative to **zwei Wochen**.

➧ **frei Haus oder ab Werk** Commercial jargon meaning 'franco domicile or ex works', which are the most and the least advantageous delivery terms for a buyer.

Wieviel Skonto räumen Sie ein? How much cash discount do you give? Note the distinction between **der/das Skonto** (cash discount) and **der Rabatt** (discount).

bei einer Zahlungsweise 10 Tage 2% for payment within 10 days 2%. (The sentence should read **bei Zahlung innerhalb von 10 Tagen 2%.**)

➧ **sonst 30 Tage netto** otherwise 30 days net

Ich werde das prüfen I shall check that. **Prüfen** here means 'to have a good look at'. **Werde ... prüfen** is a form of the future tense (see the grammar summary at the end of the book).

➧ **und ich gebe Ihnen in einer Woche Bescheid** and I'll let you know in a week's time

Practise what you have learned

1 Study the list of words below and make sure you know what they mean. Then cross out those which were *not* mentioned in the dialogue. (Answers on p. 186.)

(a) **Abnahme** (b) **Anfrage** (c) **Angebot** (d) **Auftrag** (e) **Bruttopreis** (f) **Einzellieferung** (g) **Fertigungsprogramm** (h) **Listenpreis** (i) **Mehrwertsteuer** (j) **Menge** (k) **Preisliste** (l) **Rabatt** (m) **Skonto** (n) **Umfang** (o) **Zahlungsweise** (p) **Zusendung**

2 Circle the phrases that occurred in the dialogue. (Answers on p. 186.)

(a) (i) **Bruttopreis pro Stück**
(ii) **Bruttopreis pro Menge**
(iii) **Bruttopreis pro Umfang**

(b) (i) **mit Einzellieferung**
(ii) **bei Einzellieferung**
(iii) **in Einzellieferung**

(c) (i) **Skonto bestellen**
(ii) **Skonto nehmen**
(iii) **Skonto einräumen**

(d) (i) **frei Haus liefern**
(ii) **im Hause liefern**
(iii) **zu Hause liefern**

(e) (i) **Bescheid finden**
(ii) **Bescheid gefallen**
(iii) **Bescheid geben**

(f) (i) **Angebot produzieren**
(ii) **Angebot prüfen**
(iii) **Angebot probieren**

3 Write down the correct beginnings for the sentences below. Say them aloud and then listen to the recording for the correct answers.

(a) ______________________ **ist im Preis nicht enthalten.**
(b) ______________________ **innerhalb von drei Wochen liefern.**
(c) ______________________ **frei Haus oder ab Werk?**
(d) ______________________ **räumen Sie ein?**
(e) ______________________ **von 10 Tagen geben wir 2% Skonto.**

4 Your turn to speak. Take the role of the saleswoman in these negotiations about terms and conditions. Use the prompts.

5 Listen to the dialogue and study the new vocabulary. Decide which of the alternatives in the sentences below are correct. (Answers on p. 186.)

New vocabulary

eindrucksvoll impressive
auf dem neuesten Stand der Technik state of the art
die Produktionsleistung output/production performance
gewähren to grant/give
nicht wahr? isn't/doesn't it?
die Bezahlung payment/settlement
das Rechnungsdatum date of invoice
bis dahin until then

(a) **Die neue Maschine ist ja wirklich sehr** (i) **interessant.** (ii) **eindrucksvoll.**

(b) **Der Preis** (i) **bringt 32.800 Mark.** (ii) **beträgt 32.800 Mark.**

(c) **Sie kaufen eine Maschine auf dem** (i) **fertigen Stand der Technik.** (ii) **neuesten Stand der Technik.**

(d) **Ist vielleicht ein kleiner** (i) **Messerabatt möglich?** (ii) **Wiederverkaufsfrabatt möglich?**

(e) **Wir können Ihnen 5% Messerabatt** (i) **gefallen.** (ii) **gewähren.**

(f) **Dann gibt es noch 3% Skonto bei Bezahlung innerhalb von** (i) **zwei Wochen.** (ii) **zehn Tagen.**

(g) **Ich muß die Angelegenheit noch in der Firma** (i) **durchrufen.** (ii) **durchsprechen.**

Dialogues

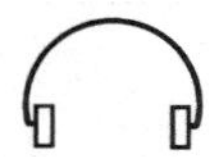

2 *Ordering from the spring collection*

Customer Ja, Frau Köpl. Ihre Frühjahrskollektion gefällt mir sehr gut – insbesondere diese gelb–weiß gestreiften Bermudas. Von denen möchte ich gerne 10.000 Stück bestellen. Wie sieht das mit dem Preis aus?

Frau Köpl Bei 10.000 Stück – 15 Mark pro Stück.

Customer Unter der Bedingung müßten Sie mir aber einen guten Mengenrabatt einräumen.

Frau Köpl Mhm, na gut, weil Sie's sind – 10%.

Customer Das ist mir ein bißchen wenig.

Frau Köpl Zusätzlich könnte ich noch das Skonto erhöhen von zwei auf drei Prozent.

Customer Unter diesen Bedingungen bin ich damit einverstanden. Und wie sieht das mit den Lieferfristen aus?

Frau Köpl Acht Wochen müssen Sie rechnen.

Customer Einverstanden. Und wie sieht das mit den Zahlungsbedingungen aus?

Frau Köpl Ja, wie gesagt, Lieferung ab Werk, einschließlich Verpackung, 3% Skonto bei Zahlung innerhalb von 10 Tagen.

Customer Sie werden in den nächsten Tagen von mir hören.

Frau Köpl Gut. Ich würde mich freuen, wenn Sie den Auftrag erteilen könnten. Wiederseh(e)n.

Customer Auf Wiedersehen, Frau Köpl.

insbesondere especially
gelb–weiß gestreift yellow-and-white striped
➧ **zusätzlich** in addition / additionally
➧ **die Zahlungsbedingungen** terms of payment
➧ **die Lieferung** delivery/shipment/supply
einschließlich inclusive
➧ **die Verpackung** pack(ag)ing
➧ **die Zahlung** payment

Ihre Frühjahrskollektion gefällt mir sehr gut I like your spring collection very much. In the garments industry, **die Kollektion** refers to a range of textiles.

von denen of those

➧ **Unter der Bedingung müßten Sie mir einen guten Rabatt einräumen** Lit. 'Under that condition must you to me a good discount grant', i.e. 'If you want such a high price you ought to give me a good discount'. **Unter der Bedingung, daß ...** (on condition that ...) is a very useful phrase.

Weil Sie's sind Because it's you. **Sie's** is short for **Sie es**.

➧ **Das ist mir ein bißchen wenig** Lit. 'That is to me a little little', i.e. 'That's not really enough for me'. A phrase commonly used to express dissatisfaction with a concession.

➧ **das Skonto erhöhen** to increase the cash discount

➧ **Unter diesen Bedingungen bin ich damit einverstanden** On these conditions I agree

Acht Wochen müssen Sie rechnen You must reckon with eight weeks. Note that **rechnen** has two different meanings: 'to calculate/do sums' and 'to reckon with/count on'.

➧ **Ja, wie gesagt, ...** Well, as I said ... A useful phrase to introduce a summary of the main points of the negotiations.

➧ **Lieferung ab Werk, ... 10 Tagen** Delivery ex factory, packing included, 3% discount for payment within 10 days. These are standard terms of payment and delivery.

➧ **Sie werden in den nächsten Tagen von mir hören** I'll let you know in the next few days (lit. You will in the next days from me hear)

➧ **den Auftrag erteilen** to place an order

Practise what you have learned

6 Can you remember what was said in the dialogue? Match the questions and answers. (Answers on p. 186.)

(a) **Was gefällt der Kundin?**
(b) **Wieviele Bermudas möchte sie bestellen?**
(c) **Was soll Frau Köpl ihr einräumen?**
(d) **Was will Frau Köpl zusätzlich noch tun?**
(e) **Wie lang ist die Lieferfrist?**
(f) **Welche Bedingungen will die Kundin noch wissen?**
(g) **Wann gibt es 3% Skonto?**

(i) **die Frühjahrskollektion**
(ii) **einen guten Mengenrabatt**
(iii) **das Skonto auf 3% erhöhen**
(iv) **10.000 Stück**
(v) **acht Wochen**
(vi) **bei Zahlung innerhalb von 10 Tagen**
(vii) **die Zahlungsbedingungen**

7 Answer the questions on the recording in full sentences. Use the prompts.

8 Study the new vocabulary before you listen to the dialogue on the recording. Then do the word puzzle below, answering the questions in German. The tinted boxes will provide the answer to the last question. (Answers on p. 186.)

New vocabulary

die Herbstkollektion autumn collection
besser better
durchgehen to go through
rechnen to calculate/add up
der Auftragswert order value
drin sein to be possible
mehr more
das Herbstgeschäft autumn trade
der Eilauftrag urgent order

(a) What has the client already seen?
(b) What does the client want to talk about?
(c) For which season are the goods intended?
(d) In what currency are the goods priced?
(e) Which period is 6–8 weeks?
(f) In which outlet will the goods be sold?

(g) What is it that amounts to 22%?

(a) (b) (c) (d) (e) (f)

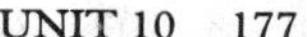

Dialogues

3 *Repairs and spare parts*

Frau Heinrich Heinrich.

Herr Schubert Guten Tag, Frau Heinrich. Hier ist Schubert von der Firma Kranz. Ich habe gestern Ihr Angebot erhalten. Und ich möchte mich jetzt gern noch mal über die Ersatzteilsituation und -versorgung mit Ihnen unterhalten.

Frau Heinrich Ersatzteile sind überhaupt kein Problem. Wir haben von allen Teilen immer ein ausreichendes Lager im Hause.

Herr Schubert Und Sie könnten auch einen 24-Stunden-Service mit ausgebildeten Servicetechnikern garantieren?

Frau Heinrich Selbstverständlich. Wir haben fünf Außendienstmitarbeiter, die immer zur Verfügung stehen – ausschließlich für Reparaturen und sonstige Kundendienstarbeiten.

Herr Schubert Ja, denn dieser Faktor wäre für uns sehr wichtig. Wissen Sie, wir können uns keinerlei Produktionsausfall erlauben und müssen dann auf ein sehr sicheres Produkt und auf eine sehr sichere Ersatzteilversorgung zurückgreifen können.

Frau Heinrich Unsere Außendienstmitarbeiter haben alle Telefon im Auto, so daß sie sehr schnell direkt zu Ihnen geschickt werden können.

Herr Schubert Ja, Frau Heinrich, das klingt sehr beruhigend. Ich denke, daß ich Ihnen dann innerhalb der nächsten Woche unseren Auftrag erteilen kann.

Frau Heinrich Das wäre sehr schön, Herr Schubert, da würde ich mich freuen.

Herr Schubert Gut, Frau Heinrich. Ich bedanke mich vielmals. Auf Wiederhören.

Frau Heinrich Ich danke auch. Auf Wiederhör(e)n.

die Ersatzteilsituation spare-parts situation
➧ **die Ersatzteilversorgung** spare-parts supply
➧ **sich unterhalten** to discuss / talk (about)
➧ **das Ersatzteil** spare part
ausreichend sufficient
➧ **der 24-Stunden-Service** 24-hour service
➧ **garantieren** to guarantee
ausschließlich exclusive(ly)
➧ **die Reparatur** repair (work)
sonstig other
➧ **die Kundendienstarbeit** service and repair work
der Faktor factor
keinerlei no ... at all
das Auto car

➧ **Ich habe gestern Ihr Angebot erhalten** I (have) received your offer yesterday.

Ersatzteile sind überhaupt kein Problem Spare parts are no problem at all

ein ausreichendes Lager im Hause sufficient stocks (lit. a sufficient stock in house). **Lager** can mean 'warehouse' as well as 'stocks'.

➧ **Sie könnten auch ... garantieren?** You would also be able to guarantee ...?

Wir können uns keinerlei Produktionsausfall erlauben We cannot afford any loss of output

und müssen dann auf ein sehr sicheres Produkt und auf eine sehr sichere Ersatzteilversorgung zurückgreifen können and (we) must be able to fall back on a secure product and a very secure supply of spare parts

➧ **mit ausgebildeten Servicetechnikern** with trained service engineers

so daß sie sehr schnell direkt zu Ihnen geschickt werden können so that they can very quickly be sent to you directly

➧ **Da würde ich mich freuen** Lit. 'There would I myself please', i.e. 'I would be very pleased about that'.

➧ **Ich bedanke mich vielmals** I thank you very much indeed (fairly formal)

Practise what you have learned

9 Build sentences by pairing up the phrases in the first list with those in the second. (Answers on p. 186.)

1. (a) **Mit dem Angebot bin ich ...**
   (b) **Wir haben von allen Teilen ...**
   (c) **Fünf von unseren Außendienstmitarbeitern ...**
   (d) **Dieser Faktor ...**
   (e) **Einen Produktionsausfall ...**
   (f) **Deswegen müssen wir ...**
   (g) **Unsere Außendienstmitarbeiter haben ...**
   (h) **Innerhalb der nächsten Woche ...**

2. (i) **... alle Telefon im Auto.**
   (ii) **... stehen ausschließlich für Kundendienstarbeiten zur Verfügung.**
   (iii) **... können wir uns nicht erlauben.**
   (iv) **... immer ein ausreichendes Lager.**
   (v) **... auf ein sicheres Produkt zurückgreifen können.**
   (vi) **... kann ich Ihnen dann unseren Auftrag erteilen.**
   (vii) **... eigentlich einverstanden.**
   (viii) **... wäre für uns sehr wichtig.**

10 Can you work out what Frau Heinrich and Herr Schubert said in the dialogue? Give the German equivalent of the following sentences. Listen to the dialogue again to check your answers.

(a) I would now like to talk to you again about the spare parts situation.
(b) Spare parts are no problem at all.
(c) We always have sufficient stocks of all parts.
(d) We have five field workers who are always available.
(e) We cannot afford any loss of output.
(f) Our field workers all have a phone in the car.
(g) I think I can give you our order within the next week.

11 Your turn to speak. Use the prompts to practise some useful phrases.

12 Some of the material in this unit has been quite difficult, so this exercise takes you back a few units to give you a breather. Listen to the message on the telephone answering machine and then answer the questions below. (Answers on p. 186.)

New vocabulary
bezüglich regarding/concerning
Angebot über offer for
die Ortsdurchwahl local number
müßte would have to
das Autohaus car dealer

(a) **Was hat Herr Jansen in der Zeitung gesehen? Die** ____________

(b) **Was möchte Herr Jansen haben?**

Ein ____

(c) **Was muß auch noch erscheinen?**

Die ____

Key words and phrases

Ich habe Ihr Angebot erhalten	I have received your offer
Besteht die Möglichkeit, ...?	Would it be possible to ...?
einen Rabatt einräumen	to give/grant a discount
Ist die Mehrwertsteuer im Preis enthalten?	Is value added tax included in the price?
die Lieferfrist abkürzen	to shorten the delivery period
Das ist ein bißchen wenig	That's not really enough
den/das Skonto erhöhen	to increase the cash discount
Unter diesen Bedingungen bin ich damit einverstanden	On these conditions I agree
unter der Bedingung, daß ...	on condition that ...
wie gesagt	as I said
Da würde ich mich freuen	I would be very pleased about that
Ich bedanke mich vielmals	I thank you very much
frei Haus oder ab Werk	franco domicile or ex works
Lieferung ab Werk einschließlich Verpackung	delivery ex works packing included
bei einer Zahlungsweise innerhalb von 10 Tagen 2% Skonto	2% discount for payment within 10 days
30 Tage netto	30 days net
den Auftrag erteilen	to place/give the order
Ich gebe Ihnen Bescheid	I'll let you know
Sie werden in den nächsten Tagen von mir hören	I'll let you know in the next few days
der Bruttopreis	gross price
pro Stück	per unit/piece
die Abnahme	purchase
die Lieferung	delivery/supply/shipment
die Einzellieferung	supply of single units
die Verpackung	packing/packaging
der/das Skonto	cash discount
der Rabatt	discount/reduction
die Zahlungsbedingungen (pl.)	terms of payment
die Zahlung	payment
wenig	little
zusätzlich	additional(ly)
zur Verfügung stehen	to be available
sich unterhalten	to discuss / talk about
sich bedanken	to say thank you / thank
garantieren	to guarantee
das Ersatzteil	spare part
die Ersatzteilversorgung	spare-parts supply
der Servicetechniker	service engineer
die Kundendienstarbeit	service and repair work
der 24-Stunden-Service	24-hour service
die Technik	technique/technology
der Produktionsausfall	loss of production/output

Grammar

More about adjectives

Adjectives are necessary if you want to make comparisons:

Der Bahnhof in Bochum ist kleiner als der Bahnhof in Düsseldorf.
The station in Bochum is smaller than the station in Düsseldorf.

Die Stadt Bochum ist größer als die Stadt Witten.
The town of Bochum is bigger than the town of Witten.

The comparative form of the adjective is usually formed by adding the ending **-er** to the basic form of the adjective. In some cases, especially in adjectives of one syllable, the vowels **a, o** and **u** change into **ä, ö** and **ü** respectively. For example, **groß** → **größer; lang** → **länger**; and **kurz** → **kürzer.**

If you want to make a comparison between *more than two* elements, you use the form of the adjective known as the superlative:

Berlin ist die größte Stadt in Deutschland.
Berlin is the biggest town in Germany.

Der Rhein ist der längste Fluß in Deutschland.
The Rhine is the longest river in Germany.

The superlative is formed by adding the ending **-te** or **-ste** to the basic form of the adjective: **groß** → **größte; klein** → **kleinste**. With adjectives ending in **d, t, s, ß, z** and **st** the superlative ending is **-est**, e.g.: **naß** (wet) → **naßeste; rasch** (quick) → **rascheste; dicht** (dense) → **dichteste**. Some forms are irregular, e.g. **gut, besser, beste.**

As with the basic adjective (see Unit 9, p. 166), both the comparative and the superlative adjectives may change their endings when they come in front of a noun.

13 Write down the comparative and superlative forms of the adjectives listed below. (Answers on p. 186.)

Example: **ruhig – ruhiger – ruhigste**

einfach – einfacher – einfachste
sicher – sicherer – sicherste

	Comparative	*Superlative*
direkt		
interessant		
leicht		
richtig		
schlecht		

14 Translate these sentences into English. Some will be familiar from the dialogues. (Answers on p. 186.)

(a) **Ich glaube, dies ist von allen die sicherste Maschine.**

____

(b) **Dies ist das schlechteste Angebot von allen.**

____

(c) **Das ist das ruhigste Zimmer im Hotel.**

____

(d) **Der 21. Juni ist der längste Tag im Jahr.**

____

(e) **Sie sind einer unseren besseren Kunden.**

____

(f) **Wir können einen größeren Rabatt geben.**

____

Adverbs

An adverb is linked to a verb and not to a noun: the *fast* train (adjective); the train travels *fast* (adverb). Adverbs are often derived from adjectives and, in fact, have the same form as adjectives. But they don't take any adjective endings. They may, however, be transformed into comparatives and superlatives and then they use the same forms as the adjectives we've just discussed. For example:

schnell fast	**schneller** faster	**am schnellsten** fastest
hoch high	**höher** higher	**am höchsten** highest
viel much	**mehr** more	**am meisten** most

Read and understand

(a)

Mit einem guten Partner geht alles!
zuverlässig
schnell
preiswert
DER BLITZKURIER
D. HERZIG
Telefon (02 34) 59 50 36 · Telefax (02 34) 59 27 82

Für das Personal sorgen wir

WP

☎ 02 34 / 6 02 89

Zeitpersonal für Büro, Industrie und Technik
Personal-Anzeigen-Service
Suche und Auswahl von Fach- und Führungskräften

(b)

(c)

Restaurant Alt Nürnberg

NEUE FRANZÖSISCHE KÜCHE

NEUE DEUTSCHE KÜCHE

Öffnungszeiten: 18.00 – 02.00 Uhr
Küche: 18.00 – 24.00 Uhr
Montag Ruhetag

Am Schauspielhaus, Königsallee 16, Telefon 31 16 98

New vocabulary

der Partner partner
zuverlässig reliable
schnell fast
preiswert reasonable prices / good value
der Blitzkurier lightning courier
das Personal staff/personnel
das Zeitpersonal temporary staff
die Industrie industry
der Personalanzeigenservice service for recruitment advertisements
die Suche search
die Fachkraft skilled worker
die Führungskraft executive manager
die Küche cooking/cuisine
die Öffnungszeiten opening/ business hours

15 What do the advertisements say? Tick the correct version. (Answers on p. 186.)

(a) **Im Restaurant Alt Nürnberg gibt es neue**
- (i) **finnische Küche.**
- (ii) **schweizerische Küche.**
- (iii) **französische Küche.**

(b) **Die Firma WP sucht**
- (i) **Fach- und Führungskräfte.**
- (ii) **Bürokaufleute.**
- (iii) **Auszubildende.**

(c) **Der Blitzkurier arbeitet**
- (i) **normal und richtig.**
- (ii) **schnell und preiswert.**
- (iii) **korrekt und teuer.**

Did you know?

Chambers of Industry and Commerce in Germany

Establishing business contacts, let alone business itself, in a foreign country is always a major undertaking. Fortunately, there are a number of government and trade bodies which can provide information, give useful addresses and in some cases even give direct help. The ministries at both federal and regional level provide literature describing the possibilities for entering new markets, giving practical advice and useful addresses. At regional, district and certainly at local level, there are offices or local government departments specifically set up to provide help with the location of new industries and the promotion of trade generally (e.g. **Kommunalverband Ruhr**, which is the association of local authorities in the Ruhr district, or the local **Amt für Wirtschaftsförderung**, 'office for the promotion of the (local) economy'). Such bodies will probably provide only general or location- or industry-specific advice; they are unlikely to be able to help you establish direct business contacts.

Industrie- und Handelskammer zu Bochum

The most immediate help in this respect is likely to come from the representative bodies of trade and industry themselves, such as the local **Industrie- und Handelskammer** or **IHK** (Chamber of Industry and Commerce), the **Handwerkskammer** (Chamber of Crafts, or Guilds) and other trade or professional bodies. At the Chamber of Commerce there are experts who not only know the local market, but are also able to help you make initial contact with institutions and, in some cases, with companies. You can also expect to be given a wide range of publications providing general information about the infrastructure of the area, its industrial and commercial base and the employment situation. The Chambers of Commerce often facilitate contacts between business people by publishing lists of services offered/required by other companies and of companies seeking joint ventures. Some organize a kind of contact fair for companies. There are a variety of names for these: **Kooperationsbörse**, **Existenzgründerbörse**, **Beteiligungsbörse**. They may also make available information about industrial or office property for sale or to let.

As German banks often work closely with business enterprises, they may in some cases be willing to give useful hints.

The Yellow Pages (**die gelben Seiten**) or the trade directories (**Branchenbücher**) provide useful addresses. Finally it might be helpful to approach your national trade federations with a view to obtaining relevant information or their counterparts in Germany, Austria and Switzerland. They certainly have a good insight into the trading conditions in their respective sectors.

It is obvious that none of these contacts will lead to quick-fix solutions to your queries. No one can do this part of market research for you. But you should be able to obtain a good deal of information and advice about entering new markets in Germany.

Your turn to speak

16

You are a sales representative. A German customer has asked you about the price and the delivery period for your product. You explain that the delivery period is four weeks and, unfortunately, you cannot shorten it.

Der Preis für ... beträgt ...
... kostet ... pro Stück / das Stück
Bei einer Bestellung von ... und mehr ...
Der Wiederverkaufsrabatt beträgt ... Prozent
Wir können die Artikel sofort / ab Lager liefern
Die Lieferzeit zur Zeit ist ... Tage/Wochen
Wir haben ... Tage/Wochen Lieferzeit
Die Lieferfrist kann ich leider nicht abkürzen

17

Your German customer has been pressing you for better terms. As this is an unusually big order, you agree to grant him a higher trade discount this time, that is to say 22% instead of 20%.

Der Rabatt ist schon sehr hoch, aber ...
Weil Sie ein guter Kunde sind ...
Weil es eine größere Bestellung ist ...
Ich kann den (Wiederverkaufs)Rabatt um 2 Prozent erhöhen
Ich kann Ihnen einen höheren (Wiederverkaufs)Rabatt von 22 Prozent einräumen/geben
Mehr kann ich aber wirklich nicht tun

Answers

Practise what you have learned

Exercise 1 You should have crossed out: (a), (b), (c), (d), (g), (h), (j), (k), (l), (n), (p)

Exercise 2 (a) i (b) ii (c) iii (d) i (e) iii (f) ii

Exercise 5 (a) ii (b) ii (c) ii (d) i (e) ii (f) ii (g) ii

Exercise 6 (a) i (b) iv (c) ii (d) iii (e) v (f) vii (g) vi

Exercise 8 (a) Ware (b) Auftrag (c) Herbst (d) Mark (e) Lieferfrist (f) Geschäft (g) Rabatt

Exercise 9 (a) vii (b) iv (c) ii (d) viii (e) iii (f) v (g) i (h) vi

Exercise 12 (a) Annonce (b) Angebot über 500 Visitenkarten (c) Adresse des Autohauses Brandes (GmbH & Co. KG.)

Grammar

Exercise 13 direkt – direkter – direkteste; interessant – interessanter – interessanteste; leicht – leichter – leichteste; richtig – richtiger – richtigste; schlecht – schlechter – schlechteste

Exercise 14 (a) I think this is the safest machine of all (b) This is the worst of all the offers (c) That is the quietest room in the hotel (d) 21 June is the longest day of the year (e) You are one of our better customers (f) We can give a bigger discount

Read and understand

Exercise 15 (a) iii (b) i (c) ii

11 TALKING ABOUT THE PAST

You will learn

- to discuss delivery problems
- to talk informally about your work and holiday/vacation
- to talk in greater detail about the activities of your company
- to understand a job advertisement and a job application

and you will also be given some information about professional training and qualifications in the German-speaking countries.

Study guide

Dialogue 1 + Practise what you have learned
Dialogue 2 + Practise what you have learned
Dialogue 3 + Practise what you have learned
Dialogue 4 + Practise what you have learned
Make sure you know the **Key words and phrases**
Study the **Grammar** section
Note the useful phrases in **Read and understand**
Read **Did you know?**
Do the exercises in **Your turn to speak**

Cochem Castle on the river Moselle, popular with holiday-makers

Dialogues

1 *Delivery problems*

Herr Weimann Ja, da kann ich Ihnen noch eine Geschichte erzählen. Ein Kunde benötigte dringend Ersatzteile für seine ausgefallene Maschine. Ich hab(e) die Produktion angewiesen, Überstunden zu fahren, der Versand hat bis in die Nacht gewartet, um die Teile einzupacken. Dann kam der Spediteur und hat das Ganze an eine falsche Adresse gebracht.

Herr Kern Um Gottes willen, da hat der Spediteur offensichtlich Mist gebaut.

Herr Weimann Das können Sie wohl so sagen. Und vor allen Dingen: der Kunde hat mir ein Riesentheater gemacht.

Herr Kern Ja, und konnten Sie das Problem nachher lösen?

Herr Weimann Ja, wir haben natürlich erst einige Tage später davon erfahren, weil die Teile ja solange woanders waren.

Herr Kern Ja, das kann ich mir gut vorstellen.

➧ **das Lieferproblem** delivery problem
die Geschichte story
erzählen to tell
➧ **einpacken** to pack
➧ **der Spediteur** forwarder/carrier
➧ **das Ganze** everything
offensichtlich obviously
vor allen Dingen above all
natürlich of course / naturally
erst only

Ja, da kann ich Ihnen noch eine Geschichte erzählen Lit. 'Yes, there can I you another story tell'. This is a typical way of introducing a story.

➧ **Ein Kunde benötigte dringend Ersatzteile** A customer urgently needed spare parts. **Benötigte** is a past tense form of **benötigen**, 'to need/require'.

➧ **für seine ausgefallene Maschine** for his broken-down machine. **Ausfallen** means 'to break down'.

➧ **Ich hab(e) die Produktion angewiesen, Überstunden zu fahren** I (have) instructed the production department to work overtime. **Habe ... angewiesen** is the perfect tense of **anweisen**, 'to instruct/order' (see the grammar section). It is fairly common in German to use an activity as a label for a business unit, e.g. **die Produktion** (production department), **die Buchhaltung** (book-keeping department). **Überstunden fahren** (lit. to go over-hours) is a colloquial form of **Überstunden machen** (to do overtime).

hat gewartet (has) waited, from **warten**, 'to wait'. This is another example of the perfect tense.

kam came – past tense form of **kommen**.

hat ... gebracht (has) taken, from **bringen**, 'to bring/take'.

um Gottes willen good God / by God. An expression of surprise in this context.

Da hat der Spediteur offensichtlich Mist gebaut The forwarder (has) obviously made a mess of things then. **Mist** literally means 'dung', but is often colloquially used to mean 'mess'; **Mist bauen** is 'to make a mess' (colloquial).

Das können Sie wohl so sagen You can say that again (lit. That can you well so say).

Der Kunde hat mir ein Riesentheater gemacht The customer (has) kicked up quite a fuss. **Ein Theater machen** means 'to kick up a fuss'.

➧ **das Problem lösen** to solve the problem

Wir haben natürlich erst einige Tage später davon erfahren Lit. 'We have, of course, only a few days later about it learnt'.

Das kann ich mir gut vorstellen I can very well imagine that. **Sich etwas vorstellen** means 'to imagine something'.

Practise what you have learned

1 See if you can complete these sentences. (Answers on p. 204.)

(a) ________________________ **dringend Ersatzteile für seine ausgefallene Maschine.**

(b) ________________________ **Überstunden zu machen.**

(c) **Um Gottes willen,** ________________________ **offensichtlich Mist gebaut.**

(d) ________________________ **mir ein Riesentheater gemacht.**

(e) ________________________ **erst einige Tage später davon erfahren.**

2 Form phrases from the dialogue by linking the appropriate words in the lists below. (Answers on p. 204.)

(a) **eine Geschichte**	(i) **lösen**
(b) **Ersatzteile**	(ii) **bringen**
(c) **Mist**	(iii) **fahren**
(d) **ein Problem**	(iv) **benötigen**
(e) **Teile**	(v) **erzählen**
(f) **an die falsche Adresse**	(vi) **bauen**
(g) **Überstunden**	(vii) **einpacken**

3 Your turn to speak. Explain what happened to a customer's order. Use the prompts.

4 Listen to the recording and then match the questions on the left with the answers on the right. (Answers on p. 204.) But first study the new vocabulary.

New vocabulary

letzte last
mir wurde ganz warm I had quite a shock
drohen to threaten
die Stornierung cancellation
die Lieferschwierigkeit supply difficulty
der Vorlieferant supplier
der Streik strike
deshalb therefore
rechtzeitig in time
der Druck pressure
ausüben to exercise/use
so schnell wie möglich as quickly as possible
der Fall case
der Zulieferer sub-supplier
mehrfach several times
draufsetzen to let down (colloquial)

(a) **Mit was drohte der Kunde?**	(i) **Beim Vorlieferanten.**
(b) **Welche Probleme hatte die Firma?**	(ii) **Lieferschwierigkeiten.**
(c) **Wo gab es die Probleme?**	(iii) **Mit der Stornierung des Auftrags.**
(d) **Welche Schwierigkeit hatte der Vorlieferant?**	(iv) **Den Vorlieferanten anrufen.**
(e) **Was mußte die Einkäuferin sofort tun?**	(v) **Der hatte einen Streik im Hause.**

Dialogues

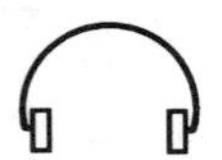

2 *Stress at work*

Herr Kemper Ach, meine Familie, die kennt mich langsam auch nicht mehr. Die Hektik und der Streß der vergangenen Monate ist langsam nicht mehr schön.

Herr Hansen Ja, du hattest, glaub(e) ich, viel mit der Messe zu tun, ja?

Herr Kemper Ja, ich war sehr engagiert auf der 'Schweißen + Schneiden' hier in Essen. Es war sehr viel vorzubereiten. Und parallel mußte ich dann noch einige Kunden im Ausland besuchen. Du weißt, unser neues Produkt mußte vorgestellt werden. Und das erforderte natürlich auch noch sehr viel Zeit.

Herr Hansen Ja, du, das geht mir ja ganz ähnlich. Wie du weißt, hab(e) ich ja die Abteilung gewechselt. Und dort hat man mir als erste Aufgabe gestellt, den Katalog zu überarbeiten. Da mußt(e) ich mit dem Drucker reden. Da mußte ein komplett neues Layout erstellt werden; dann mit der Graphikanstalt. Das war schon ziemlich stressig.

Herr Kemper Ja, ich kann mir vorstellen, das sind einige sehr wichtige Besprechungen, die Ihr machen mußtet. Naja, ich denke, der Streß hat jetzt wahrscheinlich bald ein Ende, und wir können uns ein bißchen auf ruhigere Zeiten freuen.

Herr Hansen Ja. Urlaub steht vor der Tür.

vergangen past
engagiert busy/committed
parallel parallel / at the same time
im Ausland abroad/overseas
➧ **überarbeiten** to revise
der Drucker printer/printer's
die Graphikanstalt the printer's / printing works
ziemlich quite
wahrscheinlich probably

➧ **Meine Familie, die kennt mich langsam auch nicht mehr** My family hardly knows me anymore (lit. My family it knows me slowly also not more). This phrase, like much of the conversation, is colloquial.

die Hektik und der Streß the hectic rush and the stress

Du hattest ... viel mit der Messe zu tun, ja? You had a lot of work to do (in connection) with the fair, didn't you? It's the intonation of **ja** that turns this statement into a question.

auf der 'Schweißen + Schneiden' Lit. 'at the Welding + Cutting'. In Germany, fairs are often referred to in this way.

➧ **Es war sehr viel vorzubereiten** There was a lot to be prepared. **Es gab viel vorzubereiten** is a more common way of saying this.

Unser neues Produkt mußte vorgestellt werden Our new product had to be introduced. Don't worry about this rather complicated passive construction. You could say the same using an **ich**-construction such as **Ich mußte unser neues Produkt vorstellen**.

➧ **Das erforderte natürlich auch noch sehr viel Zeit** Lit. 'That required of course also still very much time'. The key words are **Zeit** (time) and **erfordern** (to require).

➧ **Das geht mir ja ganz ähnlich** It's much the same with me

➧ **Dort hat man mir als erste Aufgabe gestellt ...** There as my first task I was given the job of ... **Die Aufgabe** means 'task/job', and 'to set a task' is **eine Aufgabe stellen**.

ein komplett neues Layout a completely new layout. **Komplett** is used as an adverb and therefore does not take any ending (as explained in the grammar section in Unit 10).

Das war schon ziemlich stressig That was really quite stressful

die Ihr machen mußtet which you had to make

Der Streß hat ... bald ein Ende The stress will soon come to an end. The adverb **bald** indicates that this refers to the future, even though the verb is in the present tense.

Urlaub steht vor der Tür Holidays are around the corner (lit '... stand in front of the door').

Practise what you have learned

5 Using the phrases from the box below, complete the following sentences. (Answers on p. 204.)

(a) ____________________ **und** ________________ **ist nicht mehr schön.**

(b) **Herr Kemper hatte viel** ____________________________ **zu tun.**

(c) **Herr Kemper mußte** __________________________________ **besuchen.**

(d) **Herr Hansen hat** ______________________________ **gewechselt.**

(e) **Herrn Hansens** ________________ **war, den Katalog zu überarbeiten.**

(f) **Herr Hansen mußte** _________________________ **reden.**

(g) **Herr Kemper und Herr Hansen freuen sich auf** ________________

(h) ___________________________________**steht vor der Tür.**

Kunden im Ausland **die Abteilung** **ruhigere Zeiten** **der Urlaub** **die Hektik** **erste Aufgabe** **mit der Messe** **der Stress** **mit dem Drucker**

6 Use the dialogue to find the German equivalents for these phrases. (Answers on p. 204.)

(a) I can imagine ... ________________________________

(b) I was very busy. ________________________________

(c) That was quite stressful. ________________________________

(d) of the past few months ________________________________

(e) There was very much to be prepared. ________________________________

(f) That required much time. ________________________________

(g) We can look forward to quieter times. ________________________________

(h) some very important meetings ________________________________

7 Your turn to speak. Take the role of the English businesswoman Mrs Swift, but speak in German, using the prompts. **Entwickeln** means 'to develop'.

Continued on next page.

8 Have a look at the new vocabulary before you listen to the dialogue on the recording. Then indicate what the people actually said by circling the appropriate phrase. (Answers on p. 204.)

New vocabulary
schlimm bad
die Panne breakdown
Warum? Why?
verärgert annoyed

(a) **War dieser** (i) **Sommer für Sie auch so stressig?**
(ii) **Winter für Sie auch so stressig?**
(iii) **Herbst für Sie auch so stressig?**

(b) **Das war wirklich ganz** (i) **schlecht.**
(ii) **schlimm.**
(iii) **schräg.**

(c) **Wir hatten verschiedene technische** (i) **Pannen.**
(ii) **Probleme.**
(iii) **Schwierigkeiten.**

(d) **Was haben die Kunden dazu** (i) **gedacht?**
(ii) **gemacht?**
(iii) **gesagt?**

(e) **Sie wollten alle ihre** (i) **Ware sofort haben.**
(ii) **Sachen sofort haben.**
(iii) **Produkte sofort haben.**

(f) (i) **Später bekamen wir falsche Ersatzteile.**
(ii) **Erst bekamen wir falsche Ersatzteile.**
(iii) **Dann bekamen wir falsche Ersatzteile.**

(g) **Ich habe immer wieder bei** (i) **der Abteilung angerufen.**
(ii) **dem Chef angerufen.**
(iii) **der Firma angerufen.**

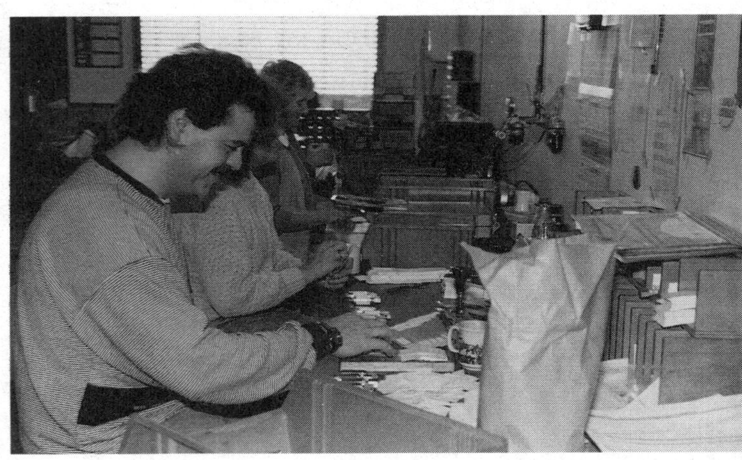

Dialogues

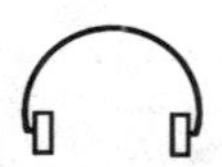

3 *What did you do in the summer?*

Herr Krause Was haben Sie im Urlaub getan?
Herr Stein Oh ja. Ich war das erste Mal auf Malta.
Herr Krause Auf Malta? Wie schön.
Herr Stein Ja, das hat mir wirklich sehr gut gefallen.
Herr Krause War es das erste Mal, daß Sie dort waren?
Herr Stein Ja, das war das erste Mal.
Herr Krause Und warum haben Sie Malta gewählt?
Herr Stein Das wurd(e) mir empfohlen wegen des milden Klimas. Nur leider war es dann nachher doch sehr heiß dort.
Herr Krause Sie sind mit Ihrer Frau, mit Ihrer Familie dort gewesen?
Herr Stein Ja, ich bin mit meiner Familie gefahren, auch mit den Kindern. Und das war auch der Grund, weshalb wir in der Hauptreisezeit und damit auch in der Hochsaison mitten im Sommer fahren mußten. Was haben Sie im Urlaub gemacht?
Herr Krause Ich bin in Schottland gewesen.
Herr Stein Oh, interessant. Wo denn in Schottland?
Herr Krause Ich bin ganz durch Schottland gefahren, sozusagen einmal an der Westküste hoch und an der Ostküste wieder runter.
Herr Stein Haben Sie sich einen Mietwagen genommen?
Herr Krause Nein, ich bin mit dem eigenen Wagen gefahren.
Herr Stein Und wo haben Sie jeweils übernachtet?
Herr Krause In Gasthäusern und privat.
Herr Stein Das klingt sehr gut.

mild mild
nachher later (on)
▸ **das Kind** child
▸ **die Hauptreisezeit** peak holiday season
▸ **die Hochsaison** peak season
sozusagen so to speak
der Wagen car

Now turn over for the notes to dialogue 3.

- **Was haben Sie im Urlaub getan?** What did you do in your holidays/vacation? **Getan** is the past participle form of **tun** 'to do'. Most people would say **Was haben Sie im Urlaub gemacht?** (used later in the dialogue).
- **Das hat mir wirklich sehr gut gefallen** I really liked/enjoyed it very much. Here again the perfect tense is used to tell about a personal experience. (For more on the perfect tense, see the grammar section in this unit.)

gewählt is the past participle form of **wählen,** 'to choose'.

- **Das wurd(e) mir empfohlen wegen des milden Klimas** It was recommended to me because of the mild climate. **Empfohlen** comes from **empfehlen**, 'to recommend', and **wegen** means 'because of'.

Nur leider war es dann nachher doch sehr heiß dort Lit. 'Only unfortunately was it then later after all very hot there.' In sentences like this you just need to pick out the key words in order to get the meaning: **leider** (unfortunately), **nachher** (afterwards), **heiß** (hot).

- **mitten im Sommer** in the middle of the summer

Das war auch der Grund, weshalb ... That was also the reason why ...

Ich bin ganz durch Schottland gefahren Lit. 'I am whole through Scotland driven', i.e. I (have) toured the whole of Scotland.

an der Westküste hoch und an der Ostküste wieder runter up the west coast and then back down the east coast

- **Haben Sie sich einen Mietwagen genommen?** Did you rent a car? (lit. Have you yourself a rented car taken?). A common alternative is **Haben Sie ein Auto gemietet?**, using the verb **mieten,** 'to rent/hire'.

Wo haben Sie jeweils übernachtet? Where did you spend the nights? **Übernachten** means 'to spend the night', and **jeweils** means 'each time'.

In Gasthäusern und privat In guest houses and in private accommodation

Practise what you have learned

9 Complete these sentences with words and phrases from the box below. You won't need to use all of them. (Answers on p. 204.)

(a) **Das hat mir wirklich ______________ gefallen.**

(b) **War es das ______________, daß Sie dort waren?**

(c) **______________ war es dann nachher doch sehr heiß.**

(d) **Ich bin mit ______________ gefahren.**

(e) **Wir mußten in der Hochsaison ______________ fahren.**

(f) **Haben Sie sich ______________ genommen?**

in der Hauptreisezeit | **einen Mietwagen** | **sehr gut** | **privat** | **erste Mal** | **Nur leider** | **meinem eigenen Wagen** | **mit den Kindern** | **meiner Familie** | **mitten in Sommer**

10

Brush up your vocabulary by finding the following German words – some of them are from the dialogue, others from earlier units. (Answers on p. 204.)

(a) The opposite of **schlecht**. ______________________

(b) Two adjectives connected with the weather. ______________________

(c) An alternative term for **Hochsaison**. ______________________

(d) The word for 'to stay overnight'. ______________________

(e) The dialogue mentions one season of the year. What are the others?

____

(f) The phrase for 'to hire a car'. ______________________

(g) The text mentions two types of accommodation. Think of a third. __________

11

Your turn to speak. Follow the prompts to take part in this discussion about your holiday or vacation.

12

Listen to the dialogue on the recording. Then match the questions and answers. (Answers on p. 204.) But first study the new vocabulary.

New vocabulary

der Berg mountain/hill
der Schwarzwald Black Forest
gewohnt lived/stayed
gewandert walked
sich erholen to have a rest
das Wandern walking
die Atlantikküste Atlantic coast
bevorzugen to prefer
das Segeln sailing
das Surfen surfing
jeden zweiten Tag every other day
mieten to rent/hire
das Boot boat
der Tourist tourist
überfüllt overcrowded
der Strand beach
sich verteilen to spread out
alt old
die Leute (pl.) people
das Glück luck
das Wetter weather

(a)	**Wo war Herr Thiel im Urlaub?**	(i)	**Am Strand.**
(b)	**Wo hat er mit seiner Familie gewohnt?**	(ii)	**An der Atlantikküste.**
(c)	**Was hat er im Urlaub gemacht?**	(iii)	**Eigentlich ja.**
(d)	**Hat er sich gut erholt?**	(iv)	**Er ist viel gewandert.**
(e)	**Wo war Frau Tonscheidt?**	(v)	**Im Hotel.**
(f)	**Was bevorzugen ihre Kinder?**	(vi)	**Im Schwarzwald.**
(g)	**Wie oft haben sie ein Boot gemietet?**	(vii)	**Jeden zweiten Tag.**
(h)	**Wo verteilen sich die Leute?**	(viii)	**Mit dem Wetter.**
(i)	**Mit was muß man Glück haben im Urlaub?**	(ix)	**Segeln und Surfen.**
		(x)	**Wahrscheinlich doch.**
(j)	**Fährt Frau Tonscheidt wieder an die Atlantikküste?**		

Dialogues

4 *Talking about the business situation*

Herr Wagner Herr Green, erzählen Sie mir doch ein bißchen, was Ihre Bank für Aktivitäten hat.

Mr Green Herr Wagner, wie Sie wissen, ist die Bank of Scotland die zweitgrößte schottische Bank. Wir haben Kundeninteressen, wir machen kurz- und langfristiges Kreditgeschäft. Wir haben vielfältige Interessen in der Industrie. Wir kümmern uns um (das) Wertpapiergeschäft. Wir haben Devisenhandel – eine Allround-Bank.

Herr Wagner Sind Sie im ganzen Land, also in ganz Schottland?

Mr Green Wir sind flächendeckend vertreten, wir haben Konzentration natürlich in Glasgow, aber wir haben auch in Edinburgh und in Dundee und überall – ich glaube, es sind 150 Zweigstellen.
Sind Sie noch bei der Westfalenbank, Herr Wagner?

Herr Wagner Ja, ich bin noch bei der Westfalenbank.

Mr Green Das Geschäft läuft gut?

Herr Wagner Das Geschäft läuft gut. Wir haben ein hervorragendes Jahr hinter uns und wir haben in den letzten Jahren uns in unseren Aktivitäten sehr stark auf das mittelständische Geschäft konzentriert. Und wir sind sehr aktiv, weiterhin natürlich, im Großfirmengeschäft.

Mr Green Das ist ja prima.

Herr Wagner Das zweite starke Feld ist das Wertpapiergeschäft. Da befassen wir uns sowohl mit den institutionellen Anlegern als auch mit den gehobenen, privaten Kunden, und das letzte starke Feld ist das Auslandsgeschäft.

- ➧ **die Geschäftslage** business situation
- **schottisch** Scottish
- ➧ **das Kreditgeschäft** credit business / lending
- **vielfältig** many/manifold
- ➧ **sich kümmern um** to look after
- ➧ **das Wertpapiergeschäft** securities business
- **die Konzentration** concentration
- **überall** everywhere
- ➧ **die Zweigstelle** branch (office)
- **hervorragend** excellent
- ➧ **stark** strong(ly)
- **sich konzentrieren** to concentrate
- **aktiv** active(ly)
- **das Großfirmengeschäft** business with corporate customers / corporate banking
- **das Feld** field
- ➧ **sich befassen mit** to deal with
- **institutionell** institutional
- **gehoben** here: higher-income
- ➧ **das Auslandsgeschäft** foreign business

was Ihre Bank für Aktivitäten hat what kind of activities your bank has. **Was für** very often replaces the word **welche** (which) at the beginning of a question.

die zweitgrößte schottische Bank the second biggest Scottish bank. Similarly: **drittgrößte** (third biggest); **viertgrößte** (fourth biggest), etc.

Wir haben Kundeninteressen We have customer interests (i.e. are involved in the private sector)

➧ **kurz- und langfristiges Kreditgeschäft** short- and long-term lending. The third such adjective is **mittelfristig**, 'medium-term'.

Wir haben Devisenhandel We have foreign exchange dealings/transactions

➧ **Wir sind flächendeckend vertreten** We are represented area-wide. A phrase commonly used in connection with market presence or the sales network.

➧ **Das Geschäft läuft gut** Business is good. The opposite would be **Das Geschäft läuft schlecht**.

➧ **das mittelständische Geschäft** business with small and medium-sized companies. **Mittelständisch** comes from **der Mittelstand**, 'middle class', originally used to describe a social class.

sowohl ... als auch as well as

Practise what you have learned

13 Which of the following statements match the information given in the dialogue? (Answers on p. 204.)

(a) **Die Bank of Scotland kümmert sich um das** (i) **Großkundengeschäft.**
(ii) **Filialgeschäft.**
(iii) **Wertpapiergeschäft.**

(b) **Sie hat** (i) **Zweigwerke in Edinburgh.**
(ii) **Zweigstellen in Edinburgh.**
(iii) **Zweigbetriebe in Edinburgh.**

(c) **Das Geschäft der Westfalenbank** (i) **läuft gut.**
(ii) **läuft schlecht.**
(iii) **läuft hervorragend.**

(d) **Die Westfalenbank hat ein** (i) **vielfältiges Jahr hinter sich.**
(ii) **schönes Jahr hinter sich.**
(iii) **hervorragendes Jahr hinter sich.**

14 Look at the words and phrases listed under the banks and cross out those items which do *not* fit in with the description in the dialogue. (Answers on p. 204.)

Westfalenbank	*Bank of Scotland*
(a) **institutionelle Anleger**	(a) **Bargeld**
(b) **Beraterbank**	(b) **Devisenhandel**
(c) **Beteiligungen**	(c) **Dienstleistungen**
(d) **Börsenbüro**	(d) **flächendeckend**
(e) **mittelständisches Geschäft**	(e) **Geldtausch**
(f) **Großfirmengeschäft**	(f) **Interessen der Industrie**
(g) **Jahresumsatz**	(g) **Privatkunden**
(h) **gehobene private Kunden**	(h) **Allround-Bank**
(i) **Wertpapiergeschäft**	(i) **Zweigstellen**

15 Your turn to speak. Use the prompts to describe some of the characteristics of the two banks.

16 Form complete sentences by matching the beginnings on the left with the endings on the right. This exercise includes words and phrases from all the dialogues in this unit. (Answers on p. 204.)

(a) **Der Kunde benötigte dringend Ersatzteile ...**
(b) **Ich habe die Produktion angewiesen, ...**
(c) **Parallel dazu mußte ich dann noch ...**
(d) **Man hat mir als erste Aufgabe gestellt, ...**
(e) **Das wurde mir empfohlen ...**
(f) **Das war auch der Grund, ...**
(g) **Wir haben uns in den letzten Jahren ...**
(h) **Im Wertpapiergeschäft ...**

(i) **... einige Kunden im Ausland besuchen.**
(ii) **... besonders auf die mittelständischen Kunden konzentriert.**
(iii) **... für seine ausgefallene Maschine.**
(iv) **... Überstunden zu machen.**
(v) **... weshalb wir in der Hochsaison fahren mußten.**
(vi) **... befassen wir uns auch mit institutionellen Anlegern.**
(vii) **... wegen des milden Klimas.**
(viii) **... den Katalog zu überarbeiten.**

Key words and phrases

Ein Kunde benötigte dringend Ersatzteile	A customer urgently needed spare parts
Überstunden machen/fahren	to do/work overtime
das Problem lösen	to solve the problem
Es war viel vorzubereiten	There was much to be prepared
Das geht mir ganz ähnlich	It's much the same with me
Es hat mir sehr gut gefallen	I liked/enjoyed it very much
Das wurde mir empfohlen	It was recommended to me
wegen des milden Klimas	because of the mild climate
mitten in	in the middle of
Was haben Sie im Urlaub gemacht?	What did you do during your holidays/vacation?
Haben Sie einen Mietwagen genommen?	Did you rent/hire a car?
flächendeckend vertreten sein	to be represented area-wide
Das Geschäft läuft gut	Business is good
das mittelständische Geschäft	business with small and medium-sized companies
das Lieferproblem	supply/delivery problem
ausgefallen	broken down
angewiesen	ordered/instructed
die Produktion	production department
der Spediteur	carrier/forwarder
einpacken	to pack
die Aufgabe	task/job
überarbeiten	to revise
vorbereiten	to prepare
erfordern	to require
sich kümmern um	to look after
sich befassen mit	to deal with
die Familie	family
das Kind	child
die Leute	people
die Hauptreisezeit	peak holiday season
die Hochsaison	peak season
das Gasthaus	guest house
die Geschäftslage	business situation
das Kreditgeschäft	lending / credit business
das Wertpapiergeschäft	securities business
das Auslandsgeschäft	foreign business
der Devisenhandel	foreign exchange dealings/ transactions
die Zweigstelle	branch
kurzfristig	short-term
langfristig	long-term
mittelfristig	medium-term
alt	old
stark	strong

Grammar

Talking about the past

In English and in German there are two ways of talking about the past. You can either say **ich habe gemietet** (I have hired) or **ich mietete** (I hired). Grammar books refer to these as the *perfect tense* and the *imperfect* (or simple past) respectively. In everyday speech the perfect is much more widely used in German than in English. There are no hard and fast rules, but it is safe to say that the perfect is used to refer to actions that are completed, whereas the imperfect is used for actions in process in the past, e.g. **Als ich ihn sah, trank er ein Bier**, 'When I saw him, he was having a beer'. We are going to concentrate on the perfect tense here. (See also the grammar summary, p. 223.)

The perfect tense

Most verbs form the perfect with the present tense forms of **haben** and the past participle of the verb. In the course of the book and especially in this unit you have come across a few such forms. The past participle is most usually formed by taking the stem of the verb, adding the prefix **ge-**, and putting a **-t** on the end. For example, the stem of the verb **wohnen** (to live) is **wohn-**. So the past participle is **ge-wohn-t** – **gewohnt**. If the stem ends in **-t**, as in **miet-en**, then **-et** is added: **ge-miet-et** – **gemietet**. Here is a full example of the perfect:

ich habe gewohnt	I have lived
du hast gewohnt	you have lived
er/sie/es hat gewohnt	he/she/it has lived
wir haben gewohnt	we have lived
ihr habt gewohnt	you have lived
sie haben gewohnt	they have lived
Sie haben gewohnt	you have lived

In German there are some verbs which use the present tense forms of the verb **sein** to form the perfect tense. This is true of all verbs of movement, e.g. **gehen, laufen, fliegen, fahren, starten** etc. But the pattern remains the same. Again the present tense is used together with the past participle of the verb.

ich bin gestartet	I have started
du bist gestartet	you have started
er/sie/es ist gestartet	he/she/it has started
wir sind gestartet	we have started
ihr seid gestartet	you have started
sie sind gestartet	they have started
Sie sind gestartet	you have started

Note that in German some verbs form the past participle with the ending **-en.** This is the case with verbs such as **fahren (ich bin gefahren)** and **kommen (er ist gekommen)**. And of course there are quite a few irregular verbs where the vowel changes, but you should be able to recognize them, e.g. **helfen** – **geholfen, gehen** – **gegangen**.

Now turn over for the grammar exercise.

17 Fill in the correct perfect tense forms of the verbs in round brackets. (Answers on p. 204.)

(a) **Wir** __________ **Überstunden** __________ (machen)

(b) **Der Versand** __________ **bis in die Nacht** __________ (warten)

(c) **Ihr** __________ **in dieser Woche gut** __________ (arbeiten)

(d) **Warum** __________ **Sie Malta** __________ (wählen)

(e) **Der Chef** __________ **mit seiner Familie** __________ (fahren)

(f) **Ich** __________ **die Abteilung** __________ (wechseln)

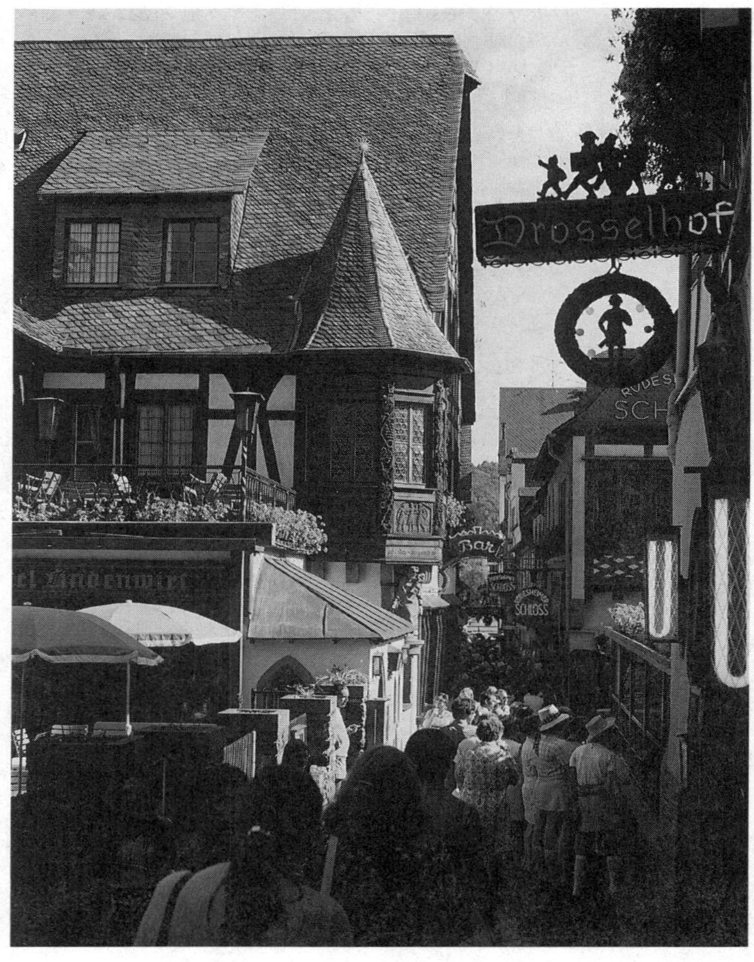

Rüdesheim on the Rhine

Read and understand

18 Study the job ad and the letter of application below. Try to learn the words and phrases that you would find most useful. There's no actual exercise here, it's just a chance to practise reading.

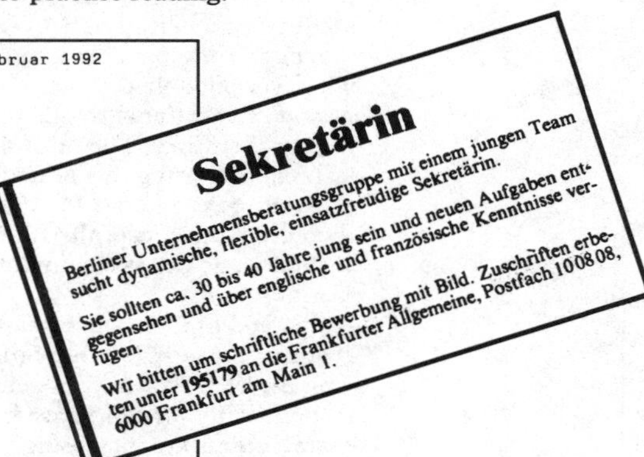

Sekretärin
Berliner Unternehmensberatungsgruppe mit einem jungen Team sucht dynamische, flexible, einsatzfreudige Sekretärin.
Sie sollten ca. 30 bis 40 Jahre jung sein und neuen Aufgaben entgegensehen und über englische und französische Kenntnisse verfügen.
Wir bitten um schriftliche Bewerbung mit Bild. Zuschriften erbeten unter 195179 an die Frankfurter Allgemeine, Postfach 100808, 6000 Frankfurt am Main 1.

Sandra Falk
Wittener Straße 121

4630 Bochum 1

Tel.: 0234/38 56 85

Bochum, den 24. Februar 1992

An die
Frankfurter Allgemeine
Zeitung
Postfach 10 08 08

6000 Frankfurt/Main

Chiffre-Nr. 195179

Betr.: Stellenausschreibung in der FAZ vom 22.2.1992 für eine Sekretärin

Sehr geehrte Damen und Herren,

Ihr Inserat in der Frankfurter Allgemeinen Zeitung vom 22.2.1992 habe ich mit Interesse gelesen. Hiermit möchte ich mich für die ausgeschriebene Stelle als Sekretärin bewerben. Die üblichen Bewerbungsunterlagen (Lebenslauf, Lichtbild, Zeugnisse) habe ich beigefügt.

Zur Zeit arbeite ich als Sekretärin des Exportleiters bei der Firma Niggemeier GmbH hier in Bochum. Ich würde mich gern verändern, um ein neues und interessantes Arbeitsfeld kennenzulernen. Deshalb würde ich mich über eine Einladung zu einem Vorstellungsgespräch sehr freuen.

Mit freundlichen Grüßen

S. Falk

New vocabulary

Berliner Berlin-based
die Unternehmensberatungsgruppe management consulting group
jung young
suchen to look for
dynamisch dynamic
flexibel flexible
einsatzfreudig keen / with drive
entgegensehen to look forward to
verfügen über to dispose of / have
die Bewerbung application
das Bild photo/picture
Zuschriften erbeten please write to
das Postfach P.O. box
Chiffre-Nr. box no.
die Stellenausschreibung job ad
hiermit herewith/hereby
die ausgeschriebene Stelle advertised position
üblich customary/usual
die Bewerbungsunterlagen application papers
der Lebenslauf curriculum vitae / résumé
das Lichtbild photo
das Zeugnis testimonial/reference
sich verändern to change job
kennenlernen to get to know
die Einladung invitation
das Vorstellungsgespräch job interview

Did you know?

Professional training and qualifications

Young people in Germany leave school at the age of 16 or 19. The vast majority will then go into training in a trade, in industry or in the service sector. For a period of between two and three and a half years they will do practical work in a company. They may receive formal training there, and wherever possible they will get experience in various departments. This period of vocational training is called **die Berufsausbildung** or simply **die Ausbildung**. The term **die Lehre** (apprenticeship) is now rather old-fashioned. During this period the trainees (**Auszubildende**) or apprentices (**Lehrlinge**) will have to attend a vocational school to learn the more theoretical aspects of their future jobs. They will also be taught subjects such as basic book-keeping, maths, German etc.

At the end of the traineeship there are practical, written and oral examinations organized by the various bodies (Chambers of Industry and Commerce etc.) which, together with the schools and firms, have the overall responsibility for this phase in a young person's education. These examinations are increasingly being standardized to ensure that the same level of competence is achieved throughout Germany. The local examination boards are made up of experts nominated by companies, the vocational schools and the trade unions. These institutions also work together to revise and update training requirements and to work out regulations for new jobs (e.g. in data processing, communications).

Young people with the **Abitur** (German equivalent of the A-level/Highers examination) often go to university to study. University courses take a minimum of five to six years and tend to be job-orientated, even in arts subjects. Graduates who find jobs with major companies are then often put on training schemes lasting anything from six months to two years. They too will spend short periods in a variety of departments before they are finally placed. Smaller firms provide training on the job for graduates from tertiary education establishments. Polytechnics and a host of other public and private training schemes offer somewhat shorter courses. The polytechnics, financed by the federal states, are becoming increasingly popular among students and employers because their courses are less academic and shorter (up to four years).

There are plenty of possibilities for further and advanced training, organized by the respective chambers, the trade federations, the trade unions and a wide variety of public and private institutions. It is worth mentioning that trade and industry offers anyone who has completed an industrial or craft apprenticeship and has had some years of practical experience on the job, the opportunity to attend certain courses in order to become a **Meister** or an **Industriemeister** (craftsman or foreman). These people form the backbone of shop-floor management in German companies.

In Switzerland and Austria the school-leaving age is 15 rather than 16. In Switzerland the tenth class is offered on a voluntary basis in some cantons. In Austria pupils who wish to go into vocational training after leaving secondary school attend a twelve-month polytechnic course. The Swiss and Austrians are proud of their dual system of vocational training (**duales Bildungssystem**), which is organized along the same pattern as in Germany and, depending on the vocational career, may take from three to five years. The regional authorities provide the school facilities and supervise the training, whereas the practical training takes place in the firms, which, via their respective trade associations, are also involved in the final examinations.

Your turn to speak

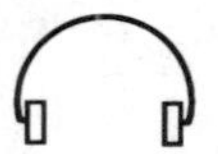

19 You are in a restaurant with a business friend. Tell him/her what you did during the summer. Say where you went, where you stayed, whether you enjoyed your stay and what the weather was like. Here are some useful phrases:

Im Sommer sind wir nach/zu ... gefahren
... sind wir in/auf/an ... gewesen
Wir haben ... Wochen Urlaub in/auf ... gemacht
Wir haben in ... übernachtet
Wir lieben das Wandern/Surfen/Segeln ...
Es hat uns sehr gut gefallen
Wir haben uns gut erholt
Das Wetter war warm/mild/heiß/kalt

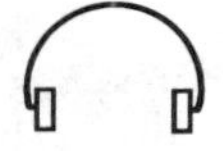

20 At a business lunch you discuss the supply and delivery problems which you have experienced recently, and the consequences to your customers.

In den letzten Wochen hatten wir einige Probleme/Schwierigkeiten mit unseren Lieferungen
Unser Zulieferer/Vorlieferant konnte wegen einer ausgefallenen Maschine nicht pünktlich liefern
... mußte(n) auf Ersatzteile warten
Wir konnten deshalb nicht normal produzieren
Unsere Kunden waren sehr verärgert
Sie haben ein Riesentheater gemacht

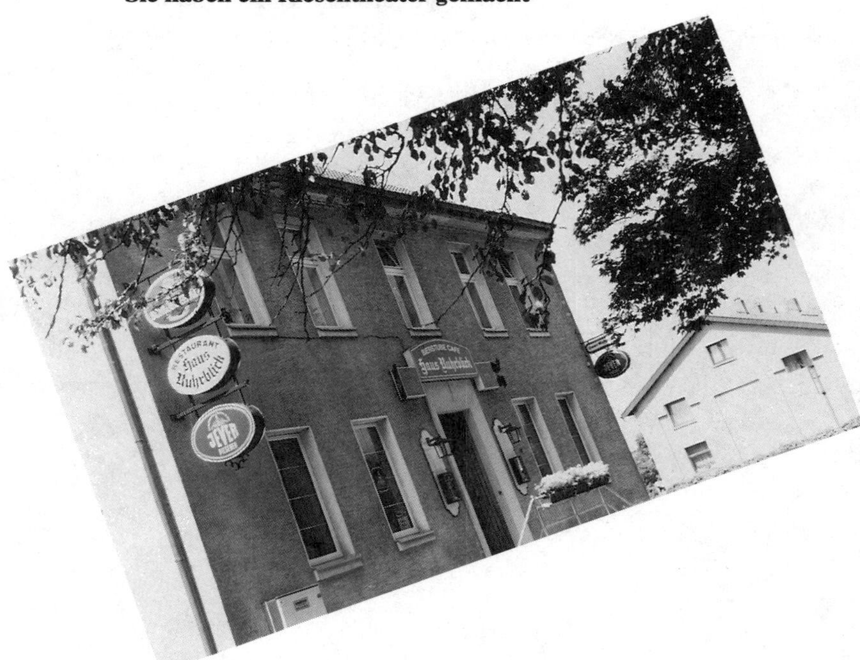

Answers

Practise what you have learned

Exercise **1**	(a) Ein Kunde benötigte (b) Ich habe die Produktion angewiesen (c) Da hat der Spediteur (d) Der Kunde hat (e) Wir haben natürlich
Exercise **2**	(a) v (b) iv (c) vi (d) i (e) vii (f) ii (g) iii
Exercise **4**	(a) iii (b) ii (c) i (d) v (e) iv
Exercise **5**	(a) die Hektik, der Stress (b) mit der Messe (c) Kunden im Ausland (d) die Abteilung (e) erste Aufgabe (f) mit dem Drucker (g) ruhigere Zeiten (h) der Urlaub
Exercise **6**	(a) Ich kann mir vorstellen (b) Ich war sehr engagiert (c) Das war ziemlich stressig (d) der vergangenen Monate (e) Da war sehr viel vorzubereiten (f) Das erforderte viel Zeit (g) Wir können uns auf ruhigere Zeiten freuen (h) einige sehr wichtige Besprechungen
Exercise **8**	(a) iii (b) ii (c) i (d) iii (e) i (f) ii (g) iii
Exercise **9**	(a) sehr gut (b) erste Mal (c) Nur leider (d) meiner Familie (e) mitten in Sommer (f) einen Mietwagen
Exercise **10**	(a) gut (b) mild, heiß (c) Hauptreisezeit (d) übernachten (e) Frühjahr/Frühling, Herbst, Winter (f) sich einen Mietwagen nehmen / ein Auto mieten (g) Hotel
Exercise **12**	(a) vi (b) v (c) iv (d) iii (e) ii (f) ix (g) vii (h) i (i) viii (j) x
Exercise **13**	(a) iii (b) ii (c) i (d) iii
Exercise **14**	*Westfalenbank:* (b), (c), (d), (g), (i); *Bank of Scotland:* (a), (c), (e), (g)
Exercise **16**	(a) iii (b) iv (c) i (d) viii (e) vii (f) v (g) ii (h) vi

Grammar

Exercise **17**	(a) haben ... gemacht (b) hat ... gewartet (c) habt ... gearbeitet (d) haben ... gewählt (e) ist ... gefahren (f) habe ... gewechselt

12 TALKING ABOUT THE FUTURE

You will learn

- to talk about your plans
- to discuss the development of a new product
- to talk about your language skills
- to understand ads for language courses

and you will be given information about foreign trade in the German-speaking countries.

Study guide

- **Dialogue 1 + Practise what you have learned**
- **Dialogue 2 + Practise what you have learned**
- **Dialogue 3 + Practise what you have learned**
- **Dialogue 4 + Practise what you have learned**
- Make sure you know the **Key words and phrases**
- Study the **Grammar** section
- Do the exercise in **Read and understand**
- Read **Did you know?**
- Do the exercises in **Your turn to speak**

Dialogues

1 *At the end of the business meeting*

Herr Karloff Ja, Mr Stevens, das war wirklich ein sehr aufschlußreiches Gespräch. Ich hoffe, Sie haben auch einige Anregungen mit nach Hause nehmen können.

Mr Stevens Ja, das Gespräch war sehr interessant. Ich habe alle Informationen, die ich erwartet habe.

Herr Karloff Ja, wunderbar. Sind Sie noch länger am Orte?

Mr Stevens Ich bin heute abend noch hier.

Herr Karloff Sind Sie hier im Parkhotel untergebracht?

Mr Stevens Ja.

Herr Karloff Ja, das ist ja das beste Haus am Platze. Haben Sie heute abend schon etwas vor?

Mr Stevens Nein, ich habe noch nichts vor.

Herr Karloff Wunderbar. Darf ich Sie vielleicht zum Essen einladen?

Mr Stevens Das würde mich sehr freuen.

Herr Karloff Prima. Ich schlage vor, wir treffen uns um 20 Uhr an der Rezeption.

Mr Stevens Ja, holen Sie mich ab?

Herr Karloff Ich hole Sie dann ab.

Mr Stevens Das wäre sehr nett.

Herr Karloff Vielleicht noch eine andere Frage: bleiben Sie noch länger hier im Ruhrgebiet?

Mr Stevens Ich werde morgen weiterreisen nach Essen und nach Düsseldorf und am Sonntag muß ich wieder zurückfliegen.

Herr Karloff Ah ja. Ist das eigentlich Ihr erster Aufenthalt in Deutschland gewesen?

Mr Stevens Nein, ich bin im vergangenen Jahr schon einmal hier gewesen, aber in München.

Herr Karloff Wunderbar. Gut, das können wir heute abend ja beim Essen dann noch vertiefen.

Mr Stevens Ja, das würde mich freuen.

➧ **aufschlußreich** informative
die Anregung idea/suggestion
➧ **nach Hause** (to) home
➧ **bleiben** to stay/remain
weiterreisen to go on to
zurückfliegen to fly back/home
➧ **vertiefen** to discuss in (more) detail

➧ **Ich hoffe, Sie haben einige Anregungen mit nach Hause nehmen können** I hope you have been able to take home some ideas. Herr Karloff is referring to the substance of the talks and the usefulness of the exchange of ideas and information.

alle Informationen, die ich erwartet habe all the information I was expecting

➧ **Sind Sie noch länger am Ort?** Lit. 'Are you still longer at the place?', i.e. 'Will you be staying here a little longer?' Note that this sentence and the next are in the present tense in German, whereas the English equivalent requires the future tense.

➧ **Ich bin heute abend noch hier** I will still be here tonight

➧ **Das ist ja das beste Haus am Platze** That's the best hotel here in Witten. Here **Haus** (lit. house) is used to mean 'hotel'; in previous units **Haus** also stood for 'company'. Both uses are business jargon.

➧ **Haben Sie heute abend schon etwas vor?** Lit. 'Intend you tonight already something?', i.e. 'Have you any plans for tonight?' **Vorhaben** means 'to have plans' or 'to intend to do': **Ich habe nichts vor** means 'I've nothing planned'; **Was hast du am Wochenende vor?** means 'What are you planning for the weekend?'

➧ **Darf ich Sie vielleicht zum Essen einladen?** May I perhaps invite you for a meal?

➧ **Das würde mich freuen** That would please me, i.e. 'Delighted, thank you very much'.

Practise what you have learned

1 Can you remember what was said in the dialogue? Complete these sentences. (Answers on p. 222.)

(a) **Das war wirklich ein ____________ Gespräch.**

(b) **Ich hoffe, Sie haben auch ____________ mit nach Hause nehmen können.**

(c) **Das Gespräch war ____________**

(d) **Sind Sie noch ____________ ?**

(e) **Ja, das ist ja ____________ hier am Platze.**

(f) **Bleiben Sie ____________ hier im Ruhrgebiet?**

(g) **War das eigentlich Ihr ____________ in Deutschland?**

(h) **Ich bin ____________ schon einmal hier gewesen.**

2 Give brief answers to these questions. (Answers on p.222.)

(a) **Wie lange ist Herr Stevens noch am Ort?** ____________

(b) **Wo ist er untergebracht?** ____________

(c) **Hat Herr Stevens am Abend etwas vor?** ____________

(d) **Zu was lädt Herr Karloff ihn ein?** ____________

(e) **Wann und wo treffen sie sich?** ____________

(f) **Wann reist Herr Stevens weiter nach Essen?** ____________

(g) **Wann fliegt er zurück?** ____________

3 Your turn to speak. Slip into the role of Herr Karloff and, following the prompts, ask some questions.

4 Listen to the recording and then circle the correct version in the sentences at the top of the next page. But first study the new vocabulary. (Answers on p. 222.)

New vocabulary
schriftlich machen to put down in writing
entscheiden to decide
irgendwelche any
verstehen to understand
eigen own
die Planung planning
selbstverständlich sein to go without saying
eigentlich nicht not really
außerhalb outside
gemütlich here: very nice
ausgebucht fully booked
bis dahin dann see you then

Continued on next page.

(a) **Damit haben wir** (i) **keine Fragen besprochen.**
(ii) **viele Fragen besprochen.**
(iii) **alle Fragen besprochen.**

(b) **Jetzt habe ich alle wichtigen** (i) **Produktionen.**
(ii) **Informationen.**
(iii) **Situationen.**

(c) **Unser** (i) **Geschäftsführer** **wird das in sechs Wochen entscheiden.**
(ii) **Abteilungsleiter**
(iii) **Gesprächspartner**

(d) **Sagen Sie mir Bescheid, wenn es** (i) **Stornierungen gibt.**
(ii) **Schwierigkeiten gibt.**
(iii) **Rückgaben gibt.**

(e) **Ich kenne da** (i) **ein kleines Hotel.**
(ii) **ein kleines Gasthaus.**
(iii) **ein kleines Restaurant.**

(f) **Das ist wirklich sehr** (i) **gemütlich.**
(ii) **nett.**
(iii) **schön.**

(g) **Ich hole Sie um** (i) **halb acht am Haus ab.**
(ii) **halb sieben am Hotel ab.**
(iii) **halb acht am Hotel ab.**

Dialogues

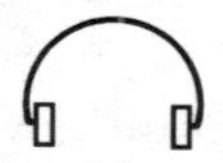

2 *Introducing a new product onto the market*

Herr Waigl Wie weit sind Sie denn mit der Entwicklung Ihres neuen Reglers?

Frau Köpl Oh, da kann ich Ihnen nur Positives berichten. Die Entwicklung ist abgeschlossen, der erste Prototyp ist erfolgreich getestet, und wir werden in Kürze in Serienproduktion gehen können.

Herr Waigl Das heißt also, daß Sie voraussichtlich nach der Messe in einem Monat mit dem Produkt an den Markt gehen?

Frau Köpl Das ist richtig.

Herr Waigl Könnten Sie mir denn in der nächsten Woche ein Muster zukommen lassen?

Frau Köpl Das sollte möglich sein, das muß ich noch überprüfen.

Herr Waigl In dem Augenblick, wo wir ein Muster haben, könnten wir natürlich auch helfen, Ihr Produkt am Markt mit zu forcieren.

Frau Köpl Das wäre sicher eine gute Idee. Wir sind im Augenblick dabei, neue Prospekte zu erstellen, Broschüren, technische Daten festzulegen und die an unsere Kunden zu verteilen.

Herr Waigl Dann möchte ich Sie bitten, mir auch da schnellstmöglich die Unterlagen zuzuschicken.

Frau Köpl Das hab(e) ich mir notiert.

Herr Waigl Okay, ich bedanke mich vielmals.

Frau Köpl Gern geschehen.

➧ **die Entwicklung** development
der Regler control device
➧ **abgeschlossen** completed/ finished
➧ **der Prototyp** prototype
➧ **getestet** tested
in Kürze shortly/soon
➧ **das heißt** that is
➧ **die Serienproduktion** mass/ series production
➧ **das Muster** sample/specimen
zukommen lassen to send / let have
➧ **überprüfen** to check
forcieren to push
➧ **am Markt** in the market
die Idee idea
➧ **die Broschüre** brochure/pamphlet
➧ **technische Daten** technical data
➧ **dabei sein** to be (busy) doing
➧ **verteilen** to distribute
festlegen to determine
➧ **die Unterlagen** documents/papers

➧ **Wie weit sind Sie denn ...?** How far have you got ...?

Da kann ich Ihnen nur Positives berichten On that count I can give you a very positive report (lit. There can I you only something positive report). **Nur** here means 'nothing but'.

➧ **der erste Prototyp ist erfolgreich getestet** The first prototype has been successfully tested

und wir werden in Kürze in Serienproduktion gehen können and we'll be able to start mass production soon. The use of the future here is not necessary because **in Kürze** (soon) indicates that the action is in the future.

mit dem Produkt an den Markt gehen to introduce a product on/to the market (lit. with the product to the market go). Another useful phrase with the same meaning is **ein Produkt auf den Markt einführen**; and **die Markteinführung** means 'introduction on the market'.

➧ **Das sollte möglich sein** That ought to be possible

In dem Augenblick, wo ... At the moment when ... A long-winded way of saying 'as soon as' or simply 'when'.

Ihr Produkt am Markt mit zu forcieren to push your product in the market. The preposition **mit** here suggests jointly with the manufacturer.

schnellstmöglich as quickly as possible

➧ **Das hab(e) ich mir notiert** I've made a note of that

Now turn over for the exercises based on dialogue 2.

Practise what you have learned

5 Can you remember who said what in the dialogue? The sentences have been rephrased but they mean the same as those spoken in the dialogue. Allocate each sentence to either Frau Köpl or Herr Waigl.(Answers on p. 222.)

		Frau Köpl	*Herr Waigl*
(a)	**Schicken Sie mir da auch bitte schnellstmöglich die Unterlagen.**		
(b)	**Ich muß noch überprüfen, ob das möglich ist.**		
(c)	**Im Augenblick sind wir dabei, neue Prospekte zu erstellen.**		
(d)	**Lassen Sie mir dann bitte in der nächsten Woche ein Muster zukommen, wenn es möglich ist.**		
(e)	**Wenn wir ein Muster haben, können wir helfen, das Produkt bei den Kunden zu forcieren.**		
(f)	**Wir haben den ersten Prototyp erfolgreich getestet und können deshalb in Kürze in Serienproduktion gehen.**		
(g)	**Haben Sie die Entwicklung des neuen Reglers schon abgeschlossen?**		

6 Join each item in the left-hand column with its partner on the right to create meaningful phrases. (Answers on p. 222.)

(a) **Positives**	(i) **testen**
(b) **technische Daten**	(ii) **zuschicken**
(c) **erfolgreich**	(iii) **verteilen**
(d) **ein Produkt**	(iv) **berichten**
(e) **an den Markt**	(v) **vorstellen**
(f) **Broschüren**	(vi) **festlegen**
(g) **ein Muster**	(vii) **gehen**

7 Your turn to speak. Take the role of Frau Köpl and say what you plan to do now that the new control device has been successfully tested and is ready for mass production. Follow the prompts.

8 Listen to the recording and then complete the sentences opposite with phrases from the box (you won't need all of them). But first study the new vocabulary. (Answers on p. 222.)

New vocabulary
vor einigen Monaten a few months ago
das Softwareprogramm software program
herzlichen Glückwunsch congratulations
umfassend comprehensive
die Bedienungsanleitung instruction manual
schreiben to write
drucken to print
vor allem above all
einsetzen to use/employ

(a) **In dem Unternehmen wird ______________________________ entwickelt.**

(b) **Das Unternehmen will das Programm erst ____________________**

(c) **Für das Computerprogramm braucht man**

____

(d) **Die Anleitung müssen Sie als nächstes ______________________ lassen.**

(e) **Wenn die Anleitung beim Drucker ist, können wir ______________**

____________ gehen.

(f) **Die ____________________ besuchen die Kunden und stellen das Programm vor.**

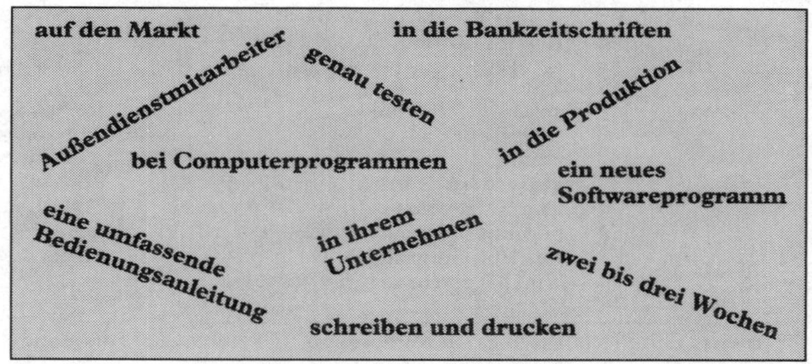

auf den Markt
in die Bankzeitschriften
Außendienstmitarbeiter
genau testen
in die Produktion
bei Computerprogrammen
ein neues Softwareprogramm
eine umfassende Bedienungsanleitung
in ihrem Unternehmen
zwei bis drei Wochen
schreiben und drucken

Dialogues

3 *Overworked and exhausted!*

Frau Reich Meine Güte, was hab(e) ich für eine stressige Zeit hinter mir. Und leider ist immer noch kein Ende abzusehen.

Herr Stoltz Das ist ja furchtbar. Aber das geht mir ja ganz genauso. Und meine Familie – samstags sieht die mich auch nicht mehr.

Frau Reich Ja, im Moment stehen so viel(e) Messetermine an. Ich muß zum Beispiel nach Birmingham zur 'Weldex' im September, und dann ist noch die 'Welding Exhibition' in St Louis. Das nimmt soviel Zeit in Anspruch.

Herr Stoltz Oh je, das geht mir ja auch so. Für mich ist außerdem noch im Dezember – und zwar am Anfang Dezember – ein Führungsseminar an einer Wirtschaftsakademie geplant. Hoffentlich muß ich das nicht ins neue Jahr verschieben auch.

Frau Reich Oh, das hört sich aber interessant an. Ich mach(e) ja jetzt auch noch einen EDV-Lehrgang Anfang Dezember. Und ich will hoffen, daß trotz der gedrängten Termine ich Zeit haben werde, daran teilzunehmen.

Herr Stoltz Ja, das muß man sehen, wie man das in die Reihe bekommt.

stressig stressful
furchtbar awful
soviel so much
außerdem furthermore/also
und zwar that is (to say)
➧ **geplant** planned/scheduled
das Führungsseminar management seminar
die Wirtschaftsakademie commercial college
➧ **verschieben** to postpone / put off
➧ **EDV-Lehrgang** EDP-course / computer course
trotz despite / in spite of

meine Güte (often seen as **du meine Güte**) goodness me / good God

➧ **Leider ist immer noch kein Ende abzusehen** Unfortunately there is still no end in sight. Cf. also **Ich kann da noch kein Ende absehen**.

Aber das geht mir ja ganz genauso It's just the same with me. **Ja** reinforces the statement.

Und meine Familie – samstags sieht die mich auch nicht mehr And my family – it doesn't even see me on Saturdays any more

Im Moment stehen so viel(e) Messetermine an At the moment there are so many visits to trade fairs planned. **Der Messetermin** usually means 'date of a trade fair' but here he is referring to the time-consuming visits to the trade fairs. **Anstehen** means 'to be scheduled/ planned/forthcoming'.

➧ **Das nimmt soviel Zeit in Anspruch** That takes (up) so much time

➧ **hoffentlich** let's hope / I hope

muß ich das nicht ins neue Jahr verschieben auch that I don't have to put that off to the new year either. The word order is unusual because **auch** comes as an afterthought. **Ins neue Jahr** means 'into the new year'.

➧ **Das hört sich aber interessant an** That sounds very interesting indeed

trotz der gedrängten Termine in spite of the tightly packed appointments. **Gedrängt** comes from **drängen**, 'to press/push'.

daran teilzunehmen to take part in it. **Teilnehmen** is 'to take part', **daran,** 'in it' (i.e. in the EDP-course). You often find prepositions such as **an, mit, vor** linked with **da**: **damit** (with it), **davor** (in front of it), **darauf** (on it). The rule is: preposition + *it* in English = **da** + preposition in German.

wie man das in die Reihe bekommt how one gets (all) that organized

Practise what you have learned

9 Can you remember what Herr Stoltz and Frau Reich said? Give brief answers to the following questions. (Answers on p. 222.)

(a) **Was hat Frau Reich hinter sich?** ________________

(b) **Was steht im Moment an?** ________________

(c) **Wohin muß Frau Reich im September?** ________________

(d) **Was ist Anfang Dezember geplant?** ________________

(e) **Was macht Frau Reich Anfang Dezember?** ________________

10 Link the phrases on the left with those on the right to form complete sentences. (Answers on p. 222.)

(a)	**Und leider ist ...**	(i)	**... ins neue Jahr verschieben.**
(b)	**Das nimmt ...**	(ii)	**... immer noch kein Ende abzusehen.**
(c)	**Hoffentlich muß ich den Termin nicht ...**	(iii)	**... wie man das in die Reihe bekommt.**
(d)	**Man muß sehen, ...**	(iv)	**... soviel Zeit in Anspruch.**

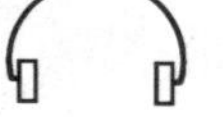

11 It's your turn to complain about life being too hectic. Use the prompts.

Ohne Gewähr

Messetermine 1992

Eine Auswahl wichtiger deutscher Messen und Ausstellungen. Nach Unterlagen der AUMA, Köln. Stand: Januar 1991. Änderungen nach Redaktionsschluß möglich.

JANUAR

8.1.–12.1.	IFR, Wiesbaden
14.1.–15.1.	It's Cologne, Köln
18.1.–26.1.	boot, Düsseldorf
21.1.–26.1.	IMM, Köln
23.1.–26.1.	Int. Lederwarenm., Offenbach
25.1.–29.1.	Int. Frankf. Messe Premiere
31.1.– 9.2.	Int. Grüne Woche, Berlin

FEBRUAR

2.2.– 4.2.	CPD, Düsseldorf
2.2.– 6.2.	ISM, Int. Süßwarenm., Köln
6.2.–12.2.	Int. Spielwarenm., Nürnberg
7.2.– 9.2.	Herren-Mode-Woche, Köln
7.2.– 9.2.	Inter-Jeans, Köln
7.2.–10.2.	inhorgenta, München
8.2.–16.2.	REISEN HAMBURG
15.2.–19.2.	Int. Frankf. Messe Ambiente
16.2.–18.2.	Mode-Woche-München
18.2.–21.2.	DOMOTECHNICA, Köln
19.2.–25.2.	IMPRINTA, Düsseldorf
27.2.– 1.3.	ispo-Frühjahr, München

MÄRZ

7.3.–12.3.	ITB Berlin
8.3.–11.3.	Igedo, Düsseldorf
8.3.–11.3.	Int. Eisenwarenmesse, Köln
11.3.–18.3.	Hannover-Messe CeBIT
13.3.–18.3.	InternorGa, Hamburg
14.3.–18.3.	Leipziger Messe, Konsumgüter
14.3.–20.3.	Leipziger Messe, Techn. Messe
14.3.–22.3.	IHM, München
20.3.–23.3.	GDS, Int. Schuhm., Düsseldorf

APRIL

1.4.– 8.4.	HANNOVER MESSE Industrie
4.4.– 6.4.	Modeforum Offenbach
7.4.– 9.4.	interstoff, Frankfurt
25.4.– 3.5.	Int. Saarmesse, Saarbrücken

MAI

1.5.– 4.5.	optica, Köln
5.5.– 7.5.	INFOBASE, Frankfurt
5.5.– 8.5.	CAT, Stuttgart
5.5.– 9.5.	METAV, Düsseldorf
9.5.–17.5.	IAA-Nutzfahrzeuge, Hannover
19.5.–22.5.	INTERFAB, Nürnberg
25.5.–29.5.	ENVITEC, Düsseldorf
27.5.–30.5.	DACH + WAND, Hannover

JUNI

9. 6.–13. 6.	Ärztekongreß Berlin
25. 6.–27. 6.	ELTEC, München

JULI

14. 7.–15. 7.	It's Cologne, Köln

AUGUST

2. 8.– 4. 8.	CPD, Düsseldorf
14. 8.–16. 8.	Herren-Mode-Woche, Köln
14. 8.–16. 8.	Inter-Jeans, Köln
16. 8.–18. 8.	Mode-Woche-München
22. 8.–25. 8.	Int. Lederw., Offenbach
22. 8.–26. 8.	Int. Frankf. Messe Herbst
30. 8.– 1. 9.	GAFA, Köln
30. 8.– 1. 9.	SPOGA, Köln

SEPTEMBER

1. 9.– 4. 9.	ispo-Herbst, München
5. 9.– 9. 9.	Leipziger Messe, Konsumgüter
5. 9.–11. 9.	Leipziger Messe, Techn. Messe
6. 9.– 9. 9.	Igedo, Düsseldorf
12. 9.–20. 9.	Haus + Heim, Chemnitz
16. 9.–22. 9.	photokina, Köln
18. 9.–21. 9.	GDS, Düsseldorf
26. 9.–28. 9.	inhorgenta-herbst münchen
30. 9.– 5.10.	Frankfurter Buchmesse

OKTOBER

10.10.–12.10.	Modeforum Offenbach
10.10.–18.10.	AAA, Berlin
19.10.–23.10.	Systec, München
20.10.–22.10.	interstoff, Frankfurt
22.10.–23.10.	EMTEC Trade Days, Hamb.
22.10.–27.10.	ORGATEC, Köln
28.10.–30.10.	IRC, Berlin
31.10.– 8.11.	hanseboot, Hamburg

NOVEMBER

10.11.–14.11.	electronica, München
12.11.–14.11.	BRAU Nürnberg
12.11.–18.11.	Art Cologne, Köln
18.11.–21.11.	MEDICA+BIOTEC, Düsseld.
21.11.–29.11.	Int. Touristica Frankfurt
24.11.–27.11.	SECURITY, Essen
26.11.–29.11.	EXPOLINGUA, Frankfurt
27.11.–29.11.	RKI, Köln
28.11.– 6.12.	HEIM+HANDW., Münch.

Dialogues

4 *Learning German*

Frau Bullmann Ihr Deutsch ist aber sehr gut!

Mr Myers Man hilft sich mit dem, was man gelernt hat. Ich würde nicht sagen, daß es sehr gut ist, oder gut. Aber vielleicht haben Sie Möglichkeiten, mir zu sagen, was man machen könnte, um gut Deutsch zu lernen.

Frau Bullmann Aber natürlich. Sie haben doch das Goethe-Institut bei sich in Chicago.

Mr Myers Oh ja. Aber ist es nicht zu teuer?

Frau Bullmann Ich glaube nicht. Sie müssen sich vor Ort erkundigen. Dort kann man Ihnen genaue Einzelheiten über die Kurse und auch über die Preise sagen. Und dann können Sie ja auch noch Zeitungen lesen, Zeitschriften oder Bücher. Das ist immer eine gute Möglichkeit, eine Sprache zu lernen. Und vielleicht gibt es ja auch deutsche Studenten, die gern Privatunterricht geben.

Mr Myers Das sind bestimmt viele Möglichkeiten, worunter ich eine auswählen könnte. Vielen Dank.

Frau Bullmann Bitte schön.

die Einzelheit detail
das Buch book
der Student student
der Privatunterricht private lesson(s)/tuition
worunter from which

Man hilft sich mit dem, was man gelernt hat Lit. 'One helps oneself with that what one has learned', i.e. 'You try and make do with what you know'. **Gelernt** comes from **lernen** 'to learn'.

Ich würde nicht sagen ... I would not say ... Note also: **Ich würde nicht teilnehmen ...** (I would not take part ...).

Aber vielleicht haben Sie Möglichkeiten ... But perhaps you have possibilities ... A complicated way of asking for information.

um gut Deutsch zu lernen to learn German well

Sie müssen sich vor Ort erkundigen You must inform yourself locally. **Sich erkundigen** means 'to get information / inform oneself'. **Vor Ort** is an idiom meaning 'on the spot / locally'.

eine Sprache lernen to learn a language

Das sind bestimmt viele Möglichkeiten These are certainly many possibilities. Note that in German **das** is singular, although it refers to several items and the verb that follows is plural.

Practise what you have learned

12 Can you remember which of these possibilities for learning a language Frau Bullmann mentioned? Mark the appropriate boxes. (Answers on p. 222.)

(a) **zum Goethe-Institut gehen** ☐

(b) **nach Deutschland fahren** ☐

(c) **Privatunterricht nehmen** ☐

(d) **Zeitungen lesen** ☐

(e) **Prospekte lesen** ☐

(f) **Fernsehen** ☐

13 Brush up your vocabulary. All the words except (g) can be found in this dialogue. Enter your solutions in the boxes provided and write down the word made up by the letters in the tinted boxes. (Answers on p. 222.)

(a) Find the word for young people who go to university.

(b) Find the word for 'detail'

(c) Find the word meaning the opposite of **preiswert**.

(d) Find a phrase in the text for 'locally'.

(e) Find the word for 'magazine'.

(f) Find the word for 'tuition'.

(g) Can you remember another word for **Kurs**.

Keyword: (a) (b) (c) (d) (e) (f) (g)

14 Your turn to speak. Take the role of the student of German in this dialogue. Use the prompts.

Continued on next page.

15

Listen to the recording and then decide which of the versions below are right. But first study the new vocabulary. (Answers on p. 222.)

New vocabulary

die Sprachkenntnisse (pl.) knowledge of a language
der Tip tip
das Radio radio
die Nachrichten news
das Hörspiel radio play
die Sportsendung sports broadcast/programme
das Kabelfernsehen cable TV
das Satellitenfernsehen satellite TV
das Tonband tape
der Videorecorder video recorder
aufnehmen to record
die Sendung broadcast/programme
der Gedanke thought/idea
unbedingt absolutely / come what may

(a) **Wenn man seine Sprachkenntnisse aufbessern will, sollte man oft Zeitungen und Zeitschriften** (i) **lesen.**
(ii) **kaufen.**
(iii) **lernen.**

(b) **Man kann auch** (i) **etwas Radio hören.**
(ii) **viel Radio hören.**
(iii) **wenig Radio hören.**

(c) **Wenn man Kabelfernsehen hat, ist das noch** (i) **schöner.**
(ii) **günstiger.**
(iii) **besser.**

(d) **Man kann eine Fernsehsendung mit dem Videorecorder**
(i) **aufschreiben.**
(ii) **aufnehmen.**
(iii) **auflegen.**

(e) **Man sollte mal** (i) **eine Reise nach Deutschland machen.**
(ii) **Urlaub in Deutschland machen.**
(iii) **einen Aufenthalt in Deutschland machen.**

(f) **Darüber sollte man mal mit der Familie** (i) **sprechen.**
(ii) **sagen.**
(iii) **lesen.**

Key words and phrases

Anregungen mit nach Hause nehmen	to take home ideas
Sind Sie noch länger am Ort?	Will you be staying here a little longer?
Haben Sie heute abend schon etwas vor?	Have you any plans for tonight?
Ich bin heute abend noch hier	I will still be here tonight
Darf ich Sie vielleicht zum Essen einladen?	May I perhaps invite you for a meal?
Das würde mich freuen	Delighted, thank you very much
Das ist das beste Haus am Platze	That's the best hotel/restaurant in town
Wie weit sind Sie denn ...?	How far have you got ...?
Leider ist immer noch kein Ende abzusehen	Unfortunately, there is still no end in sight
Das nimmt soviel Zeit in Anspruch	That takes (up) so much time
Das hört sich sehr interessant an	That sounds very interesting
Das sollte möglich sein	That should be possible
Das habe ich mir notiert	I've made a note of that
Unser Produkt muß dieses Jahr noch auf dem Markt eingeführt werden	Our product must be introduced/ launched on the market this year
um gut Deutsch zu lernen	to learn German well
eine Sprache lernen	to learn a language
aufschlußreich	informative
die Einzelheit	detail
vertiefen	to discuss in (more) detail
die Markteinführung	introduction on the market
der Messetermin	date of the trade fair / planned date for a visit to the trade fair
am Markt	in the market
die Entwicklung	development
abgeschlossen	completed/finished
der Prototyp	prototype
getestet	tested
überprüfen	to check
die Serienproduktion	mass/series production
technische Daten	technical data
das Muster	sample/specimen
die Broschüre	brochure/pamphlet
verteilen	to distribute
die Unterlagen	documents/papers
dabei sein	to be (busy) doing
nach Hause	(towards) home
bleiben	to stay/remain
das heißt (d.h.)	that is (i.e.)
anstehen	to be scheduled/planned/ forthcoming
geplant	planned
verschieben	to postpone / put off
der EDV-Lehrgang	EDP-course

Grammar

Talking about the future

In this unit, and in one or two earlier units, you have come across different ways of talking about events in the future. If you want to say 'Tomorrow I'll go into town', you can use either of the following:

Morgen gehe ich in die Stadt.
Morgen werde ich in die Stadt gehen.

In the first example the present tense is used together with an adverb (**morgen**) which indicates that the action will take place later. In the second example the future tense is used.

The future tense is formed with the forms of **werden** in the present tense and the infinitive, i.e. the basic form of the verb. In this case **werden** has the meaning of 'shall', 'will', or 'going to'. Note that when **werden** is used the verb goes to the end of the sentence.

Here are the forms of **werden** in the present tense:

ich werde	I shall / I'll
du wirst	you will / you'll
er/sie/es wird	he/she/it will / he'll/she'll/it'll
wir werden	we shall / we'll
ihr werdet	you will / you'll
sie werden	they will / they'll
Sie werden	you will / you'll

As you will have noticed in the dialogues, Germans prefer to use the present tense when talking about the future. Nowadays the future tense is used much more often in written German and to emphasize statements about future events.

So people will tend to say:

Wann treffen wir uns? When shall we meet?
Dann besuche ich Kunden. Then I'll go and see customers.
Im Sommer fahre ich nach Berlin. I'll go to Berlin in the summer.

You can also use **möchte** or **wollen** to state a future intention.

Im Herbst möchte ich einen Spanisch-Kurs besuchen.
In the autumn I'd like to attend a Spanish course.

Im nächsten Monat will ich mir ein neues Auto kaufen.
Next month I want to buy a new car.

Note that **ich will** means 'I want' and is not equivalent to 'I will'.

16 Form the future tense of the verb **trinken**. (Answers on p. 222.)

ich	____________	**wir**	____________
du	____________	**ihr**	____________
er/sie/es	____________	**sie/Sie**	____________

Read and understand

17 Read the ad for adult language courses and then answer the questions below. But first study the new vocabulary. (Answers on p. 222.)

New vocabulary

der Wohn- und Studienkomplex housing and study complex
gestaltet designed
konzentriert concentrated
eigenständig independent/free
das Sprechen speaking
maximal in the best possible way
gefördert promoted
einzigartig unique
das Ambiente ambience
geglaubt believed
das Leistungsprogramm here: teaching programme
aufwärts upwards
der Bedarf need/requirement(s)
zugeschnitten tailored
die Umgangssprache everyday language
ausschließlich exclusive(ly)
die Zielsprache target language
die Lehrperson teacher
auf Grund von because of
begeistert enthusiatic
die Erfolgsbotschaft success story
der Kursteilnehmer course participant
der Sprachkurs language course
der Ferienkurs holiday/vacation course
der Bildungsurlaub study leave
anerkannt recognized
berufsbezogen job-related
der Einzelunterricht individual tuition

(a) What are promoted in the best possible way?

____

(b) What is the programme tailored to? ______________________________

(c) What is the target language? ______________________________

(d) From whom do they hear success stories? ______________________________

(e) Who are the Ceran courses aimed at? ______________________________

(f) Which is the course to take if you are in a hurry? ______________________________

(g) What is **Einzelunterricht**? ______________________________

(h) What's in the catalogue? ______________________________

____

Did you know?

Foreign trade

The economies of all three German-speaking countries, Austria, Germany and Switzerland rely heavily on foreign trade. Most of their trade is done with their immediate neighbours – Austria with Germany and Italy; Switzerland with Germany, Italy and France; and Germany with the Netherlands, France, Italy and the Benelux countries. Thus Austria's trade with Germany accounts for roughly a third of its total trade volume, more than 50 per cent of trade is with the members of the European Community (EC) and some 12 per cent with countries of the European Free Trade Association (Finland, Iceland, Norway, Sweden and Switzerland). Switzerland too does about a third of its trade with Germany, while trade with all the EC countries together accounts for almost two-thirds and trade with EFTA countries for about 8 per cent of the total. Japan and the USA are also important trade partners.

Germany's trade patterns are changing as a result of German reunification in 1990. A higher percentage of industrial output is now consumed in the enlarged Federal Republic and, as a result of this and the recessionary tendencies in other industrialized countries, Germany had to report current account deficits for 1990 and 1991 for the first time in more than a decade. Far more than 50 per cent of Germany's trade is with its EC partners, and about 15 per cent with the EFTA countries. The USA, Japan and the CIS also have a considerable share of Germany's foreign trade. The vast majority of goods bought and sold by Austria, Germany and Switzerland are manufactured goods. This is all the more surprising as none of these countries has any raw materials worth mentioning. They therefore have to import most of the ores, oil and agricultural goods.

The banks in all three countries are closely involved in these transactions as it is they who provide the important back-up facilities for foreign trade. Their services include the provision of security for foreign trade bills and foreign trade transactions as well as short-term credit finance. They also arrange medium- to long-term financing instruments for exporters and importers and are involved in forfaiting and export credit activities. And, of course, they also help with a lot of the paperwork, documentation and the necessary payment transactions, the collection of bills, cashing of cheques, the buying and selling of foreign exchange on behalf of their clients, currency hedging, counter-trade transactions etc.

Your turn to speak

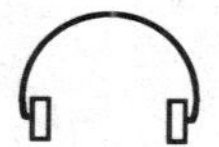

18 You are talking to a German business friend and explaining to him/her what your company is going to do in order to launch a new product in the autumn. Here are some useful phrases:

Wir haben den Prototyp getestet
Wir beginnen mit der Serienproduktion
Jetzt bereiten wir den neuen Katalog / die Broschüre / den Prospekt vor
Wir werden das Produkt / die Maschine / das Gerät auf der nächsten Messe in ... zeigen/vorstellen
Unsere Außendienstmitarbeiter werden dann alle unsere Kunden besuchen
Wir können den Kunden auch ein Muster zuschicken/zusenden

19 You are talking to a German business friend. The discussion is coming to a close and he or she asks you about your plans for the rest of your business trip. Give a detailed reply.

Heute nachmittag besuche ich dann noch ...
Heute nachmittag stehen noch Kundenbesuche in ... an
Ja, dann muß ich heute noch die Firmen ... besuchen
Und morgen fahre ich nach ...
Danach muß ich noch zur Messe in ...
Am Freitag geht es dann wieder zurück nach Hause

Answers

Practise what you have learned

Exercise **1** (a) sehr aufschlußreiches (b) einige Anregungen (c) sehr interessant (d) länger hier am Ort (e) das beste Haus (f) noch länger (g) erster Aufenthalt (h) im vergangenen Jahr

Exercise **2** (a) Heute abend noch (b) Im Parkhotel (c) Nein (d) Zum Essen (e) Um 20 Uhr an der Rezeption (f) Morgen (g) Am Sonntag

Exercise **4** (a) iii (b) ii (c) i (d) ii (e) iii (f) i (g) i

Exercise **5** *Frau Köpl:* (b), (c), (f); *Herr Waigl:* (a), (d), (e), (g)

Exercise **6** (a) iv (b) vi (c) i (d) v (e) vii (f) iii (g) ii

Exercise **8** (a) ein neues Softwareprogramm (b) genau testen (c) eine umfassende Bedienungsanleitung (d) schreiben und drucken (e) in die Produktion (f) die Außendienstmitarbeiter

Exercise **9** (a) Eine stressige Zeit (b) So viele Messetermine (c) Nach Birmingham zur 'Weldex' (d) Ein Führungsseminer (e) Einen EDV- Lehrgang

Exercise **10** (a) ii (b) iv (c) i (d) iii

Exercise **12** (a), (c), (d)

Exercise **13** (a) Stu**d**enten (b) Einz**e**lheit (c) te**u**er (d) vor Or**t** (e) Zeit**s**chrift (f) Unterri**c**ht (g) Le**h**rgang; keyword: **deutsch**

Exercise **15** (a) i (b) ii (c) iii (d) ii (e) ii (f) i

Grammar

Exercise **16** ich werde trinken, du wirst trinken, er/sie/es wird trinken, wir werden trinken, ihr werdet trinken, sie/Sie werden trinken

Read and understand

Exercise **17** (a) concentrated learning and independent speaking (b) to your needs (c) everyday language (d) previous participants (e) motivated people (f) **Crashkurs** (g) individual tuition (h) detailed information

Grammar summary

Below you will find a short summary of what we think are the most important grammar points occurring in this course. Some useful grammar terms will also be explained.

VERBS

infinitive

stem

A verb is a word denoting action or being, e.g. I *am*, he *goes*, she *loves* him. The simplest form of the verb is called the *infinitive*. In English this form is preceded by *to: to love, to go, to be,* etc. In German all verbs in the infinitive end in **-en** or **-n**, e.g. **gehen** (to go), **tun** (to do). These endings change according to the subject of the verb, i.e. who or what acts: **ich gehe** (I go), **du gehst** (you go), **wir gehen** (we go), etc. In the present tense (see 'tenses' below) these endings are the same for most verbs (see Unit 1, p. 17), but sometimes the vowel in the *stem*, or main part of the verb, changes in the **du, er, sie** and **es** forms, e.g. **sprechen** (to speak): **du sprichst, er/sie/es spricht; fahren** (to go, to drive): **du fährst, er/sie/es fährt**. These verbs are called *strong verbs* (see below).

use of verbs

Remember that in English there are two ways of expressing an action, e.g. 'I eat' and 'I am eating'. In German there is only one: **ich esse**. This applies to all tenses.

tenses

A tense says *when* you are doing something, e.g. now (in the *present*), some time ago (in the *past*) or at some point sooner or later (in the *future*).

perfect

past participles

There are two ways of talking about the past in German: the *perfect* tense and the *imperfect* tense. The perfect tense is explained in Unit 11, p. 199. It is more widely used than the imperfect, so it is more important for you to learn. The perfect is formed with the present of **haben** or **sein**, e.g. **ich habe gewohnt, ich bin gereist** (I have lived, I have travelled). **Gereist** and **gewohnt** are the *past participles* of the verbs **reisen** and **wohnen**. Remember that the participles of regular verbs are formed by putting **ge-** in front and **-t** after the stem: **gereist, gewohnt**, but that there are also irregular forms: **ich bin gekommen** (I have come), **ich habe unterrichtet** (I have taught).

imperfect

The imperfect is used to describe actions which happened quite a long time ago, e.g. **vor zehn Jahren wohnte er in Ulm** (ten years ago he lived in Ulm), or which are in process in the past. Regular verbs form their imperfect by inserting **-t** after the stem: **ich wohnte, du wohntest**, etc.

strong verbs

These are verbs such as **fahren: ich fuhr, du fuhrst, er/sie/es/fuhr, wir fuhren, ihr fuhrt, sie fuhren**. Instead of inserting **-t** in the imperfect tense, these verbs change their stem altogether. Note that closely related English verbs often do the same, e.g.

singen	**sang**	**gesungen**	(sing, sang, sung)
trinken	**trank**	**getrunken**	(drink, drank, drunk).

Dictionaries usually list all strong verbs.

use of the past tenses

The perfect in German often has to be the imperfect in English:
Gestern habe ich bis elf Uhr geschlafen Yesterday I *slept* till eleven o'clock.

future

The future is formed in German with the present of **werden** and the infinitive of the verb, e.g. **ich werde gehen, du wirst gehen**, etc. (I'll go, you'll go, etc.) (see Unit 12, p. 218). In German you can often use the present tense to state future intentions:
Morgen fahre ich nach Hause Tomorrow I'll go home.

modal verbs

These are verbs such as **müssen** (must), **können** (can), **dürfen** (may), **wollen** (to want to), **sollen** (shall, ought to). They are explained in Unit 7, p. 129.

verbs with separable prefixes

These are verbs such as **anfangen** (to begin), **zumachen** (to shut), **aufhören** (to stop), etc. They consist of two parts, a short *prefix* (such as **an, auf, zu,** etc.) and then a verb. In the infinitive these two parts appear together, but otherwise they are split up: **ich fange an** (I begin), **wir machen zu** (we shut). In longer sentences the prefix goes right to the end:
Wir fangen um neun Uhr an We start at nine
Wir hören am 12 Uhr auf We stop at 12.
Note: If there is also a modal verb, the separable verb is joined up again, e.g. **Ich möchte aufhören** (I want to stop), **Wir wollen jetzt anfangen** (We want to start now). (See also Unit 5, p. 93.)

NOUNS

A noun is the name of a person or thing, e.g. 'James', 'dog', 'book', 'fun'. In German all nouns have a capital initial letter: **Da ist ein Mann** (There's a man); **Siehst du die Frau?** (Do you see the woman?). (See Unit 3, p. 55.)

genders

All German nouns are either masculine, feminine or neuter, i.e. they have a *gender*. You can tell the gender of a noun when it is used with the words for 'the' (**der/die/das**) and 'a' (**ein/eine/ein**). (See Unit 3, p. 55.)

articles

The following words are articles:

masculine:	**der/ein Mann**	the/a man
feminine:	**die/eine Frau**	the/a woman
neuter:	**das/ein Kind**	the/a child

subject/object

In German the article often undergoes a change according to the function a noun has in a sentence. It can, for example, be the *subject* or the *object*. A subject is a person or thing that acts, e.g. '*The woman* is reading'. The object is the person or thing affected by the action of the subject. 'The woman reads *the paper*'. Whereas in English *the* or *a* is used regardless of whether a noun is a subject or an object, the articles often change in German when a noun becomes an object, i.e. when its function or *case* is changed (see Unit 3, p. 55).

cases

There are four cases altogether:

1. the *nominative*, e.g. **Der Mann ist hier** *The man* is here
2. the *accusative*, e.g. **Ich sehe den Mann** I see *the man*
3. the *genitive*, e.g. **das Foto des Mannes** *the man's* photo/the photo *of the man*
4. the *dative*, e.g. **Ich gebe dem Mann das Buch** I give *the man* the book/I give the book *to the man*.

Here are the nominative, accusative, genitive and dative forms for **der/die/das**:

	singular			plural
	masculine	feminine	neuter	all genders
nom.	**der Mann**	**die Frau**	**das Kind**	**die Männer/Frauen/Kinder**
acc.	**den Mann**	**die Frau**	**das Kind**	**die Männer/Frauen/Kinder**
gen.	**des Mannes**	**der Frau**	**des Kindes**	**der Männer/Frauen/Kinder**
dat.	**dem Mann**	**der Frau**	**dem Kind**	**den Männern/Frauen/Kindern**

Here are the forms for **ein/eine/ein**:

	masculine	feminine	neuter
nom.	**ein Mann**	**eine Frau**	**ein Kind**
acc.	**einen Mann**	**eine Frau**	**ein Kind**
gen.	**eines Mannes**	**einer Frau**	**eines Kindes**
dat.	**einem Mann**	**einer Frau**	**einem Kind**

The negative of **ein/eine/ein** is **kein/keine/kein** (no/none) and follows the same pattern. So do **mein** (my), **dein** (your) and **sein** (his).

PRONOUNS

Pronouns stand for a noun, e.g. '*Mary* loves *Fred* – *she* loves *him*'. Here are the nominative, accusative and dative personal pronouns:

nominative		accusative		dative	
ich	I	**mich**	me	**mir**	(to) me
du	you	**dich**	you	**dir**	(to) you
er	he	**ihn**	him	**ihm**	(to) him
sie	she	**sie**	her	**ihr**	(to) her
es	it	**es**	it	**ihm**	(to) it
wir	we	**uns**	us	**uns**	(to) us
ihr	you	**euch**	you	**euch**	(to) you
Sie	you	**Sie**	you	**Ihnen**	(to) you
sie	they	**sie**	them	**ihnen**	(to) them

Note that the dative is often translated by 'to' + pronoun in English, e.g.
Er gab es mir He gave it *to me* **Wir sagten es ihm** We said it *to him.*
Often you will find the dative form of pronouns in phrases such as **Es gefällt mir, Es schmeckt Ihnen, Wie geht es dir?** etc. (See Unit 8, p. 147.)

PREPOSITIONS

Prepositions are words such as 'near', 'by', 'in', 'to', 'through', 'over', etc. (see Unit 4, p. 73). In German certain prepositions take certain cases, e.g. **aus** (out of/from) takes the dative:
Er kommt aus dem Norden He comes from the north.
And **durch** (through) takes the accusative:
Wir gehen durch den Garten We go through the garden.

prepositions with the dative

Prepositions which take *only* the dative:

- **von** from/of
- **zu** to/at
- **nach** to/after
- **bei** at
- **aus** out of / from
- **seit** since, for
- **mit** with
- **gegenüber** opposite
- **außer** except

prepositions with the accusative

Prepositions which take *only* the accusative:

- **durch** through
- **entlang** along
- **für** for
- **gegen** against, towards
- **ohne** without
- **um** around/at

prepositions with the dative or accusative

Prepositions which take the dative *or* the accusative:

- **in** in/into
- **an** on/to/at
- **auf** on/onto
- **vor** in front of / ago
- **hinter** behind
- **neben** next to
- **zwischen** between
- **über** over/across
- **unter** under/below

With these prepositions the accusative is used if there is *movement* to a place, e.g.
Er ging in den Garten He went *into* the garden.
The dative is used if there is *no movement*, e.g.
Er stand im (**= in dem**) **Garten** He was standing *in* the garden.

ADJECTIVES
comparisons

Adjectives are words such as 'good', 'bad', 'red', 'pretty', etc. (see Units 9 and 10, pp. 166 and 181). You use adjectives if you want to describe and compare things, e.g.
Das Kind ist groß The child is tall
Die Frau ist größer The woman is taller
Der Mann ist am größten The man is tallest.

Be aware of the fact that adjectives, like articles, change if they are in front of the noun in certain cases, as shown in the table below.

	singular			plural
	masculine	feminine	neuter	all genders
nom.	**der kleine Mann**	**die kleine Frau**	**das kleine Kind**	**die kleinen Männer**
acc.	**den kleinen Mann**	**die kleine Frau**	**das kleine Kind**	**die kleinen Männer**
gen.	**des kleinen Mannes**	**der kleinen Frau**	**des kleinen Kindes**	**der kleinen Männer**
dat.	**dem kleinen Mann**	**der kleinen Frau**	**dem kleinen Kind**	**den kleinen Männern**
nom.	**ein kleiner Mann**	**eine kleine Frau**	**ein kleines Kind**	**kleine Männer**
acc.	**einen kleinen Mann**	**eine kleine Frau**	**ein kleines Kind**	**kleine Männer**
gen.	**eines kleinen Mannes**	**einer kleinen Frau**	**eines kleinen Kindes**	**kleiner Männer**
dat.	**einem kleinen Mann**	**einer kleinen Frau**	**einem kleinen Kind**	**kleinen Männern**

WORD ORDER
simple sentences

In simple sentences (i.e. sentences which contain only one verb), the most important rule is that the main verb always goes in second position, e.g.
Ich fahre nach London I travel to London.
Mein Haus ist groß My house is big.

This rule also applies when the sentence begins with an expression of time, place, or even the object, e.g.
Im September fahre ich nach London
Das Auto nehme ich (I take that car)

In questions, the subject is in second position, or in third position after a question word plus verb.

Vocabulary

The German–English and English–German vocabulary is a reference tool for use with the course. It is not intended to be a dictionary. Therefore the meanings given below are the ones that relate to the context in which the words occur in the text. The same words may have a slightly different meaning in another context.

Plurals

If a German word changes in the plural, these changes are shown in brackets. For example:

Abend(e) – add **e** to make the plural **Abende**
Abfahrt(en) – add **en** to make the plural **Abfahrten**
Absatz (-sätze) – change **a** to **ä**, and add **e** to make the plural **Absätze**
pl. – word used in the plural only

Gender

The gender of nouns – *m.*, *f.* or *n.* – is given in italics after the plural, or straight after the noun if there is no change in the plural.

German–English

ab from / as of/from
Abend(e) *m.* evening
abends in the evening(s)
aber but
abfahren to depart/leave
Abfahrt(en) *f.* departure
abgehakt here: dealt with
abgeschlossen completed / finished
abhängen von to depend on
abheben to withdraw (money)
abholen to meet/fetch
abkürzen to cut short / shorten
ablegen to take (off)
Abnahme(n) *f.* purchase
abnehmen to take/buy/purchase
Abreise(n) *f.* departure
absagen to cancel
Absatz (-sätze) *m.* sales
abschätzen to estimate
abschließen to conclude/enter into (a contract)
absehen to see/foresee
sich abstimmen to discuss and agree
Abteilung(en) *f.* department
Abteilungsbesprechung(en) *f.* departmental meeting
Abteilungsleiter *m.* head of department
ach ja yes, of course
ach so oh, I get it
addieren to add
Adresse(n) *f.* address
AG(s) (**Aktiengesellschaft(en)**) *f.* public limited company (plc) / stock corporation
ähnlich similar
aktiv active
Aktivität(en) *f.* activity
alkoholfrei non-alcoholic / alcohol-free
alle all
allein alone
allerdings however
Allerheiligen All Saints
alles all / everything
alles klar all right / everything OK
allgemein general(ly)
im allgemeinen generally
allzu (all) too
als as
also well / therefore / thus
alt old
Alt(bier) *n.* ale
das Ambiente *n.* ambience
an at/near
an ... vorbei past
Analysator(en) *f.* analyzer
Analysestation(en) *f.* analyzer
Ananas *f.* pineapple
Anbau(ten) *m.* annex
anbieten to offer
Anbieter *m.* supplier / offerer
andere/anderer/anderes other
anders different
anerkannt recognized
Anfahrt(en) *f.* journey (here/to)
Anfang (-fänge) *m.* beginning / start
anfangen to begin/start
Anfrage(n) *f.* enquiry / inquiry
angeben to state/give
Angebot(e) (**über**) *n.* offer (for)
Angelegenheit(en) *f.* matter / problem / question
Angenehm How do you do? / Pleased to meet you / pleasant
angeschlossen linked (up)
angesetzt planned / fixed / scheduled
Angestellte(r) *f./m.* (salaried) employee
angewiesen instructed / ordered
angezeigt shown
sich gut anhören to sound good
ankommen to arrive
Ankunft (-künfte) *f.* arrival
Ankunftszeit(en) *f.* time of arrival
Anlage(n) *f.* enclosure
Anleger *m.* investor
Anmeldeformular(e) *n.* registration form
sich anmelden to enrol / put one's name down
Anmeldung(en) *f.* letter announcing the arrival
Annonce(n) *f.* ad
Anregung(en) *f.* idea / suggestion
anreisen to travel (to) / arrive
Anruf(e) *m.* (telephone) call
Anrufbeantworter *m.* telephone answering machine / answerphone
anrufen to ring/call/phone
anschließend and then / which is followed by
Anschluß (-schlüsse) *m.* connection / telephone (line)
Anschrift(en) *f.* address
ansonsten otherwise

anspruchsvoll demanding
Antragsformular(e) *n.* application form
anweisen to instruct/order
Anzeige(n) *f.* ad
Apfelsaft (-säfte) *m.* apple juice
Apparat(e) *m.* device / machine
am Apparat speaking (on the phone)
Apparatebau *m.* instruments engineering
April *m.* April
arbeiten to work/operate
Arbeitnehmer *m.* employee
Arbeitsfeld(er) *n.* task / job
Arbeitsvorbereitung(en) *f.* production/work scheduling
Armatur(en) *f.* fixture / fitting
Art(en) *f.* type / kind
aller Art of all kinds
Artikel *m.* article / item
Assistent(en) *m.* assistant
Atlantikküste(n) *f.* Atlantic coast
auch also / too
auf on / to
Aufenthalt(e) *m.* stay
Aufgabe(n) *f.* task / job / duty
auflegen to put down the receiver
aufnehmen to take/note down/ record
aufrichtig really / genuinely
aufschlußreich informative
aufschreiben to write down
Auftrag (-träge) *m.* order
im Auftrag von on behalf of
Auftragslage *f.* order book situation / level of orders
Auftragswert *m.* order value
aufwärts upwards
Aufzug (-züge) *m.* lift / elevator
Augenblick(e) *m.* moment / minute
einen Augenblick, bitte just a moment, please
im Augenblick at present / at the moment
August *m.* August
aus from
ausbauen to expand
ausdrucken to print out
ausfallen to break down
ausführlich exhaustive / full / complete
ausfüllen to fill in/out
ausgebildet trained
ausgebucht fully booked
ausgefallen broken down
Ausgleich *m.* balancing out / evening out
auskommen to manage
Auskunft (-künfte) *f.* information

Ausland *n.* foreign countries
ins/im Ausland abroad / overseas
Auslandsgeschäft(e) *n.* foreign business
Auslandsgespräch(e) *n.* foreign/ international call
Auslandsmesse(n) *f.* foreign trade fair/exhibition
Auslandsreise(n) *f.* trip abroad
ausmachen to arrange/fix (a date)
ausrechnen to work out / calculate
ausreichend sufficient
ausrichten to pass on (a message)
ausschließlich solely / exclusively
aussehen to look
wie sieht es aus mit ...? how about ...?
Außendienstmitarbeiter (*m. sing./pl.*) field worker / field staff
außer except (for)
außerdem furthermore / also
außerhalb outside
äußerst utmost / extreme / best
ausstellen to exhibit/show
ausüben to exercise/use
Auswahl(en) *f.* selection / choice
zur Auswahl haben to have to offer / have a choice of
auswählen to choose/select
auswärtig outside the company / external
ausweiten to expand
auszahlen to pay out
Auszubildende(r)(-en) *m./f.* trainee / apprentice
Auto(s) *n.* car
Autohaus (-häuser) *n.* car dealer
automatisch automatic(ally)
Autotelefon(e) *n.* carphone

Bäckerladen (-läden) *m.* baker's (shop)
Bad (Bäder) *n.* bath(room)
Badewanne(n) *f.* bath tub
Badezimmer *n.* bathroom
Bahnbeamter (-en) *m.* railway official/clerk
Bahnhof (-höfe) *m.* station
Bahnhofstraße(n) *f.* station road
Bank(en) *f.* bank
bar cash
Bargeld *n.* cash
Beantwortung(en) *f.* reply
sich bedanken to say thank you / thank
Bedarf *m.* need / requirement(s)
bedienen to operate/control
Bedienung *f.* waiter/waitress/ service (charge)
Bedienungsanleitung(en) *f.* instruction manual

bedingt durch due to / caused by
Bedingung(en) *f.* condition
unter der Bedingung, daß on (the) condition that
bedrucken to print
sich befassen (mit) to deal with
sich befinden to be
es befindet sich there is/are
begeistert enthusiastic
begrüßen to greet/welcome
bei at / on / with / for
bei uns in our company
beide both
beigefügt enclosed
beispielsweise for example
bekommen to get/obtain
sich belaufen auf to amount to
Beleg(e) *m.* receipt
Belgien Belgium
benötigen to need/require
benutzen to use/utilize
Benzin *n.* petrol / gasoline
Benzol(e) *n.* benzene
Berater *m.* adviser / consultant
Beraterbank(en) *f.* consulting/ counselling bank
Bereich(e) *m.* field / area / sector / section
bereits already
Berg(e) *m.* mountain / hill
berichten to report/tell
Beruf(e) *m.* job / profession / occupation
berufsbezogen job-related
beruhigend reassuring
beschäftigen to employ
sich beschäftigen mit here: to manufacture and to deal in
beschäftigt employed / engaged
Bescheid(e) *m.* information
Bescheid bekommen to be notified/informed
Bescheid geben/sagen to tell/ inform/notify
Bescheid wissen to know (what to do) / everything
besetzt sein to be occupied/ staffed/manned
Besichtigung(en) *f.* visit / guided tour
besondere/besonderer/ besonderes special / particular
besonders especially
besprechen to discuss
Besprechung(en) *f.* meeting
besprochen discussed
besser better
beste/bester/bestes best
am besten (the) best
bestehen to be/exist
bestellen to order/retain/book/ reserve

Bestellung(en) *f.* order
bestimmt certain(ly) / definite(ly)
Besuch(e) *m.* visit
besuchen to visit
Besucher *m.* visitor
Besuchstermin(e) *m.* appointment for a visit
Beteiligung(en) *f.* participation
Betrag (-träge) *m.* amount
angezeigter Betrag amount shown
betragen to be/amount to
Betreuung(en) *f.* looking after
Betrieb(e) *m.* factory / plant / premises / business
außer Betrieb out of operation/use / not operating
in Betrieb in operation/use
beurteilen to assess
bevorzugen to prefer
Bewerbung(en) *f.* (job) application
Bewerbungsunterlagen *pl.* application papers/file
bezahlen to pay/settle
bar bezahlen to pay cash
Bezahlung(en) *f.* payment / settlement
bezüglich regarding / concerning
Bild(er) *n.* picture/photo
Bildungsurlaub *m.* study leave
bis until / to
bis dahin until then/later / see you then
bis gleich see you later
bis zu until / up to
bisher up to now / hitherto
ein bißchen a little (bit)
bitte (sehr) / bitteschön please
bitten to ask/request
bleiben to remain/stay
der Blitzkurier(e) *m.* fast courier
Blumenladen (-läden) *m.* flower shop / florist's shop
Boot(e) *n.* boat
Börse(n) *f.* stock exchange / market
Branche(n) *f.* industry / (industrial) sector
Brathähnchen *n.* fried chicken
Brathering(e) *m.* grilled herring
Bratkartoffel(n) *f.* fried potato
Bratwurst (-würste) *f.* fried sausage

brauchen to need/require
Brauerei(en) *f.* brewery
Briefpapier(e) *n.* writing paper / company stationery
bringen to bring
Broschüre(n) *f.* brochure / pamphlet
Brot(e) *n.* bread
Brötchen *n.* roll
brutto gross
Bruttopreis(e) *m.* gross price
Buch (Bücher) *n.* book
buchen to book/reserve
Buchhalter *m.* bookkeeper
Buchhaltung(en) *f.* bookkeeping (department) / accounting (department)
Buchhaltungsabteilung(en) *f.* bookkeeping/accounting department
Buchung(en) *f.* booking / reservation
bundesweit at federal level / national(ly)
Büro(s) *n.* office
Büroausstattung(en) *f.* office furniture and equipment
Bürogehilfe(n) *m.* office junior
Bürokauffrau(en) *f.* qualified (office) clerk (female)
Bürokaufmann (-leute) *m.* qualified (office) clerk
Bürostuhl (-stühle) *m.* office chair
Busbahnhof (-höfe) *m.* bus/ coach station
Buß- und Bettag *m.* Day of Penitence and Prayer

Chance(n) *f.* chance / opportunity
Chef(s) *m.* boss / head
Chemieprodukt(e) *n.* chemical product
Chiffre-Nummer(n) *f.* box no.
& Co. (Compagnie) and partners
Computer *m.* computer
Computerprogramm(e) *n.* computer program
Computertechnik(en) *f.* computer technology

da there
da oben up there
da unten down there
dafür for that
daher therefore
Dame(n) *f.* lady
damit with it / thus
daneben in addition / besides
Dänemark Denmark
Dank *m.* gratitude

besten/vielen Dank many thanks
herzlichen Dank very many thanks
danke / danke schön / danke sehr thank you (very much)
dann then
daran on/in that
darauf after that
daraus from that
darüber about that
das heißt (d.h.) that is (i.e.)
daß that
Daten *pl.* data / details / information
dauern to last/take
Dauerstandplatz (-plätze) *m.* overnight taxi rank
davon of whom/them/these
davonlaufen to run away
dazu to it
dein(e) your
denken to think
Denkmal (-mäler) *n.* monument
denn then
der/die/das the / which
derzeitig present / current
deshalb therefore
deswegen therefore / that's why
Detail(s) *n.* detail
Detailinformation(en) *f.* detailed information
detailliert in detail / detailed
deutsch German
deutschsprechend German-speaking
Devise(n) *f.* foreign currency
Devisenhandel *m.* foreign exchange dealing
Devisenkurs(e) *m.* foreign exchange rate
Devisenschalter *m.* foreign exchange counter
Dezember *m.* December
d.h. (das heißt) i.e. (that is)
Dienstag(e) *m.* Tuesday
dienstags on Tuesdays
Dienstleistung(en) *f.* service/ facility
Dienstleistungsabend(e) *m.* late closing day
diese/dieser/dieses this
Dieselkraftstoff(e) *m.* diesel fuel
diesmal this time
Ding(e) *n.* thing
vor allen Dingen above all
geschäftliche Dinge business matters
Diplom-Betriebswirt(e) *m.* qualified business administrator
Diplom-Kaufmann (-leute) *m.* qualified commercial clerk
Diplomkurs(e) *m.* diploma course

Diplom-Volkswirt(e) *m.* qualified economist
direkt direct(ly) / immediate(ly) / straightaway
Direktor(en) *m.* director / head
doch after all / of course
Doktor(en) *m.* doctor
Dolmetscher *m.* interpreter (male)
Dolmetscherin(nen) *f.* interpreter (female)
Donnerstag(e) *m.* Thursday
donnerstags on Thursdays
Doppelzimmer *n.* double room
dort (over) there
drängen to press/push
draufsetzen (*colloquial*) to let down
draufstehen to be written/printed on
draus (*colloquial*) from that
draußen outside
Drehteil(e) *n.* lathe work, turned piece
drin sein (*colloquial*) to be possible
dringend urgent
drohen to threaten
drüben (over) there
Druck *m.* printing / the printer's / pressure
drucken to print
drücken to press/push
Drucker *m.* printer
du you
durch by/through
durchgehen to go through
durchgehend through / direct
durchrufen to ring/call
Durchschnitt(e) *m.* average
durchsprechen to discuss (in detail)
Durchwahl(nummern) *f.* extension (number)
dürfen may / to be allowed
Dusche(n) *f.* shower
dynamisch dynamic
D-Zug (-Züge) *m.* express train

eben just / simply / quickly
ebenfalls also
Edelstahl (-stähle) *m.* special steel
Edelstahlarmatur(en) *f.* special steel fitting
EDV-Anlage(n) *f.* EDP-equipment
EDV-Lehrgang (-gänge) *m.* EDP-course
egal no matter
Ehefrau(en) *f.* wife
Ehemann (-männer) *m.* husband
am ehesten probably the easiest/ quickest
Ei(er) *n.* egg
eigen own
eigenständig independent(ly) / free(ly)
eigentlich actual(ly) / really
eigentlich nicht not really
Eilauftrag (-träge) *m.* urgent order
Eilzug (-züge) *m.* fast train
ein/eine/einer a / one
einbauen to fit
einbehalten to retain/keep
Eindruck (-drücke) *m.* impression
eindrucksvoll impressive
einfach simple / absolutely / quite (simply)
einführen to introduce
eingefahren arrived
einhalten to meet/keep
einige some / a few
sich einigen to agree
Einkauf (-käufe) *m.* buying (department) / purchasing (department) / purchase
einkaufen to buy/purchase
Einkäufer *m.* buyer / purchasing officer/manager
Einkaufsleiter *m.* chief buyer / purchasing manager / head of the purchasing department
einladen to invite
Einladung(en) *f.* invitation
einmal once / just
Einmarkstück(e) *n.* one-mark coin/piece
einpacken to pack
einräumen to grant/give
einrichten to furnish
sich einrichten lassen to be possible
Einrichtung(en) *f.* facility
einsatzfreudig keen / with drive
einschließlich inclusive (of)
einsetzen to employ/use
einsteigen to board / to get onto the train
eintauschen to (ex)change
eintragen to enter/fill in
sich eintragen to register/enter one's name
eintreffen to arrive
eintreten to enter/come in
einverstanden agreed
einverstanden sein to agree
einwandfrei faultless
einwerfen to insert
Einzelanfertigung(en) *f.* single-unit production / customized manufacturing / single unit
Einzelheit(en) *f.* detail
Einzellieferung(en) *f.* supply of a single unit / supply of individual pieces
Einzelunterricht *m.* individual tuition
Einzelzimmer *n.* single room
einzigartig unique / singular
Eis *n.* ice-cream
Eisbecher *m.* ice-cream sundae
elektrisch electrical
elektronische Datenverarbeitung electronic data processing
empfangen to receive/get
Empfang (-pfänge) *m.* reception(ist)
empfehlen to recommend
Ende(n) *n.* end
engagiert busy / committed
englisch English
Englischkenntnisse knowledge of English
englischsprechend English-speaking
entgegensehen to look forward to
enthalten contained / included
entlang along
entlanggehen to walk/go along
entscheiden to decide
Entscheidung(en) *f.* decision
sich entschuldigen to apologize
entschuldigen Sie! sorry / excuse me
Entschuldigung(en) *f.* excuse / apology / sorry! / excuse me!
sich entsinnen to remember
entstehen to arise/emerge
entwickeln to develop
Entwicklung(en) *f.* development
er he
erarbeiten to work out
erfahren to learn
Erfahrung(en) *f.* experience
erfolgreich successful
Erfolgsmeldung(en) *f.* success story
erfordern to require
erfüllen to meet/satisfy
Ergebnis(se) *n.* result
erhalten to get/receive
erhältlich available
erheblich considerable / considerably
erhöhen to increase
sich erholen to have a rest/ recover
erklären to explain
sich erkundigen to enquire/ inform oneself
sich etwas erlauben to afford something / to permit oneself to do something
zur Erläuterung to explain / by way of explanation

Erntedankfest *n.* Thanksgiving Day
errechnen to calculate/work out
erreichen to reach/get to
Ersatzteil(e) *n.* spare part
Ersatzteilsituation *f.* spare parts situation
Ersatzteilversorgung *f.* spare parts supply
erscheinen to seem/appear
ersehen to see/make out/gather
erst first / only
erste/erster/erstes first
erstellen to prepare
als erstes first (of all)
erteilen to place/give
ertragreich profitable
Erwachsene(r) **(-e)** *f./m.* adult
erwarten to expect
erzählen to tell
es it
essen to eat
Essen *n.* meal
Etage(n) *f.* level / floor
Etagenbad **(-bäder)** *n.* bathroom on each floor (i.e. shared bathroom)
etwa approximately
etwas a little / something
Europa Europe
Europasekretärin(nen) *f.* Euro-secretary
evangelisch Protestant
im Export *m.* in the export department
Exportabteilung(en) *f.* export department
exportieren to export
Exportkaufmann **(-leute)** *m.* export clerk/merchant
Exportleiter *m.* export manager
extra extra / in addition / separate(ly)

fabelhaft splendid / excellent
Fachkraft **(-kräfte)** *f.* skilled worker
fahren to go/drive/ride/travel
Fahrstuhl **(-stühle)** *m.* lift /elevator
Fahrt(en) *f.* journey / travel / trip
Fahrtrichtung(en) *f.* direction
Faktor(en) *m.* factor
Fall **(Fälle)** *m.* case
auf jeden Fall in any case
falsch wrong
Familie(n) *f.* family
Familienname(n) *m.* family name / surname
Fastnacht *f.* carnival
Fax(e) *n.* fax
Faxgerät(e) *n.* fax machine
Februar *m.* February
Feiertag(e) *m.* public holiday
Feld(er) *n.* field / area
Ferien *pl.* holidays / vacation
Ferienkurs(e) *m.* holiday / vacation course
Fernbedienung(en) *f.* remote control
Fernsehen *n.* television (set); tv watching
Fernseher *m.* television set
Fernsehgerät(e) *n.* television set
fertig finished / completed / ready
fertigen to make/produce/ manufacture
Fertigung(en) *f.* production / manufacturing
Fertigungsleiter *m.* production manager
Fertigungsprogramm(e) *n.* production programme
fest firm / solid / sturdy
festlegen to determine
Feuerwehr(en) *f.* fire (and ambulance) service
Filiale(n) *f.* branch (office)
finden to find
zu etwas finden to get to something / find one's way to
Firma **(Firmen)** *f.* firm / company
Firmenkunde(n) *m.* corporate customer
flächendeckend area-wide
Flasche(n) *f.* bottle
Fleischwurst **(-würste)** *f.* pork sausage
flexibel flexible
fliegen to fly/go by air
Flug **(Flüge)** *m.* flight
Flughafenhalle(n) *f.* airport lounge
Flugnummer(n) *f.* flight number
Flur(e) *m.* corridor
folgend following / next
Formular(e) *n.* form
Frage(n) *f.* question
fragen to ask
Franken *m.* franc
Frankreich France
französisch French
französischsprechend French-speaking
Frau(en) *f.* woman / Mrs / Ms
Fräulein(s) *n.* Miss / waitress
frei free
frei Haus franco domicile
freigeben to clear
Freitag(e) *m.* Friday
freitags on Fridays
Fremde(n) *m./f.* stranger
Fremdsprachenkorrespondent **(en)** *m* foreign-language correspondent
sich freuen to be pleased
sich freuen auf to look forward to
freundlich friendly / kind
freut mich pleased to meet you
Fronleichnam *m.* Corpus Christi
früh early
Frühjahr *n.*; **Frühling** *m.* spring / Lent
Frühjahrskollektion(en) *f.* spring collection/range
Frühstück(e) *n.* breakfast
frühstücken to have breakfast
Führungsseminar(e) *n.* management seminar/course
Fünfmarkstück(e) *n.* five-mark coin/piece
führend leading
Führungskraft **(-kräfte)** *f.* executive / manager
Funktion(en) *f.* function / position
funktionieren to work/function
für for
furchtbar awful
Fußgängerzone(n) *f.* pedestrian precinct

Gang **(Gänge)** *m.* corridor
ganz quite / whole / all
das Ganze everything
ganztägig all day / the whole day
gar nicht not at all / not ... anything
Garantie(n) *f.* guarantee
garantieren to guarantee
die Garderobe(n) *f.* coat stand
Gas(e) *n.* gas
Gasarmatur(en) *f.* gas instrument
Gasmischer *m.*; **Gasmischgerät(e)** *n.* gas mixing unit
Gast **(Gäste)** *m.* guest / visitor / customer (in a restaurant)
Gasthaus **(-häuser)** *n.* inn / guest house
geben to give
gebracht brought / delivered / taken
Gebühr(en) *f.* charge / fee
Geburtsdatum **(-daten)** *n.* date of birth
Geburtsort(e) *m.* place of birth
Geburtstag(e) *m.* birthday
Gedanke(n) *m.* thought / idea
gedrängt packed
gefallen to like
gefördert promoted
gegenüber opposite
gegenwärtig at present
gegründet founded
gehen to go/walk / be possible
nicht gehen to be impossible
wenn das geht? if that's possible?

gehoben here: higher-income
gelb yellow
Geld(er) *n.* money / cash
Geldschein(e) *m.* banknote
Geldtausch *m.* exchange of money
gelten to be valid
gemäß according to
gemeinsam together
Gemüseladen (-läden) *m.* greengrocer's (shop)
genau exact(ly)
ganz genau quite right
genauso exactly/also
genug enough / sufficient
genügen to be enough
genutzt used
geöffnet open / opening hours
geplant planned / scheduled
gerade just now
geradeaus straight ahead
Gerät(e) *n.* device / machine
gern it's a pleasure / with pleasure
gern geschehen you're welcome
gern haben to like
gesamt total / overall
Gesamtumsatz (-sätze) *m.* total turnover/sales
Geschäft(e) *n.* shop / store
geschäftliche Dinge business matters
Geschäftsbesprechung(en) *f.* business talks
Geschäftsführer *m.* general manager
Geschäftsführung(en) *f.* business management
Geschäftskontakt(e) *m.* business contact
Geschichte(n) *f.* history / past / story
Gespräch(e) *n.* conversation / talk / call
ins Gespräch gehen to start negotiations
Gesprächspartner *m.* opposite number / contact
gestaltet designed
gestern yesterday
gestreift striped / with stripes
getestet tested
Getränk(e) *n.* drink / beverage
Getränkekarte(n) *f.* list of beverages
gewähren to grant/give
gewandert walked
gewöhnlich usual(ly)
gewohnt lived / stayed
glauben to believe/think
gleich same / immediately / at once / straightaway / in a minute / in thesame way

Gleis(e) *n.* platform
Gleitzeit(en) *f.* flexitime
Glück *n.* luck
GmbH(s) (Gesellschaft(en) mit beschränkter Haftung) *f.* private limited company (Ltd/Inc.)
Goldkarte(n) *f.* gold card
um Gottes willen by God / good God
grade *see* **gerade**
Graphikanstalt(en) *f.* printing works / printer's
größ big / great / large
Großbritannien Great Britain
Großfirmengeschäft(e) *n.* business with corporate customers / wholesale banking
Großraumbüro(s) *n.* open-plan office
grün green
Grund (Gründe) *m.* reason / cause
auf Grund von because of
Gruppe(n) *f.* group
mit freundlichem Gruß yours sincerely/faithfully
Grüß' Gott Hello!
gucken to look
Gulaschsuppe(n) *f.* Hungarian soup
gültig valid / current
günstig favourable / low-priced / competitive
gut good
guten Abend good evening
guten Morgen good morning
schönen guten Morgen a very good morning
gute Nacht good night
guten Tag good day

haben to have (got)
ich hätte gern I would like
halb half
Halbjahr(e) *n.* half year
hallo hello
halten to keep
halten für to think/consider (something to be)
sich links/rechts halten to keep (to the) left/right
Hand (Hände) *f.* hand
linker/rechter Hand on your/the left/right
zu Händen von (z.Hd.) care of (c/o) / for the attention of (Attn. / f.a.o.)
sich handeln um to involve / be concerned
Handelsvertreter *m.* representative / travelling salesman

Handtuch (-tücher) *n.* towel
handvermittelt operator-connected
Hannover Messe *f.* Hannover trade fair
sich häufen here: to come on top of one another
Hauptbahnhof (-höfe) *m.* main/central station
Haupthaus (-häuser) *n.* main building
Hauptpost *f.* main post office
Hauptreisezeit(en) *f.* peak holiday season
Hauptversammlung(en) *f.* (annual) general meeting
im Hause here: on the company premises / in the office
ins Haus here: to us/you
in unserem Hause / hier im Hause in our company/firm
nach Hause (to/towards) home
Hausnummer(n) *f.* street number
Hawaii Toast *m.* Hawaiian toast
Heilige Drei Könige Epiphany
Heimatstadt (-städte) *f.* home town
heiß hot
heißen to be called
Hektik *f.* (hectic) rush
helfen to help
heraufschicken to send up
herausbringen to bring out
herausgehen to leave / to go out
herausholen to get out
Herbst *m.* autumn/fall
Herbstgeschäft(e) *n.* autumn trade
Herbstkollektion(en) *f.* autumn range/collection
herein in(to)
Herr(en) *m.* Mr / gentleman
herstellen to make/manufacture/produce
hervorragend excellent
herzlich cordial / hearty
herzliche Glückwünsche congratulations
herzlichen Dank (very) many thanks indeed
heute today
heute abend tonight / this evening
heute früh (early) this morning
heute mittag today at lunchtime
heute morgen this morning
heute nachmittag this afternoon
heute nacht tonight
hier here
hier oben up here
hier unten down here
hier vorn right here
hierher here

hiermit herewith / hereby
hiesig local / domestic
hin there
hinaufschicken to send up
im Hinblick auf with regard to / in view of
Hinfahrt(**en**) *f.* journey there / outward journey
Hin- und Rückfahrt return journey / journey there and back
hinkommen to be entered/put
sich hinsetzen to sit down
hinten over there / at the back
hinter behind / after
hinterlassen to leave (behind)
hinzählen to pay out
sich hinziehen to take time / drag on
hinzu additionally / in addition
hoch high / up
Hochsaison *f.* peak season
hoffen to hope
hoffentlich I/let's hope
in Höhe von amounting to
Holland Holland
hören to hear/listen
Hörer *m.* receiver / listener
Hörspiel(**e**) *n.* radio play
Hotel(**s**) *n.* hotel
Hotel der Mittelklasse middle-range hotel
Hotelhalle(**n**) *f.* hotel lobby
Hotelrezeption(**en**) *f.* hotel reception
Hotelübernachtung(**en**) *f.* hotel accommodation / overnight stay (in a hotel)
Hühnersuppe(**n**) *f.* chicken soup

ich I
ideal ideal
Idee(**n**) *f.* idea
ihn him
Ihnen (to) you
ihr you
ihr(**e**) you / their / her
immer always
immer noch nicht still not
in in / into
individuell individual / customized
Industrie(**n**) *f.* industry
Industrie- und Handelskammer(**n**) (**IHK**) *f.* Chamber of Industry and Commerce
Industriekaufmann (**-leute**) *m.* (qualified) industrial clerk
Information(**en**) *f.* information
Informationsmaterial(**ien**) *n.* information material / literature
(**sich**) **informieren** to inform (oneself)
inklusive (**inkl.**) inclusive
Inlandsgespräch(**e**) *n.* domestic/ national call
innerhalb von within
insbesondere especially
Inserat(**e**) *n.* ad
insgesamt altogether
institutionell institutional
Intensivkurs(**e**) *m.* intensive course
InterCity-Zuschlag (**-schläge**) *m.* intercity supplement
interessant interesting
Interesse(**n**) *n.* interest
interessieren to interest
sich interessieren für to be interested in
intern internal, in-house
international international(ly)
irgendeine/irgendeiner/ irgendeines some/any
irgendwelche/irgendwelcher/ irgendwelches any
Irland Ireland
Italien Italy

ja yes
Jägerschnitzel *n.* pork chop with mushroom sauce
Jahr(**e**) *n.* year
pro Jahr per annum/year
Jahresplanung(**en**) *f.* budgeting for the year
Jahresumsatz (**-sätze**) *m.* annual turnover/sales
Jahreszeit(**en**) *f.* season / time of the year
Jahrzehnt(**e**) *n.* decade
Januar *m.* January
jawohl yes
jede/jeder/jedes every / each
jedoch however / but
jemand someone / anyone
jetzt now
jeweils each / every time
Juli *m.* July
jung young
Juni *m.* June

Kabelfernsehen *n.* cable television
Kaffee *m.* coffee
Kalender *m.* diary/calendar
kalt cold
etwas Kaltes something cold
Kännchen *n.* pot (of tea/coffee)
Karfreitag *m.* Good Friday
Karneval *m.* carnival
Karte(**n**) *f.* card / menu
Kartentelefon(**e**) *n.* cardphone
Kartoffelsalat(**e**) *m.* potato salad
Kartonage(**n**) *f.* cartons / carton material
bar kassieren to ask someone to pay cash
Kassierer *m.* cashier
Katalog(**e**) *m.* catalogue
Kataloganforderung(**en**) *f.* request for a catalogue
Kaufen *n.* buying
kaufen to buy/purchase
Kaufmann (**-leute**) *m.* clerk / merchant
kaufmännisch commercial
kein/keine/keiner no (one)
keinerlei no ... at all
kennen to know
(**sich**) **kennenlernen** to get to know (one another)
Kenntnis(**se**) *f.* knowledge
KG(**s**) (**Kommandit-gesellschaft**(**en**)) *f.* limited partnership
Kind(**er**) *n.* child
Kirche(**n**) *f.* church
klar of course / understood / clear
klar gehen to be OK
klar sein to be clear
sich über etwas im klaren sein to realize/be aware of something
klären to clear up/clarify/discuss
klein small / little
Klima *n.* climate
klingen to sound
Knopf (**Knöpfe**) *m.* button
Kollektion(**en**) *f.* collection / range
kommen (**aus**) to come (from)
kommen (**zu**) to come/get (to)
kompetent competent
komplett complete / full
Konferenzraum (**-räume**) *m.* conference room
können can / could / to be able to
Kontinent(**e**) *m.* continent
Konzentration(**en**) *f.* concentration
sich konzentrieren (**auf**) to concentrate
Konzept(**e**) *n.* concept
Kopie(**n**) *f.* copy
Kopiergerät(**e**) *n.* (photo)copier
Korn *m.* corn schnapps
korrekt correct / that's right
Korridor(**e**) *m.* corridor
kosten to cost
was kostet das? how much is it? / how much does it cost?
Kraftstoff(**e**) *m.* fuel
Kraftstoffvertriebsgesellschaft(**en**) *f.* petrol/gasoline distributor
Krankenhaus (**-häuser**) *n.* hospital

Kreditgeschäft(e) *n.* lending / loan business
Kreditkarte(n) *f.* credit card
Küche(n) *f.* cuisine / cooking
sich kümmern um to look after
Kunde(n) *m.* client / customer
nach Kundenangaben according to customer's specifications/ requirements
Kundenbesuch(e) *m.* visit by/to customers
Kundenbesuch haben to have visitors
Kundenbetreuer *m.* sales clerk
Kundendienst(e) *m.* customer service
Kundendienstarbeit(en) *f.* service work
Kundendiensttechniker *m.* service engineer
Kundeninteressen *pl.* involvement in retail banking / private customer banking activities
Kurs(e) *m.* exchange rate / course
Kursteilnehmer *m.* (course) participant
Kurswagen *m.* through carriage
kurz short(ly) / quick(ly) / brief(ly)
in Kürze soon/shortly
kurzfristig short-term

Laden (Läden) *m.* shop / store
Lager (Läger) *n.* stock(s) / warehouse
ab Lager ex warehouse
am Lager (haben) (to have) in stock
Land (Länder) *n.* country
Ländersachbearbeiter *m.* person responsible for a country
lang long
langfristig long-term
langsam slow(ly)
lassen to let/drop
laufen to go/walk/run
lauten here: to be
Lebenslauf (-läufe) *m.* curriculum vitae (CV) / résumé
lecker nice / tasty
Lehrer *m.* teacher
Lehrperson(en) *f.* teacher
leicht easy / light
leid tun to be sorry
leider unfortunately
leisten to perform
Leistungsprogramm(e) *n.* here: teaching programme
Leiter der Finanzen *m.* head of finance / finance manager
Leiter Marketing *m.* head of marketing / marketing manager
Leiter des Versands *m.* dispatch manager / head of the dispatch department
lernen to learn
lesen to read
letzte/letzter/letztes last (few)
Leute *pl.* people
Lichtbild(er) *n.* photo
lieber preferable / rather / preferably
liefern to supply/deliver
Lieferfrist(en)/Lieferzeit(en) *f.* delivery period
Lieferproblem(e) *n.* delivery problem
Lieferschwierigkeit(en) *f.* delivery/supply difficulties
Liefertermin(e) *m.* delivery date
Lieferung(en) *f.* delivery / shipment / supply / consignment
liegen here: to be
links left / on the left
Listenpreis(e) *m.* list price
Liter *m.* litre
Lizenz(en) *f.* licence
Lohn (Löhne) *m.* wage
Lösung(en) *f.* solution
LPG(s) *n.* liquefied petroleum gas
Luxemburg Luxembourg

machen to make/do
machen Sie ... d(a)raus call it
das macht... that is/costs
Mahlzeit(en) *f.* meal / mealtime
Mai *m.* May
Maifeiertag *m.* Labour Day
Mal(e) *n.* time
mal just / once
mal eben quickly / briefly
Malz(bier) *n.* malt beer
man one / people
Mantel (Mäntel) *m.* coat
Mariä Himmelfahrt *f.* Assumption Day
Mark *f.* mark
Marketing-Assistent(en) *m.* assistant to the marketing manager / clerk in the marketing department
Markstück(e) *n.* one-mark coin/ piece
Markt (Märkte) *m.* market
Markteinführung(en) *f.* introduction on the market
Marktplatz (-plätze) *m.* market square
März *m.* March
Maschine(n) *f.* machine
Maschinenfabrik(en) *f.* engineering works
Material(ien) *n.* material
maximal here: in the best possible way
mechanisch mechanical(ly)
Mediaberater *m.* media consultant
mehr more
mehrere several
mehrfach several times
Mehrwertsteuer(n) (MWSt) *f.* value-added tax (VAT)
mein(e) my
(du) meine Güte goodness me
meist(en) most
sich melden to report (to) / call
Menge(n) *f.* quantity / lot
Mengenrabatt(e) *m.* quantity discount
Messe(n) *f.* trade fair / exhibition
Messerabatt(e) *m.* trade-fair discount
Messetermin(e) *m.* date of the trade fair / visit to the trade fair
Meter *m./n.* metre
Metzgerladen (-läden) *m.* butcher's (shop)
mieten to rent/hire
Mietwagen *m.* hired/rented car
Milch *f.* milk
mild mild
Milliarde(n) (Mrd.) *f.* billion / thousand million
Million(en) (Mio.) *f.* million
Mineralwasser (-wässer) *n.* mineral water
Minibar(s) *f.* minibar
Minimum (Minima) *n.* minimum
Minute(n) *f.* minute
mischen to mix
Mischung(en) *f.* mixture
Mist! *m.* Damn it! / Blow!
Mist bauen (*colloquial*) to make a mess of things/mess things up
mit with
Mitarbeiter *m.* employee / member of staff / staff
mitkommen to come along (with someone)
mitnehmen to take (away)
Mittag(e) *m.* midday / lunchtime
Mittagessen *n.* lunch
Mittagspause(n) *f.* lunch break
mittelfristig medium-term
Mittelklasse(n) *f.* middle class
mittelständisch small/and medium-sized (business)
mittlere/mittlerer/mittleres medium(-sized)
Mittwoch(e) *n.* Wednesday
mittwochs on Wednesdays
Möbelfabrik(en) *f.* furniture factory
mögen to like/want
gern mögen to like (to do)
möglich possible

Möglichkeit(en) *f.* possibility / way
möglichst if (at all) possible
möglichst schnell as quickly as possible
Moment(e) *m.* moment
(**einen**) **Moment** (**bitte**) just a minute/moment (please)
Monat(e) *m.* month
monatlich per/every month
Montag(e) *m.* Monday
montags on Mondays
morgen tomorrow
morgens in the morning
morgens früh/spät early/late in the morning
motiviert motivated
mühelos without any problem
Münze(n) *f.* coin
müssen must / to have to
Muster *n.* sample / specimen
Mutter (**Mütter**) *f.* mother

nach to(wards) / after
nachfragen to enquire/ask
nachher afterwards / later on
Nachmittag(e) *m.* afternoon
nachmittags in the afternoon
Nachname(n) *m.* family name / surname
Nachricht(en) *f.* message / news / information
nachschauen to check/have a look
nachschlagen to look up
nächste/nächster/nächstes next / following
Nacht (**Nächte**) *f.* night
nachteilig detrimental / disadvantageous
nachts at night
Nähe *f.* proximity
in der Nähe near / close by
Name(n) *m.* name
nämlich for / namely
Nationalität(en) *f.* nationality
natürlich naturally / of course
nehmen to take
nein no
nennen to state/give
nett nice / kind
netto net
neu new
neuest newest
Neujahr *n.* New Year('s Day)
nicht not
Nichtraucher *m.* non-smoker
nichts zu danken you're welcome
Niederlassung(en) *f.* branch office
noch yet / still
noch einmal / nochmal once again

normal normal
Norwegen Norway
notiert noted (down) / written down
Notruf(e) *m.* emergency call
November *m.* November
Nummer(n) *f.* number
nur only

ob whether
oben above/up / at the top
obwohl although
oder or
offen open
offensichtlich obvious(ly)
Öffnungszeit(en) *f.* opening/ business hours
oft often / many times
des öfteren from time to time
öfter frequently / time and again
OHG(s) (**Offene Handelsgesellschaft(en)**) *f.* general partnership
ohne without
Oktober *m.* October
Omnibusbahnhof (**-höfe**) *m.* bus/coach station
Orangensaft (**-säfte**) *m.* orange juice
in Ordnung understood / OK
in Ordnung bringen to put right
Ort(e) *m.* place
Ortsdurchwahl(en) *f.* local number (code)
Ortsnetz(e) *n.* local network
Österreich Austria
Ostermontag *m.* Easter Monday
Ostertag *m.* Easter
Ostküste(n) *f.* east coast

ein paar some
Packpapier(e) *n.* wrapping paper
Panne(n) *f.* breakdown
parallel parallel / at the same time
Park(s) *m.* park / garden
Parkhaus (**-häuser**) *n.* multi-storey car park
Parkplatz (**-plätze**) *m.* car park
Partner *m.* partner
Passant(en) *m.* passer-by
passen to suit / be OK
Pause(n) *f.* break / interval
per by
Person(en) *f.* person / people
Personal *n.* personnel / staff
Personalanzeigenservice *m.* service for recruitment ads
Personalleiter *m.* personnel manager / head of personnel
persönlich personal(ly)
Pfennig(e) *m.* pfennig
Pfingstmontag *m.* Whit Monday

Pfingstsonntag *m.* Whit Sunday
Photokopie(n) *f.* photocopy
Plakat(e) *n.* poster
planen to plan
planmäßig scheduled
Planung(en) *f.* planning
Platz (**Plätze**) *m.* place / square / seat
Platz nehmen to take/have a seat / sit down
plötzlich sudden(ly)
Polizei *f.* police
Pommes frites *pl.* chips / French fries
Portugal Portugal
Position(en) *f.* position
Post *f.* post office / postal service
Postamt (**-ämter**) *n.* post office
Postfach (**-fächer**) *n.* P.O. box
Postleitzahl(en) *f.* post code / ZIP code
Präsident(en) *m.* president
Preis(e) *m.* price
Preisliste(n) *f.* price list
Preisverhandlung(en) *f.* price negotiations
preiswert good value
prima fine/splendid
im Prinzip in principle / theoretically
privat private(ly)
Privatkunde(n) *m.* private customer
Privatkundengeschäft(e) *n.* business with private customers / retail banking
Privatunternehmen *n.* private company/enterprise
Privatunterricht *m.* private tuition/lessons
pro per
probieren to try/attempt
Problem(e) *n.* problem
kein Problem that's no problem
Produkt Manager *m.* product manager
Produkt(e) *n.* product / article
Produktgruppe(n) *f.* product group
Produktinformation(en) *f.* product information
Produktion(en) *f.* production / manufacturing / production department
Produktionsausfall (**-fälle**) *m.* loss of output/production
Produktionsgrenze(n) *f.* production limit / target
Produktionsleistung(en) *f.* output / production performance
Produktionsleiter *m.* production manager

Produktionsprogramm(e) *n.* production programme
Produktionszahl(en) *f.* production figure
Produktlinie(n) *f.* product line
Produktpalette(n) *f.* product range/mix
produzieren to produce/ manufacture
Professor(en) *m.* professor
Programm(e) *n.* programme
Prospekt(e) *m.* leaflet / brochure
Prospektblatt (-blätter) *n.* leaflet / flyer
Prototyp(en) *m.* prototype
prüfen to check/examine / have a good look at something
Prüfeinrichtung(en) *f.* testing device
Pumpe(n) *f.* pump
Pumpenproduktion(en) *f.* production of pumps
Punkt(e) *m.* point
pünktlich punctual(ly)

Qualitätskontrolle(n) *f.* quality control

Rabatt(e) *m.* discount / rebate
Rabattstaffel(n) *f.* schedule of discounts
Radio(s) *n.* radio
Rathaus (-häuser) *n.* town hall
Rathausplatz (-plätze) *m.* town hall square
rausgehen to leave/go out/face
rausholen to get out
rechnen (mit) here: to get/count on/reckon with/calculate/add up
Rechnung(en) *f.* bill
Rechnungsdatum (-daten) *n.* date of invoice
das ist recht that's fine
ist das recht? is that OK/ all right?
rechts right / on the right
rechtzeitig in time
Reformationstag *m.* Reformation Day
regelmäßig regularly
Regeltechnik(en) *f.* control engineering
Region(en) *f.* region / area / district
Regionalbank(en) *f.* regional bank
Regler *m.* controlling device
reichen to be sufficient/enough
eine Reihe von a number/ series of
eine ganze Reihe quite a few
rein in / into
reinkommen to come in
Reise(n) *f.* journey / trip
Reisebüro(s) *n.* travel agent's / travel agency
Reiseinformation(en) *f.* travel information
reisen to travel
Reklame *f.* advertising
Reparatur(en) *f.* repair work
Repräsentanz(en) *f.* representative office
Rest(e) *m.* remainder/rest
Restaurant(s) *n.* restaurant
Restbetrag (-beträge) *m.* remainder
Rezeption(en) *f.* reception (desk)
sich richten nach to depend on
richtig right / correct
Richtung(en) *f.* direction
in Richtung for / in the direction of
Riesentheater *n.* **machen** to kick up a fuss
Rohstoff(e) *m.* raw material / commodity
Rolle(n) *f.* role
keine Rolle spielen not to matter
Rückfahrt(en) *f.* return journey/ trip
Rückflug (-flüge) *m.* return flight
Rückgabe(n) *f.* return / refund
Rufnummer(n) *f.* subscriber's/ phone number
Ruhetag(e) *m.* closing / rest day
ruhig quiet / calm / also: as well
Rührei(er) *n.* scrambled egg
Ruhrgebiet *n.* Ruhr area/district
runter down

Sachbearbeiter *m.* clerk / officer
Sache(n) *f.* thing / item / matter
sagen to say/tell
Sahne *f.* cream
Saison *f.* season
Salatteller *m.* mixed salad
Samstag(e) *m.* Saturday
samstags on Saturdays
sämtlich all
Satellitenfernsehen *n.* satellite television
Satz (Sätze) *m.* typesetting
S-Bahn-Haltestelle(n) *f.* suburban railway stop
schade it's a pity
schaffen to manage
Schein(e) *m.* banknote
schicken to send
Schild(er) *n.* sign
Schinken *m.* ham
Schinkenteller *m.* plate of boiled and smoked ham
Schlafzimmer *n.* bedroom
schlecht bad
schließen to close/terminate
schließlich finally
schlimm bad(ly)
Schlitz(e) *m.* slot
Schlüssel *m.* key
schmecken to taste (nice)
schnell quick(ly) / fast
Schnellzug (-züge) *m.* express train
Schokolade(n) *f.* chocolate
schon already
schön nice
schottisch Scottish
schräg diagonal(ly)
Schrank (Schränke) *m.* cupboard
schreiben to write
Schreibmaschinentisch(e) *m.* typewriter desk
Schreibtisch(e) *m.* desk
Schreibwarenladen (-läden) *m.* stationer's (shop)
schriftlich written / in writing
schriftlich machen to put down in writing
Schule(n) *f.* school
schulen to train
schwarz black
Schwarzwald *m.* Black Forest
Schweden Sweden
schweißen to weld
Schweiz *f.* Switzerland
schweizer(isch) Swiss
Segeln *n.* sailing
sehen to see
sehr very
Sehr geehrte Damen und Herren Dear Sir or Madam / Dear Sirs
sein to be
sein(e) his
seit for / since
Seite(n) *f.* side
Sekretär(e) *m.* secretary
Sekretärin(nen) *f.* female secretary
Sekunde(n) *f.* second
selber/selbst myself / yourself (etc)
selbstätig automatic(ally)
selbstverständlich of course / naturally / certainly
selbstverständlich sein to go without saying
Sendung(en) *f.* consignment / broadcast / programme
September *m.* September
Serienproduktion(en) *f.* mass/series production
Service *m.* service / servicing
Servicetechniker *m.* service engineer
sicher certain(ly) / safe(ly)
Sicherheitsarmatur(en) *f.* safety valve

sicherlich surely
Sicherungsautomat(en) *m.* automatic flashback arrester
Sicht(en) *f.* sight
aus der Sicht von from the point of view of
Sie you
sie she/they/(to) her/(to) them
Situation(en) *f.* situation
Sitz(e) *m.* seat
mit Sitz in based in
Sitzplatzreservierung(en) *f.* seat reservation
Sitzung(en) *f.* meeting
Sitzungszimmer *n.* conference room
Skonto (Skonti) *m./n.* cash discount
so daß so that
so schnell wie möglich as quickly as possible
sofort immediately / at once
Softwarehaus (-häuser) *n.* software company
Softwareprogramm(e) *n.* software program
sogar even / indeed
solange until then / as long as
solch such
sollen shall / to be to
Sommer *m.* summer
sondern but
Sonderpreis(e) *m.* special price
Sonnabend(e) *m.* Saturday
sonnabends on Saturdays
Sonntag(e) *m.* Sunday
sonntags on Sundays
sonst otherwise / apart (from that)
sonstig other
sorgen für to provide
Sorte(n) *f.* currency
Sortenschalter *m.* foreign exchange counter
Soße(n) *f.* sauce
soweit on the whole / by and large
sowie and also / as well as
sozusagen so to speak
Spanien Spain
Spanischkurs(e) *m.* Spanish course
Sparkasse(n) *f.* savings bank
Sparte(n) *f.* line / field
spät late
Spediteur(e) *m.* forwarder / carrier
Speditionskaufmann (-leute) *m.* freight merchant/clerk
Speisekarte(n) *f.* menu
Spezialfrage(n) *f.* special problem
Spezialist(en) *m.* specialist
speziell special
spielen to play
Spinnerei(en) *f.* spinning mill
Sportsendung(en) *f.* sports broadcast/programme
Sprache(n) *f.* language
Sprachkenntnisse *f.pl.* knowledge of a language
Sprachkurs(e) *m.* language course
sprechen to talk/speak
Sprechen *n.* speaking
Stadt (Städte) *f.* town / city
Stand der Technik *m.* state of the art
Standort(e) *m.* location
stark strong(ly)
starten to begin/start
stecken to put in/insert
stehen to stand/be
Stelle(n) *f.* post / position
stellen to set
Stellenangebot(e) *n.* vacancies / jobs offered
Stellenausschreibung(en) *f.* job ad
Stellenmarkt (-märkte) *m.* job/ labour market
stimmen to be right/correct
Stock *m.* level / floor
Stornierung(en) *f.* cancellation
Störung(en) *f.* fault / defect
Strand (Strände) *m.* beach
Straße(n) *f.* street / road
Streik(s) *m.* strike
Stress *m.* stress
Stück(e) *n.* piece / item
Stückchen *n.* little bit / small piece
Stückpreis(e) *m.* unit price
Stückzahl(en) *f.* number (of pieces) / amount
stückzahlbezogen quantity-related
Student(en) *m.* student
Studienkomplex(e) *m.* study complex
Stunde(n) *f.* hour
in einer halben Stunde in half an hour
Suche *f.* search
suchen to look for
Summe(n) *f.* sum / total / amount
Summton (-töne) *m.* buzzing sound
Superkraftstoff(e) *m.* premium petrol / gasoline
Surfen *n.* surfing

Tabelle(n) *f.* table
Tag(e) *m.* day
jeden zweiten Tag every other day
14 Tage a fortnight / two weeks
Tagesnotiz(en) *f.* note for the day
täglich daily
Tankstelle(n) *f.* petrol / gasoline station
Tasse(n) *f.* cup
Tasse Kaffee cup of coffee
Taste(n) *f.* button
tätig active
tätig sein to operate
Team(s) *n.* team
Technik(en) *f.* technology / technique
technisch technical
Technischer Leiter *m.* engineering manager
Tee(s) *m.* tea
schwarzer Tee black tea
Teil(e) *n.* (spare) part
teilnehmen to take part/ participate
Telefon(e) *n.* telephone
Telefonat(e) *n.* telephone call / conversation
Telefonauftrag (-aufträge) *m.* telephone service
Telefonauskunft (-künfte) *f.* telephone enquiries
Telefonbuch (-bücher) *n.* telephone directory
Telefongespräch(e) *n.* telephone call / conversation
telefonieren to telephone
telefonisch by phone / on the phone
Telefonnummer(n) *f.* telephone number
Telefonzelle(n) *f.* telephone box/ booth
Telefonzentrale(n) *f.* switchboard
Telegramm(e) *n.* telegram
Termin(e) *m.* appointment / date / deadline
Terminabsprache(n) *f.* making an appointment
Terminkalender *m.* appointments/business diary
Terminplan (-pläne) *m.* appointments/business diary
Terminvereinbarung(en) *f.* (fixing of an) appointment
teuer expensive / dear
Textilien textiles
Theaterkarte(n) *f.* theatre ticket
Tiefgarage(n) *f.* underground car park
Tip(s) *m.* tip
zu Tisch sein to be away for lunch / at lunch
Toilette(n) *f.* toilet / WC
Ton (Töne) *m.* tone
Tonband (-bänder) *n.* tape
Tourist(en) *m.* tourist
Traubensaft (-säfte) *m.* grape juice
(sich) treffen to meet
trinken to drink

trotz despite / in spite of
trotzdem nevertheless
Tschüß! Bye!
tun to do
zu tun haben to be busy
Tür(en) *f.* door

U-Bahn-Haltestelle(n) *f.* underground station
über across / above / about
überall everywhere
überarbeiten to revise
überfüllt overcrowded
überhaupt nicht not at all
sich etwas überlegen to think something over
übermorgen day after tomorrow
übernachten to spend the night/stay overnight
übernehmen to do/take care of
überprüfen to check
übersteigen to exceed
Überstunde(n) *f.* (hour of) overtime
Überstunden fahren to work/ do overtime
üblich customary / usual
übrigens by the way
Uhr(en) *f.* clock / watch
um ... Uhr at ... o'clock
Uhrzeit(en) *f.* time
um for
Umfang *m.* volume / size / amount
umfassend comprehensive
Umgangssprache(n) *f.* everyday language / language of communication
umrechnen to convert
Umrechnungstabelle(n) *f.* conversion table
umsteigen to change (trains)
umtauschen to (ex)change
unbedingt absolute(ly) / come what may
und and
und so weiter (usw.) and so on (etc.)
und zwar that is
ungefähr approximately
Uni(versität(en)) *f.* university
unmöglich impossible
unser our
unten below / at the bottom / down
unter below / under / on
unterbringen to house/ accommodate
untergebracht sein to be staying/stay
sich unterhalten to discuss/talk about
Unterlage(n) *f.* document / paper
Unternehmen *n.* enterprise / company
Unternehmensberatungsgruppe(n) *f.* management consulting group
Unterschied(e) *m.* difference
unterschreiben to sign
Unterschrift(en) *f.* signature
unterwegs away (on business)
unverändert unchanged
Urlaub *m.* holiday(s) / vacation
Urlaub machen to go on holiday

Vater (Väter) *m.* father
verabschieden to say goodbye
sich verändern to change
verantwortlich responsible / in charge
verärgert annoyed
verbessern to improve
verbinden to connect/put through
verbindlich firm / binding
Verbindung(en) *f.* connection
verbleiben to remain
verdienen to earn
vereinbaren to arrange/fix
verfügen über to have/dispose of
zur Verfügung stehen to be available
zur Verfügung stellen to make available
vergangen past / last
Vergangenheit(en) *f.* past
vergeblich in vain
verhindert sein to be engaged/ busy/have another appointment
Verkauf (-käufe) *m.* sale(s department) / selling
verkaufen to sell
Verkaufen *n.* selling
Verkäufer *m.* salesman/assistant
Verkaufsinnendienst(e) *m.* sales office / office-based sales staff
Verkaufsleiter *m.* sales manager/ director
Verkaufsmenge(n) *f.* quantity sold
Verkaufsvereinigung(en) *f.* sales association
verkauft sold
Verkehrsverein(e) *m.* tourist information (office)
vermögend wealthy
Verpackung(en) *f.* packing / packaging
Verpackungsmaterial(ien) *n.* pack(ag)ing material
Versand *m.* dispatch (department)
Versandabteilung(en) *f.* dispatch department
verschieben to postpone/put off
verschieden several / different
Verspätung(en) *f.* delay
verstanden understood / OK
Verständnis *n.* understanding
verstehen to understand
sich verstehen to apply/be
versuchen to attempt/try
verteilen to distribute
sich verteilen to spread out
vertiefen to discuss in more detail/go into something in depth
vertreten represented
Vertreter *m.* representative
Vertriebsabteilung(en) *f.* distribution department
Vertriebsingenieur(e) *m.* distribution engineer
Vertriebsleiter *m.* distribution manager
Verwaltung(en) *f.* administration
verzögert delayed
Videorecorder *m.* video recorder
viel(e) much / many
das ist sehr viel that's quite a lot
vielfältig many / manifold
vielleicht perhaps
vielmals here: very much
Vierteljahr(e) *n.* quarter (of the year)
Visitenkarte(n) *f.* business card
Vizepräsident(en) *m.* vice-president
vollständig complete / full / entire
vom/von...her as regards / as far as ... is concerned
von from
von denen of those
vor ... ago
vor allem above all
Voraussetzung(en) *f.* precondition / requirement
voraussichtlich probably
vorbei past/over
vorbeikommen to come/walk past / come and see
vorbeischicken to send round
vorbereiten to prepare
Vorbesprechung(en) *f.* briefing, preliminary discussion
vorbestellt booked/ordered in advance
vorgenannt above-mentioned
vorhaben to intend/plan to do
vorher before
vorhin earlier / before
vorinformieren to inform in advance
vorläufig for the time being
Vorlieferant(en) *m.* supplier
vorliegen to be available
Vormittag(e) *m.* morning
vormittags in the morning
vorn in front / ahead
Vorname(n) *m.* first name
vornehmen to make/do

vornehmen to make/do
vorschlagen to suggest/propose/recommend
Vorsicht *f.* care / attention
Vorsitzender (-sitzenden) *m.* chairman
vorstellen to introduce/show
sich vorstellen to introduce oneself/imagine
Vorstellungsgespräch(e) *n.* (job) interview
Vorwahl(nummer(n)) *f.* area code
vorziehen to prefer
Vorzimmer *n.* anteroom / secretary's office

Wacholder *m.* juniper schnapps
Wagen *m.* car
wählen to choose/select/dial
Wählton (-töne) *m.* dialling tone
wahrnehmen to avail oneself of
wahrscheinlich probable
Wandern *n.* walking
wann? when?
Ware(n) *f.* goods
warm warm
warten to wait
Wartung(en) *f.* maintenance
Wartungsvertrag (-verträge) *m.* maintenance agreement
warum(?) why(?)
was(?) what(?)
was für(?) what kind of (?)
Wasser *n.* water / mineral water
WC *n.* WC / toilet
Weberei(en) *f.* weaving mill
Wechselkurs(e) *m.* exchange rate
wechseln to (ex)change
Wechselschicht(en) *f.* shift work
Weg(e) *m.* way
wegen because of / regarding
erster Weihnachtstag Christmas Day
zweiter Weihnachtstag Boxing Day
weiß white
weit long / far
so weit ready
weiter (nach) on (to) / further
weitere/weiterer/weiteres further
weiterfahren to go on/continue the journey
Weiterfahrt(en) *f.* continuation of the journey
weitergehen to go on
weiterhin further(more)
weiterreisen to travel/go on
welche/welcher/welches(?) which(?)
Welt(en) *f.* world
wem(?) (to) whom(?)
sich wenden an here: to be directed to
wenig little, few
wenigstens at least
wenn if/when
wer(?) who(?)
Werbeabteilung(en) *f.* advertising department
Werbefachmann (-leute) *m.* advertising expert
Werbegeschenk(e) *n.* (free) gift / gift for advertising purposes
Werbeleiter *m.* advertising manager
werden will / would / to become
Werk(e) *n.* factory / plant
ab Werk ex factory / works / plant
Werktag(e) *m.* workday
Wertpapiergeschäft(e) *n.* securities business
weshalb(?) why(?)
westdeutsch west German
Westküste(n) *f.* west coast
Wetter *n.* weather
wichtig important
wie(?) how(?) / what(?) / as
wie wäre/ist es (mit)? how about?
wie gesagt as I said (before)
wieder again
wiederholen to repeat/say again
(auf) Wiederhören goodbye
wiederkommen to come again/back
(auf) Wiederschauen goodbye
(auf) Wiedersehen goodbye
Wiedervereinigung *f.* reunification
Wiederverkaufsrabatt(e) *m.* trade discount
wieviel(?) how much(?) / which(?)
wievielte/wievielter/wievieltes(?) which(?)
Winter *m.* winter
wir we
wirklich really
Wirtschaftsakademie(n) *f.* commercial college
wissen to know
wo(?) where(?)
woanders elsewhere
Woche(n) *f.* week
Wochentag(e) *m.* day of the week
wohin(?) where(?)
wohl possibly
wohnen to live/inhabit
Wohnkomplex(e) *m.* housing complex
Wohnort(e) *m.* place of residence
wollen to want / intend/would
womit(?) with what(?)
worunter(?) from which(?)
wunderbar wonderful / splendid / fine
wünschen to wish/want
würde(n) would
Würstchen *n.* sausage

Zahl(en) *f.* number / figure
zahlbar payable
zahlen to pay
Zahlung(en) *f.* payment
Zahlungsbedingung(en) *f.* term(s) of payment
Zahlungsweise(n) *f.* mode/method of payment
z.B. (zum Beispiel) e.g. (for example)
Zeichen *n.* signal
zeigen to show/demonstrate
Zeit(en) *f.* time
zur Zeit at present
einen Moment Zeit haben to have a minute to spare
Zeitansage(n) *f.* time signal / speaking clock
Zeitpersonal *n.* temporary staff
Zeitschrift(en) *f.* journal / magazine / periodical
Zeitung(en) *f.* (news)paper
zentral central(ly)
Zentrale(n) *f.* head office / headquarters
Zeugnis(se) *n.* testimonial / reference
Zielsprache(n) *f.* target language
ziemlich quite / rather
Zigeunerschnitzel *n.* pork chop with peppers and tomatoes
Zimmer *n.* room
Zimmer frei haben to have vacancies
Zimmernummer(n) *f.* room number
zu to
Zucker *m.* sugar
zuerst (at) first
Zug (Züge) *m.* train
Zugauskunft (-künfte) / Zuginformation(en) *f.* train information
zugesagt promised
Zugrestaurant(s) *n.* train restaurant
Zugverbindung(en) *f.* train connection
zukommen lassen to send/let have
zukünftig (in) future
zulaufen (auf) to walk towards
Zulieferer *m.* sub-supplier
zunächst (at) first
zurück back

zurückfliegen to fly back/home
zurückrufen to call back
zusammen together
Zusammenarbeit *f.* cooperation
zusammenrechnen to add up
im Zusammensein mit together with
zusammenstellen to put together/arrange
zusätzlich additional(ly) / in addition
zuschicken to send
Zuschlag (-schläge) *m.* supplement, surcharge, extra income
zuschneiden auf to tailor to
Zuschrift(en) *f.* **erbeten** please write to
zusenden to send
Zusendung(en) *f.* sending / forwarding
um Zusendung bitten to ask to be sent
zuständig responsible / in charge
zuverlässig reliable
zwar in fact / actually
und zwar that is
zwar ... aber it is true that ... but ...
Zweigbetrieb(e) *m.* branch plant / factory
Zweigstelle(n) *f.* branch (office)
Zweigstellennetz(e) *n.* branch network
Zweigwerk(e) *n.* branch plant/factory
zweimal twice
Zweimarkstück(e) *n.* two-mark coin/piece
zweitgrößte second biggest
zweiwöchig of two weeks
Zwiebelsuppe(n) *f.* onion soup
zwischen between
in der Zwischenzeit *f.* in the meantime
zwo (zwei) two (when said over the phone)

English–German

a ein / eine / einer
be able to können
about über
about that darüber
above oben / über
above all vor allen Dingen / vor allem
above-mentioned vorgenannt
abroad im/ins Ausland
absolute(ly) unbedingt / einfach
accessories Zubehör *n.*
accommodate *verb* unterbringen
according to gemäß
accounting (department) Buchhaltung(en) *f.* / Buchhaltungsabteilung(en) *f.*
across über
active aktiv / tätig
activity Aktivität(en) *f.*
actual(ly) zwar / eigentlich
ad Annonce(n) *f.* / Anzeige(n) *f.* / Inserat(e) *n.*
add *verb* addieren
add up *verb* zusammenrechnen / rechnen (mit)
in addition extra / hinzu / zusätzlich
additional(ly) zusätzlich/hinzu
address Adresse(n) *f.* / Anschrift(en) *f.*
administration Verwaltung(en) *f.*
adult Erwachsener (Erwachsenen) *m.*
advertised ausgeschrieben
advertisement Annonce(n) *f.* / Anzeige(n) *f.* / Inserat(e) *n.*
advertising Reklame *f.*
advertising department Werbeabteilung(en) *f.*
advertising expert Werbefachmann (-leute) *m.*
advertising manager Werbeleiter *m.*
adviser Berater *m.*
afford something *verb* sich etwas erlauben
after hinter / nach
after all doch
after that im Anschluß (dar)an
afternoon Nachmittag(e) *m.*
in the afternoon nachmittags
afterwards nachher
again wieder
...ago vor
agree *verb* einverstanden sein / sich einigen
agreed einverstanden
ahead vorn
airport lounge Flughafenhalle(n) *f.*
alcohol-free alkoholfrei
ale Alt(bier) *n.*
all ganz / alle / alles / sämtlich
all day ganztägig
(all) too allzu
be allowed *verb* dürfen
All Saints Allerheiligen
alone allein
along entlang
already schon
Is that all right? Ist das recht?
also auch / ebenfalls / außerdem
although obwohl
altogether insgesamt
always immer
ambience Ambiente *n.*
amount Betrag (Beträge) *m.* / Summe(n) *f.* / Stückzahl(en) *f.* / Umfang (Umfänge) *m.*
amount to *verb* sich belaufen auf / betragen
amounting to in Höhe von
amount shown angezeigter Betrag
and und
and also sowie
and partners & Co (& Compagnie)
and so on (etc.) und so weiter (usw.)
and then anschließend
annex Anbau(ten) *m.*
annoyed verärgert
annual general meeting Hauptversammlung(en) *f.*
annual turnover/sales Jahresumsatz (-umsätze) *m.*
per annum pro Jahr
anteroom Vorzimmer
any irgendeine / irgendeiner / irgendeines / irgendwelche / irgendwelcher / irgendwelches
anyone jemand
apart (from that) sonst
apologize *verb* sich entschuldigen
apology Entschuldigung(en) *f.*
appear *verb* erscheinen
apple juice Apfelsaft (-säfte) *m.*
(job) application Bewerbung(en) *f.*
application form Antragsformular(e) *n.*
application papers Bewerbungsunterlagen *pl.*
apply *verb* sich verstehen
appointment Termin(e) *m.*
appointments Terminplan (-pläne) *m.* / Terminkalender *m.*
have another appointment verhindert sein
appointment for a visit Besuchstermin(e) *m.*
(fixing of/making an) appointment Terminvereinbarung(en) *f.* / Terminabsprache(n) *f.*
apprentice Auszubildender (-bildenden) *m.*
approximately etwa / ungefähr
April April *m.*
area Region(en) *f.* / Bereich(e) *m.* / Feld(er) *n.*
area code Vorwahl(nummer(n)) *f.*
area-wide flächendeckend
arise *verb* entstehen
arrange *verb* ausmachen / vereinbaren / zusammenstellen
arrival Ankunft (-künfte) *f.*
arrive *verb* ankommen / anreisen / eintreffen
arrived eingefahren / eingetroffen
article Produkt(e) *n.* / Artikel *m.*
as als / wie
as far as ... is concerned vom/von ... her
as from/of ab
as I said (before) wie gesagt
as long as solange
as quickly as possible so schnell wie möglich
as regards vom/von ... her
as well ruhig (*colloquial*)
as well as sowie
ask *verb* bitten / fragen / nachfragen
ask someone to pay cash *verb* bar kassieren
ask to be sent *verb* um Zusendung bitten
assess *verb* beurteilen
assistant Assistent(en) *m.*
assistant to the marketing manager Marketing-Assistent(en) *m.*
at an / bei
at first zuerst / zunächst
at least wenigens
at ... o'clock um ... Uhr
at once sofort
Atlantic coast Atlantikküste(n) *f.*
attempt *verb* probieren/versuchen
attention Vorsicht *f.*

(for the) attention (of) (Attn. / f.a.o.) zu Händen von (z.Hd.)
August August *m.*
Austria Österreich
automatic(ally) selbsttätig / automatisch
autumn Herbst *m.*
autumn collection/range Herbstkollektion(en) *f.*
autumn trade Herbstgeschäft(e) *n.*
avail oneself of *verb* wahrnehmen
available erhältlich
be available *verb* zur Verfügung stehen/vorliegen
make available *verb* zur Verfügung stellen
average Durchschnitt(e) *m.*
be aware of something *verb* sich über etwas im klaren sein
away (on business) unterwegs
away for lunch zu Tisch
awful furchtbar

back zurück
at the back hinten
bad(ly) schlecht / schlimm
baker's (shop) Bäckerladen (-läden) *m.*
balancing out Ausgleich *m.*
bank Bank(en) *f.*
regional bank Regionalbank(en) *f.*
banknote Schein(e) / Geldschein(e) *m.*
bath(room) Bad (Bäder) *n.*
bathroom Badezimmer *n.*
bathroom on each floor Etagenbad (-bäder) *n.*
be *verb* sein / betragen / stehen / sich befinden / liegen / bestehen
be to *verb* sollen
beach Strand (Strände) *m.*
because of auf Grund von/wegen
become *verb* werden
bedroom Schlafzimmer *n.*
before vorher / vorhin
begin *verb* anfangen / starten
beginning Anfang (-fänge) *m.*
on behalf of im Auftrag von
behind hinter
Belgium Belgien
believe *verb* glauben
below unten / unter
besides daneben
best am besten / beste / bester / bestes / äußerst
better besser
between zwischen
beverage Getränk(e) *n.*
big groß
bill Rechnung(en) *f.*
billboard advertising Großflächenwerbung(en) *f.*
billion Milliarde(n) (Mrd.) *f.*
birthday Geburtstag(e) *m.*
little bit Stückchen *n.*
a little bit ein bißchen
black schwarz
Black Forest Schwarzwald *m.*
black tea schwarzer Tee
blow! *(exclamation)* Mist! *m.*
board *verb* einsteigen
boat Boot(e) *n.*
book Buch (Bücher) *n.*
book *verb* bestellen / buchen
booked in advance vorbestellt
fully booked ausgebucht
booking Buchung(en) *f.*
bookkeeper Buchhalter *m.*
bookkeeping (department) Buchhaltung(en) *f.* / Buchhaltungsabteilung(en) *f.*
boss Chef(s) *m.*
both beide
bottle Flasche(n) *f.*
(at the) bottom unten
box no. Chiffre-Nummer(n) *f.*
Boxing Day zweiter Weihnachtstag
branch (office) Filiale(n) *f.* / Zweigstelle(n) *f.*
branch factory/plant Zweigwerk(e) *n.* / Zweigbetrieb(e) *m.*
branch network Zweigstellennetz(e) *n.*
bread Brot(e) *n.*
break Pause(n) *f.*
break down *verb* ausfallen
breakdown Panne(n) *f.*
breakfast Frühstück *n.*
have breakfast *verb* frühstücken
brewery Brauerei(en) *f.*
brief(ly) kurz / mal eben
briefing Vorbesprechung(en) *f.*
bring *verb* bringen
bring out *verb* herausbringen
broadcast Sendung(en) *f.*
brochure Prospekt(e) *m.* / Broschüre(n) *f.*
budgeting for the year Jahresplanung(en) *f.*
main building Haupthaus (-häuser) *n.*
bus station (Omni)Busbahnhof (-höfe) *m.*
business Betrieb(e) *m.*
small (and medium-sized) business mittelständisches Unternehmen *n.*
business with corporate customers Großfirmengeschäft(e) *n.*
business with private customers Privatkundengeschäft(e) *n.*
foreign business Auslandsgeschäft(e) *n.*
business administrator (qualified) Diplom-Betriebswirt(e) *m.*
business card (Visiten)/Karte(n) *f.*
business contact Geschäftskontakt(e) *m.*
business diary Terminkalender *m.* / Terminplan (-pläne) *m.*
business hours Öffnungszeit(en) *f.*
business management Geschäftsführung(en) *f.*
business matters geschäftliche Dinge *pl.* / das Kaufmännische *n.*
business talks Geschäftsbesprechung(en) *f.*
busy engagiert
be busy *verb* verhindert sein / zu tun haben
but aber / sondern / jedoch
butcher's (shop) Metzgerladen (-läden) *m.*
button Knopf (Knöpfe) *m.* / Taste(n) *f.*
buy *verb* einkaufen / kaufen / abnehmen
buyer Einkäufer *m.*
chief buyer Einkaufsleiter *m.*
buying Kaufen *n.*
buying (department) Einkauf (-käufe) *m.*
buzzing sound Summton (-töne) *m.*
by durch / per
by and large soweit
by the way übrigens
bye! Tschüß!

cable television Kabelfernsehen *n.*
calculate *verb* errechnen / rechnen (mit)
call Gespräch(e) *n.*/ Anruf(e) *m.* / Telefonat(e) *n.*
domestic/national call Inlandsgespräch(e) *n.*
foreign/international call Auslandsgespräch(e) *n.*
call *verb* anrufen / durchrufen / sich melden
call back *verb* zurückrufen
call it ... machen Sie ... draus
be called *verb* heißen
calm ruhig
can *verb* können
cancel *verb* absagen
cancellation Stornierung(en) *f.*
car Auto(s) *n.* / Wagen *m.*
hired car Mietwagen *m.*
car dealer Autohaus (-häuser) *n.*
car park Parkplatz (-plätze) *m.*

multi-storey car park Parkhaus (-häuser) *n.*
underground car park Tiefgarage(n) *f.*
card Karte(n) *f.*
cardphone Kartentelefon(e) *n.*
care Vorsicht *f.*
care of (c/o) zu Händen von (z.Hd.)
take care of *verb* übernehmen
carnival Fastnacht *f.* / Karneval *m.*
carphone Autotelefon(e) *n.*
carrier Spediteur(e) *m.*
carton material Kartonage(n) *f.*
cartons Kartonage(n) *f.*
case Fall (Fälle) *m.*
in any case auf jeden Fall
cash (Bar) Geld(er) *n.* bar
pay cash *verb* bar bezahlen
cash discount Skonto (Skonti) *m./n.*
cashier Kassierer *m.*
cause Grund (Gründe) *m.*
caused by bedingt durch
central(ly) zentral
central station Hauptbahnhof (-höfe) *m.*
certain(ly) sicher / selbstverständlich / bestimmt
chairman Vorsitzender(-en) *m.*
Chamber of Industry and Commerce Industrie- und Handelskammer(n) (IHK) *f.*
chance Chance(n) *f.*
change *verb* sich verändern
change (money) *verb* eintauschen / umtauschen
change (trains) *verb* umsteigen
charge Gebühr(en) *f.*
extra charge Zuschlag (-schläge) *m.*
in charge verantwortlich / zuständig
check *verb* nachschauen / prüfen / überprüfen
chemical product Chemieprodukt(e) *n.*
fried chicken Brathähnchen *n.*
chicken soup Hühnersuppe(n) *f.*
child Kind(er) *n.*
chips (French fries) Pommes frites *pl.*
chocolate Schokolade(n) *f.*
choice Auswahl(en) *f.*
have a choice of *verb* zur Auswahl haben
choose *verb* wählen / auswählen
Christmas Day erster Weihnachtstag
church Kirche(n) *f.*
city Stadt (Städte) *f.*
clarify *verb* klären
clear *verb* freigeben
clear klar
clear up *verb* (explain) klären
clerk Sachbearbeiter *m.* / Kaufmann (-leute) *m.*
clerk in the marketing department Marketing-Assistent(en) *m.*
industrial clerk Industriekaufmann (-leute) *m.*
commercial clerk (qualified) Diplom-Kaufmann (-leute) *m.*
(office)clerk (qualified) Bürokaufmann (-leute) *m.*
(office) clerk (qualified) (female) Bürokauffrau(en) *f.*
client Kunde(n) *m.*
climate Klima *n.*
clock Uhr(en) *f.*
at ... o'clock um ... Uhr
close *verb* schließen
close by in der Nähe
closing day Ruhetag(e) *m.*
coach station (Omni)Busbahnhof (-höfe) *m.*
coat Mantel (Mäntel) *m.*
coat stand Garderobe(n) *f.*
coffee Kaffee *m.*
coin Münze(n) *f.*
one-mark coin Markstück(e) *n.*
cold kalt
something cold etwas Kaltes
collection Kollektion(en) *f.*
come (from) *verb* kommen (aus)
come again *verb* wiederkommen
come along with someone *verb* mitkommen
come in *verb* eintreten / hereinkommen
come past vorbeikommen
come and see *verb* vorbeikommen
come to *verb* kommen (zu)
come what may unbedingt
commercial kaufmännisch
commercial college Wirtschaftsakademie(n) *f.*
committed engagiert
commodity Rohstoff(e) *m.*
company Firma (Firmen) *f.* / Unternehmen *n.*
in our company bei uns / hier im Hause / in unserem Hause
outside the company auswärts
private limited company (Ltd/Inc.) GmbH(s) (Gesellschaft(en) mit beschränkterHaftung) *f.*
public limited company (plc) AG(s) (Aktiengesellschaft(en)) *f.*
on the company premises hier: im Hause
company stationery Briefpapier(e) *n.*
competitive günstig
complete vollständig / ausführlich / komplett
completed fertig / abgeschlossen
comprehensive umfassend
computer Computer *m.*
computer program Computerprogramm(e) *n.*
computer technology Computertechnik(en) *f.*
concentrate (on) *verb* sich konzentrieren (auf)
concentration Konzentration(en) *f.*
concept Konzept(e) *n.*
be concerned *verb* sich handeln um
as far as ... is concerned vom/von ... her
concerning bezüglich
conclude *verb* (Vertrag) abschließen
condition Bedingung(en) *f.*
on (the) condition that unter der Bedingung, daß
conference room Konferenzraum (-räume) *m.* / Sitzungszimmer *n.*
congratulations herzliche Glückwünsche
connect *verb* verbinden
connection Verbindung(en) *f.* / Anschluß (-schlüsse) *m.*
considerable(-ly) erheblich
consignment Sendung(en) *f.* / Lieferung(en) *f.*
consultant Berater *m.*
contained enthalten
continent Kontinent(e) *m.*
continuation of the journey Weiterfahrt(en) *f.*
continue (the journey) *verb* weiterfahren
control (operate) *verb* bedienen
control engineering Regeltechnik(en) *f.*
remote control Fernbedienung(en) *f.*
conversation Gespräch(e) *n.*
conversion table Umrechnungstabelle(n) *f.*
convert *verb* umrechnen
cooking Küche *f.*
cooperation Zusammenarbeit *f.*
copier Kopiergerät(e) *n.*
copy Kopie(n) *f.*
cordial herzlich
corn schnapps Korn *m.*
Corpus Christi Fronleichnam *m.*
correct richtig/korrekt
be correct *verb* stimmen
corridor Gang (Gänge) *m.* / Flur(e) *m.* / Korridor(e) *m.*
cost *verb* kosten
how much does it cost? was kostet das?

that costs... das macht...
could *verb* können
count on *verb* rechnen mit
country Land (Länder) *n.*
foreign countries Ausland *n.*
fast courier Blitzkurier(e) *m.*
course Kurs(e) *m.*
course participant Kursteilnehmer *m.*
intensive course Intensivkurs(e) *m.*
cream Sahne *f.*
credit card Kreditkarte(n) *f.*
cuisine Küche(n) *f.*
cup Tasse(n) *f.*
cup of coffee Tasse Kaffee
cupboard Schrank (Schränke) *m.*
currency Sorte(n) *f.*
foreign currency Devise(n) *f.*
current (valid) gültig / (contemporaneous) derzeitig
curriculum vitae (CV) Lebenslauf (-läufe) *m.*
customary üblich
customer Kunde(n) *m.* / (in restaurant) Gast (Gäste) *m.*
customer service Kundendienst(e) *m.*
corporate customer Firmenkunde(n) *m.*
private customer Privatkunde(n) *m.*
private customer banking activities Kundeninteressen *pl.*
customized individuell
customized manufacturing Einzelanfertigung(en) *f.*
cut short *verb* abkürzen

daily täglich
Damn it! Mist!
data Daten *pl.*
date Termin(e) *m.*
date of birth Geburtsdatum (-daten) *n.*
date of invoice Rechnungsdatum (-daten) *n.*
date of a/the trade fair Messetermin(e) *m.*
day Tag(e) *m.*
day after tomorrow übermorgen.
every other day jeden zweiten Tag
good day guten Tag
late closing day Dienstleistungsabend(e) *m.*
deadline Termin(e) *m.*
deal with *verb* sich befassen
dealt with here: abgehakt
dear teuer
Dear Sir or Madam Sehr geehrte Damen und Herren
decade Jahrzehnt(e) *n.*
December Dezember *m.*
decide *verb* entscheiden
decision Entscheidung(en) *f.*
defect Störung(en) *f.*
definite(ly) bestimmt
delay Verspätung(en) *f.*
delayed verzögert
deliver *verb* liefern
delivered gebracht
delivery Lieferung(en) *f.*
delivery date Liefertermin(e) *m.*
delivery difficulties Lieferschwierigkeit(en) *f.*
delivery period Lieferfrist(en) *f.* / Lieferzeit(en) *f.*
delivery problem Lieferproblem(e) *n.*
demanding anspruchsvoll
demonstrate *verb* zeigen
Denmark Dänemark
depart *verb* abfahren
department Abteilung(en) *f.*
departmental meeting Abteilungsbesprechung(en) *f.*
departure Abreise(n) *f.* / Abfahrt(en) *f.*
depend on *verb* abhängen von / sich richten nach
go into depth *verb* vertiefen
designed gestaltet
desk Schreibtisch(e) *m.*
despite trotz
detail Detail(s) *n.* / Einzelheit(en) *f.*
details Daten *pl.*
detailed/in detail detailliert
determine *verb* festlegen
detrimental nachteilig
develop *verb* entwickeln
development Entwicklung(en) *f.*
device Apparat(e) *m.*/ Gerät(e) *n.*
diagonal(ly) schräg
dial *verb* wählen
dial(ling) tone Wählton (-töne) *m.*
diary Kalender *m.*
diesel fuel Dieselkraftstoff(e) *m.*
difference Unterschied(e) *m.*
different verschieden / anders
diploma course Diplomkurs(e) *m.*
direct direkt / durchgehend
be directed to *verb* here: sich wenden an
direction Fahrtrichtung(en) *f.* / Richtung(en) *f.*
in the direction of in Richtung
director Direktor(en) *m.*
disadvantageous nachteilig
discount Rabatt(e) *m.*
discuss *verb* besprechen / klären / sich unterhalten
discuss and agree *verb* sich abstimmen
discuss in detail *verb* durchsprechen
discuss in more detail *verb* vertiefen
preliminary discussion Vorbesprechung(en) *f.*
dispatch Versand *m.*
dispatch department Versandabteilung(en) *f.*
dispatch manager Leiter *m.* des Versands
dispose of *verb* verfügen über
distribute *verb* verteilen
distribution department Vertriebsabteilung(en) *f.*
distribution engineer Vertriebsingenieur(e) *m.*
distribution manager Vertriebsleiter *m.*
district Region(en) *f.*
do *verb* machen / tun / übernehmen
doctor Doktor(en) *m.*
document Unterlage(n) *f.*
domestic hiesig
door Tür(en) *f.*
down runter / unten
down here hier unten
down there da unten
drink Getränk(e) *n.*
drink *verb* trinken
drive *verb* fahren
with drive einsatzfreudig
drop *verb* lassen
due to bedingt durch
duty Aufgabe(n) *f.*
dynamic dynamisch

each jede / jeder / jedes
each time jeweils
early früh
earlier vorhin
earn *verb* verdienen
east coast Ostküste(n) *f.*
Easter Ostertag *m.*
Easter Monday Ostermontag *m.*
easy leicht
probably the easiest am ehesten
eat *verb* essen
economist (qualified) Diplom-Volkswirt(e) *m.*
EDP (electronic data processing) EDV (elektronische Datenverarbeitung) *f.*
EDP-course EDV-Lehrgang (-gänge) *m.*
EDP-equipment EDV-Anlage(n) *f.*
e.g. (for example) z.B. (zum Beispiel)
egg Ei(er) *n.*
scrambled egg Rührei(er) *n.*
electrical elektrisch
elevator Aufzug (-züge) *m.* / Fahrstuhl (-stühle) *m.*

elsewhere woanders
emerged entstanden
emergency call Notruf(e) *m.*
employ *verb* beschäftigen / einsetzen
employee Mitarbeiter *m.* / Arbeitnehmer *m.*
employee (salaried) Angestellte(r) (-en) *f./m.*
enclosed beigefügt
enclosure Anlage(n) *f.*
end Ende *n.*
engaged beschäftigt
be engaged *verb* verhindert sein
engineering manager Technischer Leiter *m.*
engineering works Maschinenfabrik(en) *f.*
English englisch
English-speaking englischsprechend
enough genug
be enough *verb* reichen / genügen
enquire *verb* nachfragen / sich erkundigen
enquiry Anfrage(n) *f.*
enrol *verb* sich anmelden
enter *verb* eintreten/ eintragen
enter into *verb* (Vertrag) abschließen
be entered hinkommen
enterprise Unternehmen *n.*
entire vollständig
enthusiastic begeistert
envisaged vorgesehen
Epiphany Heilige Drei Könige
especially besonders / insbesondere
estimate *verb* abschätzen
Europe Europa
Euro-secretary Europasekretärin(nen) *f.*
even sogar
evening Abend(e) *m.*
in the evening(s) abends
good evening guten Abend
this evening heute abend
every jede / jeder / jedes
everything alles / das Ganze
everything('s) OK alles klar
everywhere überall
ex factory/plant/works ab Werk
ex warehouse ab Lager
exact(ly) genau
exactly genauso
examine *verb* prüfen
for example beispielsweise
in exchange als Ausgleich
exchange of money Geldtausch *m.*
exchange *verb* eintauschen / umtauschen/wechseln
foreign exchange counter Sortenschalter *m.* / Devisenschalter *m.*
foreign exchange dealing Devisenhandel *m.*
exchange rate Wechselkurs(e) *m.*
foreign exchange rate Devisenkurs(e) *m.*
exceed *verb* übersteigen
excellent fabelhaft / hervorragend
except (for) außer
exclusively ausschließlich
excuse Entschuldigung(en) *f.*
Excuse me! Entschuldigung! / Entschuldigen Sie!
executive Führungskraft (-kräfte) *f.*
exercise *verb* ausüben
exhaustive ausführlich
exhibit *verb* ausstellen
exhibition (trade) Messe(n) *f.*
foreign exhibition Auslandsmesse(n) *f.*
exist *verb* bestehen
expand *verb* ausbauen / ausweiten
expect *verb* erwarten
expensive teuer
experience Erfahrung(en) *f.*
expert Spezialist(en) *m.*
explain *verb* erklären
by way of explanation zur Erläuterung *f.*
export *verb* exportieren
export clerk Exportkaufmann (-leute) *m.*
export department Exportabteilung(en) *f.*
in the export department im Export *m.*
export manager Exportleiter *m.*
export merchant Exportkaufmann (-leute) *m.*
express train D-Zug (Züge) *m.* / Schnellzug (-züge) *m.*
extension (number) Durchwahl (-nummer(n)) *f.*
external auswärtig
extra extra
extreme äußerst

facility Einrichtung(en) *f.* / Dienstleistung(en) *f.*
in fact zwar
factor Faktor(en) *m.*
factory Werk(e) *n.* / Betrieb(e) *m.*
fair (trade) Messe(n) *f.*
foreign fair Auslandsmesse(n) *f.*
fall Herbst *m.*
family Familie(n) *f.*
family name Nachname(n) *m.* / Familienname(n) *m.*
far weit
fast schnell
father Vater (Väter) *m.*
fault Störung(en) *f.*
faultless einwandfrei
favourable günstig
fax Fax(e) *n.*
fax machine Faxgerät(e) *n.*
February Februar *m.*
at federal level bundesweit
fee Gebühr(en) *f.*
fetch *verb* abholen
few wenig(e)
a few einige
quite a few eine ganze Reihe
field (of business) Sparte(n) *f.* / Feld(er) *n.* / Bereich(e) *m.*
field staff Außendienstmitarbeiter *pl.*
field worker Außendienstmitarbeiter *m.*
figure Zahl(en) *f.*
file Bewerbungsunterlagen *pl.*
fill in *verb* eintragen / ausfüllen
fill out *verb* ausfüllen
finally schließlich
finance manager Leiter *m.* der Finanzen
fine prima / wunderbar
that's fine das ist recht
finished fertig / abgeschlossen
fire (and ambulance) service Feuerwehr(en) *f.*
firm Firma (Firmen) *f.*
in our firm in unserem Hause / hier im Hause
firm fest / verbindlich
first erste / erster / erstes / erst
(at) first zuerst
first name Vorname(n) *m.*
first of all als erstes
fit *verb* einbauen
fix *verb* ausmachen / vereinbaren
fixed angesetzt
flexible flexibel
flexitime Gleitzeit(en) *f.*
flight Flug (Flüge) *m.*
flight number Flugnummer(n) *f.*
floor Stock(werk(e)) *m./n.* / Etage(n) *f.*
florist's (shop) / flower shop Blumenladen (-läden) *m.*
fly *verb* fliegen
fly back/home *verb* zurückfliegen
flyer Prospektblatt (-blätter) *n.*
foil Folienträger *m.*
which is followed by anschließend
following folgend / nächste / nächster / nächstes
for in Richtung / bei / für / um / nämlich
for that dafür
foresee *verb* absehen

form Formular(e) *n.*
continuous form Endlosformular(e) *n.*
a fortnight 14 Tage
forwarder Spediteur(e) *m.*
forwarding Zusendung(en) *f.*
founded gegründet
franc Franken *m.*
France Frankreich
franco domicile frei Haus
free frei
freight clerk/ merchant Speditionskaufmann (-leute) *m.*
French französisch
French fries Pommes (frites) *pl.*
French-speaking französischsprechend
frequently öfter
Friday Freitag(e) *m.*
on Fridays freitags
friendly freundlich
from von / aus / ab
from that daraus / draus (*colloquial*)
from which worunter
in front vorn
fuel Kraftstoff(e) *m.*
full vollständig / ausführlich / komplett
function Funktion(en) *f.*
function *verb* funktionieren
furnish *verb* einrichten
furniture factory Möbelfabrik(en) *f.*
further weitere / weiterer / weiteres / weiter (nach)
further(more) weiterhin
furthermore außerdem
kick up a fuss *verb* Riesentheater *n.* machen
(in) future zukünftig

garden Park(s) *m.*
gas Gas(e) *n.*
gasoline Benzin *m.*
gasoline station Tankstelle(n) *f.*
gather *verb* ersehen
general(ly) allgemein
generally im allgemeinen
gentleman Herr(en) *m.*
genuine(ly) aufrichtig
German deutsch
German-speaking deutschsprechend
get *verb* empfangen / bekommen / erhalten / rechnen (mit)
oh, I get it ach so
get out *verb* herausholen
get to *verb* erreichen
get to something *verb* zu etwas finden
(free) gift Werbegeschenk(e) *n.*
give *verb* geben / angeben / nennen / gewähren / erteilen / einräumen
given gegeben
go *verb* gehen / fahren / laufen
go along *verb* entlanggehen
go by air *verb* fliegen
go on *verb* weitergehen / weiterfahren / weiterreisen
go out *verb* herausgehen
go through *verb* durchgehen
by God um Gottes willen
good God um Gottes willen
gold card Goldkarte(n) *f.*
gone gefahren
good gut
goodbye (auf) Wiederhör(e)n / (auf) Wiederschau(e)n / (auf) Wiederseh(e)n
say goodbye *verb* verabschieden
Good Friday Karfreitag *m.*
goodness me (du) meine Güte
goods Ware(n) *f.*
grant *verb* gewähren / einräumen
grape juice Traubensaft (-säfte) *m.*
gratitude Dank *m.*
great groß
Great Britain Großbritannien
green grün
greengrocer's (shop) Gemüseladen (-läden) *m.*
greet *verb* begrüßen
gross brutto
guarantee Garantie(n) *f.*
guarantee *verb* garantieren
guest Gast (Gäste) *m.*
guest-house Gasthaus (-häuser) *n.*

half halb
ham Schinken *m.*
hand Hand (Hände) *f.*
Hannover Fair Hannover Messe *f.*
have (got) *verb* haben / verfügen über
have to *verb* müssen
Hawaiian toast Hawaii Toast *m.*
he er
head Chef(s) *m.* / Direktor(en) *m.*
head of department Abteilungsleiter *m.*
head of the dispatch department Leiter *m.* des Versands
head of finance Leiter *m.* der Finanzen
head of marketing Leiter *m.* Marketing
head of personnel Personalleiter *m.*
head of the purchasing department Einkaufsleiter *m.*
head office/headquarters Zentrale *f.*
hear *verb* hören
hearty herzlich
hello hallo / grüß Gott
help *verb* helfen
her sie / ihr(e)
here hier / hierher
right here hier vorn
up here hier oben
hereby hiermit
herewith hiermit
grilled herring Brathering(e) *m.*
high hoch
higher-income here: gehoben
hill Berg(e) *m.*
him ihn
hire *verb* mieten
his sein(e)
history Geschichte(n) *f.*
hitherto bisher
holiday(s) Urlaub(e) *m.*
holidays Ferien *pl.*
go on holiday *verb* Urlaub machen
public holiday Feiertag(e) *m.*
holiday course Ferienkurs(e) *m.*
peak holiday season Hauptreisezeit(en) *f.*
Holland Holland
home (direction) nach Hause
home town Heimatstadt (-städte) *f.*
hope *verb* hoffen
I/let's hope hoffentlich
hospital Krankenhaus (-häuser) *n.*
hot heiß
hotel Hotel(s) *n.*
middle-range hotel Hotel der Mittelklasse
hotel accommodation Hotelübernachtung(en) *f.*
hotel lobby Hotelhalle(n) *f.*
hotel reception Hotelrezeption(en) *f.*
hour Stunde(n) *f.*
in half an hour in einer halben Stunde
hour of overtime Überstunde(n) *f.*
house *verb* unterbringen
housing complex Wohnkomplex(e) *m.*
how(?) wie(?)
how about ...? wie sieht es aus mit...? / wie wäre/ist es (mit)?
how do you do? angenehm
how much? wieviel?
how much is it? was kostet das?
however allerdings / jedoch
Hungarian soup Gulaschsuppe(n) *f.*
husband Ehemann (-männer) *m.*

I ich
ice-cream Eis *n.*
ice-cream sundae Eisbecher *m.*

idea Idee(n) *f.* / Gedanke(n) *m.* / Anregung(en) *f.*
ideal ideal
i.e. (that is) d.h. (das heißt)
if wenn
imagine *verb* sich vorstellen
immediate(ly) direkt
immediately gleich / sofort
important wichtig
impossible unmöglich
be impossible *verb* nicht gehen
impression Eindruck (-drücke) *m.*
impressive eindrucksvoll
improve *verb* verbessern
in in / rein
in(to) herein
in that daran
included enthalten
inclusive (of) inklusive (inkl.) / einschließlich
increase *verb* erhöhen
indeed sogar
independent(ly) eigenständig
individual individuell
industry Industrie(n) *f.* / Branche(n) *f.*
inform *verb* Bescheid geben / sagen / informieren
inform oneself *verb* sich erkundigen / sich informieren
inform in advance *verb* vorinformieren
information Information(en) *f.* / Bescheid(e) *m.* / Auskunft (-künfte) *f.* / Nachricht(en) *f.* / Daten *pl.*
information material Informationsmaterial(ien) *n.*
detailed information Detailinformationen *pl.*
informative aufschlußreich
be informed *verb* Bescheid *m.* bekommen
inhabit *verb* wohnen
in-house intern
inquiry Anfrage(n) *f.*
insert *verb* einwerfen / stecken
institutional institutionell
instruct *verb* anweisen
instruction manual Bedienungsanleitung(en) *f.*
instruments engineering Apparatebau *n.*
intend *verb* wollen / vorhaben
intercity supplement InterCity-Zuschlag (-schläge) *m.*
interest Interesse(n) *n.*
interest *verb* interessieren
be interested in *verb* sich interessieren für
interesting interessant
internal(ly) intern
international(ly) international
interpreter *verb* Dolmetscher *m.* / Dolmetscherin(nen) *f.*
interval Pause(n) *f.*
(job) interview Vorstellungsgespräch(e) *n.*
into in
introduce *verb* einführen
introduce (oneself) *verb* sich vorstellen
introduction on the market Markteinführung(en) *f.*
investor Anleger *m.*
invitation Einladung(en) *f.*
invite *verb* einladen
involve *verb* sich handeln um
involvement in retail banking Kundeninteresse(n) *n.*
Ireland Irland
it es
Italy Italien
item Sache(n) *f.* / Stück(e) *n.* / Artikel *m.*

January Januar *m.*
job Beruf(e) *m.* / Arbeitsfeld(er) *n.* / (task) Aufgabe(n) *f.*
job ad Stellenausschreibung(en) *f.*
job application Bewerbung(en) *f.*
job interview Vorstellungsgespräch(e) *n.*
job market Stellenmarkt (-märkte) *m.*
jobs offered Stellenangebot(e) *n.*
job-related berufsbezogen
journal Zeitschrift(en) *f.*
journey Reise(n) *f.* / Fahrt(en) *f.*
journey (to) Anfahrt(en) *f.*
journey there Hinfahrt(en) *f.*
journey there and back Hin- und Rückfahrt(en) *f.*
outward journey Hinfahrt(en) *f.*
return journey Hin- und Rückfahrt(en) *f.*
July Juli *m.*
June Juni *m.*
juniper schnapps Wacholder *m.*
just mal / eben / einmal
just now gerade

keen einsatzfreudig
keep *verb* halten / einbehalten / einhalten
keep (to the) left/right *verb* sich links/rechts halten
key Schlüssel *m.*
kind Art(en) *f.*
of all kinds aller Art
kind nett / freundlich
know *verb* kennen / wissen
know everything/know (what to do) *verb* Bescheid wissen
get to know *verb* kennenlernen
get to know one another *verb* sich kennenlernen
knowledge Kenntnis(se) *f.*
knowledge of English Englischkenntnisse *pl.*
knowledge of a language Sprachkenntnisse *pl.*

Labour Day Maifeiertag *m.*
labour market Stellenmarkt (-märkte) *m.*
Ladies and Gentlemen Sehr geehrte Damen und Herren
lady Dame(n) *f.*
language Sprache(n) *f.*
language course Sprachkurs(e) *m.*
language of communication Umgangssprache(n) *f.*
everyday language Umgangssprache(n) *f.*
foreign language correspondent Fremdsprachen-korrespondent(en) *m.*
large groß
last *verb* dauern
last vergangen
last (few) letzte / letzter / letztes
late spät
later (on) nachher
lathe work Drehteil(e) *n.*
leading führend
leaflet Prospekt(e) *m.* / Prospektblatt (-blätter) *n.*
learn *verb* erfahren / lernen
leave *verb* rausgehen / abfahren / herausgehen / hinterlassen
left links
on the/your left linker Hand
lending Kreditgeschäft(e) *n.*
lent Frühjahr *n.* / Frühling *m.*
lessons (private) Privatunterricht *m.*
let *verb* lassen
let down draufsetzen (*colloquial*)
let have *verb* zukommen lassen
letter announcing the arrival Anmeldung(en) *f.*
letter paper Briefpapier(e) *n.*
level Stock(werk(e)) *m./n.* / Etage(n) *f.*
level of orders Auftragslage *f.*
licence Lizenz(en) *f.*
lift Aufzug (-züge) *m.* / Fahrstuhl (-stühle) *m.*
light leicht
like *verb* gefallen / gern haben
like (to do) *verb* (gern) mögen
I would like ich hätte gern
line (of business) Sparte(n) *f.*
linked (up) angeschlossen
liquefied petroleum gas LPG(s)

list of beverages
Getränkekarte(n) *f.*
list price Listenpreis *m.*
listen *verb* hören
literature
Informationsmaterial(ien) *n.*
litre Liter *m.*
little klein / wenig
a little etwas
live *verb* wohnen
loan business Kreditgeschäft(e) *n.*
local hiesig
location Standort(e) *m.*
long lang/weit
long-term langfristig
have a look *verb* nachschauen
have a good look at something
prüfen
look *verb* aussehen / gucken
look after *verb* sich kümmern um
look for suchen
look forward to *verb* sich freuen
auf / entgegensehen
look up *verb* nachschlagen
looking after Betreuung *f.*
loss of output/production
Produktionsausfall (-fälle) *m.*
lot Menge(n) *f.*
that's quite a lot das ist sehr viel
low-price günstig
luck Glück *n.*
lunch Mittagessen *n.*
lunch break Mittagspause(n) *f.*
lunchtime Mittag(e) *m.*
Luxembourg Luxemburg

machine Maschine(n) *f.* /
Apparat(e) *m.* / Gerät(e) *n.*
made gefertigt/hergestellt
magazine Zeitschrift(en) *f.*
maintenance Wartung(en) *f.*
maintenance agreement
Wartungsvertrag (-verträge) *m.*
make *verb* machen / vornehmen /
fertigen / herstellen
make out *verb* ersehen
manage (to do) *verb* auskommen /
schaffen
management consulting group
Unternehmensberatungs-
gruppe(n) *f.*
management course/seminar
Führungsseminar(e) *n.*
manager Führungskraft (-kräfte) *f.*
general manager
Geschäftsführer *m.*
manifold vielfältig
be manned *verb* besetzt sein
manufacture *verb* fertigen /
herstellen / produzieren
manufacture and deal in *verb*
here: sich beschäftigen mit

manufacturing Fertigung(en) *f.* /
Produktion(en) *f.*
many viel(e) / vielfältig
March März *m.*
mark Mark *f.*
market Markt (Märkte) *m.*
market square Marktplatz
(-plätze) *m.*
marketing manager Leiter *m.*
Marketing
mass production
Serienproduktion(en) *f.*
material Material(ien) *n.*
matter Sache(n) *f.* /
Angelegenheit(en) *f.*
no matter egal
not to matter *verb* keine Rolle
spielen
may *verb* dürfen
May Mai *m.*
meal Mahlzeit(en) *f.* / Essen *n.*
in the meantime in der
Zwischenzeit *f.*
mechanical(ly) mechanisch
media consultant Mediaberater *m.*
medium-term mittelfristig
meet *verb* abholen / sich treffen /
(fulfil) erfüllen / einhalten
meeting Besprechung(en) *f.* /
Sitzung(en) *f.*
member of staff Mitarbeiter *m.*
menu Speisekarte(n) *f.* / Karte(n) *f.*
merchant Kaufmann (-leute) *m.*
**mess things up/make a mess of
things** *verb* Mist bauen
message Nachricht(en) *f.*
method of payment
Zahlungsweise(n) *f.*
metre Meter *m./n.*
midday Mittag(e) *m.*
mild mild
milk Milch *f.*
million Million(en) (Mio.) *f.*
mineral water Wasser *n.* /
Mineralwasser (-wässer) *n.*
minibar Minibar(s) *f.*
minimum Minimum (-a) *n.*
minute Minute(n) *f.* /
Augenblick(e) *m.*
in a minute gleich
just a minute (please) (einen)
Moment (bitte)
have a minute to spare *verb* einen
Moment Zeit haben
Miss Fräulein(s) *n.*
mix *verb* mischen
mixture Mischung(en) *f.*
moment Moment(e) *m.* /
Augenblick(e) *m.*
at the moment im Augenblick
just a moment (please) (einen)
Moment (bitte) / (einen)
Augenblick (bitte)

Monday Montag(e) *m.*
on Mondays montags
money Geld(er) *n.*
month Monat(e) *m.*
per/every month monatlich
monument Denkmal (-mäler) *n.*
more mehr
morning Vormittag(e) *m.*
in the morning (s) morgens /
vormittags
this morning heute morgen
(early) this morning heute früh
early/late in the morning
morgens früh / spät
good morning guten Morgen
a very good morning schönen
guten Tag
most meist(e(n))
mother Mutter (Mütter) *f.*
motivated motiviert
mountain Berg(e) *m.*
Mr Herr(en) *m.*
Mrs/Ms Frau(en) *f.*
much viel(e)
very much here: vielmals
must *verb* müssen
my mein(e)
myself selber / selbst

name Name(n) *m.*
enter one's name *verb* sich eintragen
put one's name down *verb* sich
anmelden
national(ly) bundesweit
nationality Nationalität(en) *f.*
naturally natürlich /
selbstverständlich
near an / in der Nähe
need Bedarf *m.*
need *verb* brauchen / benötigen
start negotiations *verb* ins
Gespräch *n.* gehen
net netto
local network Ortsnetz(e) *n.*
nevertheless trotzdem
new neu
New Year('s Day) Neujahr *n.*
newest neuest
news Nachricht(en) *f.*
newspaper Zeitung(en) *f.*
next folgend / nächste / nächster /
nächstes
nice schön / nett / lecker
night Nacht (Nächte) *f.*
at night nachts
good night gute Nacht
spend the night *verb* übernachten
no nein
no (one) kein / keine / keiner
no ... at all keinerlei
non-alcoholic alkoholfrei
non-smoker Nichtraucher *m.*

normal normal
Norway Norwegen
not nicht
not ... anything gar nicht
not at all gar nicht / überhaupt nicht
note for the day Tagesnotiz(en) *f.*
noted (down) notiert
notify *verb* Bescheid *m.* geben / sagen
be notified *verb* Bescheid *m.* bekommen
November November *m.*
now jetzt
number Zahl(en) *f.* / Nummer(n) *f.*
number (of pieces) Stückzahl(en) *f.*
a number of eine Reihe von
local number/code Ortsdurchwahl(en) *f.*
opposite number Gesprächspartner *m.*

obtain *verb* bekommen
obvious(ly) offensichtlich
occupation Beruf(e) *m.*
be occupied *verb* besetzt sein
October Oktober *m.*
of course selbstverständlich / natürlich
offer (for) Angebot(e) (über) *n.*
offer *verb* anbieten
have to/on offer *verb* zur Auswahl *f.* haben
office Büro(s) *n.*
in the office here: im Hause
open-plan office Großraumbüro(s) *n.*
representative office Repräsentanz(en) *f.*
office chair Bürostuhl (-stühle) *m.*
office furniture and equipment Büroausstattung(en) *f.*
office junior Bürogehilfe *m.*
officer Sachbearbeiter *m.*
often oft
OK (ein)verstanden / in Ordnung
be OK *verb* klar gehen / passen
is that OK? ist das recht?
old alt
on bei / auf / unter / daran
on (to) weiter (nach)
once mal / einmal
once again noch einmal / nochmal
at once gleich
one ein / eine / einer / man
onion soup Zwiebelsuppe(n) *f.*
only nur / erst
open offen / geöffnet
opening hours Öffnungszeit(en) *f.* / geöffnet
operate *verb* bedienen / arbeiten / tätig sein
not operating außer Betrieb
in operation in Betrieb
out of operation außer Betrieb
operator-connected handvermittelt
opportunity Chance(n) *f.*
opposite gegenüber
or oder
orange juice Orangensaft (-säfte) *m.*
order Bestellung(en) *f.* / Auftrag (-träge) *m.*
order value Auftragswert *m.*
urgent order Eilauftrag (-träge) *m.*
order *verb* bestellen/anweisen
order-book situation Auftragslage *f.*
ordered in advance vorbestellt
other andere / anderer / anderes / sonstig
otherwise ansonsten / sonst
our unser(e)
output Produktionsleistung *f.*
outside draußen / außerhalb
over vorbei
over there hinten
overall gesamt
overcrowded überfüllt
overnight stay (in a hotel) Hotelübernachtung(en) *f.*
overnight taxi rank Dauerstandplatz (-plätze) *m.*
overseas im/ins Ausland
to do overtime *verb* Überstunden fahren / machen
own eigen

pack *verb* einpacken
packaging Verpackung(en) *f.*
packed (schedule) gedrängt
packing Verpackung(en) *f.*
packing/packaging material Verpackungsmaterial(ien) *n.*
pamphlet Broschüre(n) *f.*
paper Unterlage(n) *f.* / Zeitung(en) *f.*
parallel parallel
park Park(s) *m.*
participate *verb* teilnehmen
participation Beteiligung(en) *f.*
particular besondere / besonderer / besonderes
partner Partner *m.*
general partnership OHG(s) (Offene Handelsgesellschaft(en)) *f.*
(spare) parts Teil(e) *n.* / Ersatzteil(e) *n.*
pass on (a message) *verb* ausrichten
passer-by Passant(en) *m.*
past Vergangenheit(en) *f.* / Geschichte(n) *f.*
past vergangen
past vorbei / an ... vorbei
pay *verb* bezahlen/zahlen
pay out *verb* auszahlen / hinzählen
payable zahlbar
payment Bezahlung(en) *f.* / Zahlung(en) *f.*
pedestrian precinct Fußgängerzone(n) *f.*
people (more than one person) Personen *pl.* / Leute *pl.* / (impersonal one) man
per pro
perform (i.e. achieve) *verb* leisten
perhaps vielleicht
period of delivery Lieferfrist(en) *f.* / Lieferzeit(en) *f.*
permit oneself *verb* sich etwas erlauben
periodical Zeitschrift(en) *f.*
person Person(en) *f.*
personal persönlich
personnel Personal *n.*
personnel manager Personalleiter *m.*
petrol Benzin *n.*
petrol distributor Kraftstoffvertriebsgesellschaft(en) *f.*
petrol station Tankstelle(n) *f.*
premium petrol Superkraftstoff(e) *m.*
pfennig Pfennig(e) *m.*
phone *verb* anrufen
by phone telefonisch
phone number Rufnummer(n) *f.*
photo Bild(er) *n.* / Lichtbild(er) *n.*
photocopier Kopiergerät(e) *n.*
photocopy Photokopie(n) *f.*
picture Bild(er) *n.*
piece Stück(e) *n.*
one-mark piece Markstück(e) *n.*
small piece Stückchen *n.*
turned piece Drehteil(e) *n.*
two-mark piece Zweimarkstück(e) *n.*
pineapple Ananas *f.*
it's a pity Schade / das ist schade
place Platz (Plätze) *m.* / Ort(e) *m.*
place (e.g. an order) *verb* erteilen
place of birth Geburtsort(e) *m.*
place of residence Wohnort(e) *m.*
plan *verb* planen
plan to do *verb* vorhaben
planned angesetzt / vorgesehen / geplant
planning Planung(en) *f.*
plant Betrieb(e) *m.*
plate of boiled and smoked ham Schinkenteller *m.*

platform Gleis(e) *n.*
play *verb* spielen
pleasant angenehm
please bitte (sehr) / bitteschön
be pleased *verb* sich freuen
pleased to meet you angenehm / freut mich
it's a pleasure / with pleasure gern
point Punkt(e) *m.*
from the point of view of aus der Sicht von
police Polizei *f.*
pork sausage Fleischwurst (-würste) *f.*
Portugal Portugal
position Funktion(en) *f.* / Position(en) *f.* / Stelle(n) *f.*
possibility Möglichkeit(en) *f.*
possible möglich
possibly wohl
be possible *verb* gehen / sich einrichten lassen / drin sein (*colloquial*)
if (at all) possible möglichst
if that's possible? wenn das geht?
in the best possible way here: maximal
as quickly as possible möglichst schnell
P.O. box Postfach (-fächer) *n.*
post Stelle(n) *f.*
post code Postleitzahl(en) *f.*
post office Post *f.* / Postamt (-ämter) *n.*
main post office Hauptpost *f.*
poster Plakat(e) *n.*
postpone *verb* verschieben
pot (**of tea/coffee**) Kännchen *n.*
potato salad Kartoffelsalat(e) *m.*
fried potato Bratkartoffel(n) *f.*
precondition Voraussetzung(en) *f.*
prefer *verb* vorziehen / bevorzugen
preferable(**-ly**) lieber
premises Betrieb(e) *m.*
prepare *verb* erstellen / vorbereiten
present derzeitig
at present gegenwärtig / im Augenblick / zur Zeit
president Präsident(en) *m.*
press *verb* drücken / drängen
pressure Druck *m.*
price Preis(e) *m.*
price list Preisliste(n) *f.*
price negotiations Preisverhandlung(en) *f.*
gross price Bruttopreis(e) *m.*
reasonable prices preiswert
special price Sonderpreis(e) *m.*
principally/in principle im Prinzip

print *verb* bedrucken / drucken
print out *verb* ausdrucken
be printed on *verb* draufstehen
printer Drucker
printer's Druck(erei(en)) *f./m.* / Graphikanstalt(en) *f.*
printing Druck(e) *m.*
printing works Graphikanstalt *f.*
private(**ly**) privat
probable wahrscheinlich
probably voraussichtlich
problem Problem(e) *n.* / Angelegenheit(en) *f.*
special problem Spezialfrage(n) *f.*
that's no problem kein Problem
without any problem mühelos
produce *verb* herstellen / fertigen / produzieren
product Produkt(e) *n.*
product group Produktgruppe(n) *f.*
product information Produktinformation(en) *f.*
product line Produktlinie(n) *f.*
product manager Produkt Manager *m.*
product mix/range Produktpalette(n) *f.*
production Fertigung(en) *f.* / Produktion(en) *f.*
single-unit production Einzelanfertigung(en) *f.*
production of pumps Pumpenproduktion(en) *f.*
production department Produktion(en) *f.*
production figure Produkionszahl(en) *f.*
production limit Produktionsgrenze(n) *f.*
production manager Fertigungsleiter *m.*
production performance Produktionsleistung(en) *f.*
production programme Fertigungsprogramm(e) *n.* / Produktionsprogramm(e) *n.*
production scheduling Arbeitsvorbereitung(en) *f.*
production target Produktionsgrenze(n) *f.*
profession Beruf(e) *m.*
professor Professor(en) *m.*
profitable ertragreich
programme Programm(e) *n.* / Sendung(en) *f.*
promised zugesagt
promoted gefördert
propose *verb* vorschlagen
Protestant evangelisch
prototype Prototyp(en) *m.*
provide *verb* sorgen für

proximity Nähe *f.*
pump Pumpe(n) *f.*
punctual(**ly**) pünktlich
purchase Einkauf (-käufe) *m.* / Abnahme(n) *f.*
purchase *verb* einkaufen / abnehmen
purchased gekauft
purchasing (**department**) Einkauf (-käufe) *m.*
purchasing manager Einkaufsleiter *m.* / Einkäufer *m.*
purchasing officer Einkäufer *m.*
push *verb* drücken / drängen
put in *verb* stecken
put off *verb* verschieben
put right *verb* in Ordnung bringen
put through (on the phone) *verb* verbinden
put together *verb* zusammenstellen

quality control Qualitätskontrolle(n) *f.*
quantity Menge(n) *f.*
quantity discount Mengenrabatt(e) *m.*
quantity-related stückzahlbezogen
quantity sold Verkaufsmenge(n) *f.*
quarter (**of the year**) Vierteljahr(e) *n.*
question Frage(n) *f.* / Angelegenheit(en) *f.*
quick(**ly**) kurz / schnell / eben / mal eben
probably the quickest am ehesten
quiet ruhig
quite (completely) ganz / (fairly) zeimlich
quite simply einfach

radio Radio(s) *n.*
radio play Hörspiel(e) *n.*
railway official Bahnbeamter (-beamten) *m.*
range Kollektion(en) *f.*
rather (fairly) ziemlich / (preferably) lieber
raw material Rohstoff(e) *m.*
reach *verb* erreichen
read *verb* lesen
ready so weit / fertig
realize *verb* sich über etwas im klaren sein
real(**ly**) eigentlich
really aufrichtig / wirklich
not really eigentlich nicht
reason Grund (Gründe) *m.*
reassuring beruhigend

receipt Beleg(e) *m.*
receive *verb* empfangen / erhalten
receiver Hörer *m.*
put down the receiver auflegen
reception(ist) Empfang *m.*
reception (desk) Rezeption(en) *f.*
reckon with *verb* rechnen (mit)
recognized anerkannt
recommend *verb* empfehlen / vorschlagen
record *verb* aufnehmen
recover *verb* sich erholen
Reformation Day Reformationstag *m.*
refund Rückgabe(n) *f.*
with regard to im Hinblick auf
regarding wegen / bezüglich
region Region(en) *f.*
register *verb* sich eintragen
registration form Anmeldeformular(e) *n.*
regular(ly) regelmäßig
reliable zuverlässig
remain *verb* bleiben / verbleiben
remainder Rest(e) / Restbetrag (-träge) *m.*
remember *verb* sich entsinnen
rent *verb* mieten
repair (work) Reparatatur(en) *f.*
repeat *verb* wiederholen
reply Beantwortung(en) *f.*
report *verb* berichten
report to *verb* sich melden
representative Handelsvertreter *m.* / Vertreter *m.*
represented vertreten
request *verb* bitten
request for a catalog(ue) Kataloganforderung(en) *f.*
require *verb* brauchen / benötigen / erfordern
requirement Voraussetzung(en) *f.* / Bedarf *m.*
reservation Buchung(en) *f.*
reserve *verb* bestellen/buchen
responsible verantwortlich / zuständig
rest Rest(e) *m.*
have a rest *verb* sich erholen
rest day Ruhetag(e) *m.*
restaurant Restaurant(s) *n.*
result Ergebnis(se) *n.*
résumé Lebenslauf (-läufe) *m.*
retain *verb* bestellen / einbehalten
return Rückgabe(n) *f.*
return flight Rückflug (-flüge) *m.*
return journey Rückfahrt(en) *f.* / Hin- und Rückfahrt *f*
return trip Rückfahrt(en) *f.*
reunification Wiedervereinigung *f.*
revise (rework) *verb* überarbeiten
ride *verb* fahren
right rechts / richtig
on your/the right rechter Hand
quite right ganz genau
be right *verb* stimmen
ring *verb* durchrufen / anrufen
road Straße(n) *f.*
role Rolle(n) *f.*
roll Brötchen *n.*
room Zimmer *n.*
double room Doppelzimmer *n.*
single room Einzelzimmer *n.*
room number Zimmernummer(n) *f.*
Ruhr area/district Ruhrgebiet *n.*
run *verb* laufen
run away *verb* davonlaufen
(hectic) rush Hektik *f.*

safe(ly) sicher
sailing Segeln *n.*
(mixed) salad Salatteller *m.*
sale Verkauf (-käufe) *m.*
sales Absatz (-sätze) *m.*
sales assistant Verkäufer *m.*
sales association Verkaufsvereinigung(en) *f.*
sales clerk Kundenbetreuer *m.*
sales department Verkauf(sabteilung) *f.*
sales director/manager Verkaufsleiter *m.*
sales office Verkaufsinnendienst(e) *m.*
(total) sales Gesamtumsatz (-sätze) *m.*
salesman Verkäufer *m.*
travelling salesman Handelsvertreter *m.*
same gleich
in the same way gleich
sample Muster *n.*
satellite television Satellitenfernsehen *n.*
satisfy *verb* erfüllen
Saturday Samstag(e) *m.* / Sonnabend(e) *m.*
on Saturdays samstags
sauce Soße(n) *f.*
sausage Würstchen *n.*
fried sausage Bratwurst (-würste) *f.*
savings bank Sparkasse(n) *f.*
say *verb* sagen
go without saying *verb* selbstverständlich sein
schedule of discounts Rabattstaffel(n) *f.*
scheduled angesetzt / planmäßig / geplant
school Schule(n) *f.*
Scottish schottisch
search Suche *f.*
season (of the year) Jahreszeit(en) *f.*
season (particular period) Saison *f.*
peak season Hochsaison *f.*
seat reservation Sitzplatzreservierung(en) *f.*
have/take a seat *verb* Platz nehmen
second Sekunde(n) *f.*
secretary (female) Sekretärin(nen) *f.*
secretary (male) Sekretär(e) *m.*
secretary's office Vorzimmer *n.*
section Bereich(e) *m.*
sector Bereich(e) *m.*
(industrial) sector Branche(n) *f.*
securities business Wertpapiergeschäft(e) *n.*
see *verb* sehen
see you later bis gleich
see you then bis dahin
seem *verb* erscheinen
select *verb* wählen / auswählen
selection Auswahl(en) *f.*
sell *verb* verkaufen
selling Verkaufen *n.* / Verkauf *m.*
send *verb* zusenden / zuschicken / schicken / zukommen lassen
send round *verb* hinaufschicken / heraufschicken
sending Zusendung(en) *f.*
separate(ly) extra
September September *m.*
series of eine ganze Reihe *f.*
series production Serienproduktion(en) *f.*
service Dienstleistung(en) *f.* / Service *m.*
service (charge) (e.g. in a restaurant) Bedienung *f.*
service for recruitment ads Personalanzeigenservice *m.*
postal service Post *f.*
service engineer Kundendiensttechniker *m.* / Servicetechniker *m.*
service work Kundendienstarbeit(en) *f.*
servicing Service *m.*
set *verb* stellen
settlement Bezahlung(en) *f.*
several verschieden/mehrere
shall *verb* sollen
she sie
shift work Wechselschicht(en) *f.*
shipment Lieferung(en) *f.*
shop Geschäft(e) *n.* / Laden (Läden) *m.*
short(ly) kurz
shorten *verb* abkürzen
short-term kurzfristig

shortly in Kürze
show *verb* zeigen / vorstellen / (exhibit) ausstellen
shower Dusche(n) *f.*
side Seite(n) *f.*
sight Sicht(en) *f.*
sign Schild(er) *n.*
sign *verb* unterschreiben
signal Zeichen *n.*
signature Unterschrift(en) *f.*
similar ähnlich
simple einfach
since seit
single-unit (production) Einzelanfertigung(en) *f.*
singular einzigartig
sit down *verb* Platz *m.* nehmen / sich hinsetzen
situation Situation(en) *f.*
size Umfang (-fänge) *m.*
slot Schlitz(e) *m.*
slow(ly) langsam
small klein
so that so daß
software company Softwarehaus (-häuser) *n.*
software program Softwareprogramm(e) *n.*
solely ausschließlich
solid fest
some (any) irgendeine / irgendeiner / irgendeins
some (a few) einige / ein paar
someone jemand
soon in Kürze
Sorry! Entschuldigen Sie! / Entschuldigung!
be sorry *verb* leid tun
sound *verb* klingen
sound good *verb* sich gut anhören
Spain Spanien
Spanish course Spanischkurs(e) *m.*
spare part Ersatzteil(e) *m.*
spare parts situation Ersatzteilsituation *f.*
spare parts supply Ersatzteilversorgung *f.*
speak *verb* sprechen
so to speak sozusagen
speaking Sprechen *n.*
speaking (answering the phone) am Apparat
speaking clock Zeitansage(n) *f.*
special besondere / besonderer / besonderes
specialist Spezialist(en) *m.*
specimen Muster *n.*
spinning mill Spinnerei(en) *f.*
splendid prima / fabelhaft / wunderbar
sports broadcast/programme Sportsendung(en) *f.*
spread out *verb* sich verteilen
spring Frühjahr *n.* / Frühling *m.*
spring collection/range Frühjahrskollektion(en) *f.*
square Platz (Plätze) *m.*
staff Mitarbeiter *pl.* / Personal *n.*
temporary staff Zeitpersonal *n.*
be staffed *verb* besetzt sein
stand *verb* stehen
state *verb* nennen / angeben
state of the art Stand *m.* der Technik
station Bahnhof (-höfe) *m.*
station road Bahnhofstraße(n) *f.*
stationer's (shop) Schreibwarenladen (-läden) *m.*
start Anfang (-fänge) *m.*
start *verb* anfangen / starten
stay Aufenthalt(e) *m.*
stay *verb* untergebracht sein / bleiben
stayed gewohnt
steel Stahl (Stähle) *m.*
special steel Edelstahl (-stähle) *m.*
still noch
still not immer noch nicht
stock(s) Lager (Läger) *n.*
(have) in stock am Lager (haben)
stock corporation AG(s) (Aktiengesellschaft(en)) *f.*
stock exchange/market Börse *f.*
store Geschäft(e) *n.* / Laden (Läden) *m.*
story Geschichte(n) *f.*
straight ahead geradeaus
straightaway gleich/direkt
stranger Fremde *m.*
street Straße(n) *f.*
street number Hausnummer(n) *f.*
stress Stress *m.*
strike Streik(s) *m.*
striped gestreift
with stripes gestreift
strong(ly) stark
student (female) Studentin(nen) *f.*
student (male) Student(en) *m.*
study complex Studienkomplex(e) *m.*
study leave Bildungsurlaub(e) *m.*
sturdy fest
subscriber's number Rufnummer(n) *f.*
sub-supplier Zulieferer *m.*
subway station U-Bahn-Haltestelle(n) *f.*
success story Erfolgsmeldung(en) *f.*
successful erfolgreich
such solch
sudden(ly) plötzlich
sufficient genug / ausreichend
be sufficient *verb* reichen
sugar Zucker *m.*
suggest *verb* vorschlagen
suggestion Anregung(en) *f.*
suit *verb* passen
sum Summe(n) *f.*
summer Sommer *m.*
Sunday Sonntag(e) *m.*
on Sundays sonntags
supplement Zuschlag (-schläge) *m.*
supplier Anbieter *m.* / Vorlieferant(en) *m.*
supply Lieferung(en) *m.*
supply *verb* liefern
supply of individual pieces / supply of a single unit Einzellieferung(en) *f.*
supply difficulties Lieferungsschwierigkeit(en) *f.*
surcharge Zuschlag (-schläge) *m.*
surely sicherlich
surfing Surfen *n.*
surname Familienname(n) *m.*
Sweden Schweden
Swiss schweizerisch
switchboard Telefonzentrale(n) *f.*
Switzerland Schweiz *f.*

table (of information) Tabelle(n) *f.*
tailor to *verb* zuschneiden auf
take *verb* nehmen / abnehmen
take (last) *verb* dauern
take away *verb* mitnehmen
take down *verb* aufnehmen
take off *verb* ablegen
take part *verb* teilnehmen
taken gebracht
talk Gespräch(e) *n.*
talk *verb* sprechen
talk about *verb* sich unterhalten
tape Tonband (-bänder) *n.*
target language Zielsprache(n) *f.*
task Aufgabe(n) *f.* / Arbeitsfeld(er) *n.*
taste *verb* schmecken
tasted nice geschmeckt
tea Tee(s) *m.*
black tea schwarzer Tee
teacher Lehrer *m.* / Lehrerin(nen) *f.* / Lehrperson(en) *f.*
teaching programme here: Leistungsprogramm(e) *n.*
team Team *n.*
technical technisch
technique Technik(en) *f.*
technology Technik(en) *f.*
telegram Telegramm(e) *n.*
telephone Telefon(e) *n.*/ Anschluß (-schlüsse) *m.*
telephone *verb* telefonieren
telephone answering machine Anrufbeantworter *m.*

telephone box/booth Telefonzelle(n) *f.*
telephone call Telefongespräch(e) *n.* / Telefonat(e) *n.* / Anruf(e) *m.*
telephone conversation Telefongespräch(e) *n.* / Telefonat(e) *n.*
telephone directory Telefonbuch (-bücher) *n.*
telephone enquiries Telefonauskunft (-künfte) *f.*
telephone line Anschluß (-schlüsse) *m.*
telephone number Telefonnummer(n) *f.*
telephone service Telefonauftrag (-träge) *m.*
television/TV watching Fernsehen *n.*
television set Fernsehgerät(e) *n.* / Fernseher *m.*
tell *verb* Bescheid geben / berichten/erzählen
terminate *verb* schließen
term(s) of payment Zahlungsbedingung(en) *f.*
tested getestet
testimonial Zeugnis(se) *n.*
testing device Prüfeinrichtung(en) *f.*
textiles Textilien *pl.*
thank *verb* sich bedanken
thanks / thank you (very much) danke/Dankeschön / danke sehr
many thanks besten/vielen Dank
(very) many thanks (indeed) herzlichen Dank
say thank you *verb* sich bedanken
Thanksgiving Day Erntedankfest *n.*
that daß
that is ... das macht ...
that is (i.e.) und zwar / das heißt (d.h.)
that's right korrekt
that's why deswegen
the der / die / das
theatre ticket Theaterkarte(n) *f.*
their ihr(e)
of them davon
then dann / denn
there da / hin
there/over there dort / drüben
there are/is es befindet sich
therefore also / deswegen / daher / deshalb
of these davon
thing Sache(n) *f.*
think *verb* denken / glauben / (consider) halten für
think something over *verb* sich etwas überlegen
this diese / dieser / dieses
of those von denen
thought Gedanke(n) *m.*
threaten *verb* drohen
through durch / durchgehend
through carriage Kurswagen *m.*
Thursday Donnerstag(e) *m.*
on Thursdays donnerstags
thus also / damit
time Zeit(en) *f.* / Uhrzeit(en) *f.* / (instance) Mal(e) *n.*
time and again öfters
time of arrival Ankunftszeit(en) *f.*
time of the year (season) Jahreszeit(en) *f.*
time signal Zeitansage(n) *f.*
for the time being vorläufig
from time to time des öfteren
in time rechtzeitig
many times oft
at the same time parallel
this time diesmal
take time *verb* sich hinziehen
tip Tip(s) *m.*
to zu/auf/bis
to it dazu
today heute
together zusammen / gemeinsam
together with im Zusammensein mit
toilet WC(s) *n.* / Toilette(n) *f.*
tomorrow morgen
tone Ton (Töne) *m.*
tonight heute nacht / heute abend
too auch
at the top oben
total gesamt
guided tour Besichtigung(en) *f.*
tourist Tourist(en) *m.*
tourist information (office) Verkehrsverein(e) *m.*
to(wards) nach
towel Handtuch (-tücher) *n.*
town Stadt (Städte) *f.*
town hall Rathaus (-häuser) *n.*
town hall square Rathausplatz (-plätze) *m.*
trade discount Wiederverkaufsrabatt(e) *m.*
trade fair Messe(n) *f.*
trade-fair discount Messerabatt(e) *m.*
train Zug (Züge) *m.*
fast train Eilzug (-züge) *m.*
get onto the train *verb* einsteigen
train connection Zugverbindung(en) *f.*
train information Zugauskunft (-künfte) *f.*
train restaurant Zugrestaurant(s) *n.*
train stop S-Bahn-Haltestelle(n) *f.*
train *verb* schulen
trained ausgebildet
trainee Auszubildender (-bildenden) *m.*
travel Fahrt(en) *f.*
travel *verb* fahren / reisen
travel on *verb* weiterreisen
travel (to) *verb* anreisen
travel agency/agent Reisebüro(s) *n.*
travel information Reiseinformation(en) *f.*
trip Fahrt(en) *f.*
trip abroad Auslandsreise(n) *f.*
it is true that ..., but zwar ... aber
try *verb* probieren
Tuesday Dienstag(e) *m.*
on Tuesdays dienstags
(individual) tuition Einzelunterricht *m.*
(private) tuition Privatunterricht *m.*
(total) turnover Gesamtumsatz (-sätze) *m.*
twice zweimal
type Art(en) *f.*
typesetting Satz *m.*
typewriter desk Schreibmaschinentisch(e) *m.*

unchanged unverändert
under unter
underground station U-Bahn-Haltestelle(n) *f.*
understand *verb* verstehen
understanding Verständnis *n.*
understood verstanden / in Ordnung / klar
unfortunately leider
unique einzigartig
unit price Stückpreis(e) *m.*
university Uni(s) / Universität(en) *f.*
until bis / bis zu
until later bis dahin
until then solange / bis dahin
up to bis zu
up to now bisher
up there da oben
upwards aufwärts
urgent(ly) dringend
to us here: ins Haus
use *verb* benutzen/ausüben
used genutzt
usual üblich
usual(ly) gewöhnlich
utilize *verb* benutzen
utmost äußerst

vacancies (jobs offered) Stellenangebot(e) *n.*

have vacancies *verb* (e.g. in a hotel) Zimmer frei haben
vacation(s) Urlaub(e) *m.*
vacation Ferien *pl.*
go on vacation *verb* Urlaub *m.* machen
in vain vergeblich
valid gültig
be valid *verb* gelten
value for money preiswert
very sehr
vice-president Vizepräsident(en) *m.*
video recorder Videorecorder *m.*
in view of im Hinblick auf
visit Besuch(e) *m.* / Besichtigung(en) *f.*
visit *verb* besuchen
visit by/to customers Kundenbesuch(e) *m.*
visit to the/a fair Messetermin(e) *m.*
visitor Gast (Gäste) *m.* / Besucher *m.*
have visitors *verb* Kundenbesuch *m.* haben
volume (amount) Umfang (-fänge) *m.*

wage Lohn (Löhne) *m.*
wait *verb* warten
waiter/waitress Bedienung *f.*
walk *verb* gehen / entlanggehen
walk past *verb* vorbeikommen
walk towards *verb* zulaufen (auf)
walked gewandert
walking Wandern *n.*
want *verb* wollen / wünschen
warm warm
water Wasser *n.*
way Weg(e) *m.*
find one's way to *verb* zu etwas finden
we wir
wealthy vermögend
weather Wetter *n.*
weaving mill Weberei(en) *f.*
WC WC(s) *n.* / Toilette(n) *f.*
Wednesday Mittwoch(e) *m.*
on Wednesdays mittwochs
of two weeks zweiwöchig
weekday Wochentag(e) *m.*
you're welcome gern geschehen / nichts zu danken
weld *verb* schweißen
well also
west coast Westküste(n) *f.*
west German westdeutsch
what(?) was(?)
what kind of(?) was für(?)
when(?) wann(?)
where(?) wo(?)/wohin(?)
whether ob
which welche / welcher / welches / wievielte / wievielter / wievieltes
Whit Monday Pfingstmontag *m.*
Whit Sunday Pfingstsonntag *m.*
white weiß
who(?) wer(?)
whole ganz
on the whole soweit
wholesale banking Großfirmengeschäft(e) *n.*
(to)whom wem
of whom davon
why(?) warum(?) / weshalb(?)
that's why deswegen
wife Ehefrau(en) *f.*
will (future tense) *verb* werden
winter Winter *m.*
wish *verb* wünschen
with mit
with it damit
with what(?) womit(?)
withdraw (money) *verb* abheben
within innerhalb von
without ohne
woman Frau(en) *f.*
wonderful wunderbar
work *verb* arbeiten
work out *verb* ausrechnen / errechnen
work overtime *verb* Überstunden fahren/machen
work scheduling Arbeitsvorbereitung(en) *f.*
workday Werktag(e) *m.*
skilled worker Fachkraft (-kräfte) *f.*
world Welt(en) *f.*
would *verb* würde(n)
wrapping paper Packpapier(e) *n.*
write *verb* schreiben
write down *verb* aufschreiben
please write to Zuschrift(en) *f.* erbeten
in writing schriftlich
put down in writing *verb* schriftlich machen
written schriftlich
be written *verb* draufstehen
wrong falsch

year Jahr(e) *n.*
half year Halbjahr(e) *n.*
yellow gelb
yes ja/jawohl
yes, of course ach ja
yesterday gestern
yet noch
you (*familiar*) ihr/du
you (*polite*) Sie
(to) you Ihnen/dir
young jung
your ihr(e)/dein(e)/Ihr(e)
yours faithfully/sincerely mit freundlichem Gruß

Index